ANDEAN EXPRESSIONS

ANDEAN

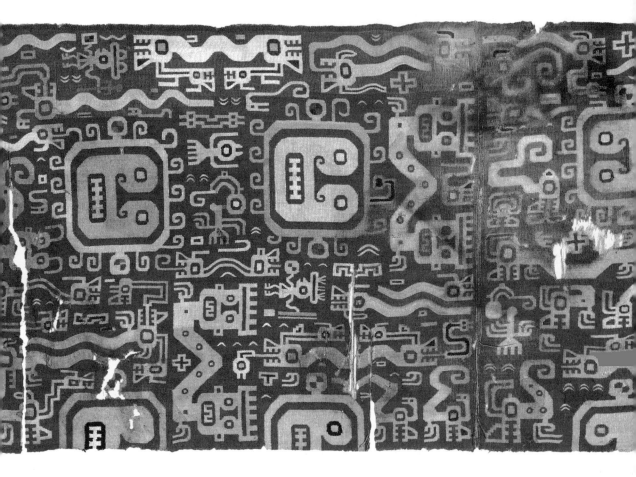

THE IOWA SERIES
IN ANDEAN STUDIES

Katharina Schreiber,
series editor

EXPRESSIONS

ART AND ARCHAEOLOGY OF THE RECUAY CULTURE

George F. Lau

University of Iowa Press
Iowa City

University of Iowa Press, Iowa City 52242

Copyright © 2011 by the University of Iowa Press

www.uiowapress.org

Printed in the United States of America

Design by April Leidig-Higgins

The University of Iowa Press is a member of Green Press Initiative and is committed to preserving natural resources.

Printed on acid-free paper

All illustrations and photographs by author unless otherwise noted.

Library of Congress Cataloging-in-Publication Data
Lau, George F., 1969–
Andean expressions: art and archaeology of the Recuay culture /
by George F. Lau.
p.   cm. — (The Iowa series in Andean studies)
Includes bibliographical references and index.
ISBN-10: 1-58729-973-9 (pbk)
ISBN-10: 1-58729-974-7 (e-book)
ISBN-13: 978-1-58729-973-5 (pbk)
ISBN-13: 978-1-58729-974-2 (e-book)
1. Recuay culture — Peru — Ancash.   2. Indian art — Peru — Ancash.
3. Indian architecture — Peru — Ancash.   4. Indian pottery — Peru —
Ancash.   5. Ancash (Peru) — Antiquities.   I. Title.
F3429.1.A45L385   2011
985'.21 — dc22   2010043206

He sees a whole that is complex and yet without disorder; he sees a city, an organism composed of statues, temples, gardens, dwellings, stairways, urns, capitals, of regular and open spaces. None of these artifacts (I know) impresses him as beautiful; they move him as we might be moved today by a complex machine of whose purpose we are ignorant but in whose design we can intuit an immortal intelligence.
— Jorge Luis Borges,
   "Story of the Warrior
   and the Captive"

A column toils at snail's pace up a mountain through narrow gorges; gunners and teamsters yell and swear as they flog their weary beasts along the rocky tracts; each broken-down wagon has to be removed at the cost of indescribable effort while behind it the rest of the column stops, grumbles, and curses.
— Carl von Clausewitz,
   On War

CONTENTS

ACKNOWLEDGMENTS

Like the story of Recuay culture that I present here, this work chronicles a peculiar journey involving engagements with all manner of persons, places, and things. I have been fortunate enough to conduct the research in a region of the world and on an ancient culture that I find extraordinary.

I first wish to acknowledge the funding for the various phases of my research in highland Ancash which forms the basis of this book's presentation and conclusions. The Chinchawas project was enabled by the support of the National Science Foundation, the Wenner-Gren Foundation for Anthropological Research, and several grants from Yale University's Department of Anthropology and Council on Archaeological Studies. The ongoing work at Yayno and in the surrounding region has been funded by the National Geographic Committee for Research and Exploration, the British Academy, the Heinz Foundation for Latin American Archaeology, and the Sainsbury Research Unit for the Arts of Africa, Oceania and the Americas (SRU).

No matter how rich field data sets can be, they are informative only through detailed documentation and study. Follow-up analyses of materials (ceramics, lithics, faunal materials, and metals) were made possible through Yale support (John F. Enders Grant program, Council on Archaeological Studies) and external small grants (Sigma-Xi GIAR). Support to complete the research as a thesis and in the form of presentations was generously provided by the Yale Graduate School of Arts and Sciences and the Department of Anthropology's Schwartz Fund. Lab work on the Yayno materials has been made possible by the British Academy and the SRU. Many individuals were involved in the administration of these awards, and I rarely have occasion to thank them properly; the ones who come to mind here are Donna del Buco, Marion Schwartz, Mary Smith, Lynne Humphreys, and Rowena Burgess. It goes without saying that without the support of these individuals and institutions, this book would have been impossible.

Peru's Instituto Nacional de Cultura (INC) has been instrumental in enabling the field research. I would like to thank the various members of the archaeological commission and associated staff in the Lima office who have assisted me on different occasions, including Lida Casas, Jorge Silva, Luis Jaime Castillo, Luis Peña, José Luis Pino, and Enrique Hulerig. The Huaraz office of the INC has been instrumental in supervising the fieldwork and in the stewardship of the project materials. I would like to thank all the directors who have been supportive of our work over the years, especially César Aguirre, César Serna, Victor Pimentel, Benjamín Morales, José Antonio Salazar, and Francisco Bazán, as well as the archaeologists and associated staff: Mirtha Antúnez, Wilder León, Lucho Burgos, Fernando Gutierrez, and Estéban Sosa.

The writing of this work began in earnest during my fellowship at Dumbarton Oaks. Its library and academic milieu fostered the first incarnations of what would become the sculpture, imagery, and architecture chapters. Many conversations with Jeffrey Quilter (then director of Precolumbian Studies), the other fellows, and the wider scholarly community there steered my research in new and productive directions. Aptly, in the Pre-Columbian tradition, it was also "formative" in transitioning me to the Sainsbury Research Unit at the University of East Anglia, Norwich, England, which widened my scholarly horizons immeasurably. Generous research time granted by the SRU and the University of East Anglia (UEA), with study leave in the fall of 2007, brought this writing project to completion.

Various people have graciously offered their time in other ways during phases of the research. In addition to the community of Chinchaywasi, Martín Justiniano, Jorge Luis Alvarez, Jim Schumacher, and Scott Hutson were instrumental during the fieldwork at Chinchawas. The Yayno work was helped out immensely by Mariano Jaramillo (our guide, cook, and curer), Julio Escudero, Silvia Milla, Nilton Luya, Katy Rodríguez, Alejandro Velasco, Italo Sauñe, Martha Bell, Philip Compton, José Luis Pino, Pomabamba's Casa de la Cultura, and the many contributions of the *comuneros* of Asuac and Huanchacbamba. George Miller kindly provided training and advice on faunal analysis; metalwork, human skeletal materials, and obsidian from Chinchawas were examined by Heather Lechtman, John Verano, and Richard Burger, respectively.

During my time in the UK and Europe, more generally, various people have been important in facilitating the practical and intellectual realization of this book. Many thanks are owed to my UEA colleagues, including Steve Hooper, Joshua Bell, Aristóteles Barcelos-Neto, Simon Dell, Margit Thøfner, Ferdinand de Jong, Sandy Heslop, John Mack, and Joanne

Clarke, who all contribute to a lively and fertile academic environment in which *things*, broadly theorized, matter in our work in the study of world cultures. Such perspectives have been enhanced by a number of our visiting fellows, and I wish to acknowledge the valuable insights of a few: Virginia Miller, Christopher Donnan, Penny Dransart, and Jeff Blomster. David Chicoine and Gabriel Ramón deserve mention for their friendship and generosity. I am also indebted to other SRU members, past and present, for their assistance in various ways, especially Pat Hewitt, Francine Hunt, Ludo Coupaye, Andy Mills, and Lisa Snell. Mary Katherine Scott assisted in the final preparation of the manuscript. Jeff Splitstoser helped with the textile descriptions. Christopher Donnan provided access to photographs of objects in several collections. Various meetings and workshops in Europe with fellow researchers Kevin Lane, Alex Herrera, Carolina Orsini, Bebel Ibarra, Doris Walter, and Wilhelm Diessl have been extremely rewarding and have resulted in thinking about the sierra of Ancash over the *longue durée*.

I would like to thank various organizations for access to collections and illustrative material: the Museum für Völkerkunde (Berlin), the Cambridge Museum of Archaeology and Anthropology, the Liverpool Museum, the British Museum, Museo Arqueológico de Ancash (Huaraz), Museo Nacional de Arqueología, Antropología e Historia (Lima), Museo de la Nación (Lima), the American Museum of Natural History (New York), and the Stuttgart Museum. I also thank Yale University's Department of Anthropology, the Peabody Museum, Kommission für Archäologie Aussereuropäischer Kulturen, Sage Publications, and Elsevier for their kind permission to reconfigure certain segments of previous work for this synthesis. The University of Iowa Press, especially Holly Carver and Kathy Lewis, also deserves thanks for all the editorial support.

Highland Ancash, particularly Huaraz and Pomabamba, has been like a second home to me. This comfort is made possible almost entirely by the hospitality and friendship extended to me by the Wegner-Oliveros, Olaza, Meza-Benway, Escudero, and Apolín-Meza families. I am especially indebted to Steve Wegner, the foremost advocate of Recuay archaeology, who has been the most invaluable colleague I could hope for in the field and in the lab. Finally, special thanks are extended to Richard Burger and Lucy Salazar-Burger for all their help and support through the years.

ANDEAN EXPRESSIONS

CHAPTER ONE

Toward a Recuay Prehistory

In this book I offer a prehistory of the Central Andes. By "prehistory" I mean the archaeological record of social and cultural developments before the written sources of the early sixteenth century. I also refer to the broad and potent spectrum of disciplines which informs our knowledge and narrative of the Andean past. This book centers on the archaeology of northern Peru but is not limited to archaeology. The insights provided by scholars in fields such as anthropology, art history, environmental and geological studies, and history are integral to advancing the current state of knowledge of developments in the prehistoric record of northern Peru.

This book proceeds with the conviction that we can advance our interpretations of ancient Andean society by developing a more generous approach to how things and spaces were complicit with humans in the events of the past. As Borges would have it, these do not necessarily regard aesthetics or function but are nevertheless provocative and informative and manage to form a complex whole, which I understand broadly as culture. In the contemplation of single facts, we can intuit some patterns and experience of their collective being. Like the observer in the epigraph, I hope to recognize in the complexities of the past — as located in ruins, statues, and urns — an enduring order and intelligence.

In recent years the pace of research for Central Andean prehistory, specifically of the first millennium A.D., has resulted in exciting and significant discoveries, many of which have revolutionized our understanding of the ancient Americas. But for various reasons the archaeology has concentrated on developments that occurred in cultures on the coast of Peru, of which Moche, Nasca, and Paracas are among the best known.

A coeval but less well-known culture, the Recuay of Peru's north highlands, forms the focus of this study (fig. 1). Like their coastal contemporaries, the Recuay people are best known for their unique art style, also

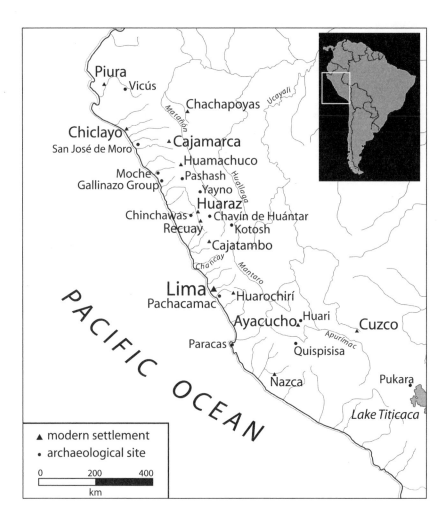

FIGURE 1. The Central Andes and places mentioned in the text.

associated with funerary pottery found in museum collections. Yet I wish to move beyond the study of the appeal of Recuay artworks to characterize the history of Recuay groups on the basis of their interaction with their distinctive environment. Recuay's most celebrated developments occurred at the foot of Peru's Cordillera Blanca, the highest and most extensive ice caps in the New World tropics and one of the most picturesque places on earth. The ecological diversity and a central geographic position in northern Peru were instrumental in the economic prosperity of Recuay groups.

Ecology and geography were also instrumental in shaping the look and distribution of the culture —"Recuayness," if you will. The rich but fragmented zones of production sustained unique centers of Recuay development and contributed to the formation of stylistic areas and boundaries that scholars are only now beginning to disentangle. Together, the groups shared similar material styles and ways of doing things, especially styles of making.

The notion of Recuayness holds a series of important implications. First, a long history of fairly insular cultural development forms the crux of the Recuay cultural tradition — patterned developments characterizing highland Ancash over the greater part of the first millennium A.D. (Lau 2004b). It is this Recuayness, in the style of material culture, which also lets us perceive interaction with other groups and, just as important, cultural changes through time. These dispositions were sometimes purposefully instantiated or employed by the Recuay to distinguish themselves from others.

To be sure, the manifestations of the tradition varied substantially. Yet Recuay's coherence was expressed as shared culture, community, and corporate identity. I reveal its diversity through time and space in order to challenge the generalized, monolithic characterizations of Recuay pervasive in the literature today.

Since its identification in the late nineteenth century (Macedo 1881), Recuay has been recognized as one of the key cultures of ancient Peru by many of the luminaries in New World archaeology (Bennett 1944; Kroeber 1944; Tello 1929). It is often considered one of the constituent cultures of the "Peruvian Co-Tradition": "the cultures included in an area co-tradition are treated as wholes. Thus each has its own history, its own persistent traditions. The coined word, co-tradition, refers, then, to the linkage, the interrelationships of these cultural traditions in time and space" (Bennett 1948: 1). New archaeological work has added greatly to the current knowledge of Recuay local groups and settlements. An overview of the current literature serves to compare patterns and fill in gaps by making analogies among a range of data sets.

Finally, this study will help to redress the lack of explicit theoretical discussion which can update our social interpretations of Recuay culture and prehistory. One of the keystones of current archaeology is a reliance on social and anthropological theory for understanding the human past. Most research on Recuay, however, has focused on culture history — the characterization of discrete cultures and their change through time. Culture history is a basic building block in archaeology, but what are the social implications of Recuay culture through time? How were Recuay groups organized, and what were the sources of social and political power? This study updates the current literature by considering Recuay prehistory through perspectives involving social complexity, economic interaction, and material culture.

Recuay "Culture"

My analysis centers broadly on the importance of *things*, especially objects and buildings, for ancient Andean groups. Such things remain our principal source of data for interpretation and identification of an archaeological culture. These things, ideas, and practices (shared cultural norms) also distinguish a culture from others. At its core, this position draws from V. Gordon Childe's famous pronouncement about the archaeological endeavor: "We find certain types of remains — pots, implements, ornaments, burial rites, and house forms — constantly recurring together. Such a complex of associated traits we shall term 'cultural group' or just 'culture.' We assume that such a complex is the material expression of what today would be called 'people'" (Childe 1929: v–vi). While most scholars reject any facile correspondence between the remains and social identity, archaeologists are still obliged to intuit the past through things — as carefully as possible.

How do investigators distinguish Recuay peoples? This is almost exclusively based on material remains, especially ceramics, architecture, stone sculpture, and other objects with imagery. Because these things participated in the everyday and ritual life of the groups who used them, they are crucial for reconstructing ancient economic and ceremonial practices. Such activities and their variability are basic in reconstructing the social organization and political complexity of Recuay societies.

Building on culture history, I offer a broad social and historical model to frame an updated, more flexible perspective on Recuay material culture. Few attempts have been made to contextualize its place and the "linkage, the interrelationships" with other Andean cultures. Little consideration has been given to Recuay culture outside its own spatial and temporal boundaries. This book therefore aims to reconstruct and evaluate the record of Recuay developments as part of a wider Andean prehistory.

Value Systems in the Recuay Tradition

José Mariano Macedo, a late nineteenth-century doctor and collector of Peruvian antiquities, noted perceptively in a discussion of prehispanic pottery: "This section [referring to a portion of his collection] is so well defined that upon seeing a Recuay pot it's not possible to confuse it with other pots from other sources; in my opinion, there existed, in Recuay, a civilization entirely isolated from the rest" (excerpted from Amat 1976b: 194, citing a letter published in *El Nacional*, 30 September 1878; my translation).

Finely made objects in a distinctive style have always been the diagnostic of the culture. In all the major media discussed in this book (architecture, stone sculpture, ceramics) and in some for which limited data are available (metalwork, textiles), the Recuay achieved a very high degree of technical sophistication, rivaling their contemporaries and other Andean cultures across time.

The study of ancient artworks forms one of the most exciting avenues of inquiry in Andean archaeology. Not only can scholars compare imagery with ancient contexts, a sort of ground-truthing, but imagery provides clues for discerning ancient patterns of behavior and belief systems. Such studies appeal because they elicit meanings which connect the past and present and show us at once how similar our situation can be to our subjects' situation and how very different.

But the study of imagery is also one of the most uncertain avenues of inquiry because of the polysemic, unstable quality of the primary data. It must be remembered that ancient artworks and imagery are neither historical archives nor a priori expressions of belief systems; they do not record (and certainly not objectively) so much as treat select themes and perspectives chosen by their artists, sponsors, and users. Their meanings also change through the process and history of their appreciation. Hence ancient images cannot be taken as impartial or complete texts of the past. Where possible, I aim to integrate different lines of contextual evidence with historical comparisons to help inform interpretations about the ancient belief systems of the Recuay.

At this juncture, I should clarify what I mean by Recuay "art," since native Andeans, and indeed most non-Western groups, do not have a comparable term. It is impossible to know for certain whether ancient Recuay peoples conceived of an art. Most items that I describe here were used in their original contexts and thus were not created as "art for art's sake" or to be appreciated for their beauty in an exhibition case. Also, most of these items do not fit easily into traditional preoccupations with verisimilitude or faithful representation. Terms such as "visual culture" and "aesthetic objects" may also be unsatisfactory: one privileges the visual in cultures that were, by obligation, multisensory, while the other favors evaluative schemes that may be more reflective of Western tastes or end in tautologies (Coote and Shelton 1992; Gell 1998; Weiner 1994). For this volume, I rely on several approaches to help distill a perspective which offers the virtues of categorical boundaries but also interpretative value for the Recuay cases.

It is useful to return to George Kubler's generous view of aesthetic behavior: "Every experience has a sense; it is rationalized; it is laden with emotion. Aesthetic behaviour is concerned with emotional states, and it marks the production of every artifact, however simple or useful it may be. Hence an aesthetic function is present in every human product, and, by extension, in all cultural behaviour" (Kubler 1962a: 17). For analyzing artworks as "products of aesthetic value," Kubler (1962a: 15) emphasized an object's perceptual quality, which derived from "a special intricacy in several dimensions: technical, symbolic and individual." This quality (expressed through the object's form and its visuality) and its varied meanings (iconography) were at the core of his endeavor.

One of the virtues of Kubler's approach is its emphasis on tracking classes and sequences of forms/meanings across great spaces and temporal durations; serial information is key, especially for discerning exceptions or deviations (Kubler 1962b: 40–49). Explaining archaeological objects as "works of art," he admitted, was a difficult task and could result in a "documentary file on cultural themes," for which he condemned archaeologists and anthropologists in particular. Yet a sort of documentary file on Recuay cultural themes, as an entry into larger questions and hypotheses, is precisely what I wish to offer here.

Subsequent studies in the anthropology of art aim to decenter the study of art from the study of aesthetics or "evaluative schemes," of both the observer and the cultures and artworks studied (Gell 1992, 1998). The criticism is leveled at scholars focused on indigenous or period-based "ways of seeing," because the simple evaluation of particular works of art sidelines some crucial issues, such as the social context of art production, circulation, and reception. For Alfred Gell, the core message in any anthropology of art is the sociality of objects: objects are engendered by and have social relationships, just like people. Eschewing issues of aesthetic behavior or symbolic meanings, Gell prefers what art objects do: it is about their agency to make things happen, to initiate "causal sequences," in the vicinity of biological persons.

The foregoing approaches need not be antithetical. Both explore how artifacts, in general, can effect outcomes in perception as well as in subsequent actions. Just as the formalism of Kubler provides a necessary methodological bridge to organize archaeological artifacts, Gell's sociology of object-person relations widens the possible range of their ancient local understandings. Throughout this work, I characterize Recuay artworks as those things and built spaces of fine quality and skill in manufacture (e.g., Lau 2006b). But I also wish to privilege local contexts for cultural elaboration — where and what people decided to value.

Labeling archaeological things as valued or as wealth entails a certain circularity. Only a fraction of the past survives in the archaeological record. And only part of that is recovered systematically enough to furnish contextual information, so the representativeness of the observations and judgments is always problematic. Not surprisingly, the best-known Recuay things are also the most durable: monolithic sculpture, stone architecture, and pottery (a form of artificial stone).

The intense seasonal rains of the Ancash highlands result in poor conditions of preservation, especially when compared to the Peruvian coast, where aridity facilitates survival of even very delicate organic remains. So it is important not to underappreciate potentially "valuable" things made out of wood, cloth, leather, sinew, and other more perishable materials. It is also clear that some Andean valuables were not highly elaborate objects at all: a simple stone could serve equally as *huaca*, a thing charged with or manifesting sacred power, like a temple or god image.

It is equally important that no informants exist today from Recuay times to help define the nature and tournaments of value (for things), which characterize any society (Appadurai 1986). The biography of an object can be tracked by ethnographers through observations and interviews. Archaeologists have no simple way to do this in the past, however, without recourse to assumptions made by implicating other (similar) objects and contexts or through fine-grain analysis of modifications or reuse of the object/building itself. Despite important attempts (Meskell 2004), it is very difficult to develop firm ancient "object biographies" (Kopytoff 1986) for the very reason that individual objects are found fossilized in time and function, as snapshots of individual states and contexts. The archaeological record may offer innumerable snapshots of other items. Some items may be reasonably similar but exist by obligation in different contexts; by identifying and assessing their relationships, archaeologists make reasonably informed comparisons. Thus they rely strongly on contexts and analogy to determine ancient value. Archaeologists generate narratives about the patterning of objects rather than object biographies per se.

Overall, greater fixity characterizes the value of ancient things as ascribed by scholars, because it is rare to have access to the whole story of any single object. This is not a cause for lament, however: the larger perspective of things in society is enhanced because of the long-term attention to changing regimes of value across object types and assemblages that archaeology is able to provide.

What did native Andeans value? In describing Andean notions of wealth, Frank Salomon (2004: 116) contends that "four semantic components — message or sign; sacred productive essence; inheritance for continuity; and reciprocity — add up to a summary of what Andean cultures traditionally treasured."[1] For archaeology, this broad statement implies that monetary or energy indices of value must be complemented by emphasis on additional classes of valuables (not currency), their properties, formal relations in and between them, and their role in the social (Graeber 2001; Munn 1986).

Those things which the ancient Recuay valued were fundamentally social artifacts. Object histories and life histories are intertwined in many societies. This is because objects and valuables more generally are created not in opposition to persons but out of and via persons. Hence people and objects are often parts of and occupy places/statuses in similar sets of social relations (Hoskins 1998; Strathern 1988). Thus the analysis of Recuay culture and Andean groups in general will be enhanced if the ascription of the social can be extended. More specifically, I employ "social relations" here in a manner which is common to Amerindian ontologies: as articulating multiple kinds of beings, including humans, animals, ancestors, divinities, and efficacious objects (see Allen 1998; Descola 2006; Viveiros de Castro 1998, 2004).

Ancient valuation systems can be approximated through another means: by judging dispositions and choices in material culture. Any single object, say a pot, is the outcome of many choices. It is a compromise out of a set of desires and constraints responding to local circumstances and previous solutions. This basic relationship of cultural choices and value has long been advocated by scholars of Andean technology (Dransart 2002; Lechtman 1984) and elsewhere (Dietler and Herbich 1998; Lemonnier 1993). Technical procedures were developed in the ancient Andes to emphasize specific physical properties or expertise for an object. Technical choices are thus critical in how makers materialize local value systems and meanings. Furthermore, technical actions within and across media can be "intertextual" across contexts; for example, motor and conceptual equivalencies made between plowing and weaving, as core transformative activities, are basic to referring to, and indeed shaping, broader social relations (e.g., Arnold 1997). Recuay groups can be said to draw on this paradigm of making in surprisingly innovative ways that emphasize certain "cross-over" techniques to render surfaces and exteriors.

It is important to note here that the making process of special things, where the purposeful inclusion of "essence" may be manifested, may be related to the Quechua term *camay*. The term is glossed by Gerald Taylor (2000: 7, note 24) as "the act of animating," as he describes the language of creation in the Huarochirí manuscript, applicable to humans, animals, and things alike. Salomon (1991: 16) adds that in camay we have "a concept to charge with being, to infuse with species specific power . . . energizing of extant matter . . . a continuous act that works upon a being as long as it exists." It may be of related importance, then, that master weavers of fine cloth (*cumbi*) were called "cumbi camayo" or "qompikamayoq" in Inka times (e.g., Cobo 1990: 225; Rowe 1979: 239–240). Simply put, certain makers were probably imbued with special qualities of creation and transformation of materials.

Artisans during late prehistoric times were themselves often sought after (D'Altroy 2002; Espinoza Soriano 1987; Rostworowski de Diez Canseco 1999). Metalworkers were brought in from many parts of the Inka empire to ply their trade for Inka nobles in Cuzco; craftspersons, sometimes in entire communities, were relocated to different parts of the empire to help with making pottery, textiles, and metalwork. Also, craft specialists sometimes transcended normal citizenry statuses and responsibilities; for example, some were exempted from the system of labor tax obligation.

Recuay cultural production consistently valued fundamental properties of materials (such as durability, color, and contrasts), qualities of form (including containment and monumentality), and decorated surfaces in addition to their functions. This book explores these properties, with a particular emphasis on their importance for past societies. The objective is to contextualize groups of solutions and observe deviations and patterns. The variability in choices can be assessed as dispositions toward value, at both the synchronic and diachronic levels.

In sum, I combine formal, technical, and agentive approaches to examine a selected corpus of archaeological material. A sustained consideration of things in Recuay contexts facilitates appreciation of their cultural value and their social roles and relationships in the past. The dynamic between things and humans sheds light on ancient conditions and contexts. Throughout this book, especially in the later chapters, I present Recuay artifacts as fundamentally social, in the sense of creating and negotiating relations among persons, places, and things.

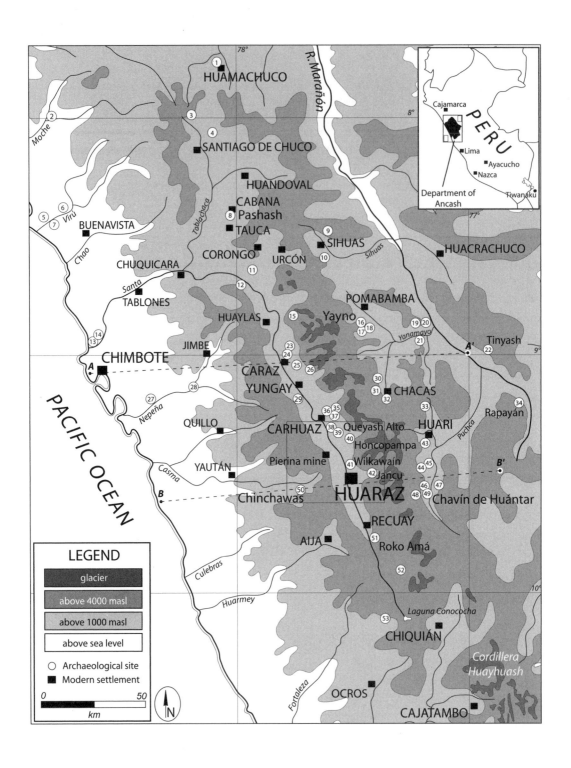

PACIFIC OCEAN

PERU

Cajamarca

Lima
Ayacucho
Nazca
Tiwanaku

Department of Ancash

HUAMACHUCO

SANTIAGO DE CHUCO

HUANDOVAL

CABANA
Pashash
TAUCA

SIHUAS

HUACRACHUCO

BUENAVISTA

Virú

Moche

Chao

CORONGO
URCÓN

Tablachaca

CHUQUICARA

Santa

TABLONES

POMABAMBA

HUAYLAS

Yayno

Sihuas

Yanamayo

Tinyash

CHIMBOTE

JIMBE

CARAZ
YUNGAY

CHACAS

Rapayán

Puchca

QUILLO

CARHUAZ

Queyash Alto

HUARI

Honcopampa

Nepeña

Pierina mine

Wilkawaín

YAUTÁN

Casma

Jancu

HUARAZ

Chavín de Huántar

Chinchawas

A   A'

B   B'

RECUAY

AIJA

Roko Amá

Culebras

Huarmey

Laguna Conococha

CHIQUIÁN

Cordillera
Huayhuash

Fortaleza

OCROS

CAJATAMBO

R. Marañón

FIGURE 2. (*Facing page*) North-central Peru, showing the location of the Department of Ancash and places mentioned in text. Transect and map inset (in dark gray) indicators refer to figures 3 and 7, respectively. Key to numbered sites: (1) Marcahuamachuco; (2) Cruz Blanca; (3) Porcón; (4) Agopampa; (5) Gallinazo Group; (6) Tomaval; (7) Huancaco; (8) Pashash; (9) Cerro Campanario; (10) Culyón; (11) La Pampa; (12) Callhuash; (13) San Nicolás; (14) Guadalupito; (15) Aukispukio; (16) Yayno; (17) Rayogaga; (18) Karway; (19) Huintoc; (20) Marcajirca; (21) Gotushjirca; (22) Tinyash; (23) Katiamá; (24) Tumshukayko; (25) Pueblo Viejo; (26) Queushu; (27) Pañamarca; (28) Huancarpón; (29) Guitarrero Cave; (30) Riway; (31) Jatungaga; (32) Chagastunán; (33) Romerojirca; (34) Rapayán; (35) Copa Chico; (36) Supaycaca; (37) Copa Grande; (38) Huaricoto; (39) Queyash Alto; (40) Honcopampa; (41) Wilkawaín; (42) Jancu; (43) Gantujirca; (44) Caunín; (45) Pariac; (46) Pojoc; (47) Warampu Patac; (48) Pucagaga; (49) Chavín de Huántar; (50) Chinchawas; (51) Roko Amá; (52) Wariraga; (53) Huambo.

The Early Intermediate Period in the Central Andes

During the early first millennium A.D. a dramatic shift toward cultural heterogeneity occurred across the Central Andes. This is expressed most clearly in the proliferation of marvelous yet remarkably different art styles, leading pioneering scholars to define the time as the Mastercraftsman Period (Bennett and Bird 1949). Most scholars attribute the transformation to the emergence of regional ethnic and political boundaries throughout the Andes (Donnan 1992; Makowski 2004; Silverman and Proulx 2002), together with innovations in technology, economic practices, and social organization.

Recuay groups developed in a part of northern Peru more or less corresponding to the modern limits of the Department of Ancash (fig. 2). Recuay culture flourished during the time known as the Early Intermediate Period, ca. A.D. 1–700 (Rowe 1967; Rowe and Menzel 1967). This period nestles between the Early Horizon (ca. 800 B.C.–A.D. 1) and the later Middle Horizon (A.D. 700–1000), which are associated with broad pan-Andean distributions of material culture.

The Early Intermediate Period has also been called the "Regional Developmental Period" (Lumbreras 1974b), referring to the prominent regionalization in cultural patterns. The north, central, and south coasts of Peru were the dominion of Moche, Lima, and Nasca groups. At the same time, the sierra saw the emergence of powerful Cajamarca, Huarpa, and Pukara groups in the north, central, and Titicaca highlands, respectively. Each of these societies developed a strong corporate style of art (Moseley 1992: 73–74).

The great diversification of cultural styles was facilitated by technical innovations and new patterns of consumption, typically associated with the display practices of local elites. New techniques of crafting were developed in the textile arts, metallurgy, and architecture (e.g., Donnan 1992; Goldstein 2000; Lechtman 1980; Moore 1996b; Paul 1990; Vaughn 2005). But many of the most notable advances occurred in ceramic production. Various groups, including the Recuay, employed new techniques, uses, and contexts for their local pottery.

Terms such as "Classic" and "Florescent" imply the widespread emergence of civilization, often associated with the rise of social hierarchies and state formation (e.g., Lanning 1967; Larco Hoyle 1966). As new data are added and models become refined, the record indicates greater variability in the social and political arrangements of the major Early Intermediate Period cultures (e.g., Castillo and Uceda C. 2008; Silverman and Proulx 2002). One primary goal of this study is to help situate Recuay culture within these new developments, elucidating how Recuay groups both participated in and contributed to the Early Intermediate Period's sociocultural dynamism.

Another major trend of the time was the widespread formation of large nucleated settlements. Urbanization was most apparent along the coast, especially the central and north coasts (Chapdelaine 1998; Schaedel 1951, 1966; Shimada 1994; Topic 1982), but the emergence of large centers also appears in the Recuay region and in other parts of the high Andes. Recuay centers took very different forms, however, and it would be premature to call them cities, either in the Western sense (see Rowe 1963) or by using a coastal Andean "desert city" analogy (Moseley and Day 1982; Shimada 1994). Investigations at Recuay centers do not readily show the functional segmentation (for example, multiethnic enclaves and areas for craft specialization and redistribution) often cited in such approximations of cities (Kolata 1983; Makowski 2008a). Nevertheless, these centers are distinguished not only by their great size and nucleation but also by a strong emphasis on large corporate projects (such as monumental temples, defenses, and irrigation systems) and distinctive funerary practices (such as ancestor veneration and great disposal of luxuries). These are highly suggestive of social hierarchies and the presence of wealthy elites.

Thus the oft-cited conundrum of Pre-Columbian urbanism in the New World resurfaces: the existence of large settlements, monumental architecture, temples, and privileged groups but uneven evidence for strong economic specialization, enclaves/barrios, and strong class systems. What were the reasons for this, and how were highland centers different from their coastal contemporaries (for example, size, architecture, communities)? What do these differences tell us about the groups and societies who made and inhabited them? The Recuay record adds insight into this process during the Early Intermediate Period.

Another major development during the period was the emergence of militaristic cultures and polities, certainly on the north coast and in the adjacent highlands. Increasingly hostile interaction occurred within and between regional groups (Bonavia 1991; Lanning 1967; Lumbreras 1974b; Makowski, Donnan, et al. 1994; Moseley 1992; Silverman and Proulx 2002; Topic and Topic 1982). The Recuay case is especially important for reckoning the early emergence of fortified centers and towns, because this pattern would characterize the Peruvian Andes until colonial times.

While intergroup violence appears to have predominated in earlier developments, the cultural emphasis on warfare during the Early Intermediate Period was unprecedented. This is most readily seen by a proliferation of defensive walled sites, often on hilltops, throughout many parts of the Central Andes, including the highlands and especially coastal areas (e.g., Willey 1953; Wilson 1988). Furthermore, a series of Early Intermediate Period cultures shared preoccupations with celebrating armed conflict in artworks and imagery (e.g., Cisneros Velarde and Lumbreras 1980; Donnan and McClelland 1999; Makowski, Amaro, and Eléspuru 1994; Menzel et al. 1964; Proulx 2006; Verano 2001). The depiction of warriors, associated clothing, weaponry, and trophies became much more frequent. Such things were often grave offerings, suggesting that important members of various Early Intermediate Period societies, including Recuay, reveled in their identity as warriors. Broadly, a warfare culture developed across the Central Andes and was emphasized in the material culture of many groups during the Early Intermediate Period.

Recuay Sociopolitical Arrangements

Archaeologists have debated about how Recuay groups were organized sociopolitically. Compared to better-known cultures, such as the Moche, Recuay has been portrayed as a static entity lacking internal variability and trajectories of change. For example, settlement survey studies and excavations commonly uncover evidence for Recuay contacts with neighboring groups, yet there is no consensus on when and whether the pattern represents territorial expansion, conflict, intensive exchange, or limited trade of prestige goods. Now, however, rich lines of evidence can be brought together to analyze Recuay's political arrangements as well as their emergence and decline.

The current evidence identifies a series of independent chiefly polities emerging in the general context of relatively dispersed egalitarian communities. Usually centered on the key settlements of large productive drainages, some of these polities fit the criteria generally ascribed to large or paramount chiefdoms: *reinos, señorios, cacicazgos,* or *curacazgos,* in the ethnohistorical parlance. Certainly size and expected population of the important Recuay sites (Yayno, Pashash, Huaraz) seem to be important indicators. Another key reason seems to be the consolidation of wealth and political power in the hands of a few, probably leaders and their close kin. Such power was manifested as unequal accumulation of rare exotics, luxury goods, and monumental architecture.

Early colonial writings of the Ancash region help shed light on Recuay developments (Espinoza Soriano 1978; Varón Gabai 1980). Ethnic lords (*curacas*) were powerful hereditary leaders who commanded rights to farmlands and other resources, such as water rights and herds of camelids. They also bequeathed their political authority and certain resource rights to their children. Their seats of power were in large nucleated settlements, although their command over labor tributaries could extend to many different communities in surrounding and frequently discontiguous areas. One cacique (chief) in northern Ancash, for example, tallied as part of his sovereignty 31 villages and 687 tribute-paying subjects in 1543, even after having suffered dramatic demographic change due to successive Inka and European interventions and subsequent developments (Cook 1977: 25, 37, 1981: chap. 11).[2] The largest Recuay settlements may have been the centers of such sociopolitical arrangements by the third or fourth centuries A.D. The regional scope for Recuay polities is mainly inferred from settlement and excavation evidence, as discussed in chapters 3 and 4; the way in which leaders were understood and construed in the past can also be analyzed through representational artworks, as discussed in chapters 6 and 7.

Little evidence suggests that Recuay groups ever coalesced into a "state." Some of the basic criteria used to distinguish this level of social complexity (such as road and storage infrastructure, formal priesthoods, bureaucracies, standing armies, and settlement hierarchies) have no archaeological correlates in Recuay culture. Not all complex social trajectories lead inexorably toward statehood; neither should we desire or expect statehood as some form of achievement or imperative for civilization (Burger 1992; Yoffee 2005). Most studies of complex societies have usually concerned their formation, especially from a comparative perspective. Equally vital questions center on the diversity, historical contexts, and interaction of complex societies. The point here is not to encourage a type of historical particularism but rather to acknowledge the basic empirical challenge of broadening our sample of the variability of complex societies, especially as it relates to their creativity and adaptation, before grand narrative schemes are presented.

One limitation of evolutionary typologies and their constituent terms such as "chiefdoms" (or any of the Spanish cognate terms) is simply that they flatten out known and potential heterogeneity in cultural assemblages and social collectivities. This occurs both synchronically and diachronically. A suspicion of evolutionary typology and globalizing ascriptions (for example, classic, florescent, and decadent) prompted John Rowe and others to eschew stage-based chronologies in favor of one based on cultural affinities and their contemporaneity. The obfuscation of variability is perhaps most apparent when trying to discuss coeval societies with different sociopolitical arrangements that share similar material cultures. Do we call all Moche groups during Middle Moche times "kingdoms"? Were all groups part of the "empire" during Inka times, and when?

My challenge is to envision a term flexible enough to describe Recuay arrangements through time and space. It is quite clear that large or "complex" chiefdoms (or even any of the Spanish terms) is inappropriate, because most areas in the Recuay heartland do not show their material correlates. Also, "complex polities" were not predominant during any period. During the Huarás period (the early part of the Recuay cultural tradition), we have hardly any evidence of chiefly societies.

For this reason, I lean toward the cultural dimensions — the boundedness, internal diversity, and dynamism — in any social organizational gloss. This is not simply out of a mistrust of broad cross-cultural labels but because we lack sufficient data to make a meaningful comparison — and the evidence that does exist fits imperfectly with any current typological schema. Even in the interest of attending to more cultural criteria, other scholars have described the Recuay case as an "interaction sphere" or "ethnic group" (Schaedel 1985; Smith 1978). I would argue that these terms are similarly problematic for the Recuay case. In the first instance, the emphasis of both terms is on the synchronic, which limits consideration of developments in the collective/phenomenon through time. Also, almost all interaction between Recuay people(s) seems to have been in terms of material style; at present we have very little evidence for intensive economic transactions. And although Recuay may certainly have been a type of regional ethnicity, it would be premature to declare this as a matter of fact, without corroborating lines of evidence on how it is like an ethnicity (Lau 2004a, 2006a). Ideal sorts of data in this regard would be language, music, and oral traditions about origins and ancestral pasts (e.g., Topic 1998). Unfortunately, these are precisely the cultural phenomena on which the Recuay prehistoric record is largely mute.

To describe the Recuay case, I do find utility in the term "commonwealth," which *The Oxford Concise Dictionary* describes as "a community or organization of shared interests in a non-political field" and *The Oxford English Dictionary* as "the whole body of people constituting a nation or state, the body politic; an independent community, esp. viewed as a body in which the whole people have a voice and interest." Despite its association with the formation of modern Western nation-states, this term is useful for the deemphasis of politics, which is alluded to but not definitive, and the greater emphasis on shared "voices" and "interests" as part of some greater social arrangement. This is the Recuayness, the materiality of shared elements and shared cultural choices, that I referred to earlier, for which we have substantially greater evidence.

Although this relieves some of the political expectations associated with terms such as "chiefdoms" and "states," my aim is to provide more specific social ascription to those cultural commonalities and shared interests that I label "Recuay." Unlike the terms *curacazgos, señorios,* or "chiefdoms" (which I have used before and will continue to use to describe specific Recuay polities), many dimensions of the Recuay tradition cannot be limited to the political leaders and elites. Because of these shared interests, Recuay as a whole can be contrasted with its contemporaries, to help bring into greater focus its regional boundaries and its linkages with other regional groups of the Peruvian Co-Tradition.

The term "commonwealth" is, for me, essentially a personal preference for referring to a large regional collectivity which is composed of multiple groups, is dispersed over a large area, and shares cultural elements that are, on the whole, different from others. Thus the common "wealth" is the constellation of things, ideas, and practices which is the stuff of Recuay culture, the social implication being the diverse relations among people who participate in this cultural universe. My use of the term presumes that it can and should be politically heterogeneous. And it connotes a cultural boundedness, a greater community, that "interaction sphere" does not. Yet by definition it is neither normative nor passive: people and their cultures within are not assumed to be the same.

Material culture is used actively and with intention by its constituents to engage in the commonwealth — both cohering and diverging from its existing properties/qualities.

On the contrary, perhaps the only inflexible criterion of definition is that the constellation of traits should be, on the whole, different from those of other commonwealths. So, for example, I would imagine a person from Huaraz, ca. A.D. 500, would have more in common with a person from Pashash than a person from Moche or Nasca. We could recognize they had similar dispositions in material culture and practice (such as wearing similar headgear or ear ornaments or carrying the same food items in their bag, prepared in a similar way) and shared local mountain divinities and religious beliefs. Perhaps they spoke the same language. In short, they would have greater cultural commonalities than people from other commonwealths.

This study illuminates how Recuay fits as an ancient Andean society — in cultural practices, social organization, and worldview. It was part of a longer trajectory of social and cultural development in the Central Andes, from which it drew inspiration, techniques, and adaptive patterns. But it demonstrates that Recuay was also very different from other Andean civilizations. Many of the Andean expressions that I term "Recuay," especially in art and cultural production, are fascinating on their own and instructive for understanding other Andean developments.

In the final analysis, the Recuay case provides new and significant evidence to evaluate models of social complexity. Recuay's development represents a notable case of adaptation to challenging highland environments, which contrasts fundamentally with earlier cases of adaptation in the north highlands. Recuay developments also differ from coeval processes on the coast. They offer key insights into the emergence of social hierarchy and chiefly leadership and the formation, interaction, and later dissolution of large discrete polities. Public art, exchange, technological innovations, warfare, and religion were key factors in Recuay organizational complexity.

The Organization of Chapters

This book offers a synthetic accounting and updating of the current archaeological record for Recuay, much of which is not widely known or accessible. Although the study emphasizes archaeological approaches, it also draws from related disciplines, especially anthropology, art history, and ethnohistory, to help theorize the range of material culture

—including sites, architecture, stone sculpture, ceramics, and other artifacts—in its social context. More precisely, I lay emphasis on what Recuay culture serves to do, as a complement to what it stands for, represents, or means. I am particularly interested in exploring how material things intervened in ancient social and political life, rather than merely being passive, epiphenomenal reflections of historical change or cosmology.

Chapter 2 introduces the backdrop for the emergence of Recuay culture, detailing the environment and traditional land use that characterized Recuay's ancient heartland in highland Ancash. I survey the region's diverse geography and paleoenvironment to describe their significance for Recuay groups. Three themes are emphasized: interactions, geographic and social boundaries, and historical forms of land use and social organization. Using a regional scheme, I review the main settlements in the ancient Recuay world, with description of formal and functional elements.

Subsequent chapters form the crux of my argument regarding the myriad interventions of artifacts and places in Recuay society. Chapters 3 and 4 focus on Recuay architecture and landscapes, by detailing variability in form and function and the chronology of Recuay settlements and constructions. In addition to discussing socioeconomic practices (agropastoralism, exchange, and defense), these chapters investigate certain buildings as vital contexts for ceremony and reinforcement of social boundaries. I conclude that special architectural contexts, especially walled enclosures and hilltop communities, were crucial for Recuay social life. Our understanding of the ancient Recuay world relies on evidence for a distinctive physical and religious engagement with the landscape.

Chapter 5 examines one of the most recognizable pottery traditions in ancient America. I provide an appraisal of Recuay ceramic technology, function, and chronology, combining relative and radiocarbon dating. The chapter discusses regional variants of the tradition (A.D. 1–700) and shows that classic Recuay fine pottery was largely limited to high-status production and use, especially for ceremonial purposes (offerings, funerary rites, display).

Chapter 6 evaluates the formal variability, contexts, and use of stone sculptures across time in the Recuay region. The analysis elucidates the changing role and symbolism of north highland sculptural traditions following the collapse of Chavín (ca. 200 B.C.). I contend that the sculptures performed as integral elements of architecture and were especially critical in interactive ceremonial practices, such as public ostentation and ancestor veneration. The production and use of stone sculptures were not limited to elites: communities of different scale and organization, from small egalitarian villages to large towns, were responsible for their manufacture.

Chapter 7 considers Recuay imagery and its implications for ritual and politics. Despite its richness (figural representations of human and animals, activities, multiple media), Recuay iconography remains one of the least understood of the major Andean art styles. The chapter highlights elements and conventions that help reconstruct highland perceptions of social roles and status, the afterlife, and divinity. It draws from the ethnohistorical literature, especially concerning religious practices in the Andean highlands, to shed light on the behavioral and cosmological implications of Recuay materials. By contextualizing their use, this chapter reveals the entangled nature of artworks and spaces in Andean belief systems and social practice.

I argue that many of the genres of representation were largely concerned with the construction of chiefly persons. Ceramic representations emphasized insular, self-sufficient collectives, under the command of chiefly elites. Different media were seen as expressions of leaders and their physical and symbolic "houses." This was effected largely through a value system greatly interested in the aesthetics of surfaces, shared in various types of Recuay making, which made bodies special and unlike. The redundancy of surficial designs helped to distinguish chiefly bodies and extend chiefly associations to different media and forms. Through various modalities of decorated bodies — persons, ceramics, sculptures, and buildings — leaders construed authority and well-being in perpetuity.

Chapter 8 synthesizes the current record for diachronic patterns in Recuay culture. It tracks the key developments during its rise following Chavín and subsequent disintegration and also emphasizes transformations in economic and geopolitical patterns, especially in relation to trade, warfare, and Wari state expansion. Lifeways are transformed during late Recuay times, as expressed through major changes in local representational systems and socioeconomic patterns. Affinities with other Andean cultures and visual systems (e.g., Wari, Moche, and Chavín) are assessed to discern long-term trajectories and contrast the relationships between changing art/technical styles and wider social transformations during the first millennium A.D. Finally, the chapter attempts a narrative regarding the end of Recuay culture, to consider the multiple factors that caused the demise and its social implications.

The chapters interweave three potent themes in understanding Andean society. The first centers on how physical things substitute, circulate, and act for political authority. My interest here is to move beyond the question of whether chiefly societies existed or not to address how they were chiefly. The chapters also examine the extent to which certain objects and built spaces emerge from and contribute to a shared idiom of materiality, common to Recuay groups. Finally, I discuss their role in Recuay ritual (ancestor cults, feasting, interment), social organization, and worldview. My objective is to situate Recuay achievements in the broader contexts of New World prehistory and the more general discussion of material culture in social complexity — in particular, artworks and monuments in power relations and social interaction. Throughout, I take it as a given that material culture actively helps shape society, just as it draws life from it.

CHAPTER TWO

Land and Settlement in Ancient Ancash

Work and daily routine are rarely easy affairs in mountainous zones. Yet Recuay groups flourished in one of the most dramatic settings in the world. Centered around the Cordillera Blanca and the Cordillera Negra, the Recuay heartland encompassed some of the most varied highland terrain in the Andes: cold, windswept steppic plateaus, glacial peaks and lagoons, verdant highland valleys, humid coastal desert canyons, and forested eastern slopes leading into Amazonia. Such diverse terrain within a highly compact zone helped shape crucial forms of economic practice as well as patterns of Recuay settlement. Most Recuay-tradition groups flourished through intensive forms of agro-pastoralism and exchange of products from different ecological zones. This setting also provided crucial locales and landscapes for events memorialized in memory and myth.

One of the great achievements of Recuay societies was their adaptation to the distinctive setting and environment of the north-central Andes. Different life zones were part of everyday existence for many Recuay groups. Each zone presented a series of unique resources for exploitation by ancient groups. Learning the ways in which ancient peoples engaged with these zones is essential for knowing about Recuay culture, especially in terms of the diverse material remains. Historically known forms of land use and records of climate change are also crucial to the analysis.

Environmental Setting

The sierra of the Department of Ancash, northern Peru, formed the Recuay heartland. Especially in the highland zone, the distribution of Recuay culture runs more or less coterminously with Ancash's modern limits. Measuring over 36,000 square kilometers, it is about the size of Switzerland. Throughout most of its prehistory, the distribution of Recuay culture rarely ventured outside of these modern political boundaries.

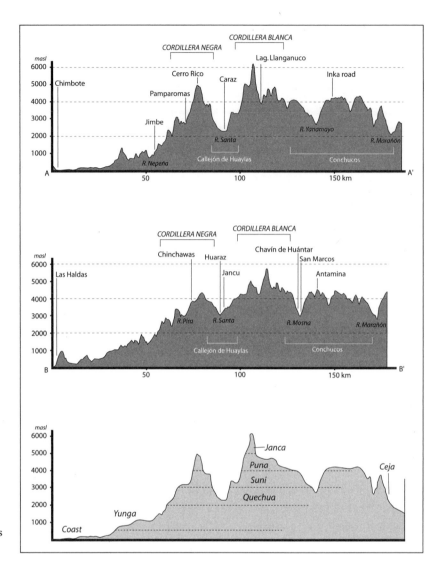

FIGURE 3. (Top and middle) Schematic profiles of transects A–A' and B–B' across Ancash Department, with transect locations found in fig. 2; (bottom) schematic profile of the vertical ecological zones in Ancash Department.

Recuay's geographic boundaries coincided with the Cordillera Huayhuash and the Pativilca Valley to the south, the Río Marañón to the east, and the Pallasca (Cabana) region in the north (fig. 2). As evidenced by their distinctive fineware pottery, Recuay people sometimes descended to different parts of the lower coastal valleys leading into the Pacific Ocean, mainly between the Huarmey and Virú valleys. But most Recuay groups in Ancash were probably limited to middle valley areas of the Pacific Andean flanks, known as the Cordillera Negra.

From the Pacific coastline, the Ancash highlands rapidly ascend over 1,000 meters above sea level (masl) in elevation, composed of the *yunga*, *quechua*, *suni*, *puna/jalca*, and *janca* life zones (ONERN 1972; Pulgar Vidal 1972; Rivera 2003; see also Tosi 1960) (fig. 3). In spite of these general terms, many areas of the highland Ancash today are characterized by great variation in local zonation and environmental conditions crucial for economic practices, seasonality, and resources.

As one moves eastward from the lands associated with coastal littoral and river mouths (*chala*), the valleys begin to narrow near the foothills of the Andes. Here the yunga life zone consists of the diverse warm and humid riverine valleys, from about 500 to 2,000 masl (fig. 4). Although the yungas do not receive much precipitation, rivers flowing down the Andean cordillera make these frequently steep canyons attractive places for settlement and resource procurement (Onuki 1985). Various animal species inhabit the zone, including birds, rodents, and deer as well as other animals such as foxes. Outside the narrow belt of land fed by the rivers, this zone is rocky and desertic. At lower elevations toward the littoral, however, the valleys widen greatly and are characterized as productive arable lands. Today the yungas (or *chaupiyungas*) are often exploited for sugarcane production, but in the past they would have been important for maize, fruits, and coca as well as matting and light building material (Marcus and Silva 1988; Rostworowski 1988). Throughout northern Peru, the middle valleys were often key zones for controlling intake canals of coastal irrigation systems (e.g., Moseley 1983; Shimada 1994).

Ascending in elevation, the yungas merge into the quechua ecological zone, roughly 2,000 to 3,000 masl. The quechua life zone consists of well-watered valley slopes and rockier tracts of cultivable land. It is

FIGURE 4. The middle Nepeña Valley. The mid-valley regions of the north-central coast are important areas for warm irrigation agriculture of crops such as maize, fruits, coca, and chili pepper. Located where the valley neck narrows and the foothills converge, the areas are also strategic places to control canal intakes of irrigation systems and access to routes for coast-highland traffic/trade.

rich in xerophytic shrubs and cactus, with occasional tough grasses and periodic rain-green plants. This ecological zone is often dedicated to planting maize and other cereals. Sugarcane, fruits, and other crops are also important in some quechua areas. High-altitude irrigation is not uncommon.

Above this zone is the suni, about 3,000 to 4,000 masl, a nonforested region of transitory grass steppe (fig. 5) with scattered shrub vegetation that is highly dependent on seasonal rains (Pulgar Vidal 1972). This was a major region for contemporary settlement, specializing in high-altitude agriculture focused on tubers such as potatoes, *olluco*, and *oca* and cereals such as wheat and barley. In the past, quinoa amaranth grain was an important crop. More diverse and dense vegetation characterizes the watercourses, which are rich in wildlife, including birds, deer, skunks, and foxes. These riverine areas, especially in steep quebradas, also support the zone's only consistent native tree, the quenual (*Polylepis* sp.) of the rose family. Today the Ancash sierra is dominated by eucalyptus trees, used for construction and firewood. In cool higher-elevation areas of the quechua and suni, a variety of legumes are cultivated, such as *habas* (fava) beans and *tarwi* (chocho), of the sweet pea family (Garayar et al. 2003; NRC 1989).

The puna (or jalca) forms the final major life zone used by humans, about 4,000 to 4,800 masl. It is essentially a cold, mountainous grassland characterized by bunch grasses, cushion and rosette-shaped vegetation, and some dwarf shrubs (Pulgar Vidal 1972). The zone furnishes natural and abundant pasturage for herd animals such as camelids or, more commonly today, sheep, cattle, and horses. Abundant water in the form of rainfall and meltwater feeds marshy lands (*pantanos* or *bofedales*) and allows for the rich plant growth favored by some animals, notably camelids. Also, where enough water is available, *Polylepis* forests thrive, especially in parts of the puna that are too inaccessible for pasturing of animals or the systematic collection of firewood. Today these stands of trees huddle around lakes, steep ravines, or cliff debris taluses.

It should be mentioned that north of Ancash the high-altitude grasslands are lower in elevation and diminish in size. By Trujillo and Cajamarca (ca. 8 degrees south latitude) geographers distinguish between the *páramo* Andes associated with the northern Andes (Ecuador, Colombia) and puna Andes associated to the south (Troll 1980). The páramos are typified by considerably more precipitation and fewer frosts and a reliance on maize agriculture as opposed to tubers. The northern part of

Ancash, in Pallasca and Corongo, trends toward páramo patterns of vegetation and topography.

Rising above the puna are the rocky mountain peaks of the janca life zone. Some peaks reach over 5,000 meters in the Cordillera Negra, while those of the Cordillera Blanca are taller; many reach over 6,000 masl, including Nevado Huascarán (6,768 masl). Today glacial tongues can be found as low as 4,100 masl, and snowlines lie at about 5,100 masl. Spectacular turquoise-colored lakes are quite common in these high areas, collecting snow or rain precipitation or crystal-clear meltwater from glaciers at their bases. Some lakes support fish and a variety of comestible plants and algae. Forests in these high areas today are the home to foxes and deer, including white-tailed and taruka varieties. Rocky taluses and overhangs are a preferred habitat of viscachas (large, chinchilla-like rodents) and some wild cats, such as the *gato montés* (Andean mountain cat) and puma, while cliffs and high overhangs provide the homes for the Andean condor and raptors.

East of the continental divide and moving north/east of the Marañón, tropical montane forest zones proliferate, especially along the peripheries of the Central Andes below 3,500 masl (Young and León 1999). These

FIGURE 5. The suni and puna life zones in the Pomabamba region. Yayno, at 4,150 masl, is located at the top of the right peak. The plots in the suni belt are cultivated up to 3,900–4,000 meters. Expansive grasslands, very suitable for herding, lie above the upper limits of agriculture.

humid woodland environments are internally diverse, again largely defined by altitude and precipitation produced by warm, rain-laden air welling up from the Amazon basin. The upper areas, called cloud forests of the *ceja de selva* or *ceja de la montaña*, are particularly rich in plants and animals.

Thus in Ancash Department the stark verticality of the Andean cordillera as it rises from the desertic coast forms a series of ecological zones, largely based on location (especially in respect to rivers and other water sources) and elevation. Each life zone presents a distinctive range of plants, animals, raw materials, and other resources, which were vital to Andean groups throughout the past.

Climate and Land Use

Due to the densely stacked zonation of Andean life zones, it was frequently either necessary or highly favorable to supplement the resources of one ecological zone or "floor" with those of other zones. In historical records, communities maintained settlements in or had regular interaction with different life zones to acquire desirable resources. Scholars have termed this economic strategy "verticality" or "ecological complementarity" (Brush 1977; Masuda et al. 1985; Murra 1972). In the vertical archipelago model, John Murra (1972) documented that settlements (conceived of as islands) of the same community or network (archipelago) could be located at different ecological floors to take advantage of each zone's unique set of resources; community self-sufficiency in resources was the ideal. Verticality is therefore a pattern of both resource acquisition and community organization, for these communities were physically separated but linked by exchange and/or kin ties. Such practices were known from different portions of the north highlands during historical times, such as in Cajamarca (e.g., Rostworowski and Remy 1992).

Some of the earliest evidence for ecological complementarity comes from highland Ancash. Early hunter-gatherers of the Callejón de Huaylas, the intermontane portion of the Río Santa which would become one of the prime areas of Recuay development, exploited the resources by making seasonal rounds to different ecological zones (Lynch 1980b). In this pattern of transhumance, Preceramic peoples were able to acquire important food and materials from coastal areas, the valley floor, and the puna region (Malpass 1985). By Chavín times, at approximately 500 B.C., camelid herding had supplanted hunting as the main source of meat protein (Miller and Burger 1995). And most later Ancash communities relied on a combination of high-altitude agriculture and the raising of livestock for their economic subsistence.

Recuay livelihood was very much dependent on the unique environmental and climatic conditions of the Ancash sierra. There is marked seasonality in the amount of precipitation and the growth of plant life. The wet season begins in highland Ancash around October, peaking from January to March and ending about April. The seasonal cycle represents the principal factor in scheduling agricultural activity in rural communities throughout Ancash. During the wet season, rains are regular and are especially strong in the late afternoons, with steady precipitation until mid-evening.

Plant life, wild and cultivated, is dependent on the rains. In April valley slopes become mosaics of verdant color. Discrete fields, known as *chakras*, are rotated with different crops, left fallow, and harvested at different times (fig. 5). By September those same slopes become sere and brown across highland Ancash.

Elevation is one of the major factors in the amount of rainfall. Lower elevations generally receive lower amounts of precipitation.[1] Most of the annual precipitation occurs during the very pronounced local wet season, roughly October to April.

Located in the tropics, highland Ancash does not see much seasonal variations in temperature (ONERN 1973: 5, 133). Considerable diurnal temperature change occurs, however, based on time of day and altitude. Although temperatures can drop below freezing at night, causing frosts particularly at higher altitudes, early afternoons can be very hot. Such temperature patterns limit intensive permanent settlement and agriculture in the high regions of Ancash but encourage some other activities, such as freeze-drying meat, and the clustering of certain tasks during the daytime.

A limited amount of cultivable land in the highland basins impedes local agricultural production. The steep gradients mean that soil horizons are shallow and often depleted in nutrients. Frequent bedrock outcrops and erosion further hinder farming. Except for the rare flat, low-lying areas close to stream bottoms, most highland regions are characterized by poor soils, such as those described for the Callejón de Huaylas and the Conchucos (ONERN 1975a, 1975b). A study demonstrated that even in the Callejón de Huaylas only a small percentage (8.1 percent) of the evaluated drainage area could be considered conducive to intensive agricultural production (ONERN 1973: 94–95). Contemporary use of land for agricultural production is especially prominent in the Conchucos provinces east of the Cordillera Blanca and in the Callejón de Huaylas (see appendix 1). Groups in the Cordillera Negra and northern Ancash farm a much smaller percentage of the land.

Despite limited cultivation and the presence of a major port city (Chimbote), the highlands are still the primary region for populations in Ancash today, making up 57.3 percent in 2002, down from 60.8 percent in 1981 (Garayar et al. 2003: 28). Modern demographic figures also point to certain regions for the highest concentrations of people in the highlands. The highest densities of people (persons per total area of the province) are in the Callejón de Huaylas, followed by the provinces east of the Cordillera Blanca. Today densities are the lowest throughout the Cordillera Negra and in far northern Ancash (Pallasca/Corongo), which have few large towns and settlements that are relatively isolated from major transport routes.

Regions, Boundaries, and Interaction

One of the distinguishing traits of the Ancash sierra and most of the Central Andean highlands consists of complex hydrological systems which serve as the breadbasket for local populations, offer courses for travel and interaction, and also form natural geographic boundaries. Just as the valleys of Ancash serve to connect different regions and peoples today, it is likely that Recuay tradition groups used these routes to their advantage in antiquity, economically and culturally.

The two major valley systems in highland Ancash are the intermontane drainages of the Río Santa and Rio Marañón, known as the Callejón de Huaylas and the Conchucos region, respectively. The Callejón de Huaylas is among the most famous Peruvian valleys due to its stunning 150-kilometer course between the Cordillera Negra and Cordillera Blanca. Quite aptly, Callejón means "large street" or "thoroughfare." It has formed a key route for exchange and interaction throughout its history. Spanish conquistadors used the Callejón de Huaylas strategically on various expeditions. And the decisive battle in Peru's War of the Confederation (1836–1839) was fought near Yungay.

The Callejón de Huaylas runs roughly southeast to northwest. At its northernmost extreme, the Río Santa veers westward as it descends toward the Pacific. The general distribution of Recuay cultural elements coincides closely with the extent of this river valley. Hence commentators have proposed alternative names such as "Huaylas" (e.g., Tello 1929) or "Santa" (Gambini 1984; Larco Hoyle 1960) in lieu of "Recuay." The

Callejón drains water coming down from both cordilleras, but mainly from the glaciers of the Cordillera Blanca. The east-west tributaries form steep valleys on the western side of the Cordillera Blanca and divide the Callejón de Huaylas at lower elevations into small, compartmentalized microregions which provide natural boundaries for towns and their hinterlands, such as Huaraz, Carhuaz, and Caraz. Huaraz receives some 700 to 800 millimeters of rainfall annually; Yungay, just 500 meters lower in elevation, receives under 300 millimeters annually.

For the tallest and most extensive mountain range in the New World tropics, the Cordillera Blanca is remarkably usable for humans, past and present. The range is narrow, and the tropical latitude prevents glaciation at lower elevations. More importantly, a series of quebradas, usually running east-west, crosses the range. Gouged into a U-shaped profile by glacial and riverine action, the quebradas (literally "breaks" or "gaps") are picturesque canyons and have the effect of articulating the western flanks of Cordillera Blanca with the eastern side (Borchers 1935; Kinzl and Schneider 1950; Ortega 1956). In addition to foot traffic, herders bring their animals to pasture in the lush, swampy bottomlands (bofedales) fed by meltwater streams. If not for these quebradas criss-crossing the giant, snow-capped mountains (nevados) of the Cordillera Blanca, it is likely that many cultural interrelationships and similarities bridging these two macroregions of Recuay culture would have been less prominent.

To the east and north of the Cordillera Blanca is the Conchucos region, a series of scenic highland basins which leads into the Río Marañón, the headwaters of the Amazon. The most important river systems, from south to north, include the Puchca, Yanamayo, and Sihuas. These were also places of Recuay development.

To the north of the Callejón de Huaylas are the regions of Corongo and Pallasca, associated with the northernmost Recuay developments. This portion of the Ancash sierra is relatively unknown archaeologically, except for a few studies (Grieder 1978; Grieder et al. 1988; Terada 1979). It remains the crucial terrain, however, for understanding Recuay's cultural interaction with the Santiago de Chuco region and Early Intermediate Period societies farther north in Huamachuco and Cajamarca. The major drainage for Pallasca is that of the Río Tablachaca, which joins the Río Santa as it descends to the coast. Current evidence suggests that this drainage was the general northern boundary for the distribution of Recuay material culture and imagery.

The area east of the Marañón has fewer signs of strong Recuay influence. Probably because of its great size, water flow, and environmental setting, the Marañón may have constituted a major boundary for Recuay culture. But archaeological knowledge of this region is also poor, due to lack of research. Highland areas on the eastern side of the Marañón do show some connections to Recuay culture, such as at Tinyash (Huacaybamba, Huánuco), but with few examples and, again, few pertinent data.

To the south of the Callejón de Huaylas, a different type of physical boundary seems to have helped define the southern distribution of Recuay culture. The Cordillera Huayhuash, just south of Chiquián, is a small but imposing mountain chain forming part of the border between southern Ancash and the Department of Lima. Together with the deep canyons of the Pativilca headwaters, the Huayhuash mountains seem to have been major obstacles for ancient interaction, as Recuay culture is much less prominent south of these geographical features. Despite its dramatic scenery of nevados and lakes, the Cordillera Huayhuash is quite different from its Cordillera Blanca counterpart, especially in geology and ecological zonation (Kinzl 1954; Rivera 2003). These natural differences apparently coincided with cultural preferences. It should be noted that very few archaeological investigations have been undertaken in this zone, and this lack also probably contributes to the underrepresentation of Recuay culture.

To the west of the Callejón de Huaylas is the Cordillera Negra. The "black cordillera" sustains no permanent glaciers at present. Pleistocene glaciation, however, was responsible for various glacial topographic formations and associated lake complexes. Compared to the Cordillera Blanca, the Cordillera Negra gives the general appearance of being less rugged and more rolling, even though it boasts many summits over 5,000 meters high. The range is generally higher along its northern segment, with a crestline varying from around 4,200 to 5,000 masl. In addition, the Cordillera Negra has undergone considerable geological metamorphism (Cobbing et al. 1981; Offler et al. 1980). For this reason, silica-rich crystalline raw materials for stone tools are very common throughout the region, such as fine quartzites and cherts (Lynch 1980b).

The western flanks of the Andes were home to at least two major areas of Recuay presence, in the Aija region and slightly farther north, in the region of Pira. Sites throughout areas of the coast, often funerary in nature, contain evidence of kaolinite pottery or other stylistic influence. Recuay groups, however, do not seem to have intervened regularly in areas below mid-valley locations.

The Cordillera Negra might be considered a natural barrier between the Recuay groups of the coast. But in fact the archaeological record shows a strategic positioning of settlements by Recuay-tradition peoples to take advantage of key routes and passes into the Callejón de Huaylas. Because the valleys of the Cordillera Negra cross the coastal desert strip before emptying into the Pacific, these formed the natural corridors for vertical forms of exchange among the coast, mid-valley, and sierra zones. There are currently three major routes into the Callejón de Huaylas: via the Pativilca River valley from the south; from Casma on the coast over the Punta Kayán pass into Huaraz; and the Cañón del Pato, in the north-ernmost part of the Callejón de Huaylas. Understandably, these consti-tute some of the lowest passes into the heart of the Ancash sierra.

Just as happens today, highland tubers, grains, and herd animals were probably exchanged for coast-grown fruits, maize, and marine foods. By the late nineteenth century scholars such as Antonio Raimondi had rec-ognized that east-west roads were natural and frequently exploited cor-ridors for coast-highland interaction (Villacorta O. 2006: 34). Julio Tello (1929: 15–16) also was cognizant of the role of economic complementarity on the Pacific Andean flanks and found that traditional socioeconomic strategies mapped onto and profited from Andean highland resource zonation.

I have described these regions in detail because the regional expres-sions and interactions of Recuay culture form key themes in the rest of this volume. At different points in time, Recuay peoples often maintained close cultural and economic ties with both the coast and neighboring highlands. Geography and environmental conditions were significant in predisposing certain forms of interregional relationships which helped to shape Recuay culture.

Historical Regions

Ancash became formalized as a department of Peru in 1839 by national decree, with Huaraz as the departmental capital. Different names have been recognized for the region. The most popular, Huaylas, is still often used today, frequently synonymously with Ancash. Indeed, the Callejón de Huaylas, the major intermontane valley through highland Ancash, was named after the ethnic group broadly known to have held dominion in the region during the time of the Inka (Espinoza Soriano 1978; Rowe 1946; Varón Gabai 1980).

Besides the Huaylas, a number of other major ethnic groups were known in the highland Ancash region during early colonial times. In the northern and eastern parts of highland Ancash, this includes the groups known as the Conchucos, Pincos, Siguas, Piscobamba, and Huari (León Gómez 2003; Schaedel 1985). Some archaeological studies of the region have tried to extend these divisions into earlier prehistory, with varying degrees of success (Ibarra A. 2003).

One of the ongoing problems with the definition of these ethnic groups, and especially their implications for ancient cultural boundaries, is the lack of systematic linguistic study in the region. Most groups in highland Ancash today speak a combination of Quechua (Ancash dialects) and Spanish (Parker and Chávez R. 1976). Quechua was probably the predominant language in Ancash even before its annexation into the Inka empire. Some posit that Quechua was spoken in Ancash by the end of the Middle Horizon, around A.D. 1000 (Torero 1974), while others prefer an earlier date, perhaps by the end of the Early Horizon (Heggarty and Beresford-Jones in press).

The historic evidence for the Culle or Culli language is very intriguing for considering northern Ancash ethnicity. Culle is often believed to be the indigenous language of Huamachuco and some neighboring areas, such as Cajamarca (Adelaar 1988; Andrade Ciudad 1995; Rivet 1949; Silva Santisteban 1986; Torero 1989). Many names of villages, mountains, rivers, and landmarks in northern Ancash are probably of Culle derivation. The spoken language is reported to have survived in remote parts of the north highlands into the early 1900s, including the northern Recuay region of Pallasca and farther south in parts of the Conchucos. It is known that some groups of northern Ancash venerated Catequil, an important oracle and huaca divinity of Peru's north highlands; the primary language of the cult was Culle (Topic 1998; Topic et al. 2002).[2]

Toponymic evidence suggests that Culle terms were integrated into place-names throughout the Pallasca area of northern Ancash and the Conchucos region, extending from a source farther north in the Huamachuco region (Lau 2009). Although we have few conclusive clues regarding the time-depth of this linguistic tradition, it does suggest that multiple languages, and perhaps ethnic groups, overlapped in geographical space during later prehistory in northern Ancash.

Climate Change

Climatic conditions in the past have fluctuated through time. The variation almost certainly affected natural resources and economic production for ancient Recuay groups. The inhabitants of Ancash must have responded to any short- or long-term patterns of change in the paleo-climate and the productive capacities of the environmental zones.

Unfortunately, paleoenvironmental conditions in the north highlands of Peru are poorly known. At present glacial ice-cores give the best evidence for local climate change during the first millennium A.D. (Thompson 2001; Thompson and Mosley-Thompson 1987, 1989; Thompson et al. 1986; Thompson et al. 1992). Two data sets are of pertinence here, the Quelccaya and Huascarán cores (Thompson et al. 2003). The Quelccaya cores provide data with annual to decadal data resolution, while only century-long data have been presented for the Huascarán cores. The Quelccaya cores cover only 1,500 years, however, while the Huascarán data extend back into the end of the Late Glacial Stage and all of the Holocene. Also, the Quelccaya ice cap is situated in southern Peru (southeast of Cuzco) and thus may be more indicative of paleoclimatic patterns associated with the south-central Andes. Nevertheless, a preliminary review of the Huascarán cores shows general correlation with overall temperature and precipitation trends previously outlined by the Quelccaya records, although local variations also occur (Thompson et al. 1995). Other studies also suggest general correspondence between changes in glacier length in the Cordillera Blanca and the changing oxygen isotope records of the ice cores (Jomelli et al. 2007; Solomina et al. 2007).

The ice cores from Huascarán, located in the heart of the Cordillera Blanca, illustrate three major patterns during Recuay times (fig. 6). First, Recuay culture seems to have emerged during a relatively cool period, in the first centuries A.D. During the fourth and fifth centuries A.D., however, the Huascarán cores suggest much milder, warmer conditions. This seems to have coincided with the florescence of Recuay culture and political integration. Mean temperatures fell greatly during the last half of the first millennium A.D., and colder conditions prevailed especially during the sixth and eighth centuries A.D. This period coincided with the demise of Recuay culture.

Over the last 1,500 years the Quelccaya cores corroborate the general patterns found at Huascarán. The Quelccaya cores provide proxy measures at an annual resolution, however, so it might be worthwhile to review these data as they pertain to the last half of the first millennium A.D. The later fifth century seems to have been characterized by wetter and colder conditions, followed by prolonged droughtlike conditions during the last half of the sixth century. Wetter conditions prevailed during the early seventh century, followed by another extended

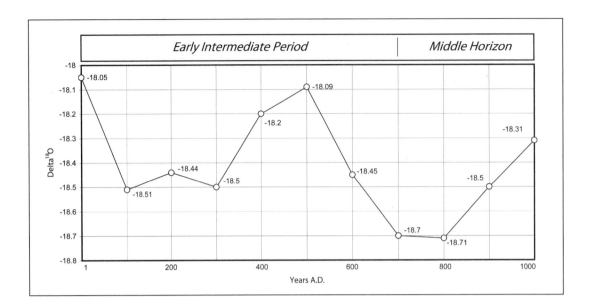

| Early Intermediate Period | Middle Horizon |

FIGURE 6. Graph plotting oxygen isotope ratios, Huascarán ice-core data, during the first millennium A.D. Ratios are expressed as $\delta^{18}O$ (the relative difference in isotopic abundance ratio $^{18}O/^{16}O$ between the sample and a standard). They represent century-long averages of the preceding 100 years (Thompson 2001). Less negative values indicate generally wetter conditions; in contrast, more negative values indicate generally drier and colder conditions. For comparison, the $\delta^{18}O$ ratio for the last 100 years measured −17.4 and the range for the Little Ice Age (A.D. 1400–1800) between −18.3 and −19.3.

period of below-normal precipitation and warmer weather. Then strong decreases in temperatures were prominent until the mid-eighth century. The Quelccaya data indicate that from A.D. 500 to 900 conditions were on average cooler than today.

The degree to which changing climatic patterns affected prehistoric groups and land use is difficult to assess, but general comparisons to the phenomena in historical times may be useful. Huascarán's century-long averages during the sixth to eighth centuries are comparable to those of the Little Ice Age, ca. 1400–1800 (Thompson et al. 1986; Thompson et al. 1992; Thompson 2001). Because of the strong relationship between altitude and temperature in the Andes, colder weather (as indicated by the Huascarán cores) probably lowered the upper limits of agriculture, displaced local vegetation, and encouraged the advance of puna-like grasslands across highland Ancash (A.D. 500–900).

Such changes were described by various commentators writing during the Little Ice Age in Peru (Cardich 1985). They note how villages in Huánuco located at 3,450 masl could only grow potatoes in sheltered areas below the village elevation; zones near 3,500 masl were avoided because they were frost-prone grasslands, whereas today a greater range of cultigens are grown and agriculture is practiced in areas far above this elevation. Historical evidence indicates that, with the amelioration associated with warming temperatures, cultivation occurs commonly as high as 4,000 masl in Huánuco and Ancash. These records as well as observations of relict plots as high as 4,300 masl suggest that the upper limits of agriculture have fluctuated between at least 400 and 700 meters between the lows of the Little Ice Age and the warm climes of the twentieth century (Cardich 1985: 304–306). Even within the Little Ice Age, major glacial advances and contractions seem to have occurred, as shown by lichen dating (Jomelli et al. 2007).

This variation needs to be taken into account when interpreting ancient land use and the elevation of settlements. Many settlement studies assume general correspondence between modern conditions and land use or across general phases, but it is clear that major transformations of the landscape can take place even within the span of a few centuries. Notably, Recuay villages and towns were very commonly located between 3,500 and 4,100 meters. On the one hand, this demonstrates a strong preference for high-altitude suni-puna ecotones. On the other, the variation may be related to climatic fluctuations.

Exploiting complementary zones is part of a broader complex of human-environment interaction focused on reducing risk. Modern farmers maintain flexible economic strategies to minimize the vagaries associated with ecological heterogeneity and climate, especially rainfall (e.g., Denevan 2001; Flannery et al. 1989; Gade 1999; Gelles 2000; Mayer 2002; Mitchell and Guillet 1993; Zimmerer 1996). The consequences of recent climatic changes can be seen in the socioeconomic practices of contemporary agro-pastoralists in Ancash (Young and Lipton 2006). Warming has resulted in shrinking glaciers and drastically modified woodland and grassland cover in the Cordillera Blanca area, forcing year-by-year assessments and adjustments of labor input for agricultural and herding pursuits: the size of crops/herds, the types of cultigens and animals, and, where possible, the location of fields/grazing areas. Another crucial point is water. As glaciers diminish in size, local people fear the lack of water for drinking and for crops (Morales Arnao 1998; Young and Lipton 2006: 72). The different responses are often compromises, with stakeholders at the community (irrigated water rights) and extracommunity level (nongovernmental organizations [NGOs], provincial governments, protected parklands).

A related aspect of highland Ancash concerns the role of extreme hazards in local settlement orientation and considerations of prehistoric landscapes. Certainly the Central Andes in general are prone to massive tectonic activity and fluvial erosion, because of the steep topography. The extensive glaciers of the Cordillera Blanca force additional forms of human-environment interaction, sometimes in tragic fashion. Climate change, in terms of fluctuating temperature and precipitation, plays a major role in the mass balance of glaciers and related hydrological activity: the amount of meltwater runoff, ice fall, and the levels of glacial lakes. In general, glacial retreat is typically associated with the formation of glacial lakes, often dammed by vulnerable terminal moraines. The combination of melting glaciers, vertical gradients, and regular tectonism fuels outburst floods and *aluvión* mudslides, which have devastated entire towns and villages. Such disasters are known historically as well as through archaeological research in the region. Water from these high-altitude sources is therefore at the same time a desirable resource and a source for cataclysms (Carey 2005; Mark 2008; Morales Arnao and Hastenrath 1998).

Geophysical research demonstrates that the second half of the twentieth century was marked by considerable climate change throughout the Peruvian Andes. Perhaps the most important pattern in recent times is warming temperatures. The effect of the warming trend is variable but is correlated with vertical structure. Warming is very prominent along the western slopes, and particularly at lower elevations, while the trend along the eastern slopes has been moderate (Vuille and Bradley 2000; Vuille et al. 2003). Research on Peruvian glaciers, including those of the Cordillera Blanca, indicates drastic reductions in size and recession, between 590 and 1,910 meters (Ames 1998; Byers 2000; Georges 2004; Hastenrath and Ames 1995; Jomelli et al. 2007; Kaser 1999). The diminishing extent of the Cordillera Blanca's glaciated zone is notable: it has reduced by approximately 15 percent over the last twenty-five years, nearly 23 percent since the 1930s, and up to 30 percent since the Little Ice Age. In addition to precipitation patterns, warming air temperature appears to be the primary agent for the recession in historic and Pleistocene times (e.g., Diaz et al. 2003; Kaser 2001; Klein et al. 1999; Mark and Seltzer 2005; Vuille et al. 2003).

Very generally, it can be postulated that changing paleoclimatic conditions affected local biodiversity and land use in the past. Under colder conditions, certain strategies were probably favored because of a downward forcing of ecological zonation. First, local peoples likely exploited lower altitude lands for agriculture. Second, glaciated areas would have advanced; an expansion of puna grasslands would have promoted camelid stock-raising at lower than current elevations. Warm periods, such as the fourth to fifth centuries A.D., probably saw the reclamation of high altitude agricultural lands and concomitant retreat upward of puna vegetation and frosts. As glaciers contracted, the warmer periods were also probably associated with greater runoff, fluvial erosion, formation of glacial lakes, and the potential for aluvión landslides.

Climate change and its consequences for coastal areas have been examined more thoroughly, especially in relation to El Niño/Southern Oscillation (ENSO). This global atmospheric pattern (Diaz and Markgraf 2000), associated with shifting oceanic currents and rising sea surface temperatures, has major repercussions for climatic conditions throughout Peru but especially in northern coastal areas (Cadier and Pouyaud 1998). Under typical La Niña phase conditions, the cold upwelling waters of the Peru or Humboldt current nurture vast quantities of low-level marine phytoplankton. Periodic ENSO phenomena displace the cold waters with warmer waters, throttling the supply of the organisms and the basis for most higher levels of the food chain, such as fish, birds, shellfish, and marine mammals. The periodicity and the severity of the phenomena are debated, but most scholars predict minor ENSO events once every two to seven years and much rarer but more catastrophic events, called "Mega-Niños," once every century or so.

The warmer waters also bring rainfall, frequently in large amounts. Along Peru's desert coast, where precipitation is scarce, such rainfall leads to flooding and wreaks havoc with riverine zones and agricultural pursuits. Combined with the collapse of marine resources, ENSO events (especially the more intense events) are disastrous for coastal human populations. Scholars have attempted to track the relationships between ENSO-related phenomena and major cultural developments some 5,000 years before the present, including the intensification of agricultural economies, the rise of monumental architecture, and the collapse of agrarian and state systems along the north coast and elsewhere (e.g., Moseley and Feldman 1982; Sandweiss et al. 2001; Shimada et al. 1991; Wells and Knoller 1999). Although ENSO events are more prominent in coastal areas, the conditions have also affected past temperature and precipitation patterns in the Andean highlands (e.g., Thompson et al. 1984; Thompson et al. 2000).

Additional research is needed to discern the correlations between changes in paleoclimate and human populations and their culture in northern Peru. Nevertheless, a crucial conclusion here is that climate and the physical environment in highland Ancash were in constant flux. Any reconstruction of Recuay settlement, land use, and landscapes must take these alterations, as well as their potential and perception, into account.

Regional Settlement Systems

Until recently Recuay settlement systems were virtually unknown outside of research done within coastal valleys, along the western limits of the culture. Over the last decade, however, intensive work has been done in different parts of highland Ancash, which elucidates what types of settlements existed, where they were located, and when and for what they were used. Data for fine-grained change through time are more limited. The literature has arisen from research investigations with archaeological reconnaissance components (Herrera 2005; Ibarra A. 2003; Lane 2006a; Lau 2010; Orsini 2003) as well as environmental impact assessments and salvage projects (Paredes et al. 2001; Ponte R. 1999a, 2001).

Many Recuay settlements converged on productive drainages, which provided the plant, animal, and water resources basic to sustaining groups in the high Andes. Like other highland groups of the Central Andes, one of the primary strategies for Recuay self-sufficiency was to locate settlements in important zones to maximize acquisition or production of resources. For example, Chinchawas, a small Recuay village at 3,850 masl, was located at the ecotone between puna and suni life zones. This allowed the inhabitants to farm nearby fields for potatoes and other high-altitude crops, such as oca and ulluco tubers, beans, or grains such as quinoa. At the same time, the residents of Chinchawas also grazed camelids in the nearby puna of the Cordillera Negra but often kept the animals in corrals near the site. Also, the strategic position of Chinchawas overlooking a trade route from the Callejón de Huaylas to the coast (Casma) facilitated access to rare goods, such as obsidian and fine ceramics. It is very likely that resources such as marine foods and lowland crops (maize, coca, and fruits) were also exchanged in this network.

Although "vertical archipelago" arrangements may have been prevalent in later prehistoric times in Ancash, very little direct evidence exists for the strategy among the Recuay. They likely practiced a form of "ecological complementarity": residents actively sourced different production zones for foods and participated in networks that allowed them access to products from other ecological floors. But regular movements were probably more circumscribed—a pattern more consistent with "compressed verticality," where different altitudinal floors are so compact that they can be managed/exploited by a fairly modest community (Brush 1976: 161–163; Murra 1972; see also Parsons et al. 2000: 119–138). This was likely the primary type of pattern for most Recuay groups.

Other variables besides complementary resources and community self-sufficiency were probably important to the character of exchange networks and settlement systems in the northern Andes, especially for the western slopes. Coast-highland interaction in northern Peru was affected by the efficiency of routes, ranked by distances to places and the character/difficulty of the terrain (Topic and Topic 1983). Specifically, factors such as distance, size/importance of interacting nodes, travel time, and efficiency help shape the scale and form of interregional interaction. The difficulty of travel and transport altitudinally between the two regions reinforces the insularity of the coast and highlands and encourages horizontal modes of movement/expansion. Thus it seems more reasonable to see small villages, especially of similar scale, networked with each other to exchange products from different ecological zones. Some scholars argue that settlements emerge and grow because of their relationships and function to other nodes in the network (Topic and Topic 1983: 255–259).

The present data indicate a number of key areas for Recuay development, in five general geographical groupings: the Callejón de Huaylas, the Cordillera Negra, the Pacific foothills, east of the Cordillera Blanca, and northern Ancash. All these loci are quite different in terms of their location and specific environmental contexts and resources.

The Callejón de Huaylas

The southern part of the Callejón de Huaylas is rich in greater expanses of high-altitude grasslands. Major Recuay developments occurred around the modern town of Katak (fig. 2). Katak is best known for a series of elaborate tombs from an extensive ancient mortuary complex, known as Roko Amá, which today is partly covered over by the modern town cemetery. Ceramics from these tombs formed the collection which would eventually lead José Mariano Macedo (1881) to designate them as "Recuay," for their proximity to the town of Recuay. Wendell Bennett (1944) later followed up on Tello's work, excavating in and around parts of Katak. Residential populations probably occupied low-lying areas near the river, now overlain by the modern settlement. Farther north, near the town of Ticapampa (Recuay Province), is a tall hilltop settlement known as Gekosh, where surface finds of kaolinite ceramics reiterate the utility and temporal precedent of the "Recuay" designation (Wegner 2003: 127, 133).

Continuing north in the Callejón de Huaylas and lower in elevation than the Katak area is the very large basin of Huaraz, where the Río Quillcay joins the Río Santa (fig. 7). Maize can be grown in the region,

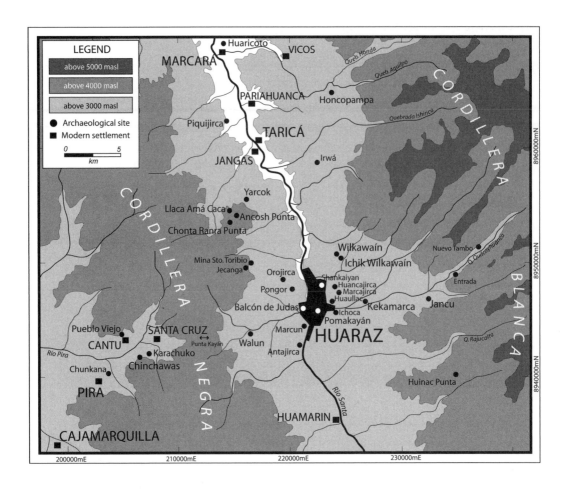

FIGURE 7. The Huaraz area, showing places mentioned in the text. The location of the region can be found as an inset within figure 2.

which was intensively inhabited at least from Chavín horizon times until the present. Greater Huaraz was likely a major hub for Recuay developments, for coeval sites within the region show very elaborate material culture. The combination of monumental architecture (Pomakayán), residential/ceremonial sites (Balcón de Judas, Kekamarca), monolithic sculpture (Huaullac, Pongor), and rich tombs and offerings (Orojirca, Ichik Wilkawaín, Wilkawaín, Pomakayán, Shankaiyan, Marian) indicates strongly graded levels of social differentiation and access to elite materials among different groups co-residing in greater Huaraz (Bennett 1944; Schaedel 1952; Smith 1978: 33–34; Soto Verde 2003; Wegner 2003). The different sites show Recuay cultural tradition ceramics associated with the Early Intermediate Period and Middle Horizon.

Just outside the limits of the modern city, many sites formed part of the economic and cultural orbit of the Recuay polity in Huaraz. To the east is the subterranean tomb of Jancu, one of the richest Recuay graves ever documented (Wegner 1988). The more prominent satellite communities include Antajirca, Pongor, and Walun, all on the western side of the Río Santa (Alcalde M. 2003; Mejía Xesspe 1941; Schaedel 1952), and, farther north, Ancosh Punta, Quitapampa, and other sites in the areas above Jangas (Ponte R. 2001). Pongor, though largely destroyed today, was occupied at least from the Early Intermediate Period until colonial times and may have been one of the main sources for the stone sculptures found in the Museo Arqueológico de Ancash, Huaraz (Espinoza Soriano 1978: 52; Soriano I. 1950).

Therefore some evidence suggests a major polity with at least a two-tier, perhaps three-tier, functional hierarchy during Recuay times. Interestingly, the area never seems to have had a classic urban center per se but a series of communities related economically and culturally. The importance of the Huaraz basin and a dispersed settlement system has historical analogues. Specifically, during the sixteenth and seventeenth centuries different areas of the modern city and the basin ("greater Huaraz") were inhabited by a series of *ayllu* (collectivities based on kinship, communal work, and ceremonialism) groups which together formed a powerful ethnic kingdom (Espinoza Soriano 1978: 50–51; Varón Gabai 1980). Lords in the area held the rights to gold and silver mines, such as Hicanga (Jecanga) just northwest of Huaraz, as part of their diverse resource base (Espinoza Soriano 1978: 109, 131; Varón Gabai 1980: 67, 73); it is not unfeasible that these were worked in earlier times.

If a Recuay-period polity was based in the Huaraz area, it is significant that many of the constituent settlements were not located in highly defensible locales such as hilltops or mountains, like other major Recuay centers. Most of the secondary sites of the polity are located on valley slopes, with little protection. This would suggest a political climate in the Huaraz basin without much overt manifestation of conflict.

Farther north in the Callejón de Huaylas is the region of Carhuaz. The early synthesis by Tello (1929) documented a rich corpus of Recuay ceramic vessels found on the former haciendas of Copa Grande and Copa Chico, above the modern city of Carhuaz. These came from subterranean tombs. Bennett (1944) subsequently documented a series of burial structures, including "box tombs" and aboveground *chullpa* mausolea at the Sahuanpuncu (Copa Chico) site. Gary Vescelius and Hernán Amat conducted settlement surveys in the Callejón de Huaylas, especially in the province of Carhuaz. Unfortunately, only secondhand summaries resulted from this work (Buse 1965: 317–333; Lanning 1965). Richard Burger and Lucy Salazar-Burger encountered Huarás-period (ca. 200 B.C.–A.D. 200) burials and midden refuse at the early ceramic site of Huaricoto, in the town of Marcará (Burger 1985a: 125). Work by Joan Gero at the nearby site of Queyash Alto recovered evidence of a ridgetop ceremonial settlement with Huarás, Recuay, and some Middle Horizon occupation (Gero 1990, 1991, 1992).

Huaylas Province includes the northern part of the Callejón de Huaylas. Recuay developments in this region are best known in two principal areas: around modern Caraz (2,296 masl) and in the Quebrada Los Cedros. By the time it reaches the Caraz juncture, the Callejón de Huaylas is dry and warm. The area today is well suited for different types of irrigation agriculture, especially maize, fruits, and beans. Recuay groups in this region were characterized by a dispersed settlement system not dissimilar to the pattern seen in Huaraz. Sites with monumental architecture within the town limits today include Inkawaín and Tumshukayko (Alcalde M. 2003). Although the area had earlier occupations, the latter site was used intensively during the Early Intermediate Period (Bueno M. 2001) and seems to have been a type of pilgrimage cult center, like Pomakayán later in its history. At the foot of the Cordillera Blanca, above Caraz, is the large settlement of Pueblo Viejo, which includes a ridgetop settlement with evidence of residential dwellings, surrounded by walled fields and concentrations of Recuay and later funerary structures (Herrera 2005: 357–358; Valladolid Huamán 1990). In the remote Quebrada Los Cedros, remains of the Aukispukio site extend from 3,800 to 4,500 masl across a rugged landscape descending from the Cordillera Blanca. The complex consists of a sector with habitations as well as Recuay cliff tombs and later aboveground chullpas (Kinzl 1935; Wegner 2001a).

The Cordillera Negra

Recuay groups were also very common west of the Callejón de Huaylas, in the Cordillera Negra. Occupation seems to have been widely dispersed throughout the region, as reflected in settlement reconnaissance, test excavations, and collections (Gambini 1984; Lane 2006a; Malpass 1985). There are at least two prominent regions of Recuay development. One of these consists of Aija province, the headwaters of the Río Huarmey. This region is best known for its stone sculptures; about fifty are known (Wegner 1982: 2). Tello (1923, 1929) reported specific sculpted monoliths in various modern villages near the town of La Merced; these were almost certainly from ancient sites within or near the settlements (see also Schaedel 1952).

When Tello encountered the Aija area sculptures in 1919, the discovery was unique. Before that time little scientific work had been done in Ancash, and Andean archaeology had focused on coastal, Tiwanaku, or Inka developments. Work in Aija essentially helped spur his theory regarding the autochthonous development of Andean civilization in the Peruvian highlands. Despite this early recognition and the presence of known sites, surprisingly little systematic work has been done in the Aija region. Sites include Chuchunpunta and Marcuncunca (Mejía M. 2006).[3] These are characterized by their defensive position as hilltop settlements and occasional finds of kaolinite ceramics.

Slightly north of Aija in the Cordillera Negra are the towns of Pira and Cajamarquilla, part of the Río Casma headwaters, where modest but very distinctive Recuay tradition groups developed (Kauffmann Doig 1966; Mejía Xesspe 1941). This area is characterized by small hilltop centers, which served as the defensive, residential, and ceremonial foci of small agro-pastoral communities. One such site, Chinchawas (fig. 8), was occupied primarily between A.D. 500 and 900 and never had a permanent population of more than a hundred people. For a small village, it was remarkable for its access to exotic goods, intensive use and consumption

FIGURE 8. Site map of Chinchawas, Sector 1 main ridgetop, showing location of constructions and stone sculptures.

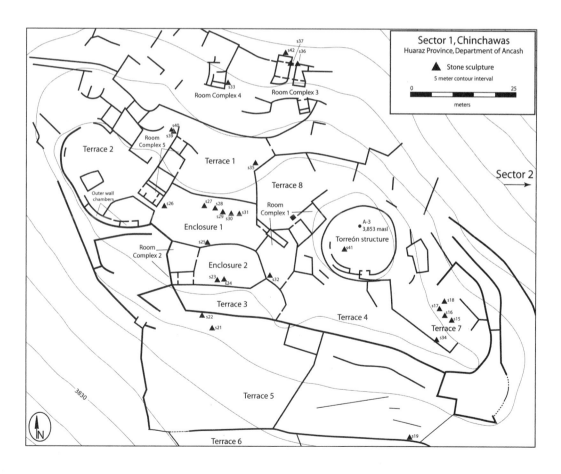

of camelids, and forms of cultural elaboration, such as tombs and mono-lithic sculptures. The site contains the largest number of in situ Recuay sculptures yet known (Lau 2002, 2005, 2006b).

Stone sculptures and surface scatters demonstrate the presence of other small centers of this kind in the region, including occupations overlain by the modern settlements of Cantu and Santa Cruz and the towns of Pira and Cajamarquilla. Most of these sites in upper Casma and upper Huarmey are located on defensible hilltops and were actively pro-ducing stone sculpture for ceremonial purposes. Because the sculptures are similar in style to those at Chinchawas, it is likely that they were at least partially coeval, probably between A.D. 600 and 900. It should be mentioned that the sculptures were used both in ancestor cults through-out the Recuay tradition and as part of high-status buildings. Finally, early Spanish documents indicate that groups of the Huaraz basin (about twenty to twenty-five kilometers due east) frequently traveled to the Pira region because of a famous oracle and huaca temple, which were used for consultations and other ceremonial occasions (Espinoza Soriano 1978: 54–63).

In general, Recuay groups of the Cordillera Negra located their settle-ments strategically along the suni/puna ecotone, roughly 3,500–4,000 masl today, to take advantage of high-altitude agricultural and pasture lands. The sites were also poised to exploit natural coast-highland routes and networks for exchange.

The Western Foothills of the Pacific Coast

Recuay culture was also prominent at lower elevations along the western Andean flanks. These groups are associated with the upper portions of the coastal valleys, from about 200 to 1,500 masl. The most important drainages with Recuay or Recuay-like ceramic evidence include the Huar-mey, Casma, Nepeña, and Santa valleys. Additional indication of Recuay influence comes from more northern valleys, including Virú, Chao, and Moche. Recuay occupations of the coastal region have been documented mainly by intensive settlement surveys. Very few sites in these valleys have been investigated through intensive excavation. Thus the discus-sion of Recuay presence in the coastal valleys is based mostly on surficial evidence, especially of kaolinite ceramics and architectural traits.

One of the most vociferous proponents for a Recuay presence on the coast was Rafael Larco Hoyle. Unlike his contemporary Julio C. Tello, who had a modest upbringing in the Lima highlands of Huarochirí, Larco was born to a wealthy hacienda family of the north coast. He ignored

Tello's theories about the role of the highlands in Peruvian civilization and actively championed a coastal origin for Recuay culture, which he called "la cultura Santa" (the Santa culture), citing a series of rich tombs found in Santa (Larco Hoyle 1948, 1960, 1962, 1966). These studies were before the impressive discoveries at Pashash and Jancu.

Larco's efforts came at a time when settlement studies were becoming increasingly important in New World archaeology, including the pioneering work in the Virú Valley (Bennett 1939, 1950; Collier 1955; Ford and Willey 1949; Strong and Evans 1952; Willey 1953). Indeed, the Virú research, as part of the Institute of Andean Research, was fueled by Larco's collaboration and initiative at the historic meeting between South and North American archaeologists at his family's hacienda in Chiclín, in August 1946 (Willey 1946). The Virú research was instrumental in showing Recuay influence on the coast, especially in ceramic style.

The coastal valleys are internally diverse, and a number of scholars have divided them into upper, middle, and lower valleys (Billman 1996; Daggett 1985; Proulx 1968; Topic and Topic 1982; Wilson 1988, 1995).[4] Recuay groups appear to have favored occupations especially in the upper to middle valleys, where the floodplain narrows considerably into the valley necks. Settlements with Recuay remains are particularly common on the foothills which border these narrow belts of arable land (fig. 4). These were away from the wide agricultural plains of the lower valleys but in close proximity to coast-highland trails and chaupiyunga lands desirable for the cultivation of valuable crops such as coca, maize, and chili peppers.

Donald Proulx and Richard Daggett (Proulx 1982, 1985) demonstrated a strong Recuay presence in Nepeña, mainly in the upper valley areas; site types, often with defensive works or placement, included occupations at large ceremonial centers such as Huancarpón (700 masl) and a series of habitation sites. The middle valley area in Nepeña seems to have been a buffer zone against coeval lower valley settlements, dominated by Moche inhabitants. Wilfredo Gambini (1984), a collector and amateur archaeologist, noted the strong interaction between Recuay and Moche cultures, especially in appraisals of grave-lots near the town of Jimbe.

Recuay-Moche interaction seems to have been somewhat different in Santa, the next valley north. As in Nepeña, sites with evidence of Recuay culture were heaviest in the middle and upper valleys, up to the confluence of the Tablachaca and Santa rivers. This seems to result from a general multiculturalism in northern Peru during the early portion of the Early Intermediate Period (Kaulicke 1992; Makowski 2004). Also, among the most common sites were fortified settlements overlooking the floodplains and habitation sites organized into settlement clusters. The defensive strategy, at least initially, appears to have been oriented to protection against incursions from the south. Thus the strategic constructions represented measures for intervalley conflict, not within the valley, as seems to be the case in Nepeña. By the middle Early Intermediate Period, associated with Moche expansion, a major shift of settlement away from the upper parts of the valley into the lower Santa Valley appears to have taken place. Interestingly, the late Early Intermediate Period is marked by an absence of fortress sites, which had been common before. Direct colonization of the Santa region by Moche invaders, probably from Virú and Moche itself, apparently provided unprecedented peace and stability for Santa groups, described as a "Pax Mochica" (Wilson 1987, 1988); a similar pattern has been described for the Casma Valley (Wilson 1995). In the Virú Valley farther north, a series of valley-neck fortified sites called *castillos* (castles) seems to have protected the lower valleys from highlanders and served to regulate access to and from the mid-valley areas and thenceforth into the highlands; this pattern characterized most north-central coast valleys (Millaire 2008).

Recuay-related settlements were also located strategically, in the middle-upper valley, for trading relations. Recuay-contemporary ceramics are not uncommon to large civic-ceremonial centers such as Huancarpón (Nepeña) and Cruz Blanca (Moche). Cruz Blanca (ca. 600 masl), at least, has been interpreted as a type of gateway community which mediated the movements of goods and people at a key bottleneck in the Moche valley (Topic and Topic 1982; Topic and Topic 1983). Huancarpón also straddles a strategic point between the junction of rivers and crossroads into different parts of the sierra (Proulx 1985).

Walled enclosures in the lower Santa Valley have been found on key coast-highland routes that contain surficial evidence of highland presence, including Recuay-related kaolinite sherds and desert ground drawings of llamas (Wilson 1988: 171–176, 189–193, 355). The enclosures probably functioned as corrals to pen transport llamas of Recuay trading caravans. Hence Recuay groups appear to have favored settlements which facilitated coast-highland relations based on exchange, probably involving cargo-bearing llamas.

The Early Intermediate Period settlements in the Casma Valley also seem to have had a strong up-valley, defensive orientation, clustering around the valley necks. Common finds of white-on-red pottery, comparable to the Huarás style of the Callejón de Huaylas, as well as highland-style chullpa tombs also indicate strong coast-highland interaction in the drainage (Wilson 1995). There are fewer reports of Recuay or highland-style pottery reaching the lower valleys farther south, notably Culebras, Huarmey, and Fortaleza (Collier 1962; Thompson 1966). In contrast to Casma, the valleys of Huarmey and Culebras show a general lack of intensive occupation during the Early Intermediate Period, but the few sites identified also focused on the middle valley sectors (Prządka and Giersz 2003).

Pallasca and Corongo

Up-valley from the lower Santa Valley is a crucial but little-investigated region which forms the northern Recuay area. This area includes several departmental provinces in the northern extreme of Ancash, including Pallasca and Corongo. In historical times this region was associated with the Conchucos curacazgo (Cook 1977; Espinoza Soriano 1964; León Gómez 2003).

The best-known settlement in the region is the large site of Pashash (3,150 masl) near Cabana, which seems to have been both a population center and a cemetery for high-status elite burials (Grieder 1978). Today Pashash measures some 10–15 hectares; like other Recuay centers, it has a prominent defensive orientation, with strategic positioning and very large, monumental walls along a strongly demarcated perimeter. On a large hilltop Pashash elites built a burial complex known as La Capilla, where archaeologists discovered the tomb and grave offerings of an important Recuay noble. It is likely that part of the ancient settlement over which Pashash had sovereignty is located under the modern town of Cabana (Grieder 1978: 17).

The area has long been known to have been the home of very elaborate stone sculptures (Grieder 1978; Larco Hoyle n.d.; Schaedel 1952; Wiener 1880). Although Pashash was probably a major center for production, other settlements made and used monoliths. Stone sculpture has been reported from different parts of the Pallasca area, including near Huandoval and Tauca (Schaedel 1952: 209–219; Wiener 1993 [1880]: 176). It is quite likely that Pashash formed the seat of a major regional polity centered in Cabana but extending into neighboring areas of the Tablachaca Valley.

What language the ancient Recuay spoke is unclear, but several scholars have suggested that some groups spoke Culle. Terence Grieder (1978) employed Culle terms for his phase names of pottery found at Pashash. And Richard Schaedel (1985: 446, 462) hypothesized that the Pashash polity spoke Culle. It should be noted that my toponymic study found that the vast majority of Recuay site names are Quechua-based. Pallasca is the only region in highland Ancash with a substantial percentage of Recuay site names (twelve of twenty-six sites) with Culle roots (Lau 2009).

The other region of note in this northern area is Corongo (Terada 1979). The Recuay presence in Corongo has been documented mainly in the form of ceramic scatters, frequently at mortuary sites with looted tombs of the subterranean or chullpa type, and sporadic finds of stone sculpture.

East of the Cordillera Blanca

The eastern side of the Cordillera Blanca forms the final major zone with Recuay tradition settlements and material culture. As is common practice today, I employ the term "Conchucos" here to refer to the river systems of the Puchca, Yanamayo, and Sihuas. Recuay settlements seem to have mapped onto the high, well-defended tracts of productive intermontane lands.

Some sites are known from the Sihuas area (Astuhuamán G. and Espinoza C. 2005), but better-known developments are located farther south. Perched above the town of Pomabamba, Yayno (ca. 4,150 masl) is the largest known Recuay tradition site, measuring ca. 30 hectares in its monumental core, and some 100 hectares when considered with associated features: corrals, looted tombs, terracing, dispersed ruins, and surface scatters. The core settlement (figs. 5 and 9) is protected by steep cliffs and in more susceptible areas by large enclosures, perimeter walls (some parapeted), walled terraces, and a series of deep dry moats and trenches.

Smaller coeval villages with similar pottery and architectural forms, all within walking distance of Yayno, suggest that the center was the seat of a major Recuay polity, with at least a two-tier settlement hierarchy focused on the northern watershed of the Yanamayo basin. Other extensive sites are known in the region around Pomabamba, with fortifications, residential compounds, funerary constructions, and other forms of monumental architecture, such as Rayogaga and Karway (Obregón Velázquez 2007; Raimondi 1873: 181–185; Wiener 1993 [1880]: 198–204), but little work has been done to evaluate their social or chronological significance.

Directly to the east, northwest of the junction between the Marañón and the Yanamayo rivers, is a rich montane region with several large sites, including Huintoc and Marcajirca (Pampachacra). Settlements here also benefited from highly defensive locations overlooking productive agro-pastoral lands. The impressive complex at Huintoc, with its arrangement of circular enclosures built of massive limestone and granite blocks, is protected on its southern flank by a sheer precipice. The more extensive Mar-

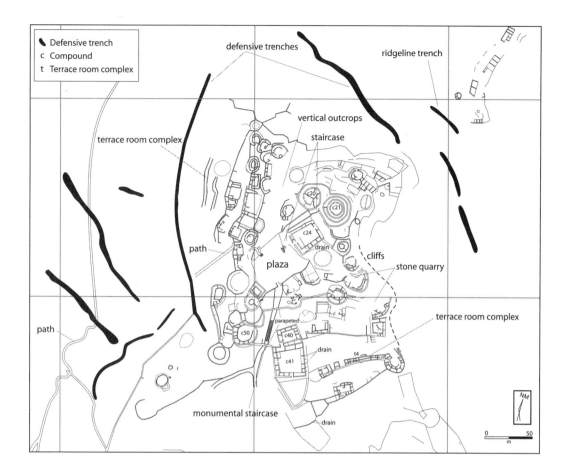

defensive trenches

ridgeline trench

vertical outcrops

terrace room complex

staircase

c20

c21

c24

path

drain

cliffs

plaza

stone quarry

path

parapeted

c50

c40

terrace room complex

c41

drain

t4

monumental staircase

drain

0   50
m

cajirca site stretches north-south along a long, narrow, and largely level ridgetop. Isolated circular constructions predominate on the ridgetop; on the adjoining slopes below is a series of limestone caves and grottoes filled with evidence of looted burials. Throughout Marcajirca are remnants of extensive quarrying, especially for gray limestone blocks.

Recuay centers are also known along the southern headwaters of the Yanamayo (the Chacas and Yanama areas), but they seem to be more in the order of small hilltop centers (ca. four to ten hectares). Some of these have been described for the Chacas area (Laurencich-Minelli et al. 2001; Orsini 2003, 2006; Wegner 2000). The precise layouts vary; but based on the current evidence, such settlements were small multipurpose hubs which serviced neighboring dispersed farmsteads. Such locations would be appropriate as places of refuge/defense during periods of conflict but also for corporate ritual purposes, especially for ancestor cults and seasonal ceremonies. Closer to the Marañón, a number of Recuay contemporary sites appear to have been established for specialized functions, such as exchange, transportation, and salt procurement (Herrera 2005).

FIGURE 9. Site map of the main archaeological sector at Yayno, showing location of constructions, access routes, and defensive features.

Farther south is the Puchca River drainage, which has its headwaters in the Mosna basin. Amat (1976a, 1976b, 2003) encountered dense Recuay-related settlement in the region (also Diessl 2004; Espejo Nuñez 1957, 1959). As in other parts of the Recuay commonwealth, settlements were strongly oriented toward dispersed habitation near fields, defensive redoubts, and cemetery sites. Subsequent work indicates a limited but palpable Recuay presence farther down-valley, in San Marcos and Huari, usually in the form of surface scatters of kaolinite pottery, occasional finds of stone sculpture, and funerary sites (Diessl 2004; Ibarra A. 2003).

The Puchca/Mosna region is perhaps best known as the heartland for Chavín civilization. Chavín de Huántar was a town and ceremonial center and was the principal cult focus for the spread of the Chavín religion and cultural elements during the first millennium B.C. (Burger 1992). The ceremonial sector is notable for its large open plazas, platform temples (highly elaborated with interior canals, galleries, and chambers), and finely sculpted monoliths, some of which are the primary cult images of the settlement. Most work in the Puchca region has taken place at Chavín de Huántar and has focused on occupations prior to the Early Intermediate Period (e.g., Kembel 2008; Lumbreras 1989; Rick 2008; Tello 1960). Later groups, however, reoccupied different portions of the settlement after its abandonment. During the last centuries B.C. people of the Huarás culture built modest stone dwellings directly atop parts of the formerly sacred center; fine sculptures were used as simple building material or fill (Lumbreras 1974a). The subsequent Recuay also interred their dead in different parts of the ceremonial sector and immediately across the Río Mosna, in the area known as La Banda. Later inhabitants appear to have had both contempt for and awareness of Chavín's ruins.

East of the Marañón, near the town of Huacaybamba, is the large settlement of Tinyash (Falcón and Díaz 1998; Kauffmann Doig 2002: 489; Ravines 1984; Thompson and Ravines 1973). It is located in the puna over 4,100 masl, with a series of construction types. In addition to its famous multistory chullpas, the site features round and rectangular constructions with high walls, which Santiago Antúnez de Mayolo (1941: 216) considered palaces and fortifications. Most scholars believe that the site dates to late prehispanic times. Stone sculpture (tenon-heads and a large vertical slab depicting a frontal warrior figure) and kaolinite surface pottery indicate that earlier Recuay tradition associations are likely (Schaedel 1952; Steven Wegner, personal communication, 2002). As in other regions, Recuay villages and central places in the Conchucos are almost always found in defensible locales and sometimes with fortifications and other evidence of warlike groups.

Recuay Settlements: Patterns and Dispositions

Site Types

Recuay settlements can be categorized according to a series of site types. Leaving aside more detailed discussion of the architecture (see chapters 3 and 4) and diachronic change (see chapter 8), the purpose of this section is to characterize the general categories of sites and range of settlement strategies prevalent during Recuay times.

The most common Recuay settlement types are multipurpose hilltop habitation sites. These can be characterized by the following designations and scales (see table 1): hamlet (up to ca. 1 ha), village (up to ca. 10 ha), and regional center (above ca. 10 ha). Hamlets and small villages are basically aggregations of houses, presumably of families and/or households. Villages and certainly the regional centers often feature additional built spaces, such as tombs, plazas for public performance, and buildings associated with status groups. Examples of small villages include Riway, Gekosh, and Chinchawas, while examples of major regional centers include Yayno and Pashash. At present, only for Yayno (fig. 9) can we appreciate the hilltop habitation type as an "urban" nucleation (Rowe 1963).

Some settlements were very large, especially the regional centers. These sites and their satellite communities can extend over great expanses of land, covering some 300–500 meters of elevation, frequently co-occupying parts of what are today puna and suni lifezones simultaneously. To do this Recuay tradition groups sometimes exploited long, tonguelike extensions of ridgetops to build extensive complexes of residential or funerary buildings, such as at Aukispukio, Chagastunán, and the later site of Katiamá. These were formal precursors for later settlements, such as Rapayán, dated to the Late Intermediate Period and Late Horizon (Mantha 2006).

While habitation sites housed a permanent residential population, they were also generally strategic locations for defense (high locations on hilltops or promontories) and were fortified with natural and/or artificial defensive features. Such sites were frequently located along major routes for interaction, especially at crossroads or river junctures, such as Balcón de Judas and Huancarpón.

Hilltop sites may also show architectural evidence for ceremonial activities, including funerary rites, offerings, and public gatherings. Resi-

TABLE 1. Major Sites of the Recuay, Late Recuay, and Wilkawaín Periods

Site	Ceramic Phase	Est. Max. Size (ha)	Elevation (masl)	Location	Modern Setting	Primary Function	Defensive Features
Recuay Period (A.D. 200–600)							
Balcón de Judas	n/a	1	3,000	Ridgetop	Quechua	Residential	—
Chinchawas	Kayán	1	3,850	Ridgetop	Suni/puna	Residential/ funerary	Perimeter walls, chambered walls
Queyash Alto	Huarás	2	2,700	Ridgetop	Quechua	Ceremonial	—
Roko Amá	Recuay	1	3,650	Ridgetop	Suni	Funerary	—
Huancarpón	Recuay	15	700	Ridgetop	Yunga	Ceremonial	Walled
Pashash	Pashash Recuay	15	3,150	Ridgetop	Quechua	Funerary/ residential	Perimeter walls, enclosures
Yayno	Rayo	30+	4,150	Ridgetop	Puna	Residential	Perimeter walls, trenches, enclosures
Late Recuay Period (A.D. 600–700)							
Antajirca	n/a	2	3,100	Ridgetop	Suni/ quechua	Funerary	—
Chinchawas	Chinchawasi 1	4	3,850	Ridgetop	Suni/puna	Residential/ funerary	Perimeter walls, chambered walls
Honcopampa	n/a	12	3,470	Ridgetop/ plain	Suni	Residential/ funerary	Perimeter walls, enclosures
Pashash	Usú	15	3,150	Ridgetop	Quechua	—	—
Pueblo Viejo (Caraz)	n/a	30	3,450	Ridgetop	Suni	Residential/ funerary	Perimeter walls
Yayno	Asuac/ Huanchac	105	4,150	Ridgetop	Puna	Residential	Perimeter walls, "moats," enclosures
Wilkawaín Period, early (A.D. 700–800)							
Wilkawaín	Wilkawaín	1	3,400	Sloping terrace	Suni	Funerary	—
Ancosh Punta	Ancosh	1.5	4,190	Ridgetop	Puna	Residential	Perimeter walls
Chinchawas	Chinchawasi 2/ Warmi	4	3,850	Ridgetop	Suni/puna	Residential/ funerary	Perimeter walls, chambered walls
Honcopampa	Honco	12	3,470	Ridgetop/ plain	Suni	Residential/ funerary	Perimeter walls, enclosures
Pueblo Viejo (Caraz)	n/a	30	3,450	Ridgetop	Suni	Residential/ funerary	Walled
Tinyash	n/a	40?	4,100	Ridgetop	Puna	Residential/ funerary	Perimeter walls, enclosures
Ichik Wilkawaín	Wilkawaín	50	3,400	Sloping terrace	Suni	Funerary	—

Sources: Bennett 1944; Gero 1991; Grieder 1978; Herrera 2005; Isbell 1991; Lau 2002, 2010; Paredes Olvera 2007; Ponte R. 1999a; Proulx 1982, 1985; Tschauner 2003.

dential hilltop settlements very commonly have discrete mortuary sectors within or near the site, often along flanking ridgetops or areas of higher ground. This occurs in village settlements (such as Chinchawas and Jatungaga) as well as in large centers (such as Pueblo Viejo and Pashash), suggesting a mutual desire among Recuay tradition groups to articulate living and ancestral populations.

Larger habitation sites often feature smaller dispersed sites, probably farmsteads, around their periphery, indicating that any given settlement also served a hinterland. Many Recuay hilltop villages and regional centers therefore provided a refuge, religious/cultural center, and node for exchanges of goods and ideas.

What is notable about the hilltop center type is the impressive range of sizes, from a few to over 100 hectares. Recuay groups were able to establish hilltop sites in most areas where they had influence, regardless of size or environmental constraint (fig. 10). Indeed, the multipurpose hilltop site is one of Recuay's cultural diagnostics. This settlement disposition contrasts with civilizations of the coast, where functionally specialized sites appear to be more common. There were probably very pragmatic reasons for this: conserving lower-lying areas for agricultural fields or reducing the danger of flooding and mudslides. Other qualities of the settlement type include its flexibility for self-sufficiency whether large or small, its insularity, and its lack of internal specialization. Overall the multipurpose habitation site type appears to have been a successful and common response to the natural and social circumstances presented to the ancient Recuay.

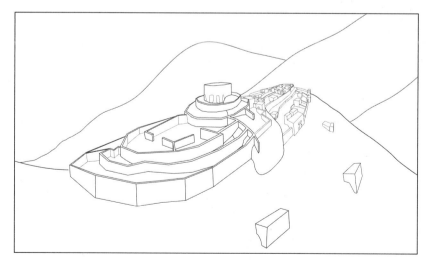

FIGURE 10. Reconstruction of Chinchawas, showing disposition of the Torreón structure and adjoining residential and ceremonial constructions (view from southeast).

Comparatively fewer habitation sites located on valley bottoms or sloping pampas are known. A good example is the dense post-Chavín squatter settlement in the temple zones of Chavín de Huántar after the Early Horizon. The Early Intermediate Period occupations of Huaricoto represent a similar context. At these sites Huarás materials were buried underneath meters of buildup resulting from subsequent occupation and natural site formation processes.

Recuay settlement of valley floors may have been more intensive than the archaeological record indicates. Centuries of erosion, agricultural activity, and mudslides obscure surface reconnaissance data. The processes bias the archaeological record toward younger and more surficial archaeological occupations. Furthermore, materials typically used for domestic housing today, wood and adobe, survive poorly in the Andean highlands.

The importance of camelids in the Recuay economy is manifested in the widespread emergence of corral sites or settlements with corral features. Specialized corrals, sometimes with a few semipermanent dwellings, are found in many parts of highland Ancash, especially in the puna belts of the Cordillera Negra and Cordillera Blanca. Large and small habitation sites, especially those in or near puna grasslands, also often have corrals attached to terraces near housing clusters — presumably to keep the animals safe when they were not grazed. Special enclosure constructions served as "ceremonial corrals," a term alluding to historically known venues for group ceremonies held to increase the size and fertility of camelid herds.

Specialized funerary sites are also quite common in Recuay culture. Although the architectural details are discussed more fully in the next chapter, it should be mentioned here that practices vary greatly, suggesting changing dispositions of the dead and their proximity to the living through time. Sites include single or several tombs as well as vast necropoli.

Mortuary sites may occur in relative isolation from residential populations, such as Jancu and Roko Amá. More commonly, cemeteries form distinct but integral parts of larger habitation sites (e.g., Pashash). Closer integration with the dead became a more prevalent pattern at the end of the Recuay cultural tradition in the Middle Horizon, when aboveground tombs, known as chullpas, became increasingly preferred over earlier subterranean chamber traditions. The superposition of funerary styles is seen both at Chinchawas and at Ichik Wilkawaín. Certainly the transformation was a complex process, but one decisive factor may have been simply a greater interest on the part of local groups to demonstrate their ties to esteemed deceased (ancestors) and territory more boldly through highly visible, durable landmarks (Lau 2000: 190–195, 2002: 298–301).

Some Recuay settlements were principally pilgrimage shrines or ceremonial centers, with restricted permanent residential occupation. One of the best known is Pomakayán, located in the heart of Huaraz. With centuries of destruction through natural disasters, looting, and robbing of building stone, the site is in a poor state today. Houses have covered over much of the site since 1970, when a giant earthquake leveled most of Huaraz. It was used in Recuay times for funerary purposes but may have been mainly a pilgrimage center (Espinoza Soriano 1978). Queyash Alto seems to have been another ceremonial complex, with little residential use. Like Recuay habitation sites, both Pomakayán and Queyash Alto occupy small promontories, which probably increased their visibility from afar.

Finally, the area also includes important places that feature rock art (pl. 2) or standing stone uprights, known as *wankas* or *huancas*. It is very difficult to date rock art; but at least some sites, especially in the Callejón de Huaylas and in the Cordillera Blanca quebradas, show painted representations with affinities to Recuay ceramic imagery. Shrines with standing stone monuments are equally hard to associate culturally, especially given the lack of systematic work conducted by archaeologists. The site of Huancajirca, just east of Huaraz, features a large stone upright, nearly five meters tall, set atop a large circular platform; preliminary work suggests use as early as the Early Horizon, continuing into the Middle Horizon (Bazán del Campo and Wegner 2006).

Social and Political Implications

Over a century of archaeological research elucidates the distinctive patterns of Recuay settlement and their implications. Probably the most common settlement pattern consists of two-tier settlement hierarchies where a number of dispersed, largely autonomous hamlets and small villages cluster around a larger center. This is most likely the case for Riway in Chacas (Laurencich-Minelli et al. 2001) and certainly the case for Chinchawas, near Pira (Lau 2002, 2005). These were at once small residential and ceremonial centers around which smaller farmsteads developed. Larger settlements with this same pattern include Pueblo Viejo, near Caraz (Herrera 2005; Valladolid Huamán 1990). Recuay collectivities were usually fairly small in scale, of variable complexity, and well distributed across highland Ancash.

The common political organization represented in the Recuay commonwealth consisted of social arrangements generally known by anthropologists as chiefdoms or ranked societies (Carneiro 1985; Earle 1987; Redmond 1994). Such societies are characterized by hereditary leaders and inequalities in wealth and status. The most frequently used material correlates for such societies include monumental/public architecture, distinctive arts, variability in consumption, and differential funerary practices.

Some highland valleys saw the rise of larger Recuay centers with wider spheres of influence. At least three seem to have been of greater scale: Pashash, Yayno, and Huaraz. Although systematic survey remains to be done to assess the precise functional and diachronic relationships of sites within their politico-economic orbits, some observations can be made. These three regions provide some evidence for subsidiary centers that would indicate more centralized forms of sociopolitical organization. The Huaraz area also has specialized ceremonial sites and satellites located away from the population centers (Lau 2005). It is now clear that Yayno was central to, and probably integrated, a network of smaller villages located lower and closer to distinct pockets of agricultural lands (Lau 2010). The evidence does not indicate that these three valley-based polities were ever in intensive contact with each other or allied for some type of integrated, pan-Ancash Recuay polity or confederation.

The Recuay commonwealth was characterized by a predominant pattern of small-scale communities. By about A.D. 300–400 several key drainages saw the emergence of a number of chiefdomlike societies. While broadly participating in similar practices, especially in the domains of ceremony, the groups of each zone maintained varying engagements with Recuay-style material culture.

Historical and Archaeological Comparisons

Historically known patterns of settlement and community organization in the north highlands and the Central Andes are useful for comparative purposes. They suggest both continuities and ruptures in the way local groups occupied and used space in ancient Ancash.

The ubiquity of the hilltop center in Recuay settlement dispositions, for example, contrasts with the picture of settlement dispositions gleaned from early historical evidence. Colonial Spanish sources describe the different types of population centers but especially those established on low-lying valley bottoms or valley flanks. This is almost surely related to initiatives during the later sixteenth century which relocated rural villages into towns (*reducciones*) near accessible roads for facilitating religious, and economic purposes (such as taxes, censuses, and missionization). For example, in the northern Recuay area of Corongo and Pallasca seventy-seven communities were reduced to five towns in the later sixteenth century (Cook 1977: 25). The reducciones also had the effect of combining and pacifying once competitive factions. Such new towns were located on valley floors or in areas central for managing formerly dispersed groups (Cook 1977; Masferrer Kan 1984; Varón Gabai 1980).

The precise extent to which reducciones transformed local or traditional patterns of settlement and land use, however, is not entirely clear. For one thing, Inka intervention in the region also certainly left its mark. The Inka made alliances with certain lords and not others, promoted building programs and other public works, and even relocated entire collectivities into the region (Hernández Príncipe 1923). New settlements were established on valley floors, some with Inka-style masonry and architectural forms, such as Pueblo Viejo (Recuay-Ticapampa).

But it is also evident that some Recuay groups prospered in low-lying valley areas. For example, the settlement cluster based in the Huaraz basin was the heart of a major Recuay polity. This area was indeed heavily settled during Inka times, but via a series of related but dispersed communities. During the sixteenth and seventeenth centuries greater Huaraz was home to groups of the large Lurinhuaylas ethnic kingdom (Espinoza Soriano 1978: 50–51; Varón Gabai 1980). These were combined in the 1572 reorganization into San Sebastián de Pampahuaraz, present-day Huaraz. In 1558 some 2,600 people resided in the zone, while in 1593 records identified some 3,400 individuals in the town (Espinoza Soriano 1978: 22ff., 72). Thus, even before formal reducciones were established, greater Huaraz and almost certainly other low-lying valley areas were important as major demographic loci.

Some Recuay settlements may be associated with patterns found in other highland cultures at the close of the Early Intermediate Period. Regional settlement investigations in the Junín highlands have documented a number of hilltop "concentric-ring" sites in the puna environmental belt (Parsons et al. 1997, 2000). In these examples, the rings describe large concentric walls which enclose the entire settlement or a large portion thereof. These sites were likely the villages of herding groups of varying size and complexity. The nested walls, sometimes four to five deep, provided secure areas for penning camelids as well as protecting residential dwellings (Parsons et al. 2000: 109–110). Such high-altitude sites, which flourished until the Inka period, were located strategically between the major production zones (suni and quechua) and dedicated to regular economic and ritual interactions between farmers and herders. They may also have been venues for ritual combat and other corporate rituals documented in historical times (see Gorbak et al. 1962; Platt 1986; Topic and Topic 1997; Urton 1993).

The development of high-altitude Recuay hilltop settlements during the mid to late Early Intermediate Period probably formed part of a widespread pattern in which highland societies became increasingly successful due to intensive herding practices. Furthermore, the emergence of major monumental centers such as Yayno indicates increasing social differentiation and the formation of large polities at least partly underwritten by herd wealth.

The ethnohistorical study of farmer-herder interaction and cosmology by Pierre Duviols (1973) is important for contextualizing prehistoric settlement patterns in Ancash. Colonial documents frequently mention the interdependent but often combative relations between paired ethnic agricultural (*huari*) and pastoral (*llacuaz*) groups in Peru's Central Highlands, reaching as far as southern Ancash (see also Duviols 1986; Hernández Príncipe 1923; Masferrer Kan 1984; Salomon 1995). Llacuaz herders are often represented as recent interlopers or "conquerors" of the region and are most often associated with the puna grazing lands. The original inhabitants known as huari, meanwhile, were said to have been cultivators of the arable lands of valley areas and montane slopes. Therefore, complementary associations existed between the upper and lower segments in terms of both social and environmental positions.

Some archaeologists working in Ancash have contended that huari-llacuaz groups coexisted in physically separate settlements (situated according to farming versus herding zones), sometimes located across valleys or as "paired settlements," but interacted through regular episodic contact for trade and ceremony (Herrera 2005: 36–38; Lane 2006a: chapter 1; Orsini 2006; see also Parsons et al. 2000: 171). Notably, documentary sources suggest co-residence within the same settlement (*llacta*) (Duviols 1986; Hernández Príncipe 1923; MacCormack 1991: 413–414; Salomon 1995: 322). This was almost certainly intensified by (if not the result of) colonial demographic reforms, which brought together dispersed populations into European-style towns for administrative purposes (Masferrer Kan 1984).

The huari-llacuaz pattern resonates with a long-standing tradition of dualism in Andean thought (e.g., Isbell 1977; Moore 1995). In essence, this principle holds that different elements of society and culture are organized according to opposing yet complementary forces (for example, black/white, male/female, right/left, sun/moon). For order or completion, one cannot exist without the other; both are needed together for balance (Burger and Salazar-Burger 1993: 97). The oppositions among the huari and llacuaz were expressed in many dimensions of culture: language, customs, creator and heroic divinities, and land use.

Recuay settlement and architectural patterns certainly manifest forms of dualism. The term used for ritual combat, *tinku* or *tinkuy*, also refers to many other phenomena characterized by the joining or union of complementary opposites, such as a marriage, the merging of paths, or the confluence of rivers. Recuay sites often overlooked the union of rivers. The pattern of establishing settlements at the confluence of rivers in highland Ancash has an early precedent in the major ceremonial center of Chavín de Huántar (Burger 1992: 130). Recuay groups also had a propensity for situating sites on ridges with two high points or prominences. Still other sites contrast discrete but complementary sectors, such as a residential (living) versus a funerary (ancestral) zone. Two different residential forms, circular and quadrangular compounds, were integrated into the overall spatial organization of Yayno.

It is perhaps axiomatic to say that the settlement patterns of Recuay groups were mapped onto key resources and landscapes, both natural and of their own making. What makes the Recuay case valuable for comparative purposes is the long duration of successful adaptation to a highly compressed and challenging environment. Furthermore, Recuay groups depended on a relatively small range of settlement types as adaptive strategies, yet they flourished in a large swath of northern Peru during the greater portion of the first millennium A.D.

Leaving aside the very important ideological component of Recuay sites and landscape for the moment (discussed further in chapter 3), four socioeconomic factors were especially important for Recuay settlement: access to farming lands, access to herding lands, capacity for defense, and capacity for trade. The few data available at present suggest that hunting had a minor role in the Early Intermediate Period diet (Lau 2007; Sawyer 1985). In general, there seems to have been little specialization in any one of the four variables. Rather, most Recuay communities focused on self-sufficiency and maintained multiple functions. Large and small Recuay communities throughout Ancash shared in this broad socioeconomic ideal.

Many Recuay settlements in highland Ancash tended to favor high-altitude zones for agriculture and herding purposes. Recuay groups often located sites directly at the crucial zonal transition, just below the ancient upper limits of agriculture and puna, where it is possible to cultivate high-altitude crops and have relatively easy access to puna grazing lands. Not only is the ecological floor economically sensible, but the natural shelter against harsher winds and frosts provided by the few hundred meters of ascent simply makes these belts of land more pleasant places for settlement.

Several notable exceptions, such as Yayno and Aukispukio, reach directly into puna-like terrain today. These are extensive sites, with client hamlet-farmsteads; indeed portions of the overall complex are located at lower elevations, closer to arable lands and flowing water. Like smaller settlements along the suni-puna belt, Recuay centers must have been sustained by plant and animal resources acquired from different ecological zones.

Other major centers in the highlands preferred lower elevations, such as in Huaraz or Caraz. Situated on valley floors, at natural crossroads, and on wide alluvial terraces, these sites flourished through a combination of farming and trade interaction, where lower-elevation crops (most notably maize) could be exchanged for animals and high-altitude tubers/cereals.

In the coastal foothills zone, major settlements with Recuay or Recuay-related occupations had different economic orientations: agriculture on adjacent ribbons of land following the watercourse and interzonal interaction with down-valley communities. Sites such as Huancarpón occupy foothill zones, which differ by some 1,500 meters of elevation from their nearest highland Recuay center. In the sierra, in contrast, Recuay settlements are found fairly continuously throughout the range between 2,000 and 4,000 masl but especially at higher elevations of this range.

The extent to which Recuay groups intensively occupied coastal mid-valley areas remains unclear. The mid-valley centers do not appear to have been part of vertical archipelagos but independent communities with both agricultural and trading interests. Regardless of their origins, they demonstrate the economic benefit and value of interzonal access to resources for Andean societies. Besides cultivation of coastal valley crops such as maize, coca, and fruits, these settlements were primary nodes for exchange. Their location by coast-highland routes and their association with corrals indicate trading practices perhaps reliant on camelid caravans. Their location also suggests an intermediate point for transactions of different kinds: marine foods and resources (shell, salt), highland crops, camelid products, luxury objects, and exotics (such as ceramics, metals, and feathers). As seen in the patterns of acquisition of even small communities, Recuay groups greatly valued coastal resources.

In sum, while it is doubtful that the Recuay actively maintained "vertical archipelagos," regular interaction certainly took place between different communities located in different environmental zones. The current evidence suggests that verticality (if present) was orchestrated at the level of individual settlements/communities rather than dispersed systematically as nodes or "islands" in noncontiguous lands. It is probable that Recuay groups practiced at least three forms of "compressed" ecological complementarity: a high-altitude form (based on tuber farming, camelid herding, and exchange); a montane valley-floor form (maize farming and trade); and a coastal middle-valley form (yunga area farming and trade).

For Recuay land and settlement, perhaps the most notable commonality was a marked concern for defense. If the archaeological record thus far provides a representative view of Recuay dispositions, it is clear that groups everywhere, from the high puna to the coastal foothills, were highly concerned about or even fearful of their neighbors. As noted, the threat derived from both Recuay and other cultures or ethnicities. We see this mainly in the position of settlements on hilltops, promontories, and other advantageous areas to defend against attack within the heartland as well as along the commonwealth's frontiers. The ancient Recuay world was fraught with conflict. Its settlement patterns reflect the anxieties of independent communities, some large and some small, interested in protecting their families, homes, and belongings.

CHAPTER THREE

Recuay Architecture

Recuay groups built some of the most outstanding buildings of ancient Peru. Like their Chavín predecessors, they are noted for the elaborate use of stone in their buildings and monuments, many generations before the most celebrated of Andean stonemasons, the Inka. Recuay peoples are best known for their mortuary architecture, but it is becoming increasingly clear that they also created other types of important structures, including shrines, defensive works, ceremonial buildings, corrals, and large housing complexes.

Having surveyed the principal patterns in settlements, in this chapter I examine the types of Recuay buildings and their associated uses. I review the most salient forms to demonstrate the variability in Recuay architectural practice. Available data on construction practices and technology are detailed to help assess their importance in comparison to other regional developments in Andean prehistory. I present the evidence in terms of functional categories and describe contexts to examine specific cases and reconstruct the geographic distribution of specific forms.

Although these categories are useful, it should be noted that many Recuay settlements were multipurpose and contained buildings with different functions. Also, some constructions almost certainly changed function over time. But only a fraction of the sites discussed here have been investigated to an extent which allows us to identify changes in the use of a building. Only a few cases provide detailed architectural histories or building biographies. In making these categories, I wish to provide a panorama of the basic types of Recuay architecture and their contexts. Where exceptions or pertinent transformations exist, they are also reviewed here to show the diversity in the form and uses of architectural types.

The analysis identifies a number of repeating themes or dispositions in Recuay architectural practice. The first concerns the focus on enclosed or contained space and its implications for defense, social life, and identity. The second addresses the use and importance of stone in the building practices and cosmology of Recuay groups. The third focuses on monumentalism and its implications for changing politico-religious organization and ideology. The fourth concerns social memory in the built environment, as instantiated through monuments and memorialized places. Each of these dimensions formed part of conventionalized dispositions toward architecture and landscape in the ancient Recuay world.

Early Descriptions of North Highlands Architecture

With some of the most impressive sites in the Andean sierra, such as Chavín de Huántar, La Galgada, and Yayno, the architecture of highland Ancash has long fascinated visitors and researchers. The famous Italo-Peruvian geographer and scientist Antonio Raimondi made various trips to the region between 1857 and 1869 (Villacorta O. 2006). Raimondi (1873) produced a monograph and detailed map of the department's geography and mineral resources. He added observations on the character and material wealth of different towns and regions in his comprehensive peregrinations across Ancash, especially the central portions (including the Callejón de Huaylas, Conchucos, and the Cordillera Negra). Raimondi's multidisciplinary coverage of Ancash was never completely published, even in other writings including the voluminous *El Perú* (Raimondi 1874–1880). For example, his notes and archives contained valuable illustrations of archaeological materials, especially Recuay stone sculpture from the Huaraz area (Raimondi 1942; Villacorta O. 2006).

The Austrian-French explorer Charles Wiener traveled through parts of Ancash in the mid-1870s. Unlike Raimondi, who journeyed throughout the department, Wiener sped through en route to the southern highlands and Bolivia. Also, unlike Raimondi's detached, scientific writing, full of dry statistics and tables, Wiener opted for a more autobiographical and candid approach. His volume *Pérou et Bolivie* (1880) was a travelogue, rife with anecdotes, one-off adventures, and impressionistic drawings. The reporting and the sense of wonder (and loss) are reminiscent of the nineteenth-century writings on ancient Mexican ruins, such as those of John Lloyd Stephens, Frederick Catherwood, and Jean-Frédéric Waldeck. Wiener's interests were manifold, including linguistics, ethnography, and history, but he focused on widening the appreciation of Peru's prehistoric past (Wiener 1993 [1880]: v–vi). Despite the brevity of his stay in Ancash, Wiener managed to record important Recuay remains, such as the sites of Pashash and Huinchuz, portable objects, and stone sculptures, now mostly lost or destroyed.

The ruins of highland Ancash became increasingly recognized on the world stage through the writings of other international traveler-scholars, such as the Englishman Reginald Enock (1907) and the Germans Ernst Middendorf (1895 [1893–1895]) and Wilhelm Sievers (1914). One of the problems of this early scholarship, quite understandably, was a lack of temporal control. These writers were not professional archaeologists, conducted little systematic work, and lacked training and data to distinguish between cultures. Cultures and time-depth were frequently conflated, and cultural achievements were attributed generally to the "Inkas" or the "ancients." This elision was not limited to Ancash Department, for it characterized many early descriptions of antiquity in the Central Andes. Nonetheless, these early descriptions helped to record the rich cultural diversity and achievements of Ancash prehistory.

Thus ancient Ancash was not undiscovered country when Julio C. Tello embarked on his archaeological expedition of 1919. But it had been neglected from the standpoint of systematic research. It must have been clear that the area had a deep history, with tangible remains and remarkable potential for data collection and synthesis. As in the case of many other dimensions of ancient Peruvian culture, it was Tello who first recognized the significance of Recuay architecture. The culture had been known primarily by a style of pottery. Tello (1929, 1930) brought the first major sites to light, including Roko Amá, Yayno, and Wilkawaín. He discussed architectural techniques and masonry and elaborated on "wanka-pachilla" (block and spall) stonework typical of Recuay and other ancient cultures of Ancash. And he reported on a typology of architectural styles, which remains fundamental in the archaeological literature and is in part followed here.

Before Tello's expedition, Andean archaeology had been dominated by coastal studies, especially of tombs and huaca ceremonial centers (e.g., see Menzel 1977; Reiss and Stübel 1880; Uhle 1903, 1914). Important highland discoveries at Machu Picchu (Bingham 1913, 1916) had been brought to light only a few years before Tello's landmark 1919 expedition. Sites that he underscored in *Antiguo Perú* (Tello 1929) — notably Chavín de Huántar, Yayno, and other places in Ancash — represented milestones in a long trajectory of cultural achievement in Peru's north highlands.

Tello (1923, 1929) championed the primacy of the highlands for Peruvian civilization, an unpopular view at the time. He understood that it was only in recent times that the demographic and economic balance had swung away from the highlands to coastal centers, with their reliance on intensive valley-wide irrigation agriculture, fishing, manufacturing, and transport industries. In addition to his familiarity with traditional cultural and economic practices, Tello was heavily influenced by colonial documents, which he cited regularly.

One of Tello's greatest contributions was his realization that Chavín had emerged quite early and adumbrated many cultural elements which would reappear in later prehistory. Architecture played a critical role in these appraisals, because Chavín architecture formed part of an archaic "Megalithic Culture" antecedent to the Inka and Wari (Tello 1930). Recuay-tradition architecture, at places such as Yayno and Wilkawaín, was lumped into this group. Tello himself, however, was quite ambiguous about the temporal or functional relationships between Recuay and Chavín constructions. Suffice it to say that for Tello architectural style was a critical, defining element of early Peruvian civilization. And Recuay expressions, in particular, were integral in this trajectory.

Subsequent research by Wendell C. Bennett (1944) disentangled Recuay pottery and architecture from Chavín. By the time of his 1938 expedition to the Callejón de Huaylas and Chavín to examine north highlands architecture and chronology, Bennett was the preeminent North American archaeologist working in South America (Willey 1988: 128). One of the enduring legacies of his research in Ancash was his wide temporal and spatial coverage. Using "pits" and "cuts," his research targeted specific contexts, stratigraphy, and features (such as tombs). Though Bennett's 1938 expedition lasted only about four months, his efficient methods allowed him to collect good samples from rather extensive areas and from complex sites in Ancash, such as Chavín de Huántar and Ichik Wilkawaín.

Bennett's stratigraphic excavations at Chavín de Huántar laid to rest the question of Chavín's chronological relationship to Recuay. In most of his pits he found later pottery cultures (Huarás and Recuay) above Chavín deposits—a pattern confirmed by other scholars in the monumental sector and in adjacent areas (Lumbreras 1970; Rick 2005; Tello 1960). Other excavations of funerary structures in the Callejón de Huaylas, with superposition of materials, complemented his theories based on stylistic data and allowed him to complete the later sequence, from Huarás to Recuay to Wari (Tiahuanacoid) and Inka period styles. His descriptions of funerary structures and their contents are invaluable, because many of those sites have since been destroyed or suffered irreversible damage due to increasing urban development in the Callejón de

Huaylas, especially around Huaraz, Carhuaz, and Katak. In effect, Bennett's investigations of highland Ancash established the foundations for current chronologies and distributions of Recuay ceramics and funerary architecture.

Residential Architecture

Relatively few data on Recuay tradition residential practices were available until the last few decades. Recent studies have brought to light new forms of spatial organization: site types as well as individual constructions and contexts. The record now features a series of well-documented cases which elucidate both local practices and regional patterns in residential architecture.

A few good examples of residential structures exist for Huarás culture. Perhaps the best known is the nucleated squatter village in the sunken circular court at Chavín de Huántar (Lumbreras 1970: 63–78, 1974a: 47–51, 1977: 7–9; Rick 2005: 74). Tightly agglutinated and irregularly shaped masonry constructions, approximately 4–5 meters wide, characterized the occupations after Chavín. Luis Lumbreras (1974a: 49) observed that each dwelling, mostly shoddily made, contained a small room which connected to a patio, storage room, and one or more small cists, often with human remains. The patios, usually slightly larger and rectangular, were the focus of food preparation and dumping of trash. Each residential complex probably served a nuclear family. Subsequent reoccupations (by Recuay and Late Recuay groups) followed similar dwelling layouts, construction methods, and activity patterns. Huarás occupations also have been isolated at Chonta Ranra Punta and at Huaricoto (Burger 1985a: 125; Ponte R. 1999a: 30–31).

At Chinchawas, a small village in the Cordillera Negra, my excavations revealed that housing mainly took the form of room clusters centered around small open spaces or patios (Lau 2001). The standard unit was a single dwelling, about 3.5 to 5 meters long and 2.5 to 3 meters wide (fig. 11a). The height of the structures is not clear, but some surviving constructions have walls over 3 meters tall and had at least two stories. Some rooms are more imposing and feature higher-quality masonry, suggesting different levels of labor investment.

As in most Recuay settlements, the village was established on a ridgetop, so the inhabitants routinely had to cope with the steep and rocky terrain, few level expanses, erosion, and different activity levels. Dwelling layouts showed persistent preferences. Each residence was usually

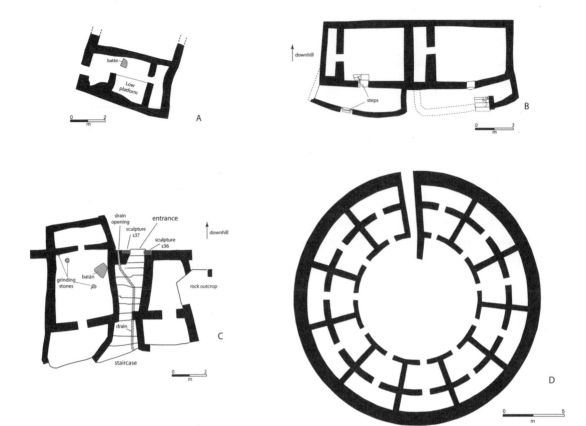

batán
Low platform

0 2
m
A

downhill
steps
B
0 3
m

drain opening
entrance
sculpture s37
sculpture s36
downhill
grinding stones
batán
rock outcrop
drain
staircase
C
0 2
m

D
0 5
m

FIGURE 11. Construction types, in plan view, based on modular dwelling-type units: (a) Room Complex 5, Chinchawas; (b) Paired rooms in Sector 1, Chinchawas; (c) northern portion of Room Complex 3, Chinchawas; (d) interior structure of the Rondán Circular Construction, near La Pampa. (Drawing by author, after Terada 1979: fig. 47, removing later additions)

subdivided into two or three chambers. The largest consisted of a main chamber, which often featured low platform areas (for example, a counter on one occasion and a small raised bench on another). The features were dedicated to food preparation activities, as evidenced by grinding stones, bone tools, and the remains of cooking and domestic discard. The main chamber usually connected to a single back chamber through a narrow threshold. Such back rooms were usually very modest, no more than a meter wide and 2 to 3 meters long; they contained little artifactual material and have been interpreted as sleeping or storage quarters. Such buildings were probably the residences of small nuclear families.

Notably, dwellings at Chinchawas were also built next to each other, sometimes sharing walls (fig. 11b). About three to six rooms/dwellings were arranged to surround small patio areas, probably associated with larger households or extended families. Each of these clusters may have serviced a group of approximately fifteen to twenty people. The most elaborate room cluster at the site featured stone staircases and stone drainage works (fig. 11c). Between two rooms is a central staircase with tall stone steps. A drainage channel flowed underneath the staircase. Set partly on bedrock with masonry channels, the drain emptied out of a nichelike outlet on the façade, directly to the left of a jamb stone carving of a female anthropomorph. The juxtaposition appears to associate the image, probably a representation of a deified ancestor, with the flow of water.

Residences at Chinchawas were sometimes isolated, freestanding structures with wide blocklike façades. The three existing examples of such platform-block buildings at Chinchawas are built into steep, sloping hillsides, so that the front façade is the tallest part of the building. Investigations in one of them (measuring 15 meters wide and 7 meters deep) revealed a unique plan of paired residences, each with a main room connected to an entry and back room. Both had staircases and entrances accessed from the rear. The Caserón at Pashash (fig. 12), measuring 30 meters wide and 15 meters high, is likely a monumental version of the platform block form.

In other regions, especially in the northern Recuay area and east of the Cordillera Blanca, there was an emphasis on the construction of discrete, walled compounds. They were circular or quadrangular (Lau 2010). Such compounds are defined by an outer perimeter wall, usually with restrictive access. Only a few of the compounds show clear entrances; access must have been above the ground floor and/or through ladders. They

FIGURE 12. The Caserón structure at Pashash.

also often feature a central open space, which is surrounded by a series of rooms or chambers. These rooms have interior doorways which connect directly into the open interior space. Some scholars have referred to such complexes as patio-groups or *kanchas* (Herrera 2006: 11; Isbell 1989: 105). I prefer the more general term "compounds," however, because the diagnostic characteristic of all these constructions is a major walled area or enclosure; furthermore, it is not uncommon to find constructions even within the courtyard/patio area.

Quadrangular or rectangular compounds are characterized by prominent exterior corners and orthogonal room layouts. Perhaps the best known are those of Honcopampa (Gary Vescelius, in Buse 1965; Isbell 1989, 1991; Tschauner 2003), referred to as patio groups and frequently associated with Wari administrative architecture. But they are also found at other large sites in the region which are pre-Wari, such as Yayno (Lau and Ramón 2007; Lau 2010).

Circular forms with curved walls are quite variable, from round to more ovoid layouts. Circular examples are also slightly more common and more widely distributed, from La Pampa to Yayno to the Chacas area (Lau 2010; Orsini 2007; Terada 1979). Areas outside the Recuay heartland also share the circular compound form, such as at Marcahuamachuco (Beckwith 1990; McCown 1945; Topic and Topic 1984) and lesser-known cases such as Tinyash (Ravines 1984; Thompson and Ravines 1973) and sites in the Santiago de Chuco area (Murga Cruz 1983; Pérez Calderón 1988, 1994).

Investigations at Yayno, near Pomabamba, illustrate dense residential occupation at the seat of an important Recuay polity. Most of its monumental sector consisted of highly protected residential compounds of different layouts. Interestingly, the stylistic and radiocarbon evidence indicates that their occupations were largely coeval, dating to the end of the Early Intermediate Period and the early Middle Horizon (ca. A.D. 400–800).

Yayno has three major residential forms (fig. 9): terrace room complexes, circular compounds, and quadrangular compounds. The most elaborate constructions are the quadrangular complexes. They show the greatest standardization in terms of layout, and the two main examples are the largest single constructions at the site. The largest (c41) measures about 35 meters on a side (pl. 1a; fig. 13). They also show the most impressive stonemasonry in terms of boulder size and quality of construction. The circular enclosures demonstrate greater variability in construction quality and size as well as diversity of activity. They range from about 8 to 25 meters in diameter and have walls up to 12 meters tall (pl. 1b). The least elaborate residences are the terrace room complexes; these are

FIGURE 13. Different wanka-pachilla masonry styles of quadrangular compounds c40 and c41 at Yayno. The east wall of c40 (right) directly abuts the earlier wall of c41 (left).

long buildings (one measures over 100 meters) which are partitioned over lengthy stretches or fully into small domestic rooms, each about 1.5 by 4 meters. One complex, about 50 meters long, features dual rows of compartments. Although they still make use of stone construction, their walls are usually fairly simple, without the boulder and spall facings and much less thick than those of the compounds.

Despite their general formal differences, the three residential types share a number of features and purposes. The first is to make bounded group spaces with contiguous walls, focusing on the containment of interior spaces. Access to the buildings is highly restrictive, usually through small thresholds or indirect passages from the rear. Some entrances are baffled. Also, many chambers and buildings must have been entered with ladders and structures made of perishable materials. They feature small apartmentlike chambers (most about 2 by 3 meters and 1.5 meters tall), constructed on top of each other, some three or four stories tall. These were presumably constructed with perishable beams lashed to tenons, some of which still remain. The interior chambers only look into the interior patio; no surviving windows look outside. Many walls of both quadrangular and circular compounds also feature small, squarish or rectangular niches. Thus far no tombs or burials have been found in Yayno's monumental sector.

The compound forms satisfied different concerns: group living, protection, formation of restricted activity areas, and privacy. The excavations demonstrate that the building types show a similar range of general activities, including food preparation and consumption, spinning fiber, and use/discard of fine ceramics. The interiors of these structures formed the focus of social life for Yayno's inhabitants. The dimensions of each compound vary, but circular compounds probably held between twenty and thirty people, while the largest quadrangular ones may have been home to up to eighty (Lau 2010: 339). The large compounds served the general residential purposes of fairly prosperous Recuay groups, probably lineages or related groupings. Variability in artifact distributions also suggests a range of high-status and lower-status contexts within the monumental sector.

At the close of the Recuay tradition, the rectangular enclosure form gained importance at another major site in highland Ancash: Honcopampa. About fourteen to sixteen rectangular structures, called "patiogroups," feature fancy megalithic stonework, often integrating large dressed boulders and other stones as wall and lintel elements; the largest block measures 4.3 meters. The constructions are characterized by a great standardization in form: some measure 30 meters on a side and are distinguished by four long halls or galleries flanking each side of a central patio. The main entrance is generally located on the east side, while the western hall is usually the widest. Hartmut Tschauner (2003: 209) found that the most elaborate masonry, often with the largest megaliths, was used for the interior patio walls directly opposite the main access into the patio. Thus the builders designed grand, visually impressive entrances within the interior spaces. Despite the formal similarities, the structures vary greatly in size and construction quality, in terms of the stonework, trueness of walls, and finish. Given the dense amounts of occupational debris (such as grinding stones and ceramics), the buildings served as high-status residences or palaces of local elites (Isbell 1991: 34–35; Tschauner 2003: 209–210).

Residential Traditions in Transformation

It is uncertain whether the circular and rectangular compounds of the Recuay tradition were local or foreign innovations (e.g., Isbell 1991: 35; Tschauner 2003: 214–217). In general, the new compound constructions formalize the pattern of situating individual structures around an open central space. They take the notion of inclusivity and boundedness one step further, however, by enclosing the entire complex. Compound structures in highland Ancash certainly had local antecedents, but none seems to have been the clear prototype.

The room cluster form at Chinchawas may have been one such antecedent. The basic modular dwelling units found at Chinchawas, with a large "front" living room with one main entrance and a narrow back sleeping room, essentially become appropriated as modules in the compounds. Perhaps this is best seen in the reconstruction of the Rondán Circular Construction (fig. 11d) at La Pampa, where the multiple dwelling units are arranged radially around the central open space (Terada 1979: 157). If the original modular unit corresponds to a space for a nuclear family, the rise of the compound form suggests a greater emphasis on a multifamily collectivity. Broadly, the compound form indicates denser living conditions, greater insularity, more restricted access, and less flexibility for addition. It also presumes a general plan before construction as well as a base and organization of sufficient labor to realize the plan.

The strong variability in the quality of the stonework, general construction, and height of walls suggests that this residential form was used by both commoner and elite groups. Where absolute dates are available, both the circular and quadrangular varieties of such compounds first became widely established by the fifth century A.D., during the latter phases of the Recuay tradition.

The rectangular compounds represent key architectural forms both at Yayno and at Honcopampa, so it may be useful to examine this comparison in greater detail. The compounds are among the most numerous and important architectural complexes at both sites. The enclosures feature roughly square or quadrangular layouts, with side rooms along each of the outer walls. In sites where other high-status architecture existed, it is notable that the enclosures were privileged in terms of stonework, finish, and overall elaboration. Their quantity also indicates a persistent local tradition of constructing and maintaining such buildings; a similar process probably accounts for the series of compounds at Honcopampa. They were not unique forms in their respective sites but part of established habits and conventions in local building.

Despite the similarities, Yayno's complexes predate the Honcopampa examples by at least a few centuries. Moreover, further analysis of the form shows important differences. For example, Honcopampa's compounds were one story tall, whereas at least some of the Yayno examples contain multiple stories, with up to three floors. Also, the side rooms at Yayno are compartmentalized, with few if any access ways that allow movements between them. Unless they were accessed by ceiling passages, it would have been necessary to exit into the open interior space and then reenter another chamber or apartment block. One of the emphases of the side rooms in the enclosures at Honcopampa was the presence of long halls or galleries (Isbell 1991: 32; Tschauner 2003: 200), which could facilitate movement around long stretches of the structures without needing to exit into the open plaza. The enclosures at Yayno lack such long passageways.

What can be gleaned from the current evidence of Recuay residential architecture? First, from the beginning the tradition seems to have emphasized small domestic groups clustered within a given hamlet or village. Groups of the Recuay tradition did not always follow today's common pattern of dispersed houses and farmsteads. This seems to have been the case from Huarás times onward. The structures also indicate an emphasis on flexibility, which allowed expansions and renovations of room clusters. Households could freely expand and adapt to new socioeconomic circumstances.

By the late Recuay period (ca. A.D. 500), some sites demonstrate a greater interest in shutting off room clusters by adding walls and separating whole groups from the rest of the settlement. Discrete compounds emerged, often with high perimeter walls, limited access, and multistory interior apartments, frequently with central open spaces. This is evident in various sites with multiple-phase occupations, such as La Pampa, Honcopampa, Yayno, and Chinchawas.

No single cause accounts for the transformation. The suite of similarities across these sites cannot be explained by simple interaction or conquest. Nor do the new forms of residential architecture mark vertical colonies or diaspora communities (Aldenderfer 1993; Goldstein 2005), for no evidence indicates any major population movements into the area or conquest, as related to these architectural forms. Moreover, the ages of these structures are sufficiently different that the transformation was not due to a single event or "horizon."

One positive factor for the change must have been increased social conflict with internal and outside factions. Access to valuable resources (including land and exotic goods), which surged in frequency during the period of Wari expansion (Lau 2005), probably contributed to the competition. Another factor seems to have been a transformation in the way in which groups organized and identified themselves, in material forms. The patterns in residential architecture are consistent with broader patterns in funerary practices, which emphasized corporate affinities while demarcating social boundaries within a given community. Groups appear to have defined themselves on the basis of architecture, through large enclosures or through chullpa monuments. The compounds integrated constituents both physically and symbolically while excluding others.

The area also shows a general trend toward increasing nucleation in settlement, especially the emergence of large centers with dense residential sectors. Corporate groups associated with individual buildings seem to have gotten larger or simply more numerous. Several compounds at Yayno were expansions, purposefully built up against existing structures. This is most clear in the addition of compound c40 directly north of c41 (fig. 13). Both are quadrangular, but each uses very different fine masonry styles; c40 includes many more wide chinking stones and fewer large colored blocks. It seems possible that the builders and users of the c40 compound, while remaining distinct as a collective, sought to show architectural relationship to the larger, older version (c41). We might conjecture that an ambitious descendant or fission group was attempting to demonstrate physical ties to the paramount "house" at Yayno.

William Isbell (1997) proposed that a particular form of Andean organization known as the ayllu (collectivities based on kinship, communalism, and ceremonialism) emerged in the north highlands and spread throughout the Andes during the late Early Intermediate Period and Middle Horizon. This pattern was manifested by its essential diagnostic: the open sepulcher tomb or chullpa (Isbell 1997: 139). While I do not agree that all ancient ayllus necessarily shared this form, chullpas (which were still nascent during the Early Intermediate Period) certainly did spread widely throughout Ancash and beyond by the Middle Horizon.

This pattern ultimately displaced or incorporated earlier mortuary traditions. This trend had social ramifications; as an ancillary development, the emphasis on group identity and intravillage factional competition was increasing by late Recuay times. It is quite possible that the strongly differentiated ayllu-like groups (as marked by co-residence, descent, and economic specialization) seen in Ancash during Inka and early colonial times may have been in existence by late Recuay.

Factional groups were probably more numerous. The earlier preference for greater insularity seems to have become more formalized and materialized in architecture. This was not a materialization of ideology or a power strategy per se, because the practices were not limited exclusively to leaders, aspiring elites, or "aggrandizers" (Clark and Blake 1994; DeMarrais et al. 1996). Rather it seems to have been a series of corporate responses (by a range of egalitarian and hierarchical groups) to the concerns and sociocultural dispositions at the time. Thus the conditions and tangible manifestations of Recuay residential life changed greatly from early to late Recuay times, with additional transformations in the Middle Horizon (discussed in chapter 8).

Constructions for Economic Production

Part of Recuay's built environment consisted of constructions which facilitated the production and management of important economic resources, sometimes called infrastructure in complex societies. This broad category includes roads, terraces, canals and water management systems, and corrals. Unfortunately, several factors hinder our current understanding. First, very little systematic work at the regional or site level exists for such contexts in highland Ancash. Significant research has been done for later periods (e.g., Lane 2006a), but most architecture of this nature has also proven to be extremely difficult to date or assign culturally, especially in reference to groups of the Recuay tradition.

Corrals for herding camelids are probably the most common form. Corrals are very prominent in higher elevations, especially within or near grasslands associated with the puna ecozone. They are frequently located next to debris taluses that were exploited for their stones; sometimes they incorporated boulders in the wall. Corrals often consist of enclosure walls in irregular layouts, which are typically fairly low, made out of piled fieldstone and without mortar. Such constructions may stand alone (Ibarra A. 2003) or may connect with part of a larger settlement, such as at Chinchawas (Lau 2007). It might be mentioned that large walled-off terrace areas of Recuay settlements probably also served as temporary pens for animals. Some settlements used perimeter walls for both defensive and herding purposes, such as at Chonta Ranra Punta (4,350 masl), which features an irregular perimeter wall enclosing approximately 1 ha of open land. A number of small structures inside it functioned as the herders' dwellings and shelter (Ponte R. 1999a).

Corral features are also known from the coastal valley areas. Walled enclosures have been found next to ancient trails in the Santa Valley, with evidence of a highland presence, including Recuay-related kaolinite sherds and desert geoglyphs of llamas. The sites were probably the llama corrals of coast-highland trading caravans (Wilson 1988: 171–176, 189–193, 355). Intensive camelid herding in Ancash in general emerged by the height of the Chavín cult (Miller and Burger 1995). And a great reliance on camelids for meat, related products (fiber, sinew, bone, dung), and use as transport animals continued as a fundamental element of Recuay-period subsistence economies (Lau 2007; Sawyer 1985).

Paths, road networks, and bridges were also very important for the Recuay, given their propensity for interregional interaction. Paths are perhaps best known from the desert coastal valleys, where simple coast to highland trails have been in use for centuries. The best-known roads in highland areas of Ancash date to Inka times, with major north-south segments of the Inka road system, the Capac Ñan, in both the Conchucos and Callejón de Huaylas. Such roads were very likely built over existing ones. One route of the Capac Ñan connected Casma on the coast with Huaraz. The best-preserved portions feature drainage channels and stone pavement typical of Inka roads, but this general route must already have been used intensively by Early Intermediate Period and Middle Horizon times (Lau 2005).

Recuay groups also built terraces to level sloping areas for different purposes. Many residential settlements in highland Ancash are located directly above their agricultural terraces, such as at Yayno (Tello 1930: 265). Not only does terracing reduce erosion and enhance thermal properties of the land, but water from canals is more efficiently distributed within terraced fields (e.g., Donkin 1979; Guillet 1987). The Recuay also built terraces or long platforms to establish level foundations for additional buildings, and these are often associated with nearby contiguous settlements (e.g., Lau 2001: 134; Proulx 1985: 121, 167). Recuay groups therefore actively engaged in reclamation projects to create more appropriate land for agricultural and building projects.

Drainage works are not uncommon in Recuay buildings, especially in residential and ceremonial structures. Small canals and drains appear to have been fairly common (for example, at Huaricoto and Chinchawas) to manage the heavy rains in Ancash. Other drainage works are larger in scale, such as the defensive ditches at Yayno, which also probably collected and channeled water downhill. Although it is likely that the Recuay had forms of irrigation agriculture, only preliminary evidence for large-scale systems is currently available. Walled areas, perhaps for reservoirs, have been recognized at Pashash and at Tinyash (Ravines 1984: 33).

Innovative large-scale water management constructions were developed at least by the Late Intermediate Period in the Cordillera Negra (Lane 2006a, 2006b: 498). Damming projects in high-altitude areas, up to 4,700 meters above sea level, helped to conserve water, fill reservoirs, and create tracts of wetland grazing land with enriched soils and the succulent vegetation preferred by camelids. They functioned as a system, and one of the "silt dams" is 80 meters wide, with a stepped revetment wall approximately 2.5 meters tall. Hence local groups actively modified existing terrain for the production of camelids. The region of Aija also had premodern systems to dam and store water, with effective strategies for wall construction (Antúnez de Mayolo R. 1986: 52–54). It is likely, but remains to be determined, that such developments also took place in earlier periods and in other parts of the Ancash highlands.

Defensive Constructions

The defensive placement of settlements is detailed in chapter 2. This section emphasizes specific architectural strategies and features that complement the general defensive location of sites. At least four broad categories of defensive measures protected different things and areas within the Recuay heartland: location, trench systems, fortification walls, and the strategic arrangements of structures. The features do not always occur altogether in one site. More commonly, only a few are observed. The diversity of strategies suggests both spatial and temporal variability in the concern for defense. Many follow defensive strategies also found elsewhere in ancient Peru (Arkush and Stanish 2005; Topic and Topic 1987). Some forms, however, may mark specific Recuay forms and innovations.

Location

Some further elaboration of the positioning of settlements might be useful, because a wide variation exists even within the category "defensive hilltop site." In terms of strategy, one of the most common defenses for Recuay groups was to position occupations at high locations, usually atop a hill, mountain, or ridgeline (table 1).

All of these sites exploit the natural higher ground, offering a commanding vantage over specific geographical features, such as nearby mountains, fields and crops, roads, and river courses. Others seem to indicate a greater emphasis on internal protection. The higher ground also impedes movement when trying to attack or carrying heavy gear. Projectiles can be thrown or shot with a greater field of vision; defenders can also lob projectiles over walls into low areas. Rocks dislodged or thrown from above can be a great advantage in steeply inclined areas.

Residential sites also often used natural features to help in their defense, whether steep drop-offs and cliffs or quebradas and rocky features. The north face of Honcopampa's residential area (a long sloping ridge called Purushmonte) is well defended because of a steep ravine to the north, leading out of the Quebrada Honda; perimeter walls defended other approaches to the settlement. Other sites, including Chinchawas, Marcajirca (Pampachacra), and Pashash's La Capilla, exploited hilltops which jut out from the surrounding topography; they provide only one relatively easy access point, through the saddle of land at the rear of the hill. Large walls fortified these areas, while the rest of the respective sites are protected simply by steep sloping drop-offs.

Trenches

Some of the most impressive Recuay defensive works included systems of trenches, purposefully excavated courses to protect vulnerable margins of a settlement. These were meant to prevent direct attacks by making it more difficult to move forward (usually upward) or by pushing attackers to lateral areas. Aggregating attackers in the ditches may have also facilitated retaliating attacks, especially with projectile weapons from above. Defensive dry moats were not uncommon in the middle and upper valleys of the Pacific flanks of the Andes, typically sealing off a protected area by cutting across the ridgeline perpendicularly (e.g., Proulx 1985: 165–168; Topic and Topic 1987: 48; Wilson 1988: 165–167, 186).

But perhaps the most extensive trench system is found at Yayno (fig. 9). Elaborate stretches protected the northern and western approaches in particular. The ditches exploited natural fractures and erosional channels of the local geological formation. In profile, they are a type of V-shaped ditch: the inner ditch side may measure up to 4 to 5 meters in height, while the exterior side may rise 2 to 3 meters. The western margins were protected by three parallel trenches, 25 meters apart. Added protection was afforded by having some sections of a trench walled across the top, providing a type of parapet. Part of the defensive system at Yayno included deep ditches cutting across the ridgelines that descend the mountaintop. Because the slopes in these areas are fairly gentle, they are the most logical places for attack. Thus the defensive features were created in these spots to slow any advance or draw any attackers to the steeper lateral ends.

Defensive Walls

Some important sites were protected by perimeter walls. This practice can protect entire settlements, with walls extending around the margins of the settlement, such as at Pueblo Viejo (Caraz) and Chonta Ranra Punta (Ponte R. 2001: 224). Sometimes perimeter walls protected important zones or other buildings within a settlement, such as the La Capilla temple at Pashash.

Perimeter walls were often made by joining a series of constructions, resulting in a long, solid wall front. The walls are not flush; they frequently have projections or are irregular. At Chinchawas, for example, the façades of dwellings and other buildings were connected to terrace walls with additional wall segments to form a single large defensive front on the entire northern side; the wall presents a formidable barrier to approaches from down-valley. Groups at Yayno employed a different strategy. Just above the long ditches builders constructed extensive gallery structures, termed "terrace room complexes." These buildings were long constructions either one or two rooms deep; one example may run over 100 meters. Not only did they essentially provide long sections of perimeter wall for Yayno's defense, but the inner spaces of the galleries were partitioned to form domestic housing and spaces for lower-status groups.

At a number of Recuay sites the walls were fitted with parapets. These are essentially short walls with long, narrow standing positions or walkways along the inner portion. Some have argued that parapeted walls are the only unambiguously defensive forms (Topic and Topic 1987: 48–49). Such features provide high, protected positions and could be used by sentries to keep watch or by defenders during attacks. Most parapeted walls have been reported from fortified sites in the coastal valleys. Yayno, however, has at least three surviving sections of parapeted walls. Two protected each side of the primary stairway that leads into the heart of the monumental sector, the main plaza. The other provided a defensible lookout near the northwest perimeter wall.

Strategic Arrangements

Some sites have a series of terrace walls or successive wall fronts. With layer-cake profiles, such constructions essentially provided multiple lines of defense. Thus the best-defended part of the site was also its most central and topmost. This architectural pattern is reminiscent of later settlements in the Junín area, known as "concentric ring sites" (Parsons et al. 2000), or large multiple-walled centers, such as Coyor in Cajamarca (Julien 1988; Wiener 1880).

Many enclosures were conjoined and connected to perimeter walls/ terraces, forming massive bastions. The most prominent examples are from Yayno, where the inhabitants joined circular enclosures along the steep ridgelines descending from the summit, most prominently on the southern and western ends. When intact, these compounds acted as formidable defenses as well as impressive monuments to local warfare ideology. Multistory towers were literally stacked on top of each other, with compounds successively built atop the rear portion of the lower structure. This strategic "chaining" served the dual purpose of exploiting the height provided by existing walls and bracing the tall, otherwise freestanding walls of the lower structures. These ridgeline bastions not only prevented lateral movements and flanking attacks but allowed inhabitants to move to higher ground and another compound if necessary, without needing to exit the complex. Ridgeline bastions also must have allowed a better view of attackers; for example, an attacker could not approach or flee through the rear flanks.

Finally, Recuay residential compounds do not often feature easy access from ground level. They were probably entered through access ways near the top of the wall, by removable ladders, or from above.

Recuay Defensive Strategies

Despite their ubiquity, Recuay defenses were usually fairly modest, practical solutions to a perennial concern about interlopers and attackers. Most groups took to high locations and exploited natural features and advantages of higher ground to help stave off potential attacks. Other low-investment measures appear to have included connecting existing structures to create long wall fronts or piling rocks to form low walls, to gain an advantage over attackers. Most commonly, defensive constructions occur alongside natural defenses, such as steep slopes, narrow ridgeline saddles, and quebradas.

Use of perishable materials to help provide expedient protection for settlement and resource areas was probably very common. This may have included piling cacti and other hard spiny vegetation, which is a common technique today to keep out unwanted visitors, human or animal.

Some Recuay groups, though, committed major corporate labor to defensive forms. The defenses at Yayno, such as the fine stone masonry of the enclosure walls, may be described as overbuilt: their elaboration far exceeds any strictly practical function. Even at the onset monumental building at Yayno strongly favored defensive measures, for its establishment on a mountaintop literally ringed with natural ditches may have exploited an ideal of a protected central or sacred place. These observations imply a valorization of warfare which is prevalent in other dimensions of Recuay culture, especially in the imagery of artworks.

Monumental fortifications were much more than mere defenses. They seem to have expressed Recuay power and identity through a type of warfare culture also prevalent in other Early Intermediate Period cultures (Lau 2004a: 163). The defensive constructions at Yayno exceed the known upper scales of Recuay labor investment and strongly suggest the presence of strong social hierarchies, led by elites with large sources of labor. As suggested by the architecture at Pashash and Yayno, lords would have actively exploited their access to local labor to construct massive buildings, both to function as defenses and as visually stunning monuments for elite aggrandizement. Tello (1930: 264–265) observed:

> [Ancient highland settlements] occupy lofty and strategic places and are defended by fortified walls and precipices. . . . Many of them arouse admiration, not only because of their perpendicular and impregnable sites, but also because of the enormous effort which their construction must have demanded. It would be difficult to explain the existence of these villages erected in rough and inhospitable places near the cordilleras — which must have sheltered a dense population to judge by the vast area they occupied — were it not for the contiguous terraced fields, which rise step by step from the bottoms of the ravines to the tops of the mountains, revealing an extraordinary mastery of nature.

Recuay hilltop architecture expressed the strength and character of the community. Similar ideas prevailed in medieval castle communities of northern Europe and Greek city-states, where a strongly defended settlement meant a healthy and prosperous community: an outward sign to others regarding the place's vitality. In the Recuay case, labor was probably drawn from nearby communities that were both subject to and protected by elites. Settlement-wide works (perimeter walls, trenching systems, drainages) were the domain of the entire community, while other structures, such as isolated enclosures, were the domain of smaller collectivities. Recuay monumental fortifications therefore served as unique expressions of both political authority and collective identity.

In part, this helps to explain the intentions and understanding of Recuay defenses, monumental or not. What did these defenses protect against, and who was meant to experience them? The settlements were most commonly strongholds or refuges in locales that were difficult to access. The available evidence does not indicate that they were ever part of an integrated network of bases for securing large territories or as bases for launching attacks. Also, the defensive systems do not seem to have defended large areas, and the forts did not necessarily work in concert. Instead they protected individual communities who were responsible for their building and upkeep.

A general emphasis on protection is manifest in the Recuay tradition, especially later in the chronology. The architectural evidence indicates both a common defense against hostile outsiders and a focus on protection against potential rival factions within the same settlement. This is consonant with a common pattern in the monumental architecture of early complex societies, where "fortresses, city walls, and enclosures around public buildings indicate a concern with defense that was already present in tribal societies, but which in the early civilizations was directed increasingly against potential internal as well as external enemies" (Trigger 1990: 121).

CHAPTER FOUR

Ritual Buildings and Landscapes

Ancient Recuay ceremonialism was manifested throughout ancient Ancash as special types of ritual places. The major categories were temples, shrines, and mortuary structures. Where relevant, specific archaeological contexts are described here to detail the range and significance of activities that occurred in these places. The chapter concludes with a consideration of the implications of Recuay architecture, including diachronic transformations, social complexity, and notions of landscape.

Temples and Shrines

Recuay religious practices regularly centered on the veneration of sacred stones and boulders. Groups in highland Ancash marked out these natural features and incorporated them as part of their ceremonial landscape.

Shrines are one general type of ceremonial space. They consist of spaces built around large standing stone uprights (wankas). The largest researched site, Huancajirca (3,290 masl), is located just above Huaraz. It features a wanka 5 meters tall, standing in the center of an earthen and walled circular/oval platform (fig. 14). The sizable platform construction, measuring 45 meters across and over 1 meter tall, evens out the natural promontory and is composed of large stones, some as tall as 1.7 meters. The central wanka itself is planted into a sturdy, low base made of cut stone masonry. Near this platform altar was a series of pits for caches and evidence of periodic burnings and offerings, indicating venerative activities from the Early Horizon onward (Bazán del Campo 2007; Bazán del Campo and Wegner 2006).

Ethnohistorical documents and archaeology elsewhere indicate that Ancash groups probably considered certain standing stones to be embodiments of supernaturals or ancestors (Duviols 1979; Falcón 2004; Lau 2000).

FIGURE 14. The standing stone (wanka) at Huancajirca. Note the row of stones which forms a small platform around the upright. Excavations determined that the shrine was used from the first millennium B.C. until the sixteenth century A.D. It forms part of a boundary wall today.

The tradition of standing sacred stone uprights in ceremonial structures has a long history in the Central Andes, from Formative to Inka times. They were often featured at the center of ritual spaces as the main cult objects of these spaces. Standing uprights can be found throughout highland Ancash, most often without the elaborate terrace platform or base (Bazán del Campo 2007: 3; Kauffmann Doig 1956). Recuay-tradition groups also erected stone uprights to mark subterranean tombs and chambers (Tello 1940: 667), such as at Jancu (Wegner 1988). At Chinchawas, a polygonal wanka signaled the location of a subterranean tomb below; a low masonry platform 5 centimeters high propped up the large reddish brown stone about a meter tall and a meter wide.

Rock art, though poorly dated, is not uncommon in highland Ancash. Some large boulders, in particular, feature rock paintings and petroglyphs which depict large anthropomorphic figures, such as at Supaycaca near Carhuaz and in the Quebrada Quilcayhuanca (pl. 2). Painted with red, yellow, and black pigments, these may possibly portray mythical figures for local groups, perhaps as early as the Early Horizon. In addition to human figures, rock art frequently depicts camelids and abstract geometric designs on caves and large overhangs (e.g., Ibarra A. 2003: fig. 19; Kauffmann Doig 2002: 490–491). Sometimes carved slabs, such as the Isabelita Stone, feature incised mythical human and animal imagery. The large stone appears to have been the main cult image of a shrine site near Jangas, which included dedicatory offerings as well as interments (Ponte R. 1999a: 51–53).

In other cases, Recuay-tradition groups emphasized outcrops of living rock. The Torreón was the most elaborate circular building on the

Chinchawas site, with at least three concentric walls of fine boulder and spall stonemasonry. One of the boulder uprights features a petroglyph of concentric circles, mimicking the architectural plan (Lau 2006b: 211, fig. 30). The walls were built around a small outcrop of light-colored andesitic rock, which rises in the central part of the interior space toward the north. Just inside the wall of the innermost room, about 5 meters in diameter, is a low but carefully made circular bench or platform, only about 10 centimeters tall, perhaps for sitting and observing rituals. Partitions between the inner and middle wall created small arclike compartments (about 30 by 80 centimeters). Entered through narrow doorways, they were probably for storing or displaying ritual objects and offerings. Excavations in the building produced fancy bowls and special objects made of rare stone, metal, and shell, which suggest activities occasioned by camelid offerings and consumption. One of the rooms just outside the interior space showed evidence of burning.

The summit of Yayno is topped by a circular building with concentric walls and curved interior rooms, like many of the site's round residential compounds. Radial partitions cut across at least three massive concentric walls of finely made wanka-*pachilla* (large block and spall) stonemasonry; some walls measure 1.2 meters thick. Tello (1929: 32) likened this structure to an "Inti Watana," alluding to circular constructions in the Inka empire associated with worship of the sun (see also Apolín G. 2004). Although work on similar structures at Yayno demonstrates their general residential character, this central building has not yet been tested for astronomical or calendrical associations. The building commands unobstructed views of the Cordillera Blanca's glaciers to the west as well as mountain ranges to the east and north, perhaps sacred peaks in local beliefs (e.g., Reinhard 1985).

These Recuay constructions are related to a widespread tradition of ritual activities in the north highlands, centered on powerful ancestral supernaturals associated with prominent stones, stone formations, and mountains (Pérez Calderón 1988, 1994; Topic et al. 2002). Other circular ceremonial structures with concentric walls include the building at Cerro Agopampa, which is built similarly around a stone outcrop (Murga Cruz 1983).

Large ceremonial constructions, built prior to the Recuay tradition, continued to be active during the Early Intermediate Period. These included the famous sites of Pomakayán and Tumshukayko. Pomakayán is located a few hundred meters east of Huaraz's central square and extends over about 2 hectares (Serna Lamas 2009). Dating to the Early Horizon, it was a temple at least partly dedicated to the Chavín cult; pottery, cult objects, and galleries in the Chavín style have been found there (Reina Loli 1959; Tello 1930, 1940). During the Early Intermediate Period the site seems to have been transformed into an important shrine and burial area for Recuay peoples. It is possible that Pomakayán was a source for many of the Recuay stone sculptures found scattered in the city and in collections (Raimondi 1873; Schaedel 1952; Wegner 2009). Some sections of curving megalithic walls, made of large round boulders, still exist on the site, but many stones have been removed for later constructions in Huaraz.

Tumshukayko also saw use during Recuay times. Like Pomakayán, it is situated within a modern city, but Tumshukayko is much better preserved. Dating mainly to the Late Preceramic period, the settlement seems to have had major occupation during the late Formative or near the end of the Early Horizon, ca. 300 B.C. (Bueno M. 2001; Tello 1960). The entire complex consists of a number of stacked terrace platforms, ringed by large masonry walls with rounded corners, elaborate staircases, and interior chambers. The stone masonry is very distinctive, often using cut teardrop-shaped stones. The builders laid them together like bricks and arranged projecting blocks on some façades to form upside-down stepped designs. Recuay-style pottery and other artifacts, including a stone *maqueta* (model)/ gaming board, have also been found at Tumshukayko, which suggests later reuse, especially for periodic offerings.

Several important conclusions can be reached regarding these data. First, older temples or shrines continued to be revered by local groups during the Early Intermediate Period, including by those associated with Recuay pottery. This would suggest that local groups were tolerant of other faiths and religious practices and perhaps incorporated elements of them into their own traditions. Second, Recuay ceremonial beliefs encompassed a pantheon of local divinities, very likely along the lines of huacas, ancestors, and mythic supernaturals documented during early historical times for the Central Highlands (e.g., Salomon 1991). Many of these were instantiated through durable features of the landscape: rock outcrops, stone uprights, and boulders.

Ceremonial Plazas and Enclosures

In contrast to other Andean cultures (Moore 1996a, 1996b), very large open plazas were not a major conventionalized form of Recuay monumental architecture. One of the most sizable plazas in the ancient Recuay world was built at Yayno, measuring roughly 45 by 55 meters. But it would only occupy a small corner of the large open plaza at Huánuco Pampa (520 by 360 meters), an Inka administrative center. Yayno's plaza, it should be mentioned, is largely artificial; it is one of the only pieces of level ground on the mountaintop settlement. Despite the lack of major standing walls, it featured very restricted access, for the plaza sits atop a terraced platform, elevated up to 8 to 10 meters in some places above the surrounding constructions. The main entrance was through a processional staircase, paved with flagstones, which led through three sets of megalithic doorways, some with parapeted walls and flanking guardian rooms. The centrally located plaza connects a series of key buildings at the site, including several high-status rectangular enclosures, and furnished further access up to the apex of the settlement through a monumental staircase. On the basis of estimates for capacity in other Pre-Columbian plazas (Inomata 2006; Moore 1996a), Yayno's plaza could have contained over 5,000 people but more likely held some 700 to 1,200 people during times of festivals and other public events.

Rather more modest walled ceremonial enclosures were typical in the Ancash highlands. The few studied through excavations are distinguished by their evidence of use during corporate gatherings. These constructions consist mainly of rectangular plaza spaces about 15 to 20 meters long enclosed by walls and appear to have formed parts of high-status architectural complexes on hilltop sites.

Queyash Alto, near Marcará, is a ridgetop settlement where excavations encountered an early Recuay civic-ceremonial settlement. In addition to a discrete high-status sector, excavations have identified ceremonial enclosures and areas associated with large-scale preparation and consumption of food and drink, especially *cuy* (guinea pig) and camelid meat. Colander sherds and large jars were probably used for the brewing of chicha maize beer, while fancy Huarás-style bowls and camelid crania ladles were used during its serving. Additional evidence for ritual activities and displays includes animal offerings, panpipe fragments, camelid figurines, and metal and shell objects (Gero 1990, 1991, 1992). The site was occupied intensively by the early part of the Early Intermediate Period until the Middle Horizon. The open feasting areas near a small mound contained evidence to indicate that new strategies of political authority associated with labor recruitment and gender divisions emerged during the early part of the Recuay tradition, in the wake of Chavín's collapse.

At Chinchawas, dense midden remains from intensive consumption activities were associated with a special walled space labeled Enclosure 2 (fig. 8). As at Queyash Alto, inhabitants located the ceremonial space just below the topmost portion of the site. The enclosure is irregularly shaped, roughly 17 by 10 meters, and had subfloor canals. Its walls were of fine stonemasonry, very likely fitted with carved stone lintels depicting ancestral themes. Sculptures were recorded within the enclosure, and others are located nearby (Lau 2002, 2006b). The enclosure was surrounded by other structures with poorer-quality stonework. Enclosure 2's size is consistent with the population estimate of about 70–100 people for the ancient village.

Excavations indicated that Enclosure 2 was a venue for periodic public ceremonies probably dedicated to ancestors (Lau 2002). Its interior space was kept relatively clean, as would befit a sacred place. Just outside the enclosure, however, was a midden, atypical for the rest of the site, where the voluminous trash from the festivities was dumped. It was especially rich in camelid remains, fancy bowls and pouring jars, and high-status items such as copper metal sheet ornaments, beads, and exotic vessels. Expedient bone implements, including pointed rib tools and cranial spoons, would have been used for serving and eating foods. On the opposite end of Enclosure 2, near its southwest corner, was evidence of intensive cooking activities, with several hearths and broken sooted jars. This was probably the main production area for the food consumed during feasting episodes.

The ceremonial practices indicated by archaeological remains accord well with historical records of Central Peru documenting the rites of highland communities after the arrival of the Spaniards (Doyle 1988; Duviols 1986). In particular, communal gatherings for ceremonies to ensure the fertility of land and camelid herds were held in special enclosed spaces.

> Apart from the numerous corrals which are found nearly everywhere in the punas . . . there are other corrals, patios, or enclosed plazas of different sizes and of rectangular or circular form, situated near the shrines or at the foot of snow-covered hills which have been taken to be pak'arinas or sacred places. The construction of these corrals must have demanded the joint efforts of an organized people, for they are formed with great stones, planted vertically and arranged in rows. . . . These corrals were sacred places where the Indians congregated for the celebration of ceremonies. (Tello 1930: 278–279)

Other ceremonial enclosures have been reported in the Conchucos and Callejón de Huaylas regions (Ibarra A. 2003). In parts of the central Conchucos region, civic architecture is characterized by "circular patio groups" (Herrera 2005: 224–243). This general form, ca. 20 to 40 meters in diameter, seems to have had both ceremonial and residential functions. Some of these structures feature raised areas for group ceremonies and feasting; one includes a ramp and a "stage" (opposite the main entrance). The stages, at the site of Gotushjirca, face upslope toward artificial cists and other natural topographic landmarks. Other circular patio groups feature interior rooms, such as those identified for the circular residential compounds at Yayno. At least part of their variability of function in the central Conchucos appears to have resulted from very long histories of use. They first appeared in the middle to late Early Intermediate Period and continued to be popular as forms until the Late Intermediate Period. The enclosures without rooms appear to be earlier, lack materials, and were used primarily for communal ceremonial activities (Herrera 2005: 229). Later ceremonial compounds seem to have combined circular compounds with orthogonal architecture typical of later periods, especially in the Callejón de Huaylas.

By the end of the Recuay tradition around A.D. 700, when Wari culture gained influence throughout the Andes, new forms of ceremonial architecture appear to have been adopted by local groups in highland Ancash. Some of the most distinctive are the D-shaped structures (Cook 2001; Meddens and Cook 2001; Ochatoma and Cabrera 2001). At least two examples have been identified at Honcopampa (Isbell 1991: 31; Tschauner 2003: 200). These tall buildings are essentially circular walled compounds, but on one side they feature a flat façade toward the south, resulting in a D-shaped plan (fig. 15). One of the examples, structure AC-13 (ca. 13 meters across, with walls 5 meters high), features an entrance on the south façade, while the other, AC-14 (ca. 8 meters across), contains four large interior niches. Other structures abut the buildings, indicating that the D-shaped buildings were special ritual structures within larger complexes.

D-shaped structures manifested the merging of local, traditional ritual activities (probably focused on funerary ceremonies, due to their frequent proximity to graves/tombs) with universalizing religious concepts and activities spread by Wari political ideology (Cook 2001: 154; González Carré et al. 1999; Meddens and Cook 2001: 227). The merging of local and foreign forms, in architecture as well as pottery, appears to have been one of the primary ways in which local groups participated in the Wari trade and political network (Lau 2002, 2005; Tschauner 2003).

FIGURE 15.
The D-shaped struc-
tures (foreground) and
the group of chullpas
(background) at Honco-
pampa. The rustic stone-
masonry of the tall
D-shaped structures
contrasts with the block-
spall style, often incor-
porating large boulders,
found in the chullpas
and compounds.

Funerary Structures

By far the most common type of Recuay ceremonial architecture consists of mortuary structures. Their widespread construction represents a
significant change from earlier periods. While few Chavín-period burials
have been discovered in highland Ancash, small-scale mortuary structures in the Recuay tradition abound throughout the north highlands.
Recuay peoples interred their dead using a variety of constructions.

Subterranean Tombs

Subterranean tombs form one broad category, which includes a number
of types. These types share one basic feature: a large portion or all of the
structure lies underground, almost always beneath stones and boulders,
or is within or adjacent to living rock.

Perhaps the simplest burials consist of those which employ a small
natural or artificial cavity in the ground for the interment. The cavity
is overlain by a large stone slab or boulder. Sometimes such stones were
moved deliberately to roof the cavity. In other cases, a cavity was excavated underneath it. In slightly more elaborate examples, low walls are
often built to make small individual chambers or to provide an even
facing (or "lining") for the interior compartment. Such burials can be

found in many parts of the Callejón de Huaylas, including Huaraz and Carhuaz (Bennett 1944: 34–36; Ponte R. 2001; Tello 1940: 665). Tombs beneath boulders are common in the Quebrada Llanganuco, dating to Early Intermediate Period occupations, probably of Huarás and later of Recuay groups (Matsumoto 2006).

Small cist or box graves represent another very common type occurring in parts of highland Ancash. They are slightly more elaborate than simple cavity tombs because they feature a more formalized compartment, often built with stone masonry or carved out of bedrock, sometimes using a combination of methods. The compartment is usually rectangular, in the form of a cist or boxlike cavity. It is fairly small, frequently no more than 60–80 centimeters in any one dimension and typically much smaller. Most cist tombs could probably have held only a single flexed interment. But some stone cist tombs are known to have had multiple interments. The structures are sometimes associated with Huarás pottery, suggesting an early Early Intermediate Period date for their first widespread use (Bennett 1944: 36; Burger 1985a: 125; Lumbreras 1974a: 49). A cluster of cist tombs, associated with Recuay pottery, was found in the western side of Pomakayán. Cist tombs continued to be employed during the late Early Intermediate Period and Middle Horizon, sometimes as part of chullpa complexes, such as at Ichik Wilkawaín and Chinchawas (Lau 2001; Paredes Olvera 2007). Most cist tombs are topped by large stone slabs or natural boulders.

Larger tombs, with discrete chambers, represent another prominent Recuay-tradition funerary structure (fig. 16). These structures are generally larger than cist or box tombs and may have multiple interment chambers. They are associated with small collective burials, given their capacity to accommodate more than one (flexed) burial or funerary bundle. Stone slabs or boulders typically served for roofing and may also have been physical landmarks for the tomb. One of the common additions to chamber tombs is a small entry space, variously called an antechamber or vestibule.

A basic subterranean chamber tomb was found at Chinchawas (Lau 2001: 156–157). This structure features an ovoid main chamber (1.9 meters long and 1.2 meters high). An east attachment serves as a small vestibule for a narrow doorway (40 centimeters wide, 80 centimeters high), while another addition functions as a small back chamber. A more elaborate example, but without the entry vestibule, was reported in the funerary sector at the site of Jatungaga. This partly subterranean octagonal structure, 1.6 meters across and 1.1 meters high, features eight finely finished

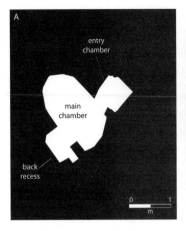

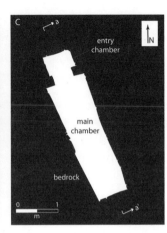

FIGURE 16. Plan views of subterranean tombs identified at Chinchawas: (a) Subterranean Tomb 1 (ST-1); (b) ST-3; (c) ST-2.

walls with wanka-pachilla masonry and rectangular niches, probably for ceremonial paraphernalia and temporary lighting while attending to the burials (Orsini 2007: 88).

Two other chamber tombs at Chinchawas are rectangular in layout (Lau 2001: 157–159). Each has an antechamber, which provides entry into the main interment space. These examples (figs. 16b, c) are comparable to the "deep stone-lined tombs" at Ichik Wilkawaín (Bennett 1944: 21ff.) in their rectangular shape, size (approximately 3–3.5 meters long by ca. 1 meter wide), and construction. Another comparable tomb was found at the site of Marcajirca in the Marian suburb of Huaraz, which features a main chamber associated with separate chambers in the form of box-like cists and antechambers, used for offerings (Ponte R. 2001: 227–228). Groups of the Recuay tradition also used tombs in the form of cylindrical or polygonal-sided shafts. Some of the more notable cases include several looted examples flanking the hilltop settlement at Chuchunpunta, located just outside the town of Aija.

Long galleries are another major form of Recuay subterranean tombs. Such constructions were built both as locales for interment/offerings and also as accessways into large tomb complexes. They are especially common near Huaraz, at sites such as Ichik Wilkawaín and Shankaiyan (Bennett 1944). Constructed by lining the side walls and roof with stone slabs, some galleries extend up to 20 meters, but most measure between 3 and 10 meters in length and about a meter in height and width. Recuay interments and offerings have even been found in galleries made by earlier cultures, such as in the Rocas gallery underneath the rectangular plaza at Chavín de Huántar (*El Comercio*, 8 April 1998).

The most elaborate Recuay burials are multichambered complexes. Even this subcategory, however, includes substantial diversity in the form and employment of unique local features. Víctor Ponte (2001: 228–229), for example, described a simple, three-chambered structure at the Quitapampa C site. The entire subterranean tomb, 3.5 meters long, was built partly of wall and partly of bedrock, with two round main chambers and a connecting antechamber. The doorways feature tall stone jambs.

Subterranean chamber tombs in the Katak region were much more elaborate. Located on a long ridgetop just southeast of modern Katak, Roko Amá is the most extensive and complex Recuay-tradition cemetery known. It is especially significant because the site was the source of the ceramic materials first used to distinguish the Recuay pottery style (Bennett 1944: 64; Macedo 1881; Middendorf 1973: 70; Tello 1930: 271). Many of Roko Amá's subterranean chambers are still partly exposed on the surface within the walls of the modern Katak cemetery. Outside are additional mounds and subterranean tombs to the east.

Tello (1929: 41) reported an astounding 148 *soterrados* (subterranean chamber tombs) in the Katak region; most of these were likely at Roko Amá. Many if not all had been excavated by a wealthy landowner some four decades before. The emptying of these tombs was so thorough that very little Recuay pottery exists today surficially on the site or even within the chambers. Given the absence of material, Bennett (1944: 64) believed that many of the subterranean structures in the Katak region were in fact residential in nature and called them "houses" and "dwellings." They are now understood to have been primarily subterranean funerary mausolea in the Recuay tradition.

Roko Amá's multichambered structures usually consist of a main central room about 2–3 meters long and over a meter wide which connects a series of smaller ancillary compartments, including entry chambers. Many of the tombs at Roko Amá feature stonemasonry interiors, roofs of large stone slabs, and interior wall niches. The tombs often had multiple floors or small chambers built directly atop each other. The multiple floors and chambers permitted internal spatial divisions and complexity, which functioned to segregate interments and forms of interaction with the deceased.

In 1939 Tello's disciple, Toribio Mejía Xesspe (1948), reinvestigated a number of the Katak tombs and also excavated two unopened tombs, in which he found Recuay pottery. Mejía categorized the tombs into four types: (1) Soterrado Simple (one story and chamber); (2) Soterrado Compuesto I (one story and chamber, topped by a structure or platform); (3) Soterrado Compuesto II (one story and multiple chambers, topped by a structure or platform); and (4) Soterrado Compuesto III (two stories with one or more chambers, topped by a structure or platform). Perhaps more importantly, Mejía (1948) called attention to their use for ritual purposes as places for storage of cult objects and paraphernalia, citing religious continuity with colonial-period idolatries in the region (e.g., Hernández Príncipe 1923).

In the nearby Yanapampa tomb (Site 1K) illustrated by Bennett (1944: 65), the western part is very similar in form to the isolated rectangular subterranean tombs at Chinchawas, with a long chamber connected to a small antechamber. The tomb also features white and red paintings of Recuay-style designs, suggesting that tomb interiors may have been a focus of mural painting, especially in the Katak region.

About 12 kilometers east of Huaraz is the large subterranean tomb of Jancu (fig. 17). Discovered accidentally in 1969 while building a school-house, it remains one of the few instances of a largely intact elite Recuay tomb. Through interviews and study of the grave offerings, archaeologist Steven Wegner (1988) has been able to reconstruct different aspects of the tomb's final disposition in form and use.

The tomb itself is situated underneath a large granitic boulder and is

FIGURE 17. Plan view of the Jancu tomb, showing the subterranean gallery into the main chamber and interior burial compartments. The entire main chamber is covered by a large boulder. (Drawing by author, after original in Wegner 1988)

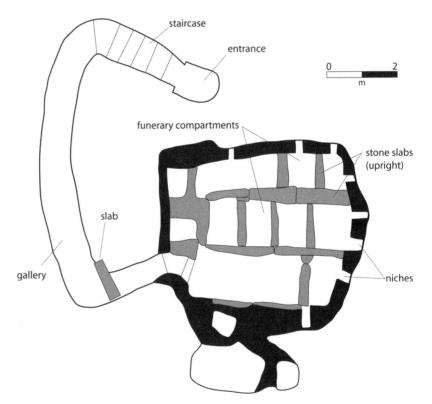

almost completely covered by it. A large standing stone upright (wanka) once marked an elaborate entrance. This featured a small vertical entryway leading into a flight of steps ending at a threshold at the base, which was once blocked with a large slab. The narrow stairway descends into a long 5-meter gallery which curls around into a short passageway, which also has steps and is closable with a heavy stone slab. Like the entranceway and gallery, the roughly quadrangular-shaped room, approximately 4 by 5 by 1.5 meters, has walls of large stone slabs with chinking masonry.

A number of features are especially noteworthy. First, Jancu's interior walls have a series of about a dozen elaborate masonry niches, squarish in shape and approximately 20 centimeters high and deep. But many are in poor condition. The niches and nearby wall ledges were used for placing grave offerings and ceremonial paraphernalia. Second, flat stone slabs, approximately 80 centimeters tall and 10–20 centimeters thick, divide the interior chamber into twelve to fourteen small and low compartments. Most of them were probably used to contain individual interments. Thus, unlike the Katak structures, where a main room connects to a series of smaller subsidiary chambers, the main space in the Jancu type is partitioned to contain the burial compartments physically. Finally, the tomb interior seems to have been purposefully made a light color, using lighter-colored stone and clay to cover dark surfaces.

The most elaborate Recuay burial ever recorded systematically was the subfloor tomb at Pashash, in one of the structures on La Capilla hill. Excavated by Terence Grieder and Alberto Bueno, the tomb was of a very high-status individual, probably a woman, who was buried with elaborate offering caches. The offerings included metal adornments, figurines, fine kaolinite vessels, and rare stone objects. The tomb itself was located inside a structure which was called a "burial temple" (Grieder 1978: 48). The back wall of the tomb doubled as the perimeter wall for the hilltop. The dimensions of the temple are unknown because it was not fully excavated. But additional burials were later found in other parts of La Capilla, indicating that the hill was used repeatedly for the interment of Recuay elites.

The portion exposed by Grieder and Bueno featured three distinct activity contexts, all with elaborate masonry and flat paving-stone floors. Underneath the floor and a stone slab lid was a small burial compartment, measuring only 60 by 55 centimeters. The primary burial was flexed but was badly preserved. Three separate offerings were associated with the burial: one directly adjacent to the flexed interment, one above the roof of the burial compartment, and another just beneath the outer threshold leading into the inner burial space. Some of the grave offerings, including garment pins, spindle whorls, and decomposed textiles, suggested that the main interment was of a mature woman (Grieder 1978: 55).

Where the natural topography permits, Recuay tombs are sometimes built directly into small spaces of grottoes in cliffs, under rock overhangs, and underneath large boulders. In these cases, it is not uncommon to find an outer wall which demarcates the primary burial space, sometimes with interior partition walls which form additional separate interment spaces. Perhaps the most notable tombs of this type include those of Aukispukio (Wegner 2001a), which features segmented funerary structures built into high, rocky overhangs. Investigations in some of the burial structures have recovered important northern-style Recuay remains, including pottery and textiles, and a complete drum. Sheltered spaces underneath boulders at Pueblo Viejo are separated formally by walls which reach from the floor to the roof/side of the boulder.

Chullpa Tombs

By about the sixth and seventh centuries A.D. peoples of the north highlands began to prefer building aboveground burial constructions (fig. 18), called chullpas (Isbell 1997). Throughout Ancash, chullpas became so

FIGURE 18. Plan views of chullpas identified at Chinchawas: (a) Chullpa Tomb 5 (CT-5); (b) CT-6; (c) CT-9; (d) CT-7; (e) CT-10; (f) CT-3; (g) CT-12; (h) CT-1. Strong variability characterizes the layout, size, and construction quality of chullpas. Some of the chullpas at Chinchawas had second stories.

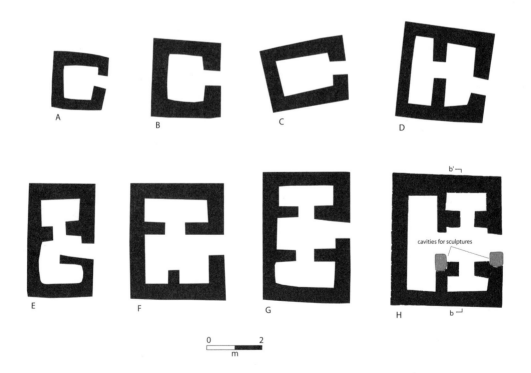

prominent across the highlands that the famous priest and Ancash historian Padre Augusto Soriano Infante (1947: 10) described them as an "infinity of chullpas."

Chullpas in Ancash were most commonly made out of stone. Builders often employed large boulders for walls and large tabular slabs for the roofs (fig. 19). The roofs of most chullpas today have collapsed, so it is difficult to discern how they might have looked like in antiquity. Evidence suggests that at least some may have been gabled with dual sloping roofs. The few surviving at Tinyash have thick, sloping rooflines (forming a triangular pediment) which employ very flat roofstones, stacked atop each other (Antúnez de Mayolo 1935, 1941; Ravines 1984; Thompson and Ravines 1973). Many roofs were formed by using a simple corbeling technique, where flat stones on opposite walls were cantilevered and then topped with stone slabs and earth. In other sites the roofs seem to have been left unelaborated, with large flat boulders spanning the burial spaces and mounded over with clay and soil. It is also clear now that chullpas in highland Ancash, like other parts of the north highlands, sometimes featured stone sculptures as architectural elements engaged physically on walls, especially as lintels and jambs in threshold areas (Lau 2000, 2006b). The elaborate use of stone led Tello (1930) to speculate that chullpas were part of the seminal Megalithic Culture in early Andean civilization.

Chullpas vary considerably in their form and features, however, like other Recuay buildings and artworks. They are typically single small, freestanding buildings, with a squarish or rectangular floor plan. The

FIGURE 19. Section drawings of Subterranean Tomb ST-2 (a) and Chullpa Tomb CT-1 (b), Chinchawas. Both constructions provided interior compartments for interments and used large stone slabs to cover the burial spaces.

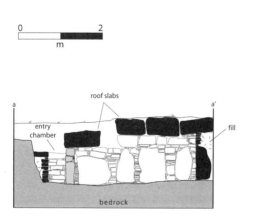

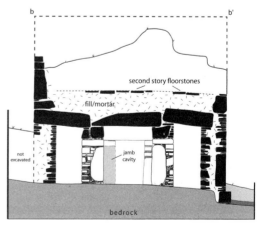

A   B

façade of the chullpa is typically on one of the longer ends. Chullpas may have one or more doorways that face cardinal directions, sometimes with an eastern exposure toward the rising sun (Isbell 1997), although this is highly variable. Doorways are also frequently located to have a vantage point over special areas. At Honcopampa, for example, many of the doorways of the chullpas face north toward the elaborate compounds in the main residential sector of the site. At Nuevo Tambo, in the Quebrada Quilcayhuanca, the chullpas are located on small terraces which rise up along the steep quebrada walls; their doorways face south, overlooking the rich pasturelands of the valley. At other sites, such as Sahuanpuncu, the chullpa groups have more idiosyncratic and variable orientations, often facing one another, or are arranged around an open patio area. In these contexts the builders may have oriented the buildings to those spaces and directions that were deemed important for continued well-being and vigilance by the deceased, whether this meant land and herds or living and other ancestral populations.

Basic chullpas have just one interior room, while more elaborate examples are partitioned into multiple chambers through use of interior walls or columns. Most chullpas in the north highlands were modest one-story buildings, such as the majority of chullpas at Chinchawas and Nuevo Tambo. The majority of these measure no more than 3–4 meters across and have only a few small chambers. Moreover, the stonework and overall building are highly variable, suggesting the practices of multiple local groups over time rather than a single integrated program.

The largest well-known chullpas have additional levels, such as at Katiamá, Queushu, Honcopampa, and Wilkawaín. Wilkawaín features the largest-known chullpa (fig. 20), approximately 10.7 by 15.6 meters, and contains three floors with a series of interior chambers. Some chullpas are also built over subterranean cavities or chambers, which are either coeval or earlier constructions. This practice has been reported, for example, at Chinchawas and Ichik Wilkawaín. Floors are often simply made of packed dirt, but the most elaborate employ flat stones to pave irregular surfaces or cover subterranean features.

Some chullpas were covered in mud-plaster and painted, such as Pueblo Viejo (Caraz). Hand and finger impressions can be seen in some of the interior chambers of several chullpas and tombs under boulders at the site. The most common colors which survive, usually in the interiors of tombs, appear to have been red and white. It is quite possible that exteriors were also given such treatment, but the facing no longer survives. Some tombs at the site are associated with light-colored boulders (prob-

ably of granite or andesite) which feature a reddish orange color, though it is not certain whether this is paint or naturally oxidized patina.

It should be noted that chullpas are characterized by their visibility. They usually occupy rocky hilltops, steep slope faces, and ridgelines. To heighten their prominence on the terrain and to even the surface for the foundations, chullpas also were often built on top of raised terrace platforms, usually about a meter or so tall. Some of the most impressive include the tall prominences for the main chullpa at Queushu, the low basal platform of Chukaro Amá at Honcopampa, and the terraced ridge for the large chullpa at Katiamá.

Finally, chullpas of Recuay-tradition groups appear in large groups (table 2). Just like the subterranean tombs, chullpas frequently occur with other chullpas, giving the impression of dense communities of the dead or necropoli. For example, Bennett (1944: 62) identified some thirty-five chullpas, which he called "house units," in the area of Sahuanpuncu. Juan Paredes (2007: 2) observed that the large cemetery complex of Wilkawaín and Ichik Wilkawaín contains over sixty chullpas. The greatest concentration of these mausolea may be at the Pueblo Viejo site, near Caraz, where Alexander Herrera (2005: 358) estimated 150 chullpas and other tomb structures. Even within such sites, perimeter walls (sometimes relatively low) appear to have grouped specific chullpa buildings together.

FIGURE 20. The east façade of the main building, Wilkawaín. Tenon-heads may have adorned the upper façades of the burial mausoleum (chullpa), the largest of its kind in highland Ancash.

TABLE 2. Recuay-Tradition Mortuary Sites and Tomb Forms

Site	Elevation (masl)	Subterranean Tombs	Chullpas
Jancu	3,800	1	—
Roko Amá (Katak)	3,650	148	—
Marcajirca A, B (Marian, Huaraz)	3,260	4+	1
Wilkawaín/Ichik Wilkawaín	3,400	15 (est.)	60+
Chinchawas	3,850	3	14
Honcopampa	3,470	—	15–16
Huallac	3,150	—	10
Sahuanpuncu (Copa Chico)	3,200	n/a	35
Yarcok	3,784	n/a	22
Pueblo Viejo (Caraz)	3,450	n/a	150

Sources: Bennett 1944; Herrera 2005; Isbell 1991; Lau 2002; Ponte R. 1999a; Tello 1929; Tschauner 2003.

This occurs, for example, at Huaullac, Honcopampa, and Tinyash and appears to indicate some social cluster within a larger collectivity.

On Recuay Architecture: Patterns and Change

Recuay architecture, not surprisingly, treats basic life concerns: habitation, defense, economic production, and ceremony. Having described the general forms of buildings, I wish to review some key points regarding the manufacture and significance of Recuay architecture. Although the architecture is characterized by considerable formal variability in time and space, Recuay groups seem to have shared similar solutions in the use of materials and techniques.

Materials, Construction Methods, and Special Architectural Features

MATERIALS

Based on the current record, Recuay architecture was very much a stone architecture. Unlike their contemporaries in the coastal valleys, who built large constructions using mud brick and organic fill materials, Recuay groups emphasized stone for their walls, foundations, fill, and even the roofs of tombs. For Recuay groups of the coastal valleys, especially in the middle and upper valley areas, stone architecture was also preferred, particularly for the larger sites.

Evidence is limited for use of perishable materials. Adobe mud bricks and *tapia* molded mud wall segments were almost certainly employed for walls and buildings. Mud bricks are employed widely today throughout highland Ancash (e.g., Doughty 1968: chapter 5); tapia is rarer and is most prominent in parts of the Conchucos. These techniques may have been preferred in the past, especially in areas which lack stone or at lower elevations, with less threat of erosion from rain. In both techniques mud is mixed with hay and grass to provide strength. Walls of this material can last up to a century or longer if covered over with clay or plaster and maintained. But very little prehistoric mud-based architecture has survived in the highlands. Low stone walls, especially those which do not rise much beyond the foundations and/or maintain a flat top, may have been used as the bases for the upper segments of adobes. Mud brick may have been more common in the Recuay-period buildings in the coastal valleys, where there is less precipitation.

Holes and projecting stones in the interior walls of compounds were likely used to support wooden rafters for the multiple floors of chambered apartments. This occurs at Yayno, and some intact beams have survived in similar compounds at the nearby Karway site. This is not to say that Recuay peoples did not use perishable construction materials. Organic products such as wood, thorny scrub, and ichu grasses were probably employed for architectural purposes (for example, for roofs, ladders, walls, and fencing). But these have not yet been found in archaeological contexts, probably because organic preservation is generally very poor in the seasonally wet highlands of Ancash.

Floors were most commonly made of packed dirt and clay. Stone pavement, while known, was less common and seems to have been reserved for special buildings such as tombs and other high-status structures. Some walls, again mainly for ceremonial buildings, were covered over with clay or plaster and sometimes subsequently painted.

STONE MASONRY TECHNIQUES

Stone was fundamental to Recuay culture. Recuay builders incorporated this abundant material into all manner of architectural projects: from temples to tombs to canals. Stone lent itself to building strong, durable monuments, but it was also highly symbolically charged, being associated with telluric divinities, ancestors, and supernatural fertility. Recuay peoples also frequently incorporated natural topographic features into their ceremonial architecture. As in the case of other Andean cultures, rocks, boulders, and stone outcrops were sometimes charged with sacred power or essence, and it is possible that the inclusion of special features served to co-opt and manage this potency.

Masons of the Recuay tradition used many types and sizes of stone. Like their Chavín forbears, Recuay builders employed stonework for their monumental buildings. Unlike the Chavín, however, who imported stone to the ceremonial center from great distances, the Recuay were in general considerably more pragmatic. Where possible, they exploited local sources of stone, including igneous and metamorphic types common throughout highland Ancash. Little work has been done on Recuay quarrying or block manufacture, but stone quarries are known, usually within and very near archaeological settlements. Light-colored granites, for example, were acquired by the builders at Yayno from quarries located at the eastern part of the site. The quarry worked a large pyramidal exposure of rock, which is fractured in large, sheetlike slabs. Outcrops of rhyolite and andesite were used at Chinchawas. Metamorphic rocks, especially schists, were used widely for the constructions at Tinyash, including the elaborate roofing of chullpas, which exploit the rock's tensile strength (Ravines 1984: 35).

Blocks were probably shaped to appropriate sizes in quarry areas, as preforms; the finer fitting work was most likely completed closer to the finished building. Evidence of production debris can be identified at Yayno near the outcrops, and Mejía Xesspe (1941) reported evidence of a quarry for monoliths at the Walun site, just west of Huaraz in the Cordillera Negra. At Marcajirca (Pampachacra), massive gray limestone blocks with white quartzlike streaks are found near rock outcrops in its southern sector. Some of these blocks have pronounced grooves on the narrow edges, which were probably made to help fasten ropes or provide leverage; once the blocks are mounted, the grooves cannot be seen. Such grooves are also sometimes identified on the exposed megalithic blocks at Yayno and nearby sites with monumental walls, so it seems to have been a shared quarrying style for different groups of the region.

Recuay buildings are commonly identified by their distinctive stone masonry. Unlike Tiwanaku or Inka styles, the Recuay did not often employ ashlar masonry (cut stone blocks without mortar). Even when stones were cut into rectangular blocks, they were often laid with mortar (Grieder 1978: 21). The best-known style, called wanka-pachilla, was employed frequently on high-status architecture, including mortuary and secular buildings (pls. 1a, 1b; figs. 12, 13). Walls are formed by aligning large stone uprights or boulders (wankas), while spaces between the wankas are filled with small, usually flat and angular chinking stones (pachillas). Most often these small stones were stacked on top of each other, carefully filling in the interstices between the large stones. The mortar was of a sandy, mud-clay matrix. It should be mentioned that this technique provided only a veneer or outer face; interior cavities were commonly filled in with rubble fill and mortar, always in more haphazard fashion.

Some surviving examples of Recuay wanka-pachilla walls reach approximately 12–15 meters high. In several buildings at Yayno, for example, masons constructed wall courses by standing large flat slabs on end to create an inner and outer face atop a basal slab laid horizontally, creating a U-shaped profile; the inside was filled in with rubble and mortar. Thus the only elements which spanned the thickness of the wall consisted of the flat basal stones laid on their sides, on which the uprights rested (fig. 13). Besides the visual effect, the combination of thin courses of basal stones underneath courses of stone uprights functioned to distribute the heavy weight above to the rest of the wall. The walls taper, narrowing at the top, which results in a sloping batter that is especially prominent on the more inclined outer faces. Although the batter forced this weight inward toward the building, it was effectively buttressed by apartment chambers built along the interior walls. It is useful to note that the sloping batter not only was a response to technical constraints or the need for stability but was apparently quite desirable in Recuay monuments. The Caserón at Pashash, for example, features a substantial batter, despite being fixed to the side of a hill (fig. 12). Perhaps a relic trait from building terrace and revetment walls, the batter formed part of the Recuay construction aesthetic.

Fine and common masonry styles were diverse in the Recuay world. The availability and properties (especially fracture pattern and the capacity to be shaped) of rock types vary, so it is not surprising that the styles themselves are quite variable and often context-specific. The differently sized courses of large stones or patterns in stonemasonry seen at the large Recuay centers are actually quite rare. Many walls are freestanding, made of piled fieldstones (*pirca*) or combined stones of varying size without emphasis on patterns, and do not feature wankas or large stones. In addition, a site may show a wide range of techniques even for similar forms of buildings, such as at Honcopampa (Tschauner 2003).

MASONRY FEATURES

Extremely large blocks were often reserved for basal parts of structures or for thresholds, staircases, and corners. A common building convention included stacking large slab blocks to form corners and external angles of walls. The two major corners of the Caserón at Pashash feature a series of stacked horizontal slabs with alternating long ends, like brickwork. For the rectangular compounds at Yayno, the builders alternated flat and vertical slabs (fig. 13), a technique also characteristic of Marcahuamachuco's fine buildings and sometimes called "long and short work" (McCown 1945: 250).

The Recuay frequently enhanced masonry surfaces. As noted, this occurs in the form of painting over clay plaster as well as stone sculptural elements embedded as architectural members. But decorative effects were also achieved through the stonework itself. The courses of similarly sized stones represent one method. The most elaborate buildings at Yayno and at Pashash feature courses of large boulders of steadily diminishing size as the wall rises. The visual effect is heightened at Yayno because builders employed boulder slabs of different colors, including red, yellow, and various hues of gray. The colors are produced by weathering effects but also by the use of differently colored stones. Another large center, Tinyash, boasts a building whose large circular wall features a light-colored band near the top. Made of white quartzlike stone, it forms a halo that contrasts with the dark stone of the rest of the building (Antúnez de Mayolo 1941: fig. 14).

The play between tonal contrasts and shadows may also have been the intention of other architectural features found on Recuay buildings. The exterior wall of the burial temple at Pashash has a stringcourse, a narrow stone band projecting from the wall. This breaks up the flat surface of the 5-meter-tall façade (Grieder 1978: 29-30). Architectural representations on pottery also depict stringcourses, usually at the juncture between floors. The stringcourses on monumental buildings do not seem to have a practical function; as suggested by the pottery representations, however, they appear to mark the transition between upper and lower stories. This was probably a conventionalized reference to the butt-ends of perishable wooden rafters. Projecting capstones and roofstones also break up the profile of wall surfaces. Flat sloping stones project outward from the tall enclosure walls at Tinyash and Yayno, probably to deflect rain.

Recuay groups often lavished elaborate stonework on staircases and thresholds. A pair of stone sculptures at Chinchawas adorns a threshold, flanking either side of a stone staircase (Lau 2006b). Stone staircases are also known at Pashash (Grieder 1978: 29). The main monumental staircase at Yayno features a stone pavement, with wide and deep flagstone steps. The staircase passes three monumental thresholds, at which massive stone blocks are laid vertically and connect with walls defending each level of the approach. This processional way leads into a large plaza but continues steeply upward through a monolithic staircase which leads to another megalithic compound, c24 (Tello 1930: 266) (fig. 9).

Stone niches were also common features in Recuay buildings, in both tombs (for example, at Katak and Jancu) and residential structures (at Chinchawas, Tinyash, and Yayno). Niches are almost always found on the interiors of Recuay constructions. In general they were made by selecting larger, usually sturdy flat stones which could be arranged to create a niche "frame" around which masonry was added to finish the wall. Niches tend to be fairly small, often no more than 30 centimeters in any dimension; they are usually taller than they are wide and sometimes quite deep. Such niches probably stored important cult objects. But some niches, such as in the D-shaped structure AC-14 at Honcopampa, can be large enough for a person to sit down or to display a large object, such as a cult effigy.

At Yayno niches are found mainly in the circular and rectangular enclosures and are associated with higher-status groups. But niches cannot be described universally as high-status features or as typical of elite architecture. Grieder (1978) noted that niches were absent at Pashash, while they seem to have been fairly abundant in small villages such as Chinchawas.

Recuay drainage works also used fine stonework. Canals and water outlets have been found in a number of sites. This seems to be a key difference from the construction at Marcahuamachuco, where stone-built drains were scarce (McCown 1945: 253). Stone-built drainage works at Chinchawas and at Yayno can be divided into three categories: underfloor canals, exposed drains on the sides of structures, and drain outlets. Underfloor canals are all covered by flat stones and drew away water into lower areas. Drain outlets are located on the floor or in parts of walls. At Yayno some outlets are quite large, measuring 40–50 centimeters wide. No stone compartments for hygienic or ritual cleansing, like the Inka baths, are yet known for the Recuay.

Clues from Pottery Representations

Some Recuay modeled ceramics depict structures and building complexes (e.g., Reichert 1977: pls. 134–144). Given the content of these representations and similarities with known archaeological contexts, it is likely that they are miniature representations of high-status buildings (figs. 21–23). Many of the building features depicted in the ceramics have correspondences in archaeological contexts. In effect, these depictions

FIGURE 21. (*Left*) Ceramic representation of a fortified enclosure, with armed sentries guarding different stations along the perimeter wall. (Museo Nacional de Arqueología, Antropología e Historia, Lima)

FIGURE 22. (*Right*) Ceramic building effigy with an exterior painted and modeled architectural ornament. Note the image of the chiefly figure in the window; a pouring spout issues from his head. (Staatliche Museen zu Berlin–Preussicher Kulturbesitz Ethnologisches Museum; photo by C. B. Donnan)

provide a mode for comparing and elucidating the archaeological record. Despite their high degree of stylization, they are significant because they provide clues to the way in which important built spaces may have looked and functioned during Recuay times. Equally important, these representations disclose clues regarding ancient thinking about the use and experience of space.

The representations seem to include at least three types of architectural references: to defensive buildings, tombs, and residential-ceremonial compounds. In the first category, warrior figures, often with weapons and shields, stand atop or inside walls in a quadrangular or circular complex (e.g., Campana 2000: 88; Lumbreras 1978: 113; Ravines 2000: 88). The walls of these architectural representations are frequently topped with triangular crenellations, suggesting that at least on one level they were considered defensive battlements. One fort representation (fig. 21) features a large rectangular enclosure, divided in two by a diagonal partition wall. Along the parapeted walls are warrior-sentries stationed at guard posts and platforms.

At least one vessel may depict a Recuay funerary building, lavish with architectural ornament (Lau 2006b: 232). The other category of architectural representations involved residential-ceremonial buildings, what Raphael Reichert (1977: 42) called "house or temple models." These vessels depict one- to three-story buildings, frequently with small human figures

FIGURE 23. Ceramic building effigy, with representations of stone statues and tenon-heads. (Staatliche Museen zu Berlin–Preussicher Kulturbesitz Ethnologisches Museum; photo by D. Graf)

presided over by a slightly larger figure of a male personage, probably a lineage founder or family head (fig. 22). The small figures frequently hold vessels, probably for some form of libation or drinking ritual associated with feasts and political leadership (Lau 2002: 297).

The representations most often have quadrangular floor plans and may be left open or partitioned into small roofed spaces or galleries, forming an interior open area either in the center or to the side. The buildings in these vessels are characterized by symmetry but some also feature unique elements such as stairways. Rooms are generally single chambered and are covered by simple roofs that are horizontal, slightly sloping, or in some cases gabled. Some vessels show complexes with as many as three floors. Superstructures, including roofs and parapets, are supported by walls, columns, pilasters, and platforms. Access is through small doors, stairways, walkways, and ladders. Most of these features have correlates in Recuay architecture.

Roofing and the tops of walls, even of these residential-ceremonial buildings, may be adorned with triangular or step-shaped crenellations. Windows are generally rectangular, but some are cross-, step-, and L-shaped. Some horizontal sections of walls have open geometric friezes. Doorways are given special attention, often with pronounced lintels and jambs. In some cases cornices or stringcourses extend around the vessel to delineate the divisions between stories.

Miniatures of stone sculptures sometimes adorn the architectural representations. Tenon-heads of humans/anthropomorphs are engaged on walls (fig. 23) (Eisleb 1987: pl. 206; Reichert 1977: 316). In addition, free-standing figures that are portrayed limbless and sculpted in the round may be depictions of statuary. They are lined up in architectural spaces facing outward with stoic, lifeless expressions and resemble some stone sculptures.

In most of the architectural effigies, buildings are painted with important symbols of highland cosmology. If the pottery representations of architecture are accurate, the upper façades of high-status Recuay structures may have combined painted decoration with stone sculpture and friezes of ornate, arabesque-type masonry. This may also explain, at least in part, why the distinctive stonemasonry of Recuay walls is so rarely depicted on the ceramic vessels.

Recuay Mortuary Practices

A great diversity existed in the burial forms and practices among Recuay-tradition groups. Recuay funerary architecture has no unitary expression. Each region seems to have had its own suite of preferences, with modifications to local practices over time. Graves and different interment spaces also existed for people of different social status, from elites to commoners. Even coeval Recuay elites (for example, of Pashash and Jancu) maintained very different practices, indicating the primacy of local preferences, which were probably associated with large kin-based collectivities. Overall, the wide variability stresses the cultural and political autonomy of local groups within a flexible, coherent tradition of mortuary practice.

Despite the formal variation of the mortuary structures, most employ comparable technical practices and address similar principles on the treatment of the dead, which constitute one of the basic characteristics of the Recuay commonwealth. In creating different solutions with the aim of disposing of their dead, Recuay groups disclose a shared set of funerary beliefs and practices centered on ancestor veneration. This is a common religious practice around the world, based on a cosmology that ancestors (known deceased) continue to maintain influence over the living. Through feasts, dances, offerings, consultations, and other venerative activities, descendants honor their deceased in return for their power and legitimacy — in particular in domains such as fertility in resources, transmission of land rights, and success in warfare.

Ancestor veneration is typically limited to the living descendants. Thus funerary cults were probably fairly localized affairs, restricted to families, lineages, or other collectivities related by descent, real or fictive. Ancestor cults also often involve a strong emphasis on place. Ancestors are connected both physically (such as tombs and relics) and figuratively to the landscape through ancestral time, via myths and deeds crucial for ancestorhood.

The set of beliefs and general practices broadly focused on ancestor veneration helps to frame some of the most salient attributes of Recuay groups. While ancestor veneration was practiced by coeval societies of the Central Andes, the material manifestations were quite different (De-Leonardis and Lau 2004). The changing beliefs about the treatment of the dead took material form in highland Ancash following the collapse of the Chavín cult. Recuay-tradition groups actively began to create and maintain special built spaces as new ceremonial dispositions took hold.

Diachronic Patterns of Funerary Structures

Recuay ritual architecture is characterized by a series of formal changes through time. Tombs with more interior space and chambers for greater numbers of interments became preferred, especially later in the sequence. As Recuay groups grew more powerful, it seems that funerary buildings became more elaborate and increasingly stressed physical access to progenitors. The trend toward larger spaces, multiple group interments, and increased ease of access is perhaps most readily expressed in the development of the freestanding chullpa burial monuments. In the north highlands, chullpas emerge at least by the Early Intermediate Period and become more widespread later in the Recuay tradition. By the Middle Horizon (A.D. 700–1000) chullpas are the predominant burial form until colonial times.

All available evidence suggests that subterranean tomb forms are in general older than chullpa forms, for three main reasons. First, the major subterranean Recuay tombs of Jancu, Pashash, and Roko Amá yielded materials which stylistically predate chullpa structures. Chullpa sites in highland Ancash very rarely contain materials of the early Recuay tradition. Instead Middle Horizon and later cultural remains predominate. Chullpa sites often have evidence for Wari cultural influence, especially in distinctive imported styles such as Cajamarca, Viñaque, Chakipampa, and Nievería, and press-molded styles (Bennett 1944; Isbell 1989; Lau 2001, 2004b; Paredes Olvera 2007; Terada 1979).

Second, in several cases chullpa-like structures are superimposed over subterranean tombs, as at Ichik Wilkawaín (Bennett 1944: 44–50) and Chinchawas (Lau 2002).

Finally, radiocarbon tests from funerary contexts or associated with material from funerary contexts indicate the temporal priority of subterranean tombs and Recuay-style contents within them. Excavations in chullpas at Chinchawas recovered materials dated after A.D. 800, while the subterranean tombs were associated with materials radiocarbon-dated to earlier occupations. Nonetheless, at least some temporal overlap and shared practices indicate that the chullpas were terminal components of a broader Recuay funerary tradition (Lau 2004b).

Location and Use of Funerary Structures

Recuay groups buried their dead in funerary buildings, often very close to the living populations. Tombs were typically established on rocky prominences, places of visual prominence, and places with good vantage points. The location of doorways is highly variable, but they often open out into shared ritual space or have a direct relation to productive lands or features. Purposeful siting of burial structures and their orientation conveyed the continuing vigilance of the deceased over their community and vital resources. This is further highlighted where the back walls of tomb structures (for example, at Pashash and Chinchawas) doubled as an outer perimeter wall protecting interior spaces or other buildings. Ancestral domains here literally protected or encompassed the living.

Individual burials were usually flexed or seated (probably in wrapped, bundled form). The bodies were most often interred in physically distinct spaces rather than ossuaries. At present we have little physical evidence to suggest cremation, defleshing, or other types of disposal.

The building practices of Recuay mortuary structures were quite flexible. They accommodated one or multiple individuals. Larger tombs, in particular, were mausolea intended for the interment of many individuals, perhaps organized on the basis of kin relationships or other group affiliations (Isbell 1997). Multiple chambers in chullpas served to house separate interments in the same manner as in the compartmentalized spaces of subterranean tombs.

Most Recuay mortuary structures, however, were not simply for interment of bodies; they were places for ancestral rites, to interact physically with forebears long after their biological death. Reuse of buildings and spaces characterized Recuay-tradition mortuary practices. They seem to have included considerable movement and treatment of the human remains after the initial interment. Antechambers provided spaces to make offerings and protracted the ritual process of accessing the interior space.

In both chullpa and subterranean tombs, small doorway openings ensured the opportunity for periodic interaction with the contents of the interment and funerary space (figs. 19, 20). Entrances and key access points in Recuay funerary structures were often not sealed by walls. They were temporarily closed off by movable stone slabs which could be repositioned, thus permitting intermittent entry to the inner chambers. The tomb entryway at Jancu had at least three thresholds at different points, and two were found with door-slabs. Besides the added protection afforded by the stone slabs, the thresholds at Jancu indicate a purposeful elongation of the burial process, which was focused on segregating the entry, opening, and closing process. Periodic access served a number of functions, including the retrieval and veneration of certain individuals, maintenance of the tomb, and additional interments. Niches in both chullpas and subterranean chambers probably functioned to hold sources of light and store ritual paraphernalia or grave goods necessary for the periodic revisitations.

Reuse also characterizes mortuary sites where local peoples returned to build new tomb structures and/or to add new interments. In such sites, formally discrete mortuary constructions and burials accumulate in the same general area over time. This is clearly the case for the numerous subterranean tombs at Katak and the repeated use of La Capilla hill at Pashash for high-status burials. The later clustering of chullpas at various sites (e.g., Honcopampa, Ichik Wilkawaín) draws from this tradition of locating or adding new interments next to existing ones. At present we can only speculate that such physical juxtapositions may have been parts of long-term mortuary traditions of local groups which mapped new interments in relation to ancestors, groups, or special sacred places.

Interestingly, later peoples sometimes intentionally built chullpas above subterranean tombs. Subterranean chambers, galleries, or cists at several sites are directly overlain by aboveground chullpa mausolea. Two observations may help to explain this pattern. First, the superposition indicates continuity in the sacredness of the burial area, for it is unlikely that people would continue to bury their dead in an area which seemed to be inappropriate. Second, chullpa builders may have desired to superimpose (literally) a new mortuary ideology. Such a practice appropriated but was still compatible with earlier funerary spaces.

Many of the various funerary structures of the Recuay tradition also share elements of architectural decoration and techniques of manufacture, which deliberately impinge on the experience and reception of these buildings. These were not houses for the living, as Bennett (1944) had postulated. They were artificial caves, repositories, and special dwellings for the esteemed dead, who would be visited and honored through periodic ceremonies.

The structures facilitate movements, but in very specific and, I would argue, prescriptive manners. Anyone who enters a Recuay-tradition subterranean tomb or chullpa is struck by the interior's dark, somber, and cramped conditions. Even the relatively ample interment spaces at Jancu and Roko Amá do not permit an adult to stand; it is necessary to crouch and move forward slowly by squatting or kneeling.[1] The experience immediately distinguishes tomb spaces from those of residential or activity areas. Inside and low to the ground, the visitor is also prompted to contemplate the stature of the tomb's occupants, the mummy bundles and other cult objects, and the objective of reentering the tomb in the first place: to interact with them. The interior spaces force the visitor to be at eye level with the bodies and to be physically closer to touch and handle them.

The disciplining of internal movements within the mortuary spaces is further highlighted by the different points or stations en route to the bodies. This is hard, physical, but rudimentary work: crawling, moving access stones, struggling to see and feel. In essence, the visitor is made deferential and vulnerable, in a type of reinfantilization. I suggest that this incorporative sequence of action is connected to the desired result of the experience: awareness of the potency of ancestors (progenitors and elders).

The process can be understood more fully by recognizing that Recuay builders, like many Amerindian societies, modeled their tombs as womblike forms — as places of emergence and regeneration and as sources of social identity (e.g., Boone 2000; Heyden 1981). The galleries and forechambers of subterranean tombs and chullpas act like connective tubes to the vital interiors, where interments — bundled, seedlike, and in fetal position — can regrow. By entering the space and making offerings and supplications, the visitor (almost certainly a descendant) is also vitalizing the ancestor in an embodied nurturing act, at once connotative of agricultural work, insemination, and reciprocity with the deceased

(Duviols 1979; Gose 1994; Weismantel 2004: 502, for example, speaks of "reproductive theory" in Moche art).

Recuay tombs also have a dense, solid quality, which can be attributed in general to their small forms and employment of natural and stone-masonry walls. The tombs frequently incorporated natural depressions or fractures in bedrock, boulders, and hilly outcrops as formal elements in the buildings. The stonemasonry ranges from high to low quality and could be employed for the entire structure or just a portion of it. Masonry walls are often used to subdivide spaces, fill in cavities in bedrock, or simply enclose a space. Large stones feature frequently as roofing stones or tomb lids and for jambs, lintels, and corner blocks. In other words, many large stones were used especially in areas which required substantial load-bearing, compressive strength. Other large stones, the wanka uprights, were selected for marking graves or sealing off entryways, while boulders were employed to locate and provide a natural roof for many burial constructions.

Subterranean chambers and chullpas were often given the same architectural decoration. In cases of exceptional preservation, it is clear that the chambers and outer walls of Recuay tombs were sometimes decorated. One method was to embed stone sculptures directly into the architecture, especially in certain areas. The jamb and lintel positions of entrances, such as on chullpas, were favored. At the subterranean tomb of Yanapampa, Bennett (1944: 64–67) reported painted scenes on the interior threshold wall. The designs, including a bicephalic creature, are quite similar to motifs found on Recuay stone sculpture. Tello (1930: 279) argued that such depictions at architectural thresholds may have had protective power to ward off enemies and malevolent spirits. It could be argued that the stone members, usually of ancestral figures, were themselves foundational "supports," both for the tomb structure and for the structure of the corporate group.

Finally, white and red seem to have been preferred colors for adorning Recuay funerary architecture. The figures in the Yanapampa tomb were painted in a brownish red over a white background. The interior of the Jancu tomb used white stones for the walls and compartment partitions and a whitish clay which covered over and lightened the interior. Red pigment or a natural red color sometimes marked tomb exteriors, such as funerary buildings at Pueblo Viejo (Caraz). Red and white seem to have been important colors on funerary buildings of other Andean cultures, such as the Moche and Chimu, and on Inka-period chullpas in

Bolivia. Red paint is also used to mark post-Recuay tombs in highland Ancash (Herrera 2005: 184). It seems possible that this ensemble of colors was especially appropriate for Recuay-tradition funerary structures, because they mirror the color range (red, white, and black) of polychrome fineware typical of Recuay grave offerings. Recuay ancestor ceremonies were lively, colorful affairs — a feast for the eyes as well as the stomach.

Transformations in Monumentalism

Although the Recuay tradition has sometimes been viewed as a legacy of Chavín (Grieder 1978: 182; Tello 1923), it largely rejected most Chavín forms and meanings, especially in architecture. When the monumental sector at Chavín de Huántar itself was reoccupied, little regard was paid to its former glory. Taking advantage of the temple's lack of vigilance, early Recuay-tradition squatter groups erected shoddy dwellings atop the sunken circular plaza, formerly one of the most sacrosanct areas of the Chavín temple and cult. The newcomers not only exploited the temple for stone and sculptures to use for fill and in their habitations but dumped trash throughout the ceremonial precinct (Bennett 1944; Tello 1960). Later reoccupations during the first millennium A.D. continued the desecration, with intrusive burials and further refuse discard (Lumbreras 1970, 1974a, 1977).

The cultural rupture is also apparent when comparing Chavín and Recuay monumental architecture. The major north highland centers of Chavín de Huántar, Kuntur Wasi, and Pacopampa shared in the Chavín cult by erecting platform-mound temples. Chavín builders created grand open plazas, monumental thresholds, and staircases for large public performances, gatherings, and processions. Narrow chambers and elaborate internal galleries and ventilation/drainage systems were committed to smaller-scale, more private rituals. These spaces enabled the interaction with priests, cult objects, and audiences crucial for the ancient function and reception of the expansive Chavín religion (Burger 1992; Kembel 2001; Lumbreras 1989; Moore 2005: chapter 3; Rick 2005).

A more fragmented landscape based on small local communities and territories emerged during Recuay times, replacing the pattern of open ceremonial centers in the north highlands. Extensive open plazas and sunken courts disappeared. Although some centers, such as Pashash, Yayno, and Tinyash, contain special monumental constructions, none of them draws from the earlier temple platform-mound model. Recuay architects in general emphasized smaller, more enclosed spaces. The emphasis on "containment" coincided with new forms such as residential compounds, discrete circular towers, defensive works, and (especially later) chullpa tombs.

Unlike the pattern at Chavín de Huántar, the Recuay also established most of their settlements atop hilltops and in defensible zones. Even ceremonial architecture manifests greater concern for defense, as reflected in perimeter walls, strategic positions, and restricted access. Much of the impulse to build elaborate architecture among the Recuay was directed toward defensive and funerary purposes. Monumentalism for later Ancash groups therefore had a profoundly different inspiration, which was not based on either previous antecedents or routines of daily life.

Architecture and Social Complexity

The wide variation in specific forms of architecture, especially in tombs and residential types, indicates a spectrum of people in Recuay society, with different economic capacities and statuses. Although it would be reasonable to attribute the largest buildings or richest graves to Recuay elites, I contend that it is also useful to consider them the work of the people who elected to make them. The former approach addresses the capacity to actualize in terms of access to labor, resources, and wealth, while the latter focuses on intentionality. Only through a flexible process where decisions on making architecture are made at the local level by capable people can the great diversity in Recuay architecture be understood.

At least two major transformations in architectural practice occurred during the period under consideration. One was during the transition between the Huarás and Recuay periods. The current record suggests that during Huarás times, by approximately A.D. 1, graves were fairly modest, with few grave offerings. At best, the cist and box tombs which characterize Huarás groups were very small corporate labor projects. By the Recuay period (A.D. 200–300), however, graves had grown increasingly monumental, and offerings (such as at Roko Amá, Jancu, and Pashash) were unprecedented in their richness and elaboration.

This pattern is also found in other forms of settlement and in the architectural evidence. Huarás-period villages were small in both size and population, with modest domestic architecture. By the middle Early Intermediate Period a number of major Recuay centers had emerged, with monumental buildings and discrete higher-status sectors. Ceremonial enclosures were used for public displays of generosity and linked to forms of ancestor veneration and fertility rituals. Not only did wealth and power become increasingly concentrated in certain groups of highland Ancash, but certain individuals and their factions began to express them through increasingly elaborate displays, through offerings, feasts, and funerary ceremony. The emergence of Recuay ranked societies in highland Ancash occurred during the first centuries A.D.

The other major architectural transformation occurred by about A.D. 600, when chullpa mortuary structures began to overtake subterranean forms in popularity. This was an uneven process, for the new practices took hold in highly specific contexts and at different times. In some places chullpas developed early (such as Wilkawaín and Honcopampa, by about A.D. 600), while it took longer for this form to take root in the smaller provincial settlements (such as Chinchawas, by about A.D. 700). Some settlements never constructed chullpas at all, such as Pashash and Yayno, which declined or were abandoned just as chullpa practices burgeoned.

The variability in the forms, construction quality, and adoption of chullpa tombs indicates different levels of investment and potential for labor mobilization. The variability also suggests a considerable degree of local choice, for each chullpa shows a propensity for being a discrete project, with different solutions and building specifications for a similar end. Despite working within shared cultural conventions, Late Recuay groups built and used tombs to distinguish themselves from other co-resident groups.

The great elaboration in chullpa mortuary architecture contrasts with the patterns of grave goods. Grave offerings in aboveground chullpa interments of highland Ancash in general are fairly modest (Lau 2002; Paredes et al. 2001; Ponte R. 2001). Earlier Recuay tombs (such as at Pashash, Jancu, and Roko Amá) contain significantly more evidence for accumulation of prestige goods, especially finely made ceramics and metal objects. During Recuay times, people apparently had a greater concern for individual elite status. Distinctions between groups of the same community appear to have been given priority by Late Recuay and the Middle Horizon times.

Recuay Landscapes: Imagined and Practiced

Now that the physical environment and architecture have been described, it is worthwhile to consider the makeup and significance of Recuay landscapes. The term "landscapes" is used broadly here to encompass the physical environment, including all human modification (e.g., Denevan 1992; Erickson 2008) and ancient imagination of it (Ashmore and Knapp 1999; Moore 2005; Tilley 1994). I find utility in the generous definition of landscape as "the world as it is known to those who dwell within, who inhabit its places and journeys along the paths connecting them" by Tim Ingold (1993: 156; also 1999) and his optimism that archaeologists can contribute to elucidating such worlds (see also Bradley 1998, 2000).

What fashions "landscape" for any group is its ensemble of activities or tasks (for example, walking, harvesting, and hunting) in any given environment: *the landscape as a whole must be understood as the taskscape in its embodied form*: a pattern of activities 'collapsed' into an array of features" (Ingold 1993: 162; emphasis in the original). Hence the goal of considering Recuay landscapes is to explore past perceptions and experience of activities in the physical world. This promises to complement our understandings of human-environment interaction, currently centered on the view of landscape as the neutral, static backdrop for human activities (usually economy-driven) or culturally specific symbolic ordering of space. Both stances have been offered in reference to ancient societies of Ancash, including Recuay (Herrera 2005; Lane 2006b; Lau 2000; Orsini 2007).

What would a Recuay landscape look like, and how was it experienced? Not all aspects of the landscape are anthropogenic: it is likely that we can only have a partial idea of how any one person, much less a group, may have experienced it in the distant past. Still, the most suitable method for approaching this question is to focus on the products of human activity in any given space, because places acquire their unique significance in the contexts of people's interaction with the world. While these form the main source of inference, complementary evidence may also be obtained from ancient imagery and ethnographic comparisons. Here I wish to outline a working framework of Recuay landscapes to help situate other cultural developments discussed in the remainder of this book.

I follow Jerry Moore (2005: 3) in his definition of the built environment as "a culturally constructed landscape that, like other cultural dimensions, includes utilitarian and nonadaptive, innovative and conservative elements" (also Lawrence and Low 1990). Through architecture, Recuay groups actively attempted to transform their natural world into something appropriate for social and economic well-being. While most scholars have focused on "sacred landscapes," fuller evaluation of the landscape concept needs to incorporate a wider range of imagination and experience, which includes more everyday and secular interactions with the ancient environment.

Another fundamental difficulty with the analysis of ancient landscape and land use in Ancash concerns paleoclimatic change. This was a major source of variability, which has not been fully taken into account in current appraisals. Settlement studies portray elevation as being decisive in the orientation of land use and suggest that this orientation remained the same over long periods (for example, over a phase). But we have no reason to believe that modern climatic conditions and land use held true for the past; indeed, it is clear that increasing warming has taken place over the last century. Further, historical records of paleoclimatic fluctuations demonstrate that puna conditions exist equally at 4,200 and at 3,500 meters, so in cooler times sites in present-day agricultural zones may have been in cold steppic grasslands associated with herding. If, as scholars advocate, our reconstruction of past landscapes needs to consider all human action on the environment, it is impossible to do this without identifying some of the potential effects of climate change.

My perspective here assumes that Recuay landscapes were neither fixed nor singular; they were always in the process of becoming, being reworked and transformed at the local level. In this flux, however, some of their most salient dimensions can be identified. The foregoing discussion has already touched upon five dimensions of the Recuay built environment: the vertical zonation and movement; the emphasis on stone; the emphasis on containment; the relationship to the past; and productive capacities. These concerns are not mutually exclusive. On the contrary, they are often entangled in the various architectural expressions already characterized. But these five qualities, writ large, also offer a quick synopsis of many salient features of any ancient Recuay landscape.

The available record indicates that Recuay peoples privileged specific interactions with their landscape. The vertical zonation of highland Ancash provided a series of distinctive possibilities and constraints and impinged on their daily experience (for contemporary perceptions in Ancash, see Walter 2002). Recuay peoples domesticated environments by establishing their dwellings and constructions in suitable regions. These areas were almost certainly perceived as places with many purposes and capacities for different life activities. Among the most important was simply the production and extraction of subsistence resources. Villages and towns were the foci of social life for Recuay groups and frequently existed side by side with their lands for agriculture and herding.

In all likelihood, the way in which the Recuay reckoned the vertical topography was not based on neat categories of environmental zonation but rather on how the topography is contemplated and routinely used as "production zones" (Mayer 1985). To be sure, physical qualities and characteristic contents affected use, but rarely do environmental zones begin and end neatly in Ancash. They are parts of ecological gradients, which are worked to varying degrees depending on local strategies and are characterized by what different zones are like (or not like) rather than by scientific, quantifiable criteria. Enrique Mayer (1985: 50) contends: "It is the contrasts (which really interest campesinos [farmer-peasants]) that can be applied to geographical areas, things, people, food, music, or whatever, in various orders of magnitude."

The features of Recuay landscapes were experienced through people's ability to move through them and actions. Trails and roads are at once the medium and result of this activity, where actions are "sedimented" over many generations (Ingold 1993: 167). From the scant archaeological evidence it is safe to say that most Recuay groups moved in fairly circumscribed ambits, presumably within an area which formed part of their community. For the Recuay, such as at Chinchawas, trail networks existed between their settlements, fields, pastures, and key places such as sources of water, canal intakes, and cemetery areas.

Beyond this area existed places that were more off limits, outside a "comfort-zone" or routine, which most likely had to do with the difficulty of distance, boundaries with other collectivities, and lack of knowledge. Less-common trails were routes between settlements and inter-Andean valleys. Natural communication routes followed river systems, and horizontal movements rather than vertical movements probably would have been favored (Topic and Topic 1983). Movement between regions was probably most common by traders of rare goods and materials, most likely in conjunction with caravans and camelid cargo animals. Trails between settlements also actively trafficked people on their way to regional pilgrimage locations: religious centers and shrines (see also Hyslop 1984; Wallace 1991).

The physical environment provided food and other materials. These were acquired through hard work and habitual engagements between people and places. Constructions such as roads, corrals, and farming terraces were fundamental to the success of Recuay subsistence and other economic practices. While studies have examined irrigation and hydraulic architecture associated with farming, Kevin Lane (2006b) notes quite rightly that not enough attention has been paid to ancient peoples' use of water in relation to herding. Elaborate silt dams or systems of damming typical for later agro-pastoralism may have been in use since Recuay times.

The importance of camelid herding all across highland Ancash (established by later Chavín times) translated into new attitudes and interactions with the physical world, especially as reflected in artworks and political ideology. Unlike Chavín imagery, which emphasized mythical hybrid creatures with relationships to the tropical lowlands (such as caymans, jaguars, and harpy eagles), the Recuay often depicted domesticated highland animals, such as dogs and camelids. Camelids in particular were represented in ceramics as explicit items of wealth and prestige for Recuay elites (Gero 1999; Reichert 1977). The changing imagery appears to coincide with widespread settlement in or near the high puna regions, with the grasslands and well-watered vegetation favored by camelids. The Recuay often settled in ecotonal areas close to both fields and pasture or developed specialized practices and institutions to exploit orientations based on camelids. Movements between ecological floors, caravans, and herding specialists must have been part of this landscape transformation.

But other dimensions of social life were probably affected, for which the evidence is more limited. Very little is known about transformations in work scheduling, a topic of major concern for agro-pastoralists, or the use of nonmeat camelid materials and development of associated technologies. In terms of new raw materials, we have evidence for camelid bone implements and spindle whorls and for the processing of camelid hair fiber. Important resources such as sinew, dung, and leather, however, must also have provided new avenues for material engagements. The few surviving Recuay textiles are of unsurpassed sophistication for the time and were the technical prototypes for later masterworks (Rodman and Fernández 2000: 126). The experience of highland Ancash as a zone for herding therefore had a number of sociocultural ramifications which scholars are only beginning to illuminate.

In most zones, another strand of human-environment interaction was prominent for groups of the Recuay tradition. We might call this their "contained landscape," because it draws from a number of exclusionary and protective dispositions regarding the environment. It almost certainly refers to a common structural distinction between interior and exterior spaces in Amerindian thought. The notion of containment can also describe the various expressions of the individual and corporate chiefly body, which I find most evident in the architectural effigies (discussed in chapter 7). In these artworks the interior scene highlights a controlled, orderly whole, the province of the family, culture, and village. This is contrasted with the world outside, an ambiguous and dangerous domain of animals and enemies (e.g., Descola 1986, 2001); it is full of resources which need to be internalized and domesticated. In essence, Recuay architecture and settlements express a strong desire to enclose and define spaces, to delimit special places and/or to keep things and people out. This occurred at the regional, settlement, and intrasite level.

Having already examined patterns at the settlement and intrasite level, we might ask: what separated people at the regional level? Recuay groups counted upon high areas, natural and artificial barriers, and remoteness as ways to manage the distance between themselves and other groups and their operational worlds. These were significant divides, both natural and culturally constructed. Major geographic barriers occur in the Ancash highlands: mountains, large rivers, and canyons, to name a few. During extended cold spells, the glaciers of the Cordillera Blanca were probably important impediments to east-west travel in highland Ancash, yet this may also have served positively for those who wished to be apart or have protection from regional threats.

Just as importantly, major cultural divides in the form of borders and boundaries also separated people. The Recuay were seen by their Moche neighbors as warlike others, and boundaries were created between highland and coastal groups (Lau 2004a; Proulx 1982). Such boundaries were reinforced by differences in religious practices, cosmology, and probably in language. Northern boundaries along Recuay's frontier with Huamachuco and Cajamarca were also maintained through active negotiation of material styles and exchange of imported goods (Lau 2006a). In many areas, social boundaries were remade through the activity of preparing for and engaging in armed conflict. Such cultural divides only gain momentum when people recognize or experience them as such as regular parts of their (contained) landscape.

Sacred landscapes remain a prominent topic in the consideration of the Americas, ancient and contemporary. Different treatments and approaches (e.g., Kosok 1965; Scully 1975; Townsend 1992) help map out the variability of the bold assertion by Mircea Eliade (1959: 34) that "to settle in a territory is, in the last analysis, equivalent to consecrating it." Many ancient and contemporary cultures of the Andes perceive the natural environment, often in divine embodiments and qualities, which are animated and spiritually potent. But in return for their resources or favor, they are in constant need of recompense, through offerings (sacrifices) and veneration. Cosmologies and ceremonies developed alongside these beliefs, and it is precisely through actions that sacred Recuay landscapes were actualized and experienced.

If monuments address the past and its imagination and experience in the present (Bradley 1998; Connerton 1989), it is noteworthy that by far the most numerous monuments in the Central Andes are the thousands of tombs and mortuary structures, especially chullpas. Each of these constructions is a testimony to a group's attentive engagement with its landscape.

Although direct information regarding Recuay myths and worldview is lacking, historical sources of indigenous highland belief systems in the Andes detail the close connections among ancestor cults, the physical terrain, and rituals of renewal (e.g., Allen 1988; Doyle 1988; Duviols 1986; Gose 1994). For many contemporary groups on either side of the Cordillera Blanca, the imagination of the landscape and the past are inextricably linked (Paredes G. 2006; Walter 2006; Yauri Montero 2000, 2004). Indeed, the landscape *is* the past, for it embodies previous work and experience as well as an ancestral history where heroic deceased and divine actions are instantiated through its physical features.

In the cosmology of many Andean groups, people and their huaca ancestors were said to have emerged from sacred spots on the landscape, known as *pacarinas*. Most often these were caves, mountains, springs, lakes, and other geological features. Mountains and rock formations were worshipped as huaca deities as well as sources of water. Anyone moving along the Callejón de Huaylas, at the base of the Cordillera Blanca, passes not only the towns and villages but also a veritable pantheon of glaciated peaks known through local oral traditions as divine embodiments — to name a few: Huantsán, Huascarán, and Huandoy. These features held significance for people because they were the sites of special actions of their heroic deceased after their emergence, such as defeat of enemies, lithomorphosis, the provision of resources, the establishment of territories, or construction of canals. The basic point is that ancestors were providers for the living and had the capacity to confer potencies and fertility on lands and herds.

The ancestral connection with the landscape is most famously recorded in the narrative of Tanta Carhua, an Inka *capacocha* sacrifice in a region of southern Ancash (Hernández Príncipe 1923). Tanta Carhua, the daughter of a provincial lord, was given up as a binding gift of diplomacy to the Inka. She was buried in a subterranean tomb and later worshipped near an irrigation canal, which was said to have been enabled by her actions (Zuidema 1977, 1990). What better form to authenticate the right to claim land or resources than an adjacent physical monument?

The ancestors themselves, not just the tombs, were integral parts of the landscape for Andean mortuary traditions. Nowhere is this more true than for Recuay groups, who, following historical traditions, celebrated stones and outcrops as ancestors. Inka and colonial documents describe the capacity of certain figures, especially those of a mytho-historical past, to turn into stone (Duviols 1977). The lithomorphosis of ancestors took the form of outcrops, boulders, or large uprights (huancas). Indeed, aboveground monoliths and subterranean mummified interments can be complementary manifestations of ancestors (Duviols 1979).

It is notable that the inhabitants of ancient Ancash placed so much emphasis on creating stone monuments and locating sacred places in durable topographic forms. Attachment to the land must be taken into account when considering why native groups in colonial times were so vehemently explicit about ancestral places; the tumults of Inka and later Spanish reorganizations almost certainly reinforced their perceptions that their land and its fruits could be wrested from them. We have little reason to believe, however, that the tussle for territory was limited to late prehispanic times. The Recuay data show that "contained" dispositions toward the landscape emerged soon after the demise of Chavín.

Recuay ceremonial places therefore charted the locales of past and present engagements with the environment but specifically through the idiom of ancestral relationships. Dotting the region with monuments represented one manner in which local groups transformed their world, for it established enduring visual cues for the interdependency between land and ancestry. Such buildings marked the boundaries of Recuay communities and their materialized past. In this way the sacred, lived, and contained dimensions of Recuay landscapes converged.

In addition to its political purpose of managing territory, making monuments was a way to fix culture and identity in a landscape that was prone to change. By this I mean the strong, even inexorable, propensities for the world to transform physically through time or culturally through the actions of people. The temporality of the rainy and dry seasons on the land is one such propensity: lands move from ranges of green to sere, productive to fallow, full to barren. Some rivers meanwhile slow from roaring torrents born of the rains to a trickle. Climatic fluctuations work to alter the patterns, bringing life zones upward and downward, changing the size of glaciers and pockets of vegetation, or prolonging and shortening seasons. Unlike the seasonal rhythm, the great dangers of highland Ancash which also transform the perception of the landscape are sudden and largely unpredictable: earthquakes, the bursting of glacial lakes, floods, and landslides.

Thus change is ubiquitous in the Ancash landscape, and everyday human interaction forms part of the movement. It could be argued that Recuay sacred places, made of stone or ascribed to topographical features, attempted to counteract this flux. The monuments anchored history and identity to given locales in a changing world, thereby deny-ing simple death, erosion, and forgetting. By building monuments the Recuay sought to deviate from customary forms of human interaction with the landscape. Or perhaps the monuments represented the finality of engaging the landscape under a different, ancestral pace.

CHAPTER FIVE

Pottery and Society

More than architecture and stone sculpture, pottery has been the hallmark of Recuay culture since the definition of the style some hundred years ago (Eisleb 1987; Grieder 1978; Reichert 1977; Smith 1978). Scholarly studies commenced at the turn of the twentieth century, with a particular emphasis on the iconography in wider discussions of Andean art and civilization (Lehmann and Ubbelohde-Doering 1924; Levillier 1926; Montell 1929; Schmidt 1929; Seler 1893; Tello 1923).

Pottery provides essential lines of evidence to understand the close relationships between Recuay material culture and society. First, at the most basic level, it facilitates study of the culture's distribution in geographical space and time: when and where people used pottery (fig. 24). Second, it allows us to characterize the cultural differences between Recuay groups: variability expressed through ceramic frequencies and style. Third, study of ceramics can investigate what people did with pottery: how they used and interacted with ceramic things. Finally, pottery is a crucial medium which is preserved in the archaeological record and carries the few remaining clues to understanding an ancient belief system.

Time and Terminology in Recuay Pottery Studies

Many different local styles existed in Ancash, leading to some debate as to what the pottery should actually be called. Few people have undertaken synthetic interregional studies of Recuay-style ceramics (e.g., Reichert 1977; Smith 1978). It is worthwhile to identify the salient differences in pottery style as well as to note potential ambiguities in cognate terms (Gambini 1984; Lau 2004b; Wegner 1982).

It was Dr. José Mariano Macedo (1881: vii) who coined the term "Recuay" for materials coming from the rich tombs of the Katak area in the province of Recuay. Some scholars have preferred "Huaylas" to describe

		North Highlands							Coast		
		Ancash	Pashash	Yayno	Pierina	Chinchawas	Cajamarca	Huamachuco	Moche	Virú	Santa
LATE INTERMEDIATE PERIOD	1200	Aquillpo			Cotojirca V	Chakwas		Toro	Chimú	La Plata	Early Tambo Real
MIDDLE HORIZON	900	Wilkawaín 2			Cotojirca IV	Warmi	Late Cajamarca	Tuscan	Transicional	Tomaval	Late Tanguche
	800	Wilkawaín 1				Chinchawasi 2	Middle Cajamarca B	Urpay / Chamis / Amaru	Late Moche V		Early Tanguche
	700	Late Recuay	Usú	Huanchac		Chinchawasi 1	Middle Cajamarca A	Huamachuco			
EARLY INTERMEDIATE PERIOD	600		Huacohú	Asuac					Middle Moche IV	Huancaco	Guadalupito
	500	Recuay 3							Middle Moche III		
	400	Recuay 2	Quimít	Rayo	Cotojirca III	Kayán	C		Early Moche II	Late Gallinazo	Late Suchimancillo
	300	Recuay 1	Yaiá				Early Cajamarca B		Early Moche I		
	200	Huarás					A	Purpucala	Gallinazo	Early-Middle Gallinazo	Early Suchimancillo
	100		Quinú		Cotojirca II						
	AD 1						Initial Cajamarca			Salinar	

(Vertical label in dark band between Ancash and Pashash: Recuay Tradition)

FIGURE 24. Regional sequences and chronology of the Recuay culture.

Recuay pottery. Tello (1923, 1929) first popularized "Huaylas." Tello (1930: 284) divided his sample of pottery from the Callejón de Huaylas into two types. The "primitive technique" type (evidenced by materials from tombs at Copa) and the "Recuay" type (Macedo collection) were "very similar and differ only in certain characteristics. [In t]he more primitive technique, the predominance of the utilitarian forms, the lack of ornamentation and the incipient form of the first type, contrast with the more advanced technique, the better material, and the variety of form and ornamentation which the second type affords." In later works he was more sanguine about a general Recuay culture and used "Huaylas" and "Recuay" synonymously (Tello 1940: 657–673, 1960: 13).

It is not exactly clear why Tello opted not to use "Recuay" regularly. At that time he may have intended to make an implicit reference to the "Huaylas" (or "Wayla") ethnic group of the Ancash highlands documented historically (e.g., Tello 1940: 652). It is possible that he also believed the distribution of the style extended to the geographic limits of the Callejón de Huaylas and beyond, so it was not just centered on "Recuay" (e.g., Tello 1929: 86, 91).

Tello (1923: 204–205, 218) regularly used the term "Huaylas" or "Callejón" to describe Recuay-style materials as a regional cultural entity or phenomenon across highland Ancash. This was a conservative designation privileging geographic provenience. Tello was never explicit in his published works about the precise pottery distinctions. He tended to use more localized terms for cognate styles from specific places, such as "Copa" (or "Kopa"), "Katak," or "Aija" (especially Tello 1923). In other words, he considered these local styles and materials under the more regional rubric of "Huaylas," which he used interchangeably with "Recuay."

In fact, it was Tello's students and disciples who were more rigorous in their pottery terminology. For example, Toribio Mejía Xesspe (1948: 9) referred to "Huaylas" pottery in tombs that he opened at Katak in 1939, while Rebeca Carrión Cachot (1955: 67–73, 1959: 24) preferred to call Recuay culture "Huaylas" almost exclusively in her influential publications on Andean ritual and cosmology (see also Espejo Núñez 1951, 1957).

When A. L. Kroeber and Wendell Bennett used "Recuay" in the mid-1940s, therefore, they were clearly going against the Peruvian orthodoxy by relying on Macedo's original designation and eschewing any of Tello's surrogate terms (Bennett 1944, 1946; Kroeber 1944). In part this was simply a reliance on the Macedo type collection and priority of existing terminology (see also Kroeber 1930: 103–107; Levillier 1926: 59ff.). Kroeber (1944: 93–96) followed Tello's insistence that Recuay was one of two types of "Callejón culture," the other being the "primitive" skeuomorphic pottery of Copa. Like "Huaylas" for Tello, "Callejón" for Kroeber was both the geographic entity referring to the Callejón de Huaylas and also a type of regional tradition, of which Recuay was a part. For Kroeber (1926: 36, 1944: 94; also 1930: 103–104), Recuay could be divided into two types: Recuay A and Recuay B. Recuay A was synonymous with Tello's "Recuay," while Recuay B focused on freestanding ceramic effigy figures and distinctions in painting.

Neither of the substyles envisioned by Tello and Kroeber could be confirmed through stratigraphic excavations by Bennett (1944: 104). In fact, Bennett includes vessels of Tello's "primitive technique" (Copa or "Andean Archaic") in his Recuay formal typology.[1] Unlike his predecessors, Bennett provided a comprehensive typology of forms, using materials from excavations and comparative collections, though no statement could be made about subphases. Curiously, Bennett (1944: 90–92) mistook a number of Recuay ceramics from Balcón de Judas and Chavín for other styles, which he called "Post-Chavín" and "San Jerónimo."

Rafael Larco Hoyle (1960, 1962, 1966) went a new direction by emphasizing the term "Santa." But scholars such as Bennett (1944: 99) already knew about Larco's somewhat radical thinking about Recuay in the 1940s.

An early mention of highland or Callejón influence on the coast appears in an essay about Virú or Gallinazo culture (Larco Hoyle 1945: 1). Larco's ideas crystallized after reconnaissance in Virú, Chao, and Santa in 1943–1944. His excavations in the Santa Valley (Larco Hoyle 1962) led him not only to observe strong Recuay (or "Santa") occupation of the coast but to claim that the style had originated in the valley.

Larco preferred the term "Santa" for at least three reasons. First, he believed that the style centered along the entire Santa Valley, not just the intermontane portion (the Callejón de Huaylas). He also felt that the origins of Recuay culture should be investigated from the lower coastal valleys, where elaborate Recuay-style grave-lots were being found in various hacienda estates in Santa, such as Suchimancillo, Vinzos, and Santa Clara (see also Clothier 1943: 241–242). At the time of his writing, the tombs that he excavated in Santa were in fact the richest and best-documented Recuay tombs, so a coastal origins model must have seemed logical. Stylistically, Recuay and coastal styles, such as Gallinazo (or Virú) and Moche, showed many connections in form and kinds of exterior decoration. Finally, "la cultura Santa" was an audacious challenge to his rival Tello and his disciples, who claimed that Recuay originated in the Ancash highlands.

Larco's definition of "Santa" is somewhat ambiguous, because he never distinguished coastal from highland expressions or provided a framework to deal with cultural variability. Subsequent proponents of the term, such as Wilfredo Gambini (1984), a collector and amateur archaeologist, strongly favored "Santa" to describe Recuay materials of the coast or the sierra. Adding to the confusion, Tello (1956: 289ff.) himself had used "Santa" to describe a completely different pottery culture associated with the mid to late Middle Horizon in the Casma Valley.

The terminology for the Recuay-style material from the coastal valleys is still debated. Proulx (1985: 283–285, pl. 7) reported on Recuay occupations in the Nepeña Valley associated with the kaolinite pottery types, such as Huancarpón White-Painted and Huancarpón Negative-Painted. In his settlement study of the lower Santa Valley, David Wilson (1988: 151–198, appendix 1) describes Recuay-related kaolinite types in his Early and Late Suchimancillo periods. These works can be compared to previous studies, especially the descriptions of "Callejón" types reported for Virú (Ford 1949: 65, 76; Strong and Evans 1952: 242; Strong et al. 1952: 347–351). The finds of pottery offerings close to the shoreline near San Nicolás, Santa, extend Recuay pottery use (probably for ceremonial displays and offerings) even into the lower coastal valleys (Choronzey 2009: 95–97).

The primacy of the sierra in Recuay studies was restored by work in the highlands in the 1960s and 1970s. The 1961–1965 archaeological investigations headed by Gary Vescelius in the Callejón de Huaylas, under the auspices of the Cornell-Vícos project, are legendary for their expertise and originality in method (Burger and Lynch 1987). Except for a few secondhand reports and references to personal communications, the work has never appeared in print (e.g., Amat 1976b; Buse 1965; Lanning 1965; Lynch 1980a; Ravines and Alvarez Sauri 1967).

In a summary of Andean research, Edward Lanning (1965) outlined Vescelius's working regional sequence. Vescelius favored "Huaylas" as the term to describe its periods, including "Early Huaylas" to refer to Huarás materials and "Middle Huaylas" for classic Recuay kaolinite materials. Various scholars (e.g., Buse 1965: 330–331; Reichert 1977: 24) eagerly awaited publication of Vescelius's Ancash sequence; but it was never published, for he died in 1982. His excavation notes and descriptions for various key sites critical to the Recuay tradition (such as Honcopampa, Queyash Alto, and Huaricoto) also remain unpublished.

In a series of overviews, Federico Kauffmann Doig (1966: 75–87, 1970: 329–344, 1980: 413–421) lobbied for Recuay pottery to be rebranded "Copa," because he felt that very little pottery of the style could in fact be traced to Recuay (town or province). Tello in particular had repeatedly employed the term "Copa" (named after the Copa Chico and Copa Grande zones near Carhuaz) to refer to the forms and imagery of vessels in the Dextre Collection, which he acquired for the Museo de la Universidad de San Marcos, Lima (Tello 1940: 664).

As work by Tello and Bennett had demonstrated, excavations at Chavín de Huántar regularly uncovered post-Chavín materials. Tello (1960: 349–352) grouped together different pottery types from the site as "Huaylas-Marañón," including kaolinite, white-on-red, and more plainware styles. The use of "Marañón," curiously, reveals Tello's ambivalence about the pottery or inability to identify it, though he knew both Cajamarca and Ancash firsthand. Bennett (1944: 89–92) recognized both a white-on-red style and also "San Jerónimo" kaolinite ceramics at Chavín. But, inexplicably, he also had trouble in distinguishing the Recuayness of the "San Jerónimo" pottery and ascribed it instead to the Inka period without detailing his rationale for likening kaolinite wares to the Inka style.

These ambiguities were overcome by investigations led by Luis Lumbreras and Hernán Amat at the Chavín site and surrounding areas during the 1960s and 1970s. They documented the stratigraphic superposition of post-Chavín phases: one associated with white-on-red (Huarás) and a later occupation associated with Mariash and Callejón pottery (Lumbreras 1970, 1974a, 1977).

The Callejón pottery of the Chavín de Huántar sequence should be distinguished from pottery groupings of the same name used by Tello (1929: 85–91), Kroeber (1944: 93–96), and scholars of the Virú Valley project (Ford and Willey 1949; Strong and Evans 1952: 242–245). Unlike Tello's definition, these scholars placed no emphasis on skeuomorph forms. This Callejón pottery of Chavín clearly emerged outside the Callejón de Huaylas, unlike Kroeber's use of the term. Rather, the intent of the designations seems to have been to relate fairly modest painted wares to similar wares from the Callejón de Huaylas (Lumbreras 1974a: 49–50).

Mariash pottery is synonymous with Tello's "Huaylas-Marañón" and Bennett's "San Jerónimo" style. It is notable that Mariash pottery appeared in both Huarás and Callejón levels, suggesting periods of cultural commingling and/or slow transition. Toward the end of the sequence, Mariash disappeared and the Callejón style predominated (Lumbreras 1974a: 48). In effect, the division of Callejón and Mariash mimics Tello's division of "primitive technique" plainware and kaolinite Recuay. Studies by Hernán Amat (1976a, 1976b) never elaborated on the "Mariash" style of Chavín de Huántar and consistently referred to "Recuay." His stylistic seriation (Amat 2003) presented five subphases (I–V: see the discussion below).

In the northern part of the Ancash highlands, Recuay pottery is best known from the site of Pashash. Curiously, the three main collaborators during the excavation of the site in 1971–75 all used different terms to describe its pottery. Terence Grieder (1978) provided the most comprehensive description with accompanying illustrations, designating a series of ceramic phases based on a type-variety system, stratigraphic excavations, and a motif-based seriation. The first phase, known as Quinú, was essentially a white-on-red style. This was followed by the main occupation of the site (with which most of the sculpture and funerary remains were associated), which was represented by three phases, from earlier to later: the Quimít, Yaiá, and Huacohú. The subsequent Usú phase followed these kaolinite wares and seems to have been a late Recuay variant.

Alberto Bueno (Bueno M. 1989: 42–43) preferred use of "Pashash Temprano (fase 1)," associated with Quinú, and "fase II de Pashash," a rubric combining Quimít, Yaiá, and Huacohú. He contended that the hearth of Recuay culture was found at Pashash itself; developments in the Callejón de Huaylas were derivative — hence the name "Pashash-Recuay."[2] The other key member of the Pashash team, John W. Smith, Jr. (1978), referred to the various ceramic wares by using a type-variety nomenclature developed for the site rather than adopting Grieder's Culle-language phase names or Bueno's groupings. In accordance with Bueno, however, he postulated that Pashash was the most important ceremonial center in the "Recuay interaction sphere" (Smith 1978: 41).

The Japanese expedition to La Pampa in northern Ancash defined a long epoch during the first millennium A.D. as the "Tornapampa period." One of its main imported types of pottery, "Tornapampa Thin Grey," may have been of Recuay style, but it could not be isolated from other pottery categories of the period.

With subsequent investigations in highland Ancash, the identification of local Recuay and cognate styles has proliferated. For example, the investigations of Balcón de Judas and Jancu have defined local Huaraz-based strains of Recuay wares (Wegner 1988, 2003). For the zone affected by the Pierina Gold Mine, Víctor Ponte (2001) referred to local Huarás and Recuay occupations as Cotojirca II and Cotojirca III, respectively. In the Cordillera Negra, Recuay developments were termed Kayán (early Recuay) and Chinchawasi phase I (late Recuay) (Lau 2004b). Other Recuay wares have been identified in the zones east of the Cordillera Blanca, particularly in the upper Mosna, Puchca drainage, and Chacas areas (Ibarra A. 2003: 305–308; Laurencich and Wegner 2001).

In summary, nearly one hundred years of work since Tello began systematic research in coastal and highland Ancash have resulted in a number of disparate terms to describe the Recuay phenomenon. The lack of regional synthesis and disparity in terminologies have hindered other critical avenues for research. Alternative terms have been proposed, and each has its virtues. Importantly, none seems sufficiently foolproof or without disadvantages to supplant the historical precedent and basic utility of "Recuay" as a culture-historical term. In earlier works (Lau 2004b, 2006a) I have provided the rationale why it makes sense to consider "Recuay" as a composite cultural tradition of a number of substyles, especially in terms of ceramics. In brief, stylistic commonalities, chronological milestones, and geographic reasons help to define the limits of the culture. A review of these reasons is useful to bring us closer to a viable Recuay sequence.

The Recuay Cultural Tradition

The history of Recuay research has been beset by a number of problems which have contributed to the lack of a good relative chronology. The scarcity of research and publication is probably the largest contributing factor. We have very few substantive data from the labors of earlier researchers (Tello, Bennett, Larco, and Vescelius), except position statements. Second, most Recuay research on pottery has focused on funerary sites, often of a single occupation, rather than on multiperiod refuse deposits. Indeed, finding a Recuay settlement with deep, intact stratigraphy has been surprisingly difficult. This is related to a third factor: classic Recuay pottery only seems to have been produced over four to five centuries, a relatively short period compared to other major styles.

The short duration of pottery production is related to the final factor: the question of sample size and the suitability of the assemblage for comparison. For cultures such as Moche and Nasca, tens of thousands of vessels from grave-lots and collections are available to enhance the representativeness of regional and diachronic groupings. Extensive sampling and archaeological assemblages help to provide relative and absolute ages. In contrast, we have considerably fewer Recuay vessels, probably no more than 3,000 whole examples. The most comprehensive study of the ceramics was conducted by Raphael Reichert (1977: 31), who was able to study 735 pots but conceded the difficulty of a temporal seriation. Perhaps more importantly, relatively few sites have been published with stratigraphic data associated with plainwares and/or radiocarbon measurements (Lau 2004b; Ziółkowski et al. 1994). Therefore a suite of reasons has caused Recuay to resist any sound chronological assessment.

A review of the current state of our knowledge on Recuay chronology is necessary to detail potential stylistic commonalities which help form units of contemporaneity. This builds on the framework and terminology used in studies on defining a Recuay "cultural tradition," dated ca. A.D. 1–800, as tracked through a series of ceramic style groupings (Lau 2004b). New work and data can be added to help define the main periods of the relative sequence.

Ceramics of the Huarás Period

The Huarás style, ca. 200 B.C.–A.D. 200, is the least well known of the pottery styles in the Recuay tradition. Huarás is synonymous with white-on-red pottery in highland Ancash, especially of the Callejón de Huaylas, northern Ancash, and portions of the Conchucos. Bennett (1944) first recognized white-on-red pottery in sites around the Huaraz, such as Wilkawaín, and called it "Huaraz." Lumbreras (1969, 1970) and Amat

FIGURE 25. Huarás-style bowls and bottles recovered in the Wilkawaín area (after Bennett 1944: fig. 12)

(1976a) employed the spelling "Huarás," which remains the commonly accepted orthography and helps to distinguish it from the city.

As suggested by the name, the Huarás White-on-Red style is typified by white painted decoration on a red background surface (fig. 25). Huarás pottery is a redware and is often slipped or simply burnished to a deep, dusky, and dark red. Surface decoration includes matte finishes and, more commonly, burnishing to a very dull gloss. Highly polished surfaces are rare. White painting is applied in fairly thin brushstrokes, with different levels of opacity. Often only faint traces of the paint survive, perhaps due to the paint or vitrification process. The most common designs are short vertical strokes, parallel diagonals, simple geometrics (sometimes nested), multiple wavy lines, and dot fields within geometrics.

The white painting almost always occurs on the exterior of vessels, most commonly along the upper rim of open bowls. Bowls are gener-

FIGURE 26. Huarás-style jar. The ear spool and the fanlike collar are elements typical for figures in later Recuay human effigy vessels. (Museo Arqueológico de Ancash, Huaraz)

ally small, typically 15 to 20 centimeters in diameter and about 5 to 8 centimeters deep. They also often have flaring or carinated profiles, with pronounced basal angles (Bennett 1944: figs. 12, 31R). Elsewhere they can be more hemispherical (Lumbreras 1974b: fig. 95). Small jars, frequently with bridges and modeled anthropomorphic figures (heads and full-bodied), are infrequently painted but are commonly identified as Huarás on the basis of the surface treatment/color (fig. 26).

Huarás pottery is generally assumed to have been the high-status pottery of the time. Not much is known about the complementary utilitarian or plainware range of pottery. It is possible the Huarás used necked and globular neckless jars (ollas), but neither is particularly restricted to Huarás assemblages. Nor are neckless ollas restricted to the Early Horizon or early Early Intermediate Period; the form has been used in highland Ancash since the first millennium B.C.

Huarás is considered a part of the Recuay ceramic tradition because Huarás forms and decorative patterns continued into the Recuay tradition (Amat 2003; Lau 2004b). These include the emphases on open bowls and small jars, red slips, and groups of vertical or horizontal bands along exterior rims. Other elements, including Huarás funerary practices, stone sculptural iconography, and masonry technique, also anticipate later Recuay practices (Bennett 1944: 36, 50; Lanning 1965: 140; Lumbreras 1970: 69–74).

Investigations at Chavín de Huántar, Huaricoto, and Pashash have encountered Huarás pottery stratigraphically below Recuay levels (Burger 1985a: 125; Grieder 1978: 63–65; Lumbreras 1974a: 46–47). Other studies helped determine the geographic distribution and functional contexts of Huarás-style pottery. Throughout the Callejón de Huaylas, white-on-red pottery has been reported variously as "Huarás," "Blanco sobre rojo" (white-on-red), "Cotojirca II," "Quinú," and "Tornapampa Thin Brown" (Gero 1992; Grieder 1978; Isbell 1989; Lynch 1980a; Ponte R. 2001; Terada 1979). These strengthen the original position of Bennett (1944: 109): that Huarás was intermediate between Chavín and classic kaolinite Recuay. Elsewhere the most reliable radiocarbon dates suggest that the Huarás style proper emerged at least by the last centuries B.C. and flourished until about A.D. 200. Finally, Lumbreras (1974a: 48) and Amat (1976a: 535) hinted at subphases of the Huarás period at Chavín de Huántar, and Amat (2003: 103) presented the brief rationale for two divisions. Analysis of ceramics at Chavín de Huántar will help clarify the start date of its Huarás occupation.

Some evidence, however, suggests that white-on-red pottery continued to be made and used well into later periods. This is in part because of widely varying radiocarbon dates for deposits containing white-on-red pottery (Lau 2004b: 191). Also, it is not uncommon to find materials that look like Huarás style with later materials. For example, Bennett (1944: 92; see also Lumbreras 1970: 41) found Huarás materials mainly in small unlined cist graves around the Huaraz region but also reported finding it associated with later kaolinite materials at Chavín de Huántar. Vescelius recovered white-on-red materials in many later deposits at Huaricoto, including Recuay and post-Recuay levels (Buse 1965: 330). White-on-red pottery was also found with kaolinite Recuay materials at Jancu. The cognate style at La Pampa, called "Tornapampa Thin Brown," could not be isolated stratigraphically from kaolinite styles (Terada 1979: 179). White-on-red pottery was found at Chinchawas in association with a late Recuay style and radiocarbon-dated to around A.D. 600–700. In general, however, the Chinchawas versions are larger and more crudely made.

These cases suggest a long period of white-on-red pottery use, in which there was no simple stylistic replacement or clear transition from Huarás to Recuay. In other words, not all white-on-red style pottery should be classified as Huarás period. Three alternatives can be presented to account for the pattern. One is the possibility that Huarás ceramics were curated and used in later activities. Another is that Huarás people continued to coexist and make their own pottery when Recuay kaolinite styles became predominant. The other alternative, perhaps the most likely, is that a type of Huarás-style archaism and emulation may have occurred in later Recuay-tradition societies (see also Vescelius, in Buse 1965: 330). The making of white-on-red pottery, probably for special ritual purposes such as funerary and offering activities, may have continued. Hence I use "Huarás" to mean only the pottery from the Huarás period, the first period in the Recuay tradition.

Ceramics of the Recuay Period

By the early centuries A.D., groups in highland Ancash and in certain parts of the coastal valleys began to make and employ fine pottery made out of kaolinite pastes. Recuay was not the only culture to begin using such clays during this time. Other groups in the north highlands also integrated this new material into their pottery production and often for similar forms, especially bowls and spoons. Recuay-period styles endured for at least four centuries, ca. A.D. 200–600.

Production and Decoration

From a technological standpoint, Recuay constitutes one of the most sophisticated and distinctive ceramic traditions in Andean prehistory (Donnan 1992). Relatively little is known about Recuay plainwares (see Lau 2001; Wegner 2003). The fine range of Recuay pottery, however, is easily recognized and is best distinguished by thin pastes, elaborate surface treatment including polychrome and resist painting, and hand-modeled sculptural decoration. Although most of the fancy pottery features oxidized light paste, reduced blackwares, burnished to a high standard, were also produced in characteristic Recuay forms (Wegner 2000, 2001b).

Recuay pottery is perhaps best known for its use of a light kaolinite clay, which fired to various colors from a chalky white to light gray. Many potters may have combined kaolinite and terra-cotta clays, as pinkish and buff pastes are not uncommon. In fact, many Recuay finewares may employ a redware paste, which is covered over with a kaolinite slip to reproduce the desired light background surface. This may have been a way to conserve the material (Reichert 1977: 34). Light slip colors include off-white, buff, and whitish pink.

Besides their visual and tactile properties, kaolinite vessels indicate that Recuay groups possessed special technologies and prehistoric access to raw materials. Kaolinite is an alumina-rich clay resulting from the advanced weathering of acid rock, such as granitic rocks (high in feldspar and quartz) or micaceous schist. It is most common in warm tropical and subtropical regions with high rainfall and good soil drainage, which results in acid leaching of the parent rock. Sedimentary deposits of kaolinite also occur (Rice 1987: 45–46). Thus kaolinite vessels imply knowledge of and access to raw clay sources, which are known from certain parts of the northern Peruvian sierra (Czwarno 1983).

In general, kaolinite is characterized by less shrinkage during drying and by low plasticity. The clay also requires a higher firing temperature than typical terra-cotta clays (Rice 1987: 45–48). Shaping and firing kaolinite ceramics thus took remarkable skill, especially for the elaborate sculpted effigies and architectural models which were made of many composite elements. Vent holes in solid or thick pieces of clay, such as figures and handles, were commonly used to ease the air pressure during firing (Reichert 1977: 32–33). Only a few wasters (pieces that fired incorrectly or broke) are known from Recuay-tradition sites. Leaving aside issues of sampling, this perhaps suggests that potters rarely failed to achieve their desired results.

The pottery production methods are not very well known. To my knowledge, no known kilns or firing areas or tools implicated in the process of production have ever been identified. The most elaborate construction of vessels was done by hand-forming, with little or no reliance on molds. Some groups may have made fine vessels, specifically ring-based bowls, using potter's wheels (Grieder 1978: 96–101), but this idea remains controversial.

The paste color left a distinctive light field on which polychrome decoration was applied. Recuay groups employed three main colors: white, red, and black. Variants of red (for example, orange, brownish red, and maroon) were also very common. Exterior painting was common on closed vessels such as jars, while both interior and exterior fields were often painted on open bowls (pl. 3). Brownish and red slips or light washes are typical, especially on the interior of bowls. Although positive black slip painting occurs (prefire), the black most often resulted from a postfire resist technique, also known as negative painting. This technique refers to the application of an organic black pigment, which, when burnt, left a black surface except in those areas without the pigment or protected by a resist coating.

Because resist decoration implies multiple firings, the overall process requires careful planning for each step in the production sequence. The designs and the addition of color in particular would have needed to be carefully worked out to complement each other. In general, a basic sequence in Recuay fancy ceramic manufacture can be outlined. After the vessels were modeled, their surfaces were modified with a combination of slip and organic black pigment. If the vessels were not made out of white kaolin clays, they were first given an overall coating of white slip to approximate the white kaolin. A reddish slip was applied to parts or all of the vessel, providing a red-on-white color scheme. Sometimes they were burnished until they acquired a smooth, matte surface. They were then fired in an oxidizing atmosphere.

After firing, a black resist decoration was added. This was achieved by either scorching the surface or painting on it directly with an organic pigment. More commonly, potters used a resist material (such as wax, resin, or slip, in solution or moldable pieces) to make the designs. After the designs were applied, the entire vessel would be dipped or given a wash with the organic black pigment. When fired, all the parts dipped and not covered by the resist material became a hazy graphite black. Once the resist material was removed, a "negative" design in the original white or red, or both, emerged on a black background. This was done to create complex geometric and zoomorphic motifs and added to the visual play between the different parts and painted layers of the vessel.

Painted designs are most often linear. They include a wide range of motifs: geometric, contrasting fields and patterns of color and figural representations (pl. 3). Brush strokes can be wide or narrow, but they usually are not combined on the same vessel. Brush strokes commonly measure 3–4 millimeters in width. Exterior and interior painting was applied to the upper portions near the rim; painters would often frame these areas with horizontal and vertical lines to form small quadrangular design fields for special figures. Painted decoration could be at once precise and untidy, in brush strokes and attention to the design panel. Even very precise painting occurred with patches of red slip paint, providing natural contrasts in color and technique. Specific colors were used purposefully: combinations of color, usually red, white, and black, were among the most favored (e.g., Hohmann 2003; Reichert 1977, 1982a).

Many fancy Recuay vessels feature prefire plastic decoration, including sculptural modeling, the addition of elements (such as figures, nubbins, and eyes), removal of elements (for example, architectural features), and incision. Some of the most common include small nubbins on the rims of open bowls, often in the shape of a stepped platform or hemispherical tab. Simple appliqué and adornos were very common, especially in later

Recuay-tradition pottery. Among the most handsome Recuay vessels are those which combine many decorative techniques on the same piece.

Clues from the pots themselves allow some tentative observations about the production process. Sometimes potters left small marks on the underside of bowls and, later in the Recuay tradition, on the strap handles of jars. This could be done using rapid paint strokes (Grieder 1978: fig. 52) or, more commonly, by using plastic decoration such as small incisions, punctations, and depressions (Lau 2005: fig. 11). These simple marks take the form of S-designs, slashes, ticks, or crosses and were almost always quickly executed.

In modern potting communities of northern Peru, marks are put on vessels to help distinguish them during the making or distribution process (Donnan 1971). Because of the cost of firewood, firing vessels is often a communal process; thus the marks help to distinguish vessels, especially those of a similar shape made by different potters. This latter point would be especially pertinent if a special type of kiln or knowledge about kaolinite firing was limited to certain production centers, as seems possible.

Given the quality of the Pashash materials, Grieder (1978: 79–83) contended that painted and incised marks on the bottom of ring-base bowls were the marks of individual Recuay artists; they functioned like signatures on master artworks. He surmised that multiple pots could be attributed to specific artists and "studios" on the basis of the style of painted decoration and quality of the finish (wall thickness, "fineness"). Perhaps more in line with a Euro-Western model of art production, Grieder conceived of a production process where specific artists were contracted by Pashash's elite patrons and made the special offerings of the La Capilla tomb. One potential difficulty is that Grieder (1978: 80) assumed that the potter and painter were one and the same: "the distinctiveness of the pottery vessel is matched by the individuality of the decoration, which shows that the whole process was carried out by one artist, without specialization in any one part of the process." This contrasts with fineware traditions in which more specialization occurred in painting and the potter and painter need not have been the same artisan (e.g., Donnan and McClelland 1999).

At this stage it may be premature to say the marks are anything more than identifiers of an artisan's hand during a stage of the manufacturing process. The abundance and exceptional fineness of the Pashash materials may suggest a model of attached craft specialization. It is interesting to note that makers' marks are also identified on some bowls at Yayno, especially simple crosses and ticks typical of Pashash (Grieder 1978: fig. 53). This perhaps suggests an elite distribution network, if the crosses are the marks of a specific workshop. Makers' marks are not limited to fine vessels in the Recuay tradition, however, so any explanation also needs to account for the marks on plainware jars and pitchers.

Patterns and Implications of Vessel Forms

Recuay potters fashioned a dizzying range of vessel forms. Among the most notable typologies are the synthetic treatments of Bennett (1944: fig. 32), Tello (1929: figs. 47–59), and Amat (2003: figs. 4–8). The appraisal of the Recuay style by Reichert (1977) remains the most comprehensive, explicit, and best-illustrated work on the ceramics. He identified over nineteen shape groupings, including forty-five variants, and several miscellaneous groupings. Rather than adding to the typology here, I only wish to highlight the most characteristic categories, notable cases, and implications of the ceramic forms, especially as they relate to contexts of use.

Broadly, the most common Recuay ceramic forms include bowls, jars, dippers, cups, and many composite shapes. Open bowls are the predominant open forms and the most popular form of all fineware pottery. They are generally small, measuring around 15–18 centimeters across and 7–10 centimeters tall. These bowls have relatively simple body shapes, usually with convex side walls and round or slightly flattened bases. Bowls very commonly feature ring or pedestal bases.

Unlike jars, open bowls are fairly regular in size and shape. Part of the explanation for this must include the general practical constraints of eating and drinking from them, so extremely large or small vessels probably did not serve the desired functions. Tiny bowls almost certainly were miniatures left with other offerings at graves. Small sculpted figures on Recuay vessels sometimes hold cups and bowls, but rarely do they have the ring base. This could simply be artistic license, but bowls with ring bases may have had a distinct function and special status. The ring bases, usually only 6–7 centimeters across and 1–2 centimeters tall, prop up the container and keep the vessel/contents still on a level surface. This accords with the presumption that such fineware bowls were left to contain offerings of food or liquids in funerary contexts. Sometimes the bowls feature an interior pedestal topped by a modeled figure, usually a bird (Reichert 1977: 39, pl. 25). In use, the bird figure would literally float atop the food or drink.

Taller-walled serving vessels also frequently have ring bases. Incurving bowls are probably the most common, often in the form of human effigy heads (fig. 27). Tall cups with a long cylindrical or elongated ovoid body were also popular. These were used for consuming food and drink and were left as containers with offerings.

Spoons and ladles also occur in Recuay serving assemblages. The handle areas are regularly modeled with human and animal figures (fig. 28). A related form is the long-handled vessel, which has two main types. The first consists of a deep everted-wall bowl with a handle and often with wide, flanging rims. The second dipper type, sometimes known as a "kanchero" or popcorn popper, features a lenticular profile (about 8 to 10 centimeters tall), with a constricted mouth and handle. Dipper handles almost always curve upward and have been referred to as "corniform" or horn-shaped (fig. 29). Dippers sometimes have short tubular spouts to pour liquids. It is notable that the corniform handle and many vessel types may have been skeuomorphic and imitated the shapes of bottle gourds and tubers (Tello 1929: 87).

Closed vessels, commonly referred to as jars and bottles, are more diverse in size and shape. Recuay jars often feature spherical, ellipsoid, or lenticular, pill-shaped bodies. They have many types of collars, but some of the most distinctive include a convex bowl-shaped neck or more commonly a wide, very everted disc rim which is nearly flat. Vessels with the disc rim are sometimes referred to as "pacchas," a Quechua term for a special container used for ritual libations and water/fertility ceremonies (Allen 2002; Carrión Cachot 1955; Gambini 1984: 143–144).

FIGURE 27. Front and side views of incurving bowl with ring base, in the form of a human head. The face is painted red, while the wavy lines (indicative of hair) are in resist black. (Museo Arqueológico de Ancash, Huaraz)

FIGURE 28. (*Top*) Ladle with handle modeled into the head of a female who wears a simple head covering, approximately 20 cm long. (Museo Arqueológico de Ancash, Huaraz)

FIGURE 29. (*Bottom*) Open bowl, polychrome, with corniform handle. The exterior features an orange slip over prefire incised designs, including a bicephalic creature. (Museo Arqueológico de Caraz)

Such jars sometimes feature a strap handle connecting the neck or rim to the shoulder of the body. Many jars have simple flaring, funnel-like spouts and take the form of an individual human or animal effigy with modeled features, especially the head. Men and women as well as felines, birds, and deer are all depicted. The body of the human or animal is represented by the vessel body. The jar may have an additional short, tubular spout to facilitate serving from a different portion of the jar. These commonly issue from the modeled heads of male humans or animals or from a vessel held by the figure.

A number of complex jars feature a globular body and a flattened top portion for positioning small human and animal figures in composite action scenes. The scenes usually depict chiefly figures interacting with other figures, centered on special activities such as sexual intercourse, veneration, dancing, and libations. Like other jars, they may have a small, tubular spout in addition to the larger flaring one.

Some very distinctive bottles have two lenticular-shaped chambers, joined at the center and also at the spout with a strap-handle bridge. Other dual-chambered vessels feature an animal effigy on one side and a human figure on the other. Pairings include male-camelid, female-bird, and male-feline.

Perhaps the most distinctive Recuay closed forms are the vessels with representations of built environments, which are called architectural models or effigies. These rank among the most complex Recuay objects, requiring hand-sculpting of figures and buildings, polychrome/resist painting, and multiple firings. The representations are important, because they give an idea about how Recuay people probably conceived of, made, and used their buildings. In general, architectural vessels include three main genres: those in which human figures are covered with a simple veranda; those in which the architecture forms a backdrop for ritual gatherings; and representations of defensive buildings protected by human figures. All three categories emphasize identity and containment, for the buildings help to mark out and protect the people inside.

Recuay groups also developed more unusual, idiosyncratic forms, such as bottles with donut-shaped bodies and the use of triple-tube spouts. Some jars or bottles are in the form of human effigies, sometimes showing a single figure (usually male) who is depicted seated, standing, or lying on his stomach. Other vessels show a male and female pair having sexual intercourse.

Several forms appear to be specific to certain regional Recuay groups. For example, Recuay groups in northern Ancash developed jars with neck flanges. The flange not only served to keep liquids from flowing down the side of the vessel but allowed an open bowl to sit, upside down, on top of the jar. Presumably the bowls would have been used in conjunction with the food/drink stored in the jar. The bowls sometimes have a small nubbin to facilitate lifting them off the jar. They were probably mainly held by hand when used (when the liquid was served), for the nubbin at the base would make the bowl wobble. Another rare form consists of a small bottle with a long, narrowing spout (fig. 30); this container features

FIGURE 30. Fine bottle with a long, narrow spout and strap handle. (Museo de la Nación, Lima)

a small bowl-shaped funnel for the mouth. At the bottom of it is a small aperture into the jar's main body. These were likely used as special vessels, perhaps for hot infusions of herbs or coca.

Northern Recuay groups also made effigy bottles of composite animals, such as the feline-serpent effigies of Pashash (Grieder 1978). Square and even triangular vessels are known, suggesting experimentation in the craft and a self-conscious mastery in the northern Recuay area.

In the Callejón de Huaylas, a characteristic form is the double-chambered bottle, usually featuring two lenticular-shaped bodies (fig. 31). These have short, flaring rim spouts, often with single animal figures. Another characteristic form for the southern Recuay area (also sometimes found in the Conchucos region) consists of a human figure leading a camelid. The figure is usually a well-attired male, always with a fancy headdress and other accouterments, standing next to a camelid.

In summary, the Recuay produced a great diversity of pottery forms for their fancy range. The diverse forms suggest that pottery manufacture among the Recuay was probably never standardized and that pottery was not mass produced. The Recuay differed from their contemporaries in this way of producing fine pottery. The use of molds, which is typical of Moche potters and other groups along the coast (Donnan 1965, 1992; Jackson 2008; Russell et al. 1998; Shimada 1994), was not a frequent mode of manufacture for Recuay groups. Furthermore, the wide range of ves-

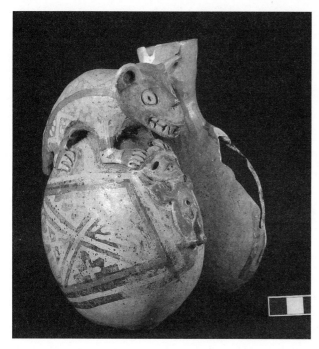

FIGURE 31. Double-chambered bottle, with modeled figures. The animal, with feline elements, grasps the splayed, moribund body of a woman by the head. The human is completely painted red, showing the color of unclothed skin. From the grave-lot of Jancu. (Museo Arqueológico de Ancash, Huaraz)

sel forms and the wide variability even in form groupings reinforce the notion that there was little centralized production of Recuay finewares (like Nasca finewares: see Proulx 2006; Silverman 1993; Silverman and Proulx 2002; Vaughn 2005).

The wide variability also suggests that the pottery served myriad purposes and circumstances. Perhaps the most basic was the use of fancy ceramics for serving and storage. No residue analysis has yet been conducted on Recuay vessels to determine their ancient contents. But it can be hypothesized that the foodstuffs and beverages were also of fine quality, suitable for the palates of high-status families, esteemed ancestors, and divinities. The elaboration and the small size of the jars, bowls, and spoons indicate that fairly small portions were being served or stored, which is consistent with their special, episodic use. To date, Recuay fancy pottery occurs most commonly in funerary sites and offering deposits and occasionally in feasting and residential contexts. In general, the ancient contexts of these ceramics reflect their importance in periodic, highly ceremonial events focused on offerings and libations, especially of elites.

Recuay Subphases

Because ceramics are vital for making inferences regarding change through time, it is useful to review in detail how previous studies have reckoned

Recuay subphases. Only a handful of people have offered a breakdown of Recuay phases. Not only have these met with some resistance, but few have been able to verify the cultural diagnostics of the sequences through excavation or pottery analysis.

The most ambitious sequences, based mainly on stylistic seriation of collections, were offered by Hernán Amat (1976b, 2003) and Wilfredo Gambini (1984). Amat proposed a five-phase Recuay sequence. Phase I is essentially a transitional phase between white-on-red pottery and Recuay kaolinite, characterized by redware jars (with modeled figures), flat-based bowls, and geometric designs — all in the manner of the Huarás style. Phase II is defined by both redware and kaolinite (terminal end) pastes and the use of zoned resist decoration, usually in geometrics. Phase III includes classic Recuay materials: polychrome and resist-painted kaolinite ceramics. Phase IV, featuring redware and kaolinite vessels, offers a wider variability of shapes, painting, and decorative modes, although the figurative modeling is of lower quality. The rims of vessels are often decorated with linear and circular motifs. The wide diversity in cultural elements is associated with an "expansive Recuay" period (Amat 2003: 117). Finally, Phase V represents the dissolution of the previous style, with new innovations, including use of reduced firing, high vessel walls, and Wari stylistic influence.

Gambini (1984: 144) modeled his sequence largely after Amat's but introduced one more subphase. Gambini felt that the Recuay or "Santa" sequence begins with an epi-Chavín style (Phase 1), with common figure modeling and stamped circles, and is associated with the Gallinazo style. Phase 2 has less plastic decoration and is associated more with white-on-red pottery, although kaolinite also appears to have been employed. Phase 3 is marked by the appearance of two-color resist painting on redware and kaolinite pastes. Phase 4 sees the emergence of the three-color resist technique with the first appearance of central male figure jars. Phase 5 is characterized by a continuation of previous decorative techniques but with greater emphasis on sculpted figures, architectural representation, and action scenes in the ceramics. Phase 6 includes positive-painted kaolinite, innovative placement of spouts, and greater emphasis on fine geometric motifs.

Although these general trends are correct (Huarás to Recuay to Late Recuay), the strict precision and the identification of diagnostics are largely untenable. First, they are essentially evolutionary trajectories of pottery, assuming an earlier, primitive technique, followed by the style's development and florescence (classic kaolinite) and then, at least in Amat's sequence, its untidy dissolution. It is clear, however, that these distinctions do not work, for "primitive" and kaolinite ceramics are often found in coeval deposits and grave-lots (e.g., Bennett 1944). Gambini's sequence marshals a range of known examples from collections; but despite the great detail, it includes no diagnostic elements which can be isolated to a single phase.

Perhaps more importantly, neither sequence relies explicitly on stratigraphic deposits, cultural associations, or radiocarbon dates. Amat's sequence is based mainly on a study of museum collections, but his field investigations in highland Ancash (specifically at Honcopampa and Chavín de Huántar) must also have informed the analysis. Regrettably, Amat has never specified the stratigraphic basis for the Recuay sequence in published form, and illustrations of pottery associated with the subphases remain unavailable. Vescelius, Amat's colleague in the field, also hinted at two Recuay subphases, as described earlier (cited in Lanning 1965).

The only well-published sequence based explicitly on stratigraphic superposition is the Pashash sequence offered by Terence Grieder (1978). In addition to the burial offerings, Grieder, Bueno, and Smith excavated pits that facilitated the formulation of three Recuay subphases (Quimít, Yaiá, and Huacohú). These were preceded by a white-on-red ceramic phase known as the Quinú phase and followed by the Usú, a Late Recuay variant. All three phases contain finewares (including kaolinite vessels) and plainwares.

The Quimít-phase finewares are typified by positive painting (most often red-on-cream), red and cream slips, and effigy figures. Resist painting and plastic decoration are rare. According to Grieder (1978: 65), the subsequent phase, the Yaiá, "represents the purest Recuay style," a courtly style of Recuay nobles. Unlike the previous phase, Yaiá is characterized by black-on-cream resist painting and various slip colors. Ring bases are the predominant basal form for cups and bowls, and the rims sometimes feature small tabs/nubbins. The subsequent Huacohú phase is best identified by a diversity of paint colors, but especially positive white designs (for example, dots on a dark band) and orange-slipped backgrounds. Resist black designs continue, and plastic decoration appears more frequently.

The last two phases at Pashash, Yaiá to Huacohú, appear to have analogues at Yayno. In particular, the Yayno finewares at least seem to show a stylistic change from polychrome/resist painted kaolinite (with characteristic Recuay designs, such as step motifs and repeating circles) to emphasis on positive painting on fine redware, usually centered on band designs (for example, white dots), white painting, and nested geometrics.

We now have enough evidence to propose, for the moment, three sub-phases for the Recuay style, based mainly on an interpretation of stylistic comparisons of fineware, stratigraphic associations, and radiocarbon dates. The preliminary sequence can only be corrected with additional chronological research.

Although other forms are informative, the open bowl (notably its shape and decoration) appears to offer the most consistent cultural elements to describe the subphases of the Recuay tradition. The Recuay open bowl might be thought of as something analogous to the Larco stirrup-spout bottle that is so essential in the Moche seriation for the Moche and Chicama valleys. As noted, Recuay pottery production was never standardized. Very fancy bottles and other special vessels probably circulated rarely outside of their use in funerary contexts. Unlike a number of the other forms with strong local idiosyncrasies, however, the open bowl seems to have been produced and used in time and space by most if not all of the groups called Recuay.

RECUAY I

This phase is represented by the early reliance and predominance of kaolinite pottery, most commonly in the form of simple kaolinite ring-based bowls and dippers with corniform handles. Bowls often feature repetitive geometric designs (circles, S-shapes, parallel hatching, meanders) on the uppermost exterior rims. Red or orange slip is often used.

Representative sites include Balcón de Judas (Wegner 2003) and Chinchawas (Kayán phase). This is not the only time that these forms appear, but they make their first appearance in Recuay I. The bowls in particular are part of widespread proliferation of positive painted kaolinite bowls in the north highlands, associated with Early Cajamarca and other early Early Intermediate Period sierra styles of highland La Libertad (Huamachuco, Santiago de Chuco) (Church 1996; Krzanowski 1986; Lau 2006a; Terada and Matsumoto 1985; Topic and Topic 1983; Topic and Topic 1984).

RECUAY II

This phase is best represented by the Yaiá phase at Pashash, the Rayo-style materials at Yayno (pl. 4a–f), and the Jancu grave-lot (pl. 5). In other words, this phase consists of the florescence of the Recuay style, with burgeoning stylistic variability. Resist and polychrome techniques are taken to a new and innovative level during this period, with common usage on the exteriors of open bowls and on jars. Negative designs are typically reserved for the exterior and include crosses, repeated dots, parallel straight and wavy bands, and zoomorphic designs. Bowl interiors may be left plain but are also sometimes painted with a thin red wash and/or often with different polychrome registers of highly repetitive designs: S-designs, eyes, dots and circles, step, and maze motifs.

The forms include similar ring-based bowls and dippers, but with time a greater diversity of other shape categories emerges as well, including the disc-rim jars (pacchas), central figure jars, and double-lenticular bottle. Although little contextual information is available, I speculate that most of the figural scenes and architectural models also belong to this phase.

RECUAY III

This phase is best represented by the Huacohú style at Pashash and Asuac-style materials at Yayno (pl. 4g–h), respectively. In addition to kaolinite wares, fine positive-painted redwares reemerge. Unlike the previous style, painting is commonly done with white pigment in bands or meanders and often in repeating dots on dark backgrounds. Designs are typically in band designs, step motifs, and geometrics on an orange slip. Unlike the narrow band widths of Recuay II, Recuay III often features wider bands in variable colors.

Around this time, especially in the northern area, certain filler elements proliferate on Recuay-style pottery (Steven Wegner, personal communication, 2007). These include hatched or lattice elements in quadrangles or in triangles as well as eye- or football-shaped elements, scored with short curvy strokes. These elements were usually applied between larger designs or on them. It is unclear what these elements represent, but the eye-shaped elements (with their scoring) resemble the Moche representations of muscoid fly larvae, typically associated with the putrefaction and defleshing of dead corpses (Bourget 2001: 104–106; compare Grieder 1978: figs. 137, 175, 182). They are most often represented as simple "footballs," but at Pashash they are sometimes represented with heads (each with a beak and perhaps antennae). It is possible that the vessels with this imagery are especially associated with death or funerary ritual.

Ceramics of the Late Recuay Period

From around A.D. 600 to 700 pottery production took a different direction stylistically throughout the Recuay heartland, with a widespread de-emphasis on kaolinite vessel production and the proliferation of coarser local-decorated wares. It remains unclear why the use of kaolinite clays across the Ancash highlands became much less prominent. Production of kaolinite vessels was not very standardized, so it was not the shutdown of a few centers that stopped their manufacture. Rather, this seems to reflect an extensive disinterest in the pottery. It apparently became less appealing or less useful across a wide spectrum of Recuay groups. Some of the socioeconomic reasons for this transformation are explored in chapter 8.

Overall, stylistic changes indicate the dissolution of the previous Recuay fineware style. Late Recuay pottery generally relies on coarser oxidized pastes, with tan to pinkish buff paste colors. On bowls, the most diagnostic vessels of the phase, the former emphasis on hemispherical shapes (with tall convex walls) gives way to larger, shallower shapes, very commonly with ring bases. Kanchero dippers and wide disc-rim pacchas become obsolete. Handled bowl dippers often take the form of effigy heads.

Decoration shows a concomitant deemphasis on resist painting and elaborate figural modeling. Painting typically occurs on the exterior of bowls and small jars. The line weights of painted designs become heavier and less meticulous; in general, fewer colors are used, including black and white but relying almost exclusively on a dark red or purplish pigment. Common designs reuse but update previous Recuay preferences: multiple horizontal meanders, groups of vertical or horizontal lines, repeating circles, and simple repeating linear and geometric motifs (such as rectangles, mazes, and triangles).

Late Recuay pottery at Chinchawas is known as Chinchawasi 1 Ware A (Lau 2004b). A related style named Usú emerged at Pashash (Grieder 1978: 70). The Pierina mining area provides examples categorized within the larger Cotojirca III and Cotojirca IV phases (Ponte R. 2001). Published examples occur as far abroad as Chacas in the Conchucos (Wegner 2000: 16) and Katak (Eisleb 1987: figs. 23, 38, 92). In addition, ceramics in the Callejón style identified for the Mosna drainage bear Late Recuay affinities (Lumbreras 1970: 67). The Huanchac style at Yayno contains some of this pottery (pl. 4i–j). These styles may therefore be considered terminal Recuay components following kaolinite wares.

Ceramics of the Wilkawaín Period

The final period of the Recuay cultural tradition, dated roughly A.D. 700–800, was a dynamic time of cultural transformation in highland Ancash, as it was for many parts of the Central Andes. It corresponds to the early to middle portions of the Middle Horizon in Andean chronology and is best understood as a period of strong local interaction with Wari culture, especially in the Callejón de Huaylas.

In a previous publication (Lau 2004b) I have described this time in relation to "early Wari influence." But for purposes of simplicity and meaning, here I turn to the "Wilkawaín" designation for this period, which follows both the historical precedent of the site and the cultural makeup typical for the period (e.g., Bennett 1944; Schaedel 1952; Wegner 1988). Ichik Wilkawaín, of course, is where Wendell Bennett recovered "Tiahuanacoid" or Wari-style materials from funerary constructions stratigraphically above Recuay materials. Investigations by Juan Paredes Olvera (2007) at the site and its surrounding region confirm the dynamism of local groups, particularly in their use of pottery, during the period of Wari expansion. Groups were taking an active interest in acquiring imported vessels and emulating foreign styles for local ceremonial uses, such as burials and offerings.

Wilkawaín-period radiocarbon dates (Chinchawas, Honcopampa, and Queyash Alto) fall largely into the eighth century A.D. and are considered roughly coeval with the early Middle Horizon. The Middle Horizon in the Callejón de Huaylas is most often associated with developments at Honcopampa, often interpreted as a Wari "administrative center" (Isbell 1989, 1991). Intensive occupation at the site began during the "Early Honco" phase, when a major building program included Wari-style D-shaped structures (Vescelius, in Lanning 1965: 140; Buse 1965: 327). Unfortunately, the pottery from Honcopampa and the Vescelius sequence has never been published, so stylistic comparisons for Honcopampa are currently unavailable.

Ceramic change is documented at Chinchawas, with the transition between Chinchawasi Phases 1 and 2. The major continuity consisted of a ware characterized by dark red painting on a light background. But the popularity of distinct vessel shapes varied. Red oxidized pastes also became more prominent, displacing the long emphasis on light kaolinite-related fabrics. Interior painting grew more popular (especially dual-face designs and interior nested diamonds), while other designs and the white-on-red pottery style fell out of favor (Lau 2004b).

During the Wilkawaín period, especially in the Callejón de Huaylas, exotic prestige ceramics became more widely used and displayed. Wari polychrome, Cajamarca, Late Moche and other north-coast styles, and non-Recuay kaolinite wares have all been documented as trade items, especially in burial contexts (Bennett 1944: figs. 9, 10, 13; Lanning 1965: 140; Lau 2005; Menzel 1964). The greater frequency of exotic pottery appears to reflect a widening of exchange relationships enabled by early Wari expansion, at least in the Cordillera Negra and the Callejón de Huaylas. We have less evidence of interaction between Wari and local groups in the Conchucos.

By the end of the Wilkawaín period the last vestiges of the Recuay tradition had been supplanted by new dispositions in making pottery. Local groups during the later Middle Horizon (Wilkawaín period), Late Intermediate Period, and Late Horizon made ceramic vessels bearing little evidence of the thin, light-colored clays, modeling, and detailed painting so characteristic of the Recuay style.

Uses and Contexts of Fancy Ceramics

The foregoing discussion has approached Recuay ceramics almost exclusively as tools of culture history. But pottery existed neither in a vacuum (without people) nor as something left purposefully by its makers and users for scholars to reconstruct their "culture." Rather, ceramics were ubiquitous and exist in such quantity through time because people found them handy for a range of purposes.

Pottery was essential in Recuay social life and served a host of purposes. People depended on ceramics for their daily activities. Besides the preparation and serving of foods, ceramic vessels must have been important for containing and hiding items and keeping them away from pests, storage of food and water, and hygiene. Pots also regularly broke, necessitating new ones. But even their fragments could be reused to make other implements, such as scrapers, spindle whorls, and projectiles. Of course, ceramics were not only for quotidian purposes but also played a role in other sociocultural domains. Recuay vessels were critical participants in trade, religious, and public ceremonies, in performances, for status display, and for social identity and memory.

This section focuses on the different uses of ceramics and their various contexts in Recuay culture. Because I concentrate on the finer range of Recuay pottery here, this discussion focuses on the contexts of use; imagery is discussed in greater detail in chapter 7.

The plainware range of pottery, such as jars and bowls, fulfilled the most common household uses: cooking, serving, and storage. Given its ubiquity in Recuay sites, plainware pottery, not surprisingly, was produced, used, and then discarded in much greater quantities than the finewares. For example, excavations at Chinchawas found a much higher percentage of plainwares, making up more than 97.5 percent of the overall pottery assemblage. In other words, for every decorated fragment recovered, about forty plain ones were found.

Plain Recuay tradition pottery is associated with different activity areas. Most commonly, plainware pottery has been recovered in cooking, food preparation, and midden areas associated with residential buildings. Jars were used mainly for storage of liquids, while wide-mouthed ollas served to heat water and cook soups and stews. Sieves were used to drain materials and perhaps for heating foods over a fire. Spoons and ladles were employed to stir and deliver the food, often in conjunction with open bowls.

Interestingly, plainwares also occur mixed in with fine ceramics in ceremonial or high-status settings, often in and around small open plazas (e.g., Amat 2003; Gero 1991; Lau 2002; Wegner 2003). Plainware ceramics were important even for those factions with greater access to finer pots. Thus the remains of jars, cooking ollas, open bowls, sieves, and ladles are not uncommon, even in and around ceremonial spaces. Elites need to eat too; finer wares must have been rarely used for cooking, storage, or other more quotidian purposes. Moreover, offering food and beverages on a suprahousehold scale was integral to the festive responsibilities and redistributive economy of Recuay leaders — what Joan M. Gero (1992) called "political meals" and Michael Dietler (1996, 2001) termed "commensal politics." Through such hospitality, sponsors (usually lineage heads or chiefs) could incur obligations from their participants, most probably in the form of labor.

Kaolinite ceramics were more specialized in distribution and scope. In general we can identify four principal uses or contexts: as funerary goods, as nonfunerary ritual offerings, for libation activities, and in feasting episodes. These activities are not necessarily mutually exclusive. For example, feasting activities are often part of funerary ceremonies, and libations are often part of the feasts. They are separated here to show the variability of uses rather than as firm categories. In general, the presence of kaolinite ceramics helps to index special activities or higher-status groups.

Recuay ceramics are most frequently found in tombs, as burial goods. All the best-known collections of Recuay ceramics, such as the Macedo, Dextre, and Pashash collections, were grave-lots. One of the basic implications of this is simply that Recuay peoples venerated their esteemed deceased with great effort, by making, handling, and offering fine ceramics in funerary contexts. The whiteness of the pots must have been important in the dark interiors of Recuay tombs. It distinguished the vessels as containers for the food and drink earmarked for the well-being of the deceased. In the Jancu tomb, for example, over fifteen vessels (some with male and female effigies) were found in various parts of the tomb. Some were left on a shelf along the outer walls and others were in niches. These were positioned by the descendants to be vigilant over and in effect interact with the interments.

It should be noted that Recuay funerary offerings were often made in pairs. Hence two bowls or jars of similar form and decoration may be found together. The vessels are very similar, but frequently one is slightly different from the other. For example, effigy offerings often represent a male and a female. Paired bowls may have slightly different painted designs; occasionally one bowl is larger than its counterpart. In other words, the offerings often show an emphasis on complementary opposites or pairs.

Recuay ceramics were also essential to offering caches. In addition to the funerary focus on offerings just noted, some offerings have no outward association to graves. These seem to be indicators of votive commitment to sacred places and things. For example, the offerings at San Nicolás (Santa) may have been meant for the religious center (huaca) near the ocean. The Usú-phase offering in the La Capilla temple at Pashash seems to have been a type of cache offered to a sacred place rather than to any one individual. This would suggest that vessels were considered appropriate gifts and agents (with suitable status and religious efficacy) for the divinities or spirits immanent in these places.

The very shapes of Recuay vessels (jars, bottles, and dippers) indicate their role in ritual toasts or offerings of drink/liquids. As in most societies, communal drinking, especially of alcoholic beverages, is critical in Andean social relations. It is not unusual to have both very elaborate equipment and also very elaborate social dispositions and behaviors dedicated to drinking (Carrión Cachot 1955; Cummins 2002; Gose 1994). In addition, some Recuay ceramic representations allude to libation ritual. Women and men hold cups presumably to mimic pouring events which the vessel itself facilitated. It is like an image within an image, constantly repeating itself in progressively smaller iterations (on related synecdochal relations, see Allen 1997).

Reichert (1977) noted the strong ritual focus of Recuay fancy pottery but also noted that the negative-painted designs can come off easily with protracted or regular use, by washing, wiping, or simply by holding.

Overall, it is likely that most of the fanciest Recuay vessels, given their excellent condition, were used on rare occasions for very special events.

Conclusions

This chapter has reviewed the forms, manufacture, and distribution of Recuay pottery, with an emphasis on complementing studies which showcase the iconography. Aside from the imagery, what can be learned about Recuay society from the evidence of ceramics? Having reviewed their production, use, and chronology, I can now offer several salient observations.

First, at present it is possible to identify four periods in the Recuay ceramic tradition: Huarás, Recuay, Late Recuay, and Wilkawaín. I have discussed these briefly, with short descriptions of their diagnostic elements. The Recuay period includes three subphases described here, using stratigraphic evidence from excavations and associated radiocarbon dates. More specialized studies on Recuay pottery-making techniques and production, especially as related to clay sourcing and production, will help to elucidate substyles and the chronology of Recuay-tradition groups.

Second, pottery production was highly heterogeneous. Coeval styles of the Recuay tradition were so different that the manufacture was probably never limited to a single production center. Rather, multiple production locales may have been associated with different politico-religious centers. Such centers in the ancient Recuay world were largely independent: each maintained ties to its own pottery workshop(s) and its own artisans. It is not known whether itinerant potters made fancy pottery.

The fanciest Recuay vessels were mainly for the ceremonial purposes of wealthy Recuay elites. These can be pinpointed further as key objects in special corporate or public events: libations, offerings, and feasts. Given their terminal original contexts, they were almost always associated with ancestor ceremonies. This also helps to explain the strong local differences in Recuay ceramic styles, for the styles are expressive of the local cultural preferences specific to each (venerating) corporate group.

Despite the prominent local flavor of each ceramic-producing area, however, the overall combination of similar stylistic dispositions (especially in forms, decoration, and imagery) and their use contexts helps to distinguish groups of the Recuay commonwealth.

CHAPTER SIX

Objects of Stone

Some of the most durable artifacts of the ancient Andes included carefully worked sculptures, implements, and related
objects made from stone. In this chapter I focus on their forms
and distribution to help explore the types of material engagements that
Recuay people had with stone things.

For Recuay groups of highland Ancash, the tradition of rendering
stone blocks into monolithic objects occurred over the better part of
the first millennium A.D. Where contextual data are available, they are
commonly associated with ceremonial buildings and spaces. Sculptures
served as structural elements on shrines or temples and tombs. Some
also stood freely as uprights. Most sculptures formed parts of episodic
building programs for different communities of the cultural tradition
and were dedicated to the ancestor ritual of local groups.

The Recuay followed on the footsteps of their Chavín predecessors
with one of the most prolific stone-carving traditions in Andean prehistory. Unlike the Chavín or Tiwanaku, however, Recuay stone-carvers
were not limited to production at major ceremonial centers. Artisans
produced Recuay-style sculptures at many different locales, from large
political centers to small hamlets, and especially for cemeteries and
shrines. By no means is the archaeological record complete, but a conservative estimate would place the total of known sculptures at around
500 to 600 examples, found scattered in different provinces throughout highland Ancash. Ongoing discoveries continue to add to current
knowledge.

Recuay sculptural compositions are blocky and stylized and treat a
narrow range of subjects. The style does not convey the same monumentality or formal complexity of composition as, for example, Chavín's
Tello Obelisk or Tiwanaku's Gateway of the Sun. The mesmerizing quality of these other traditions has been a source of enchantment for the ancients and scholars alike (Gell 1992; Urton 1996: 237). Recuay sculptures

remain provocative, nevertheless, precisely because of their simplicity, accessibility, and candor.

Through centuries of weathering and destruction, most Recuay sculptures have been relocated or rendered undetectable. The market for desirable Pre-Columbian antiquities also fosters problems in conservation and theft. Their valuable archaeological contexts, in particular, have been or are in danger of being lost. Only a small number of Recuay sites have been identified with sculptures, and only a few have in situ examples. Sculptures are frequently dislodged, transported to other locations without systematic documentation, or simply removed illegally. A small percentage of the Recuay sculpture corpus can be attributed reliably to the original provenience, and only a fraction of those survive at the site or in situ. Archaeologists rely on those few well-investigated cases and careful study of existing collections and literature to help understand these works in their prehistoric contexts.

Distribution and Sculpture Areas

What is sculpture? The *Oxford English Dictionary* defines the term: "Originally, the process or art of carving or engraving a hard material so as to produce designs or figures in relief, in intaglio, or in the round — now chiefly used with reference to work in stone and bronze, and to the production of figures of considerable size." While noting the difficulties of cultural categories (Kubler 1962b; Paternosto 1996), this chapter in essence proceeds with this definition in mind. The principal objects under discussion are of stone, feature relief or carving which resulted in designs, and are fairly large.[1] The following discussion charts the major sculptural areas in the Recuay tradition and reviews the associated literature, taking special note of the patterns and peculiarities of form and design in each geographical area.

The Callejón de Huaylas and Cordillera Negra

THE SOUTHERN CORDILLERA NEGRA (AIJA, LA MERCED)
Stone sculpture in the Recuay style has been recognized since the late nineteenth century. Foreign travelers described impressive Recuay remains throughout the north highlands, including stone monoliths (e.g., Middendorf 1895 [1893–1895]; Raimondi 1874–1880; Sievers 1914; Wiener 1880). But it was Tello's archaeological expedition in 1919 that established highland Ancash as one of the major archaeological regions of Peru. Tello (1929: 55–116) also recognized, for the first time, the cultural association

A   B

C   D

FIGURE 32. Carved monoliths of the Aija–La Merced region: (a) statue of female figure from Mayakayán, height 1.31 m; (b) statue of female figure from Arway, height 1.1 m; (c) statue of male warrior from Tarushkawanan, height 1 m; (d) statue of male warrior from Rurek, height 1.31 m. (Redrawn from Tello 1929: Figs. 40, 42–45)

between Recuay stone-carving, pottery, and ceremonial architecture. Tello visited a number of sites in the region but placed special emphasis on various stone sculptures in and around the highland towns of Aija and La Merced, to the west of Recuay in the Cordillera Negra. Over forty sculptures were reported (Schaedel 1952: 135–136).

The best-known material from this region consists of a series of about thirty impressive anthropomorphic sculptures of male and female individuals (fig. 32). Tello (1923: figs. 39–44, 1929: figs. 40–45, 1930: figs. 15–16) brought these "statues" to popular attention and associated them with local shrines and temples. The figures are represented in seated position, usually measuring around 0.9–1.3 meters tall and 25–30 centimeters wide. They were often carved from grayish igneous rock, probably granites. The men are adorned with clothing, accessories, and weapons (such as shields, clubs, bags, headdresses, and trophy heads) which suggest that they were important warriors or had warrior identities. The women are represented with elaborate hairstyles, shawl pins, and finely decorated textiles, including mantles and head wraps equally denotative of high status. The statues also feature specific designs typical of Recuay ceramic imagery: double-headed serpents, birds, and feline heads with appendages. For Tello, this not only confirmed the cultural affiliation between pottery and the monoliths; the imagery emphasized, across media, fertility and celestial references to the sun, moon, and lightning.

Tello (1929: 73–81; Mejía Xesspe 1941: 22) also recognized that the stone sculpture occurred both purely as statues (sculpted and viewed in the round) and as architectural elements. Tenon-heads, for example, sometimes adorned the façades of shrines and monuments, and lintels spanned important thresholds. These lintels, sometimes measuring up to 2 meters across, frequently depicted a single central frontal anthropomorph, flanked on either side by a feline creature (Tello 1923: figs. 33–34). He contended that the lintels or horizontal slabs, later called "puma slabs" by Schaedel, magically protected the inhabitants of the buildings against enemies and malevolent spirits (Tello 1929: 73).

Perhaps most importantly, Tello (1930: 280) introduced a model for the function and social context of the stone sculpture:

> One notes a close relationship between the statuary sculpture and the structures called shrines.... These consist... of small pyramids, subterranean chambers, enclosed patios, and other special depositories. The pyramids are adorned with stone statues, representing warriors and women; the subterranean chambers served for the preparation of the mummified bodies of the immediate ancestors; the patios were devoted to the care of llamas and other animals destined for sacrifice, and the buildings especially to [sic] storing of food offerings and the various objects of idol worship, such as gall-stones, small idols or konopas, and probably also ceremonial pottery vessels.

Hence seemingly unrelated elements of Recuay culture were recognized as vital and integral components of local religious practices: ancestor cults.

THE CENTRAL CALLEJÓN DE HUAYLAS (HUARAZ)

The best-known Recuay stone sculpture comes from the area in and around Huaraz, in the heart of the Callejón de Huaylas. Today the Museo Arqueológico de Ancash of Huaraz boasts proudly that its Parque Lítico (sculpture park) features one of the largest collections of monoliths in the Americas (figs. 33, 34).

Several of the earliest descriptions of Recuay stone sculpture were of examples found in and around the Huaraz region (e.g., Raimondi 1874–1880; Sievers 1914). Spurred on by Tello's discoveries but lack of chronological precision, Bennett (1944) initiated studies in the north highlands specifically to elucidate the character and position of highland cultures, including Recuay, in the Andean sequence. Much of his work on the Recuay period focused on sites in the Callejón de Huaylas: in the region of Katak, Carhuaz, and especially Huaraz. Bennett (1944: 104–105) corroborated the association between Recuay ceramics and stone sculpture and developed a simple classification for the sculptural types: two statue types (Huaraz and Aija), relief slabs (fig. 35), and tenon-sculptures (fig. 36). Based on his experience in Bolivia and many parts of Peru, he conjectured that the last two forms also had strong relationships to Tiahuanacoid (Wari) cultures. Kroeber (1944: 93–96) concurred that Recuay culture had strong ties to Wari, as reflected in stone sculpture.

Bennett's student Richard Schaedel (1948b, 1952) provided the first systematic classification of Recuay tradition monoliths as well as the first synthetic treatment on Central Andean stone sculptures. The work relied on descriptions and stylistic groupings of sculptures from differ-

FIGURE 33. (*Left*) Stone sculpture of male figure with crossed legs. The pose resembles the body disposition of mummy bundle interments. (Museo Arqueológico de Ancash, Huaraz)

FIGURE 34. (*Right*) Stone sculpture of male figure with crossed legs. The figure features many articles of warrior dress, including a headdress with a forehead crescent and trophy hand designs (on the sides). On the right arm is a club, while the left carries a shield and a small bag (also on the side), perhaps for coca. (Museo Arqueológico de Ancash, Huaraz)

FIGURE 35. (*Top*) Sculpture of profile felines facing each other. (Museo Arqueológico de Ancash, Huaraz)

FIGURE 36. (*Middle, bottom*) Tenon-sculptures: (a) feline head with large mouth, whiskers, and interlocking fangs; (b) human head, with trophy hand motifs on the forehead band. The rear extensions would be inserted into the façade, so that the heads could be suspended from walls. (Museo Arqueológico de Ancash, Huaraz)

ent regions to discern cultural and chronological relationships. Writing from a pan-Andean perspective, Schaedel (1948a) maintained that Recuay was one of the most diverse and prolific stone-sculpting traditions in the Central Andes.

Schaedel's studies on sculpture were exercises in classification, which sought to rectify Tello's broad-brush characterizations of function and cultural affiliation. Like Bennett, Schaedel (1948b: 76–78) categorized the sculpture into three formal groups (human statues, "puma slabs," and heads/tenon-heads) and associated Aija type sculptures with classic Recuay pottery and tenon-heads with "Wilkawaín-Tiahuanaco" or Wari affiliation.

Schaedel's doctoral dissertation (1952) provided an extensive inventory by making stylistic groupings ordered according to geographic regions. He defined centers of sculptural production (such as the "Huaraz central area"); areas in the immediate vicinity of each center (such as the "Circum-Huaraz area"); and areas considered associated but more distant (such as the "Huaraz Peripheral Area"). Key centers in Ancash included Aija, Huaraz, and Cabana (Pashash, Pallasca). Subsidiary areas included Huambo, Huántar, and Pomabamba. The objective was to compare stone sculpture, like pottery, on the basis of clinal stylistic relationships and regional variability. In many ways these groupings still hold, although subsequent work has helped to update the overall distribution.

Despite the extensive distribution of Recuay-tradition sculpture, the "Huaraz area" and "Huaraz Peripheral Area," which Schaedel (1948b: 69, 1952: 175) used together to describe developments in the Callejón de Huaylas, contained the largest clustering of specimens and the widest stylistic variation. Overall, Schaedel (1948b: 78) believed that Huaraz, though a "center of aesthetic developments," received strong influences from the areas to the north, including Pashash.

Schaedel (1948b: 77–78) attempted to divide Recuay sculpture into subphases on the basis of motifs and relief carving techniques. For the Huaraz area sculptures, for example, the "Huaraz General Style" included the Realistic, Convex, and Diminutive substyles; the Realistic substyle antedated the Convex (Schaedel 1952: 143–176). Unfortunately, he had little contextual evidence to verify the periodization. Relief slabs with feline heads, depicted frontally, could be considered Recuay, while feline heads in profile could be regarded as "Recuay-Tiahuanaco" (see also Schaedel 1993). Given the emphasis on classification, he offered very little discussion about the function or social significance of Recuay stone sculpture.

Schaedel's research drew broadly from his collaboration with Padre Augusto Soriano Infante, the founder of the Huaraz archaeological museum, who was responsible for amassing its large sculpture collection (Schaedel 1948a; Soriano I. 1940, 1941, 1950). By 1950 Soriano had catalogued over four hundred specimens in the Huaraz museum, most with information on dimensions, general provenience, and notable features. He conceived of six principal groups: "monolitos" (monoliths: nonfigural pieces), "litoesculturas" (stone sculptures: representational pieces), "estatuas" (statues: humans), "cabezas felínicas" (feline tenon-heads), "estelas de empotradura" (wall stelae), and "estatuas zoomorfas" (zoomorphic statues). Soriano defined these categories based partly on shape and partly on their iconography. Subcategories (for example, of anthropomorphic statues) were based on the design, such as raised arms and crossed legs. Using the displays of sculpture in the Museo Arqueológico de Ancash, Steven Wegner (1988) updated the typology for the Huaraz corpus and Recuay stone sculpture more generally into five major forms: statues, vertical slabs, horizontal slabs, tenon-heads, and quadrangular panels.

THE CENTRAL CORDILLERA NEGRA (CHINCHAWAS, PIRA)

A related sculpting tradition developed in the Cordillera Negra just north of Aija. In and around Pira, a small town near the Punta Kayán pass to the west of Huaraz, a series of prehistoric communities actively produced carved monoliths. These include archaeological sites in Pira (Lau 2004a: fig. 6b), Cajamarquilla (Kauffmann Doig 1970: 340), Santa Cruz, Cantu, and Yaután (Schaedel 1952), and Chinchawas (Lau 2006b; Mejía Xesspe 1941).

Tello's students continued his intellectual legacy by emphasizing the stone sculpture of the Cordillera Negra as one of the most distinctive expressions of highland Andean art and cosmology. The social contexts for Recuay tradition stone sculpture were emphasized, such as funerary structures at Chinchawas and Karachuko and a possible production area at Walun (Mejía Xesspe 1941, 1957). The imagery of horizontal slabs and their cosmological meaning were also assessed (Carrión Cachot 1955, 1959).

In a number of short descriptions, Kauffmann Doig (1966, 2002) also drew attention to the sculptural tradition of the Cordillera Negra, with a special focus on lesser-known styles. He described a variant style that proliferated in the area around the modern settlements in Cajamarquilla and at Santa Cruz, near Chinchawas, which contained large carved monoliths, some embedded as decorative elements. Kauffmann Doig (1966: 82) suggested that the sculptures may be portraying mummy bundles. In the area around the town of Marenayoc, within the zone affected by the Pierina Gold Mine, Víctor Ponte (1999a: 70–72) documented five previously unreported stone sculptures. The assemblage included four feline tenon-heads and one quadrangular panel of a profile feline, typical of the Huaraz group sculptures.

The site of Chinchawas contained over forty different specimens (Lau 2000, 2002, 2006b). Twenty-six sculptures were identified from the main hilltop, including nine horizontal slabs, the largest and most elaborately carved monuments at the site. The main sector also contained seven quadrangular panels, six vertical slabs, and four tenon-head sculptures. Nearly all of the quadrangular panels depict a single profile feline, while the horizontal slabs show the pervasive theme of a central figure, usually a male with warrior accouterments, flanked by feline creatures (fig. 37). Two vertical slabs adorned a high-status residence, as jambs on either side of a central entrance/staircase into a room complex (fig. 38).

Another vertical slab formed part of the Torreón structure, a circular towerlike construction on the highest part of the settlement. Most of the sculptures are therefore associated with walled enclosures and important adjacent buildings on the central ridgetop. The walled areas were used for group ceremonies centered on public displays and ancestor veneration. Large amounts of bone refuse and broken drinking vessels

FIGURE 37. Horizontal slab sculptures documented at Chinchawas: (a) sculpture s19; (b) sculpture s17; (c) sculpture s16; (d) sculpture s26. The conventional arrangement was a central frontal anthropomorph, flanked on either side by a feline or feline-creature. Like the humans, the felines usually show male genitalia. Some figures feature supernatural elements, such as animal head appendages and bicephalic bodies.

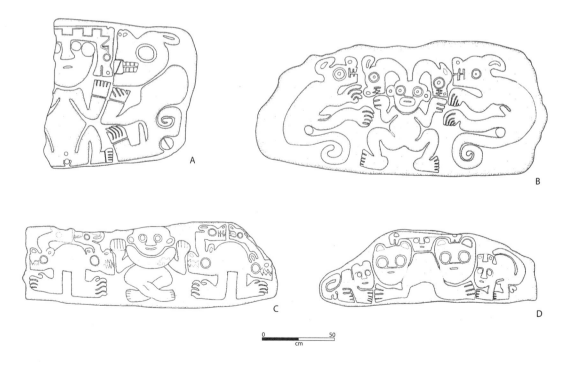

A

B

C

D

0   50
cm

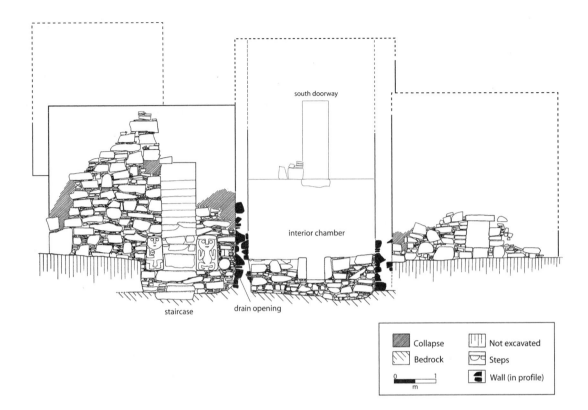

south doorway

interior chamber

staircase   drain opening

▨ Collapse		▥ Not excavated	
▧ Bedrock		▱ Steps	
0 — 1 m		◧ Wall (in profile)	

FIGURE 38. North façade of Room Complex 3, a high-status residence at Chinchawas. The low and even stone wall of the interior room (right) may have been surmounted by adobe mud bricks. On either side of an entrance and staircase into the complex is a vertical slab sculpture, depicting frontal anthropomorphs. On the west side (figures' left) is a splayed female figure and on the east side (figures' right) a male warrior figure. Adjacent to the female figure is an opening to drain rainwater.

suggest that camelid consumption and feasting were key elements of the group activities. In the cemetery area of Chinchawas were seventeen additional sculptures, sixteen of which were vertical slabs (fig. 39), all of which were associated with later Middle Horizon chullpa tombs. Given their form, it is very likely that vertical slabs, most depicting a single frontal anthropomorph, were structural elements.

For a single site, considerable variability characterized the degree of detail and skill in sculptures at Chinchawas. In general, the finer sculptures employ higher relief, include more intricate carving, and have flatter, more even surfaces. The larger specimens, especially those containing the larger scenes, probably required more investment to carve and mount. The less elaborate sculptures show more economical treatment, relying on incised detail rather than fuller relief. Several resemble the "Diminutive style" sculpture. Although their execution differed, they suggest a conservative approach to formal proportions and suitable representations, which lasted some 300–400 years at Chinchawas.

In shape and relief style, the sculptures from Chinchawas and its vicinity are most similar to the sculptures of the Huaraz area (for example,

A   B   C   D

0   40
cm

Antajirca and Pongor) and from the Cordillera Negra to the south (for example, Cajamarquilla and Marcacunca). All four major Huaraz formal types are represented in the Chinchawas assemblage: vertical slabs, horizontal slabs, quadrangular panels, and tenon-sculptures. Most of these sculptures are decorated only on one face with bas-relief carving and incision. One notable difference, however, is that anthropomorphic statues sculpted in the round, common to the Huaraz and Aija area, are not found at Chinchawas.

FIGURE 39. Vertical slab sculptures documented at Chinchawas: (a) sculpture s38; (b) sculpture s9; (c) sculpture s10; (d) sculpture s14. Nearly all vertical slabs depict frontal anthropomorphs and are associated with the chullpa tombs in the funerary sector.

The data suggest the existence of a local Recuay sculptural tradition linking sites in Aija, Cajamarquilla, Chinchawas, and Huaraz. It appears to be most concentrated in a zone encompassing the Cordillera Negra region between the Casma and Huarmey headwaters and greater Huaraz. Typically associated with elites and political-religious centers, the monoliths at Chinchawas and other nearby sites demonstrate that even small village settlements made and used sculptures in the Recuay tradition.

THE NORTHERN CALLEJÓN DE HUAYLAS

Fewer sculptures are known from the northern Callejón de Huaylas. The more prominent cases include tenon-heads at a number of chullpa sites. Six large heads were reported during investigations at the large complex of Katiamá near Caraz (Zaki 1987). Photographs of the large chullpa at Katiamá featured three or four heads in situ. They are rectangular-block feline heads typical of the Callejón de Huaylas and specifically of chullpa mortuary monuments. Similar tenon-head sculptures are known from other chullpa sites, such as Sahuanpuncu and Wilkawaín. Little is known about the sculpture in the northern Cordillera Negra (upper Nepeña, Santa).

East of the Cordillera Blanca

Recuay stone sculpture from the region east of the Cordillera Blanca is much less well known and documented than for the Callejón de Huaylas and the Pallasca region. Nevertheless, it is possible to chart regional developments centered on certain river drainages.

THE PUCHCA DRAINAGE

In the southern portion of the Conchucos, Schaedel (1952: 188–196) reported approximately fifty sculptures with "Huántar" and "Huántar peripheral area" provenience, associated mainly with the towns of Huántar, Huari, and San Marcos in the Río Puchca drainage. The style is mainly composed of small, flat vertical slabs, which combine simple bas relief and decorative incision (also Diessl 2004: 112–113; Espejo Núñez 1957). The slabs mainly feature a single anthropomorphic figure. Special emphasis is given to the head and facial features; the neck is often graced with a fanlike collar or neck ornament. Limbs and hands are rendered in a simple manner: thin and with few curves. In technique and design they resemble some of the "Diminutive style" sculptures of the Callejón de Huaylas and Huaraz. Overall, Schaedel (1952: 196) attributed "Huántar style" sculptures to Recuay groups.

THE YANAMAYO-SIHUAS DRAINAGES

A small corpus of known sculptures in the northern Conchucos region has important relationships and implications for Recuay-period groups. Collections in Pomabamba and Piscobamba include several realistic tenon-head sculptures of humans, probably male warriors with elaborate helmets/headdresses characteristic of the northern Ancash area and farther north (Horkheimer 1944; Kroeber 1950).

The region around the towns of Yanama, San Luis, and Chacas has also produced stone sculpture with relationships to the Recuay tradition (Márquez Zorilla 1965; Schaedel 1952; Wegner 2000, 2001b, 2002). These include vertical and quadrangular slabs and tenon-heads. Although anthropomorphic depictions predominate, a number of notable representations of mythical and zoomorphic figures are also present. The felines, serpents, and frontal heads with appendages, in particular, have strong associations with Recuay-tradition imagery (Herrera 1998: figs. 5, 6). The carving includes a range of techniques and is of variable quality. Some of the less elaborate designs use low incisions. This can be attributed to the time depth of the sculptures as well as the lack of a strongly unified style. Nearly fifty sculptures have been identified in the region, with local specimens of the Pallasca style and two new stylistic groupings. The diverse styles of sculptures are most likely the result of multiple independent production centers (Herrera 2003: 123).

Pallasca

One of the most vibrant Recuay sculptural styles developed in northern Ancash, in the province of Pallasca. It centered in the Cabana region, especially in and around the vicinity of the Pashash site. Impressive sculptures had already been reported from the region by Charles Wiener (1880), who had illustrated various examples in his travel volume *Pérou et Bolivie*. Schaedel (1952) later compiled a detailed description and analysis of over eighty sculptures under the category of "Pallasca style." These included a number of sculptures found in the modern town of Cabana, many of which were said to have been from the nearby site of Pashash (fig. 40).

The stylistic and chronological relationships of the corpus were fur-

FIGURE 40. Vertical slab sculpture, probably from Pashash. The low relief shows typical features of splayed anthropomorphs: a central cross, serrated head appendages, and a diamond-shaped torso. Above the figure are several bodiless heads. (Museo Arqueológico de Cabana)

FIGURE 41. (*Left*) Vertical slab sculpture showing a warrior figure, probably from Pashash. The figure holds a long mace and trophy head, wears a headdress with a forehead crescent and upturned feather-like elements, and chews a wad of coca in his right cheek. (Museo Arqueológico de Cabana)

FIGURE 42. (*Right*) Sculpture of a Recuay crested animal, probably from Pashash. Note the head and tongue appendages which terminate as triangular heads. (Museo Arqueológico de Cabana)

ther clarified by archaeological excavations (Grieder 1978; Smith 1978). Through iconographic analysis, the researchers were able to make comparisons between the sculptures and stratified Recuay ceramic materials. This correlation helped to demonstrate the contemporaneity of different pottery types with the sculptural imagery.

The Pallasca area assemblage includes very fine pieces of sculpture, including tenon-sculptures, vertical slabs (figs. 40 and 41), and quadrangular panels. The relief carving is especially notable for its variable depth and precision (fig. 42). Schaedel (1952: 202) reported on a Pallasca-style sculpture of a standing warrior figure from Urcón, which he praised as "one of the most impressive bas-reliefs of South America." The stone-carving techniques were also varied, leading Schaedel to suggest different styles based on the height, finish, and degree of realism of the reliefs.

The form and design of Pallasca-style sculptures and those of the Callejón de Huaylas differ in many ways. Tenon-heads are common in both areas; but while feline heads are more common in the southern Recuay area, for example, they are less frequent in the Pallasca region. In contrast, human tenon-heads of warriors, sometimes very naturalistic in finish, are more prominent in the Pallasca style (Tello 1929; Wiener 1880: fig. 46). Horizontal slabs or lintels are not as common in the northern

Recuay area and, when present, rarely show the central figure theme of a frontal anthropomorph flanked by two felines. Finally, sculptures in the round (statues) were apparently not popular outside the Huaraz and Aija areas.

The Pallasca sculptures demonstrate a great range of designs and themes. In addition to themes shared by other sculpture-producing Recuay groups (such as splayed anthropomorphs on vertical slabs, double-headed figures, and crested animals), Pallasca sculptors preferred different sorts of images, including birds, bodiless heads, heads with appendages (fig. 43), and more abstract motifs (for example, step designs, rainbows, and whirling crosses) (fig. 44). Owls (for example, on tenon-sculptures) are far less prominent elsewhere in the ancient Recuay world.

Because analogous motifs could be found on the pottery, Grieder (1978: 183–184) postulated that the ceramic designs of Pashash owed their character to representational standards set by local stone sculpture. Given the strong Recuay association with imagery, as well as the association with extremely wealthy offerings in the La Capilla tomb, Grieder (1978: 182) concluded that the production and use of Recuay monolithic stone-carving and other "Great Art" resulted from the rise of theocratic elites and their patronage of the arts (also Smith 1978: 53).

FIGURE 43. (*Left*) Quadrangular panel sculpture of a bodiless head with four appendages, probably from Pashash. The head appendages emerge out of the ears and take the form of profile creatures. (Museo Arqueológico de Cabana)

FIGURE 44. (*Right*) Quadrangular panel sculpture of a whirling cross, probably from Pashash. Several of these sculptures are known, suggesting they were mounted together for an impressive façade. (Museo Arqueológico de Cabana)

Related Areas

Stone sculpture was also produced in various areas near the margins of the Recuay heartland. In the Santiago de Chuco area (southern La Libertad department, just north of Ancash), sculptures resembling those of the Pallasca style have been reported, though none were found in situ. These include realistic tenon-heads of helmeted warriors, images of crested animals, and panels with geometric designs that sometimes have associations with Recuay-related pottery (Horkheimer 1944; Pérez Calderón 1988, 1994; Wiener 1880).

The sculpture area of Huambo, named after a village near Conococha along the southern margins of Ancash Department, is known for a series of stone heads and relief panels, including zoomorphic figures and geometric designs. The heads are without tenons, with simple carving emphasizing the nose and eyes. Many of the sculptures were said to have come from the site, also known as Huambo, probably from the walls of a circular structure (Schaedel 1952; Soriano I. 1947). Although the heads are not common, slabs with profile felines and geometric designs (for example, the rainbow design) connect Huambo to sculptural traditions in Huaraz and the Cordillera Negra, such as Chinchawas.

Tenon-sculptures and slab sculptures have been reported at Tinyash (Antúnez de Mayolo 1941; Falcón and Díaz 1998; Ravines 1984). The tenon-sculptures are of two types: anthropomorphic heads, which are heavily eroded, and "rosetones," round blocks with a flat frontal surface. Several horizontal slabs with depictions of bodiless heads as well as a profile feline have been found. Finally, the best-known monolith at Tinyash is a large vertical slab (2.5 by 0.9 meters) with a representation of an anthropomorph carrying a long club with a mace-head and a trophy head.

These cases are not well defined enough to warrant definitive conclusions regarding cultural affiliations, but they are important to show the forms of stylistic interaction at the margins of the ancient Recuay world. What seems to relate the sculptural production especially to Recuay in these three cases is a common interest in mounting sculptures on walls of special constructions and a shared iconographic inventory of feline and warrior imagery.

Manufacture and Materials

Culture history and iconography have dominated the discussions of Recuay stone sculpture, while their production has received only limited attention. In particular, relatively little information is available on how raw blocks were quarried, transported, and then worked. Recuay carvers used a range of stone for the sculptures. They preferred igneous rocks, especially those with fine-grain mineral matrices: granites, granodiorites, trachytes, andesites, and porphyritic andesites. Most sculptures use stone which ranges from a light gray to gray to greenish gray in color (Lau 2006b; Schaedel 1948b: 70, 1952: 301ff.; Soriano I. 1950; Tello 1929: 76).

It is possible that special types of blocks of exotic stone were preferred, but the available evidence indicates that most carvers probably acquired blocks from nearby quarries, given the costs of transport. The likely use of local stone stands in contrast to other major sculptural programs, such as at Chavín de Huántar and Tiwanaku (e.g., Rowe 1967). In these cases, large blocks of specially valued material were imported at great expense and labor. Fine-grained andesites and other light-colored igneous rocks were used at Chinchawas, though sandstones, limestones, and shales are also available locally (Bodenlos and Straczek 1957; Cobbing et al. 1981). Although suitable rock can be found nearby as outcrops, the investigations did not encounter evidence for local quarrying.

Large quantities of rock debris and possible monolith preforms may be evidence of production at the Walun site on the eastern side of the Cordillera Negra, near Huaraz (Mejía Xesspe 1941). The site, near multiple ancient and modern roads, consists of several large, domelike geological formations, with suitable outcrops for quarrying.

With the exception of the tenon-sculptures and statues sculpted in the round, the wide majority of Recuay monoliths are sculpted only on one side. This is consistent with the interpretation that most Recuay sculptures were mounted on walls of special constructions. While some sculptures were almost certainly load-bearing, such as horizontal slab lintels and large jamb sculptures, many monoliths are fairly thin and decorated on only one face, suggesting that they were mounted as veneerlike elements on masonry walls.

For larger assemblages, a comparison of dimensions indicates that certain groups or regions shared basic formal tendencies. For example, Schaedel (1952: 166) noted that the width of anthropomorphic sculptures (statues) of the Huaraz Convex style was very often approximately two-thirds their height. This is consistent with the data from nearby Chinchawas, where vertical trapezoidal slabs showed a proportion of roughly 3:5. For horizontal slabs, the ideal width to height proportion is slightly under 3:1 (Lau 2006b).

Recuay tradition sculpture is characterized by a diversity of finishes. Presumably this is due to a number of interrelated factors: the type of stone, local traditions in making, and the ability/dispositions of the sculptor. For example, some areas are typified by higher relief, such as the Bold Flat or Bold Salient styles described for the Pallasca/Cabana region. In these styles the sculpted image extends toward the viewer from the background. The Pallasca region is also known for a "negative" style, where the bas-relief design is produced by careful removal of rock in the background (Schaedel 1952: 214).

Still other areas preferred sculpting "in the round": removal of rock and/or the carving occurs on all surfaces. Sculptures using this technique were presumably freestanding and were made to be appreciated by people circulating around them. Decorative treatment on the sculptures from the Huaraz and Pira areas favored very low bas-relief carving and/or incision techniques. With the exception of the Pallasca corpus, Recuay sculptors in general did not aim for perfectly flat surfaces or especially high relief.

Some sculptures may have been painted, although only a few examples have ever been reported (e.g., Schaedel 1952: 130). Certain sculptures also have recessed areas (for example, in the eyes or ears) that would have been appropriate to inlay with colored materials such as stones, marine shells, or other items.

The quarrying of the blocks was probably very similar to the process used to acquire material for stone constructions, at least in the initial stages. For the sculpting itself, copper metal tools were known and available to Recuay groups. But it is more likely that a combination of stone hammers made of hard stone was employed. For coarser work other rocks were probably used to chip away and even irregular surfaces. Flat surfaces were most likely created by using abrading blocks and sand, a technique popular among the Inka (Protzen 1992).

Surviving details on some monoliths provide clues to the process. Large grooves found on the lateral ends or the back side of several worked blocks at Chinchawas may be evidence of quarrying or transport methods. Unfinished sculptures, which may have been broken or abandoned in process, have also been found, as well as instances of errant gouges, mistakes, and initial stages of work (Lau 2006b). On several blocks it is possible to discern that during the initial stage the artist mapped out the composition and committed certain parts of the working surface for elements such as the body, head, and appendages. Completing the figures would consist of filling in the blocks with detail, through incision and general reduction.

Overall, the variability indicates that the stone-carving was not strongly regulated by stringent production criteria or rules. At least some variability may be due to changing stylistic preferences over the long duration of Recuay sculptural production. But the differences in form, representation, and quality also argue against mass production or distribution — for example, for a single center or from a single workshop. It seems more likely that the corpus of Recuay-tradition stone sculpture resulted from sporadic production, perhaps by part-time artisans affiliated with various coexisting social groups.

Other Stone Objects and Uses

Architectural Ornament

In addition to the monoliths with carved figures, collections and archaeological sites throughout highland Ancash include worked stones which were probably elements of architectural decoration, such as dressed stones and miscellaneous ashlars with straight bands and carefully cut holes. The stones were probably combined with other stones of the same kind to form masonry patterns or highlight specific places on walls.

Such blocks are of geometric designs, such as step motifs, whirling crosses (fig. 44), and rainbows. The pieces were almost certainly mounted on walls as architectural decoration. Little can be said of their meaning, but their symbolic significance should not be overlooked. Similar designs occur on ceramics, suggesting an importance across media (Grieder 1978).

Ground Stone Tools

The most prominent Recuay stone objects were carved monolithic blocks, but other types of notable stone artifacts are known. Broadly, these are classed as ground stone implements, some of which are large and bulky and some of which are more portable. Most likely served for everyday purposes, while others had more special episodic function. They are important because they constitute basic indices of the commitment to stone typical of Recuay groups.

Stone was especially useful in tasks at the household level. As in most ancient agrarian societies, the Recuay used stone for various household implements to transform different types of material for consumption or other purposes. These included manos (hand grinding stones) and *morteros* (mortars) of various shapes and sizes, usually made out of specially selected river cobbles. Larger tools included rocker grinders, used with both hands in a rocking motion, and *batanes* (large flat, stationary grinding slabs). The implements are commonly found in the food preparation areas of domestic dwellings and open spaces (fig. 11a, c).

The great range of ground stone tools reflects the diverse resources and ecological niches exploited. Batanes have been found as high as 4,150 masl (Yayno), which implies that local groups were actively processing crops such as maize and quinoa, probably cultivated at lower altitudes. Such slabs may also have provided surfaces to grind minerals and other materials, such as tempering inclusions for ceramics. Small morteros, with small but deep receptacles, likely served to process materials such as chili peppers, herbs, and roots; some may have been used in the preparation of hallucinogenic snuff and infusions.

Elaborate ground stone objects are also known. These seem to have been luxury items or to have been associated with elite prerogatives. Stone bowls, some plain and some depicting faces, are known from Pashash. Perhaps the most common luxury object in the Recuay world was the stone piruru (spindle whorl). Although some were made using fired clay, recycled sherds, or bone, the fanciest whorls were ground down from small pebbles, of different rock types and colors. They were sometimes decorated with small incisions and holes.

The Recuay also produced a range of fancy hafted forms. These include discoidal or ovoidal stone axe heads used for chopping trees or as a weapon. Another common mace-head form is star-shaped, for bludgeoning enemies with one of the pointed ends. Great care was given to selecting appropriate stones (often green or black) and producing lustrous weapons, which served in physical combat as well as in funerary practices as grave offerings.

Maquetas or Gaming Boards

The so-called maquetas (models) are another class of carved monoliths made by the Recuay. These are typically flat, rectangular stones, with a top surface featuring a number of squarish compartments arranged with a pair of opposed or complementary raised areas (fig. 45a). Some maquetas are circular, with round compartments. Notwithstanding the form, the arrangement of compartments is always symmetrical. Not only did their makers painstakingly carve the compartments out of stone, but their sides are occasionally decorated with incision or low-relief carvings (fig. 45b).[2] Most are fairly small and portable, measuring 30 centimeters on a side. The larger examples, about 50 cm long, are heavy and cannot be carried easily by one person.

At least eleven examples of maquetas have been reported, nearly all

FIGURE 45. Carved stone slabs, probably gameboards and/or schematic architectural representations: (top) ca. 30 cm long (Municipality of Chacas Collection); (bottom) ca. 24 cm long, from Pashash, showing incised bicephalic creature with tripartite body. The compartments and raised corner zones are symmetrically arranged and are carved with great precision, suggesting activities/spaces which engage opposing or complementary sides. They may be generic images of paired and dueling hilltop communities. (Museo Arqueológico de Cabana)

from the Ancash highlands (Bankmann 1981; Diessl 2004: 163; Smith 1977; Wegner 2000).[3] Several dozen more exist in Ancash collections. The few with good proveniences derive from Recuay contexts. Where present, the carved designs also bear similarity to imagery on Recuay pottery and stone sculpture. Besides their cultural affiliation, scholars debate whether such objects represent architectural models, counting devices (Wiener 1880), or gaming boards (Smith 1977; Wegner 2001b).

Architectural models and representations are not uncommon among ancient Andean cultures. A number of Central Andean groups, including the Moche, Chimu, Tiwanaku, and Inka, appear to have made models of constructions in stone, wood, and other materials. Many other cultures, including contemporaries of the Recuay (Moche, Gallinazo, and later Wari), represented architecture in three-dimensional modeled ceramics.

A problem with this architectural hypothesis is that, to date, no known Recuay complex matches any of the models (e.g., Castillo et al. 1997; Goldstein 1993; Swenson 2006). Given the consistent layouts of the objects, it would be expected that one or more Recuay sites would have a comparable arrangement. Indeed, the consistency of the plan suggests a more repetitive, systematic activity focused on the individual compartments. For this reason, people have suggested (e.g., Wiener 1880) that the maquetas were elaborate counting devices, to be used in conjunction with small pebbles, beans, or grains of maize, like a type of abacus.

The other likely alternative for their consistent symmetrical arrangement is that they were gaming boards (Smith 1977). The known specimens always have two opposable "home" areas, on opposite corners or adjacent to each other. These areas are usually raised and may consist of multiple levels or terraces. Each home area connects typically to seven compartments and a middle shared area, with one to four compartments. Most have a total of twenty-one compartments; at least one has twenty-five. In a reconstruction of "the religio-social-political structure that characterized the Recuay culture just prior to the Tiahuanaco [Wari] expansion," John W. Smith, Jr. (1977: 123) proposed that the game was probably played with dice and/or used game pieces (jaguars and soldiers) to kill opposing pieces and capture spaces. Smith compared the game to Aztec *patolli* and called the elevated compartments the "home" areas and the central compartments the "zone of conflict."

Like many other aspects of Recuay culture, the boards allude to the importance of warfare in local social life and cosmology. The two elevated areas (often stepped) probably refer generically to paired, perhaps dueling, hilltop mounds or centers rather than being a prototype for one specific settlement. The compartments around the raised portions may be modeled on plazas and walled enclosures typical of Recuay sites. The objects may follow a common pattern in board games of the ancient world (Finkel 2007), which uses the idiom of warfare for play (for example, a battle, enemy sides, pieces as warriors, and capture), in this case between two opposing but complementary communities. The notion of conventionalized encounters based on violence and complementarity is also fundamental to ritual combat events (tinku) known through ethnography of the Andean highlands (e.g., Gorbak et al. 1962; Platt 1986; Topic and Topic 1997; Urton 1993).

In some ways, focusing on or presuming only one purpose diminishes the significance of these objects as meaningful artifacts in their own right, each with its own history and context. For example, regardless of their exact function, given their rarity and occasional association with elaborate burials and politico-ceremonial centers, it is likely that the carved slabs were high-status items, probably limited to production and use by specific individuals of high rank.

It is also clear that the orderly, symmetrical arrangement probably relates to a general Recuay emphasis on duality in visual culture as well as the built environment. If the maquetas were in fact gaming boards, it is tempting to imagine elites, perhaps chiefly leaders, enjoying a confrontation of wits and chance on a gaming board. This might be considered a tinkuy, the term used to describe the union or common place for two complementary opposites. The relationship with funerary practices is also particularly suggestive: "death games," often played during the wake with dice or other thrown objects (such as beans and bones), are known from different parts of the Andes. It has been argued that the purpose of death games is to reestablish social order during times of loss. The games help to redefine social roles, while reinforcing sociocultural oppositions and providing opportunities for the chance determination of fates (e.g., Paerregaard 1987).

Stone Sculpture and Its Implications

Chronological and Formal Considerations

Because very few examples have been found in their original contexts or in excavations, stone sculptures throughout the Andes remain very hard to date. Most scholars rely on a combination of surface associations and comparison of imagery between sculptures and other media. On rare occasions sculptures can be associated with specific buildings, ceramics, stratigraphy, and absolute ages from radiocarbon data.

On the basis of stylistic seriation and associations, Schaedel (1948b: 77) offered a three-phase Recuay sequence for the Callejón de Huaylas. Phase 1 consists of mainly freestanding sculptures worked in the round, with continuous curvilinear incisions, often in serpentiform designs. Phase 2 includes freestanding sculptures with clearly defined anatomical lines and slab sculptures featuring felines but also sees the emergence of "puma slabs" showing central figures with flanked felines. In phase 3 sculptures evidence greater dependence on deeper relief and less emphasis on incision, and the representation of felines becomes more conventionalized. This phase reproduces many of the motifs found on Pashash pottery. Panels/slabs with framing borders and motifs such as the frontal head with appendages are common. Later developments include the use of tenon-heads.

The present evidence, including excavation data and radiocarbon associations, can clarify some of the culture-historical distinctions. Schaedel's phase 1 was essentially a stylistic hunch on the transition between Chavín and Recuay-style sculpture, which he surmised was associated with Huarás white-on-red pottery. A number of sculptures physically associated with white-on-red pottery do not feature the continuous curvilinear incisions, such as at Kekamarca and Marenayoc (Ponte R. 1999b; Roosevelt 1935: fig. 18).

The archaeological data from Chinchawas also help to illuminate chronological relationships of certain sculptural forms. It is clear now that monolithic stone-carving at the site extended beyond kaolin-producing cultures after A.D. 600. Horizontal slabs, tenon-heads, and panels with feline representations were produced and used during the late Early Intermediate Period into the Middle Horizon. Notably, the sculptures also feature various representations which combine elements of different "puma slab" types and periods. Meanwhile, the vertical slabs from the funerary sector of Chinchawas, almost all depicting single anthropomorphs, correspond mainly to the building and use of the chullpa monuments associated with the later Middle Horizon.

Fewer chronological associations for the sculptural styles of the northern Recuay area and east of the Cordillera Blanca have been found. This is in part due to lack of work, but the known corpus is also considerably smaller and varied in style. The sculptures from Pashash which bear iconographic similarities to the local pottery almost certainly date to the site's Recuay period, with absolute age associations ranging from A.D. 400 to 700. Later sculptures within this range may have certain design elements resembling those of late-period ceramic designs. This includes images of a profile zoomorphic figure with a crest head appendage with step designs and a triangular torso, sometimes bearing a cross motif.

Tenon-heads have a wide distribution in Recuay culture and are part of a broader north highland tradition of sculptural production. Their use began as early as Chavín (Bennett 1942; Burger 1992; Tello 1960). Examples from more distant Early Intermediate Period and Middle Horizon cultures occur in the highlands due north of Ancash and farther into the eastern interior (Bonavia 1968; Horkheimer 1944; Kroeber 1950; McCown 1945; Pérez Calderón 1988).

In the Recuay-tradition cases, some tenon-sculptures almost certainly adorned mortuary constructions in highland Ancash. In situ examples are known from chullpas at Tinyash (Ravines 1984; Thompson and Ravines 1973) and Katiamá (Alba H. 1946). Excavations at Katiamá also discovered a number of feline tenon-heads (Zaki 1987).[4] Miniature human tenon-heads also appear on the high-status architecture portrayed on Recuay modeled vessels. In general, positive correlations have been found between feline tenon-heads and chullpa constructions, especially in the Callejón de Huaylas. The distribution of anthropomorphic heads was more extensive, but they have few direct associations with funerary buildings. They also seem to have been produced throughout the Early Intermediate Period and into the Middle Horizon.

Variability and Social Differentiation

A number of regions in the Recuay heartland show particularly vigorous stone sculptural traditions. The most important include the areas of Pashash and Huaraz, with a smaller center in Aija. It is clear now that smaller agro-pastoral communities, with limited evidence for political centralization, also produced stone sculpture. This would imply that such groups recognized and shared the cosmology of the cult imagery found at political centers.

Yet it is important to note that not all Recuay groups relied on stone sculpture as a source of social identity. At some primary centers (such as Yayno) they are absent altogether or represent minor aspects of the material culture, suggesting that stone-carvings were local prerogatives rather than being a compulsory or necessarily emulated practice. The wide variation may be at least partly attributed to a pattern in which groups of different means and social standing participated in common cultural practices. Groups of varying status and resources supported the production of sculptures that distinguished each group. This was expressed particularly through their association with architectural spaces and formal properties of the sculptures, such as size, elaboration, and innovation in the carving.

Not surprisingly, a similar type of distribution and variability characterizes funerary structures, notably the chullpa mortuary monuments. Here the form, size, and quality of construction differ substantially, indicating contrasting scales of investment on the part of the ritual collective group (Lau 2006c). Local kin groups, most likely extended family or lineages, were probably responsible for their construction and maintenance. Like chullpas, the sculptures signaled the autonomy and distinction of specific collectivities.

The religious system in which monoliths took center stage facilitated a shared cultural identity with other groups of the Recuay commonwealth. Groups with very localized stone sculptural traditions were nested within this larger entity. By the same token, because each community's set of cult objects and ceremonial spaces was different, they were also a source of difference and exclusion. This is precisely because Recuay social identity and ways of doing things were bound to local ancestors.

Ancestor Effigies

Set in architecture and ceremonial spaces, the sculptures were objects of cult and veneration. The current evidence resonates with the model, first offered by Julio C. Tello, that most Recuay-tradition sculptures were integral elements of small but widespread cult practices. The human figures in the stone-carving likely represent deceased ancestors — specifically, deified leaders or important progenitors, who were venerated after death as sources of fertility, well-being, and sociopolitical legitimation (DeLeonardis and Lau 2004; Isbell 1997). In part this would help explain their occurrence in and around mortuary structures (Lau 2006b), as commemorative monuments of persons who built, used, or became interred in the chullpa (fig. 46).

Besides their physical associations, distinctive formal features of the carved figures support this interpretation. For one thing, each sculpture or figure is unique. The depiction of elements such as headdresses, crosses, and trophy heads may be related to the unique properties or achievements of specific individuals. Carved elements are also executed in variable configurations and quality; groups of effigy sculptures are rarely so standardized in style that they can be considered part of a single program or workshop of sculptural production. Rather, it is more reasonable to believe that sculptures were produced at different times, one by one, most likely following the irregular patterns associated with death and local dispositions to apotheosize known deceased.

The rendering of the figures' bodies is also instructive. The splaying of the figure, for example, constitutes a common way of denoting being

FIGURE 46. Pottery vessel showing a representation of ceremonial activity, likely a form of ancestor veneration, in front of a building. Three female figures raise cups to a male figure, who also holds a drinking vessel and presides in front of a heavily adorned building. Birds perch on the flat roof. The painted designs of the vessel and building resemble the frontal figures of vertical slab sculptures. (Museo Nacional de Arqueología, Antropología e Historia, Lima)

dead and/or honored in Andean art (Fraser 1966; Hill 2000). In some statues the seated position and placement of the hands and legs appear to reference the disposition of mummy bundles (Kauffmann Doig 1966: 82). This is further enhanced by the wide, masklike countenances with large eyes, jutting jaws, and a slit mouth, which resemble the statuelike figures on Recuay ceramic architectural scenes and ancient Peruvian mummies more generally. The wide, fanlike collars found on many sculptures were probably distinctive pieces of funerary apparel,[5] while the headdresses mark the transformation into an ancestral divinity.

Mimesis and the Materiality of Monoliths

In construing ancestors as being of stone, the Recuay drew from general Andean ontologies about divinity and ancestral bodies. Significant comparisons can be offered between Recuay practices and ancestor cults documented in the highland regions of Ancash and neighboring areas. In particular, colonial writings record the centrality of stone monoliths in native religion of the north-central highlands; they detail how Andeans considered stones and rock outcrops, modified or not, to be petrified ancestral persons and forces (Doyle 1988; Duviols 1977, 1986, 2003; Hernández Príncipe 1923).

One noted inquisitor wrote tersely about the practical logic of this view: "The Indians have histories of these idols, known by the elders in their traditions, and they say that the idols have inside them, though they may be of stone, a certain divinity that turned into stone, and for this reason they worship it" (Avendaño 2003 [1617]: 713, my translation). The stones were frequently located in the landscape, marking notable locales where momentous acts by the ancestor transpired, such as pacarinas (places of emergence), the establishment of villages and fields, and the opening of irrigation canals. The stone embodiments therefore establish the very grounds (both the physical place and the rationale) for ancestorhood.

For example, in the community of Cochillas (near Ocros), in southern Ancash, extirpators reported on local practices, describing "a large guanca of stone with the stature of a person, and it seemed that the stone had a hat on its head, and they called the idol Llacsachuco, who represented a Guari Indian who opened that irrigation canal // first and for this reason they worship it and in the same way they showed another idol named Nuñuyoq guaca who was a guanca two varas tall of a shrouded corpse [mummy?] and they worshipped him and had him in the middle of the fields because he was the first Guari Indian who worked those fields" (cited in Doyle 1988: 64–65). In essence, Recuay stone-carving materializes the unique potential of certain Andeans to transform into stone, the "lithomorphosis" frequently ascribed to ancestors (Duviols 1977, 1979). No doubt people were comparing ancestors to general physical qualities of the material: hard, of calm and unyielding bearing, enduring, and, where appropriate, anchored in the landscape (Tilley and Bennett 2004).

But stone as a substance was also valued for specific physical properties, such as the individual color, patterning, and surfaces. Native informants of the Cajatambo region recalled that their stone idols/petrified ancestors had the color of "partridge eggs" and "glowed like fireflies" (Doyle 1988: 65). In like manner, besides the mummy effigies, the sacred objects of idolatrous groups in the Recuay area often included crystals, unusual outcrops, and stones that were red and/or had peculiar forms; the shape of birds was often referenced (e.g., Hernández Príncipe 1923: 29–36). This point was almost certainly part of a wider ontology and materiality in the Andes, imagining the status of emergence, growth, and fertility through ovate, inchoate forms (such as eggs, seeds, potatoes, pebbles, and bundles), situated in earthly, womblike spaces (Allen

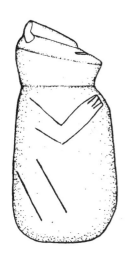  

front

FIGURE 47. Front and side views of a stone miniature, showing a seated anthropomorphic figure, recovered during excavations at Chinchawas; height 6.4 cm. Its form resembles flexed mummy bundles or Recuay statues representing ancestor bundles.

1997; Kemper Columbus 1990; Lau 2008; Makowski 2005; Salomon and Urioste 1991; Sillar 1996).

The excerpts cited above and the idolatries testimonies, more generally, indicate the main quality that I wish to ascribe to Recuay stone-carving and other images: they were animated or infused by supernatural potencies. The potency characterized certain things and places but also was able to flow from context to context. When mummies were burned outright by the Spanish priests, for example, the ashes and unburned remains were retrieved and treated as relics. At other times they were replaced by stone surrogates, transferring the potencies into other objects, generally smaller and concealable, for furtive rites. This capacity may be expressed in a miniature Recuay figurine found at Chinchawas, made of light gray stone, which appears to depict a mobile, pocket-sized mummy bundle (fig. 47). As an effigy of an effigy, it almost certainly served as a potent extension of the original.

The ascription of supernatural qualities to certain Recuay stone objects resonates with their archaeological contexts. The placement of sculptures in ceremonial spaces, for example, was to enable the interaction of the living with the figures in stone. To be sure, this occurred largely through the actions of the living participants, in the form of offerings, libation, and other venerative activities. But the sculptures also participated, for they were recipients and witnesses of the action. Further analogies with the early Spanish records suggest that Recuay effigies may have been consulted, dressed, danced with, and indulged as if they were living (e.g., Arriaga 1968 [1621]; Cobo 1990 [1653]). The agency of Recuay monoliths derived from their status as mediators for crucial physical interactions between social beings, made of stone or of flesh (Gell 1998).

To learn how the Recuay understood the stone sculptures we need to consider their production and use contexts as well as what the Recuay did with them. But if the basic questions of where and how Recuay sculptures were made remain unclear, we have even less evidence regarding the sculptor. Unlike the pottery vessels, sculptures never have explicit maker's marks. One Spanish inquisitor, however, noted that the making of the stone and metal idols was accomplished by specialists and that they were frequently "sold" (Avendaño 2003 [1617]: 715–716); in another passage, he wrote that the painting and fashioning of cult objects were accomplished by the specific ritual group (ibid.: 718).

Recuay sculptures, in the last analysis, are artifacts made by human hands and knowledge. Even beyond qualities attributed to "lithomorphosis," stone should not be regarded as an inert material (Allen 1998; Paternosto 1996; Protzen 1992). It is actively invested with labor, being quarried, transported, modified, fitted, and carved. Stone-carving likely drew from local value systems which articulated technical knowledge and finely made things in the Central Andes. The classic examples of this are expressed in metalwork or textiles, where certain technical procedures were adopted to highlight specific physical properties or expertise, frequently unnecessarily or at high costs. A key desire was to introduce or enhance a "technological essence" (for example, the color gold or a woven design) throughout the substance and structure of an object, animating seemingly inanimate substances (Lechtman 1980, 1984, 1993). For example, Penny Dransart (2002) compares camelid fleece to water. In stone-carving, as a reductive technique, the essence of the material is neither alloyed nor woven into the object. But this essence may be a latent potency that emerges in the object's creation through work. Recuay stone-carving, like other Andean technical systems, probably imparted specific meaning to key materials in art and technology when converted and fashioned into artifact forms.

Discussions of native beliefs about materials and creation are critical here (Duviols 1978; Salomon 1991; Taylor 1976). In the native Quechua myths and traditions of Huarochirí, compiled in the early seventeenth century, Frank Salomon (1991: 16) notes that "all things have their vitalizing prototypes or *camac*, including human groups; the *camac* of a human group is usually its *huaca* of origin. Religious practice supplicates the *camac* ever to vitalize its *camasca*, that is, its tangible instance or manifestation." For example, the small camelid and maize figurines typical of many late prehistoric sierra sites were made specifically to increase the fertility of camelid herds and maize yields, respectively. The practice of ancestor cults and creation of stone effigies in Recuay culture was probably related to this pattern, whereby the living, by way of descent and access to ancestral camac, were charged with the right of creating simulacra of their ancestors: bringing entities of the same group into being.

This helps to explain not only the practice of effigies but also their particular form. Michael Taussig (1993: 8, 13, 16) considered why the wooden curing figurines among the Cuna in Panama assume the appearance of Europeans. His explanation is relevant here:

> Why bother carving forms at all if the magical power is invested in the spirit of the wood itself? And indeed, as our puzzling leads to more puzzling, why is embodiment itself necessary? . . . the important point about what I call the magic of mimesis is the same — namely . . . the making and existence of the artifact that portrays something gives one power over that which is portrayed . . . the model, if it works, gains through its sensuous fidelity something of the power and personality of that of which it is a model.

In the Recuay case, the "power" resides not in the alterity of ethnic others but in divine progenitors. Like the animal and plant effigies, the human images are to intervene, with effect, in their domain of the living. Just as the descendants realize ancestral effigies in image and thought, they are their progeny, the beneficiaries of their desirable, vitalizing interaction, past and present.

Conclusions

Since the time of Tello, stone sculpture has been critical to the analysis of Recuay art and culture. Although early works focused nearly exclusively on their stylistic classification, chronology, or iconography, subsequent literature examines the functions and significance of the monoliths in Recuay society. The social role of Recuay-tradition sculptures, especially in ceremonial practices and in reckoning identity, has played an increasing part in interpretation.

This chapter has focused on the distribution and social significance of Recuay stone sculpture. The great variability in the distribution and character of stone sculpture relates to widespread but highly localized religious practices based on ancestor veneration. The Recuay case demonstrates that monolithic stone sculpture is not limited to strongly differentiated societies and that production is not associated exclusively with central places.

The foregoing discussion has reviewed the distinctive forms and contexts of the sculptures. The ways in which they were used and received provide a fuller account of things and spaces in ancient Recuay society. I argue that the stone-carvings (of humans) were not simply perceived as representations of ancestors but served as ancestors. Thus they are reimagined as active and actively experienced things.

Ultimately, the social interactions between humans and monoliths form only part of a larger and distinctive system of material engagements with stone. In all these cases the Recuay endeavored to employ stone in various modes to alter the nature of other, usually more pliant and susceptible, things: grinding stones for plants, stones for walls, maceheads for dealing a killing blow, whorls for camelid fibers, and mimesis of fleshly bodies.

CHAPTER SEVEN

Chiefly Worlds in Artworks and Imagery

Imagery is understood here broadly as the iconographic, decorative, and formal elements of objects, especially those which have representational effect or desire. Shared imagery was vital to Recuay social life, being pervasive in the look and practice of community ceremony and politics. In one sense, it is the fundamental element of a Recuay corporate art style. This is somewhat paradoxical since the imagery was crucial in fashioning social selves in Recuay society, distinguishing individual rank, identity, and authority within and between communities. On another level, because of the emphasis across multiple media, many of the analytical categories used in this evaluation (such as "sculpture," "style," "art," "chiefship," and "feasting") can now be explored as intermingled elements of small but integrated cultural projects in which objects and their imagery were vital.

My general proposal is that Recuay artworks — sculptures, figural ceramics, monuments, textiles — centered on chiefs and their social relations. They often adorned and represented chiefs but in doing so helped to make them as well. This proposal fuels a principal methodological assumption of this book: the interpretation of the individual objects of different media is enhanced when they are studied together.

One of the bases for chiefly status in Recuay society was warfare. Leaders construed themselves as warriors (fig. 48). And a warrior or warfare "culture"— manifested in weapons, imagery, and fortified architecture — emerged among groups to negotiate identity within a political milieu rife with conflict. The rise of Recuay political complexity coincided with a warfare aesthetic.

The Recuay also developed a concern for the human body and its capacity for action and symbolism. Much of the imagery was to commemorate specific individuals and their networks of social relations; the representations followed a number of shared formal conventions for portraying the human body and its potential for ancestorhood. Furthermore,

FIGURE 48. Modeled effigy jar of a chiefly warrior figure. The figure holds a weapon and shield and wears ear spools and a headdress adorned with trophy hands, all denoting his high warrior status. (Museo Nacional de Arqueología, Antropología e Historia, Lima)

complex surficial imagery covered or affiliated bodies, physical and symbolic, with a "social skin," which extended forms of chiefly agency and helps to explain their ubiquity.

In this chapter I focus on the miniature worlds represented on ceramics. The pots were not simply vessels for liquids. They were perceived as embodiments of chiefly leaders, their physical and symbolic houses, and containers for their potency. Recuay groups trusted in the notion that their chiefly leaders were the physical representatives of their community (house) and its prosperity. The chiefly imagery works in bold homologies, marking and promoting certain equivalencies among vessels, bodies, and buildings. This occurs both in formal terms and in the technology of making, which privileged key materials and special enriched surfaces.

The final section of this chapter examines the imagery of animals and humans. We see intertwined relationships, especially between human and feline figures. It is an imagery of authority and transformation, of potent beings with mutable forms or beings who exert change to other subjects, often through violence. I contend that these are in essence chiefly metaphors.

The veneration of ancestor effigies was central to the religion of Recuay groups. Their presence was vital, because political ideology, art production, and the products of labor mobilization were invested in leaders who drew legitimation and economic power from genealogy. What "made" a chief in Recuay culture was a special engagement with other social beings: subjects, women, animals, and divinities.

The main venues for the use of Recuay artworks were funerary ceremonies and festive public events. Their imagery and objects mediated relations between people and things as well as between people and people. In examining the images, I attempt to explain the need and function of artworks in Recuay society and also the specific character of their forms and imagery.

About Recuay Chiefs

This chapter pivots on the discussion of chiefly representations, so it is useful to be explicit about what I mean here by the term "chief." First, it is a contrivance derived from a number of comparative examples and personal choices to help understand Recuay archaeological patterns. Perhaps the most valuable comparisons are to be found in early colonial documents about the caciques and curacas (native lords) of Ancash (Cook 1977; Espinoza Soriano 1964, 1978; Hernández Príncipe 1923; Millones 1979; Varón Gabai 1980, 1993) and of neighboring highland and coastal areas (Julien 1993; Netherly 1977; Ramírez 1996; Topic 1998). Particularly important are the references to the socioeconomic foundations of local authority — herds, land, and kin — as well as their spatio-demographic arrangements.

I also find compelling the various documentary accounts of chiefly leaders in other parts of South America, especially in the Northern Andes and lowland Amazonia (Heckenberger 2007; Reichel-Dolmatoff 1985; Salomon 1986; Steward 1946; Steward and Faron 1959) as well as farther abroad (Oliver 2005; Sahlins 1985; Valeri 1985). Their physical and symbolic status at the head of descent groups and estates (corporate bodies and corporations, such as "houses") is also relevant to the Recuay case (Carsten and Hugh-Jones 1996; Gillespie 2000; Houston and Cummins 2004; Lévi-Strauss 1983; Moore 2005; Oyuela-Caycedo 1998). Thus I employ the terms "chiefs" and "native lords" (curacas/caciques) somewhat synonymously in this chapter. These terms draw attention to what such postholders do and represent rather than where their respective societies might fall in some evolutionary ladder or time line.

In short, Recuay chiefs were leaders of large and small communities who drew socio-religious authority through specific ancestors. They were physical, biological beings, but I suggest that they were also embodiments of ancestors, as special representatives of a genealogical line. Thus Recuay chiefs were part of historical flows but were implicated in, indeed perpetuated, a mythical kin-based order in which they assumed roles as symbolic centers of a given group articulated by real or fictive descent.

My use of the term "chiefs" presumes their capacities in political and ritual domains, especially in public, funerary, and commensal ceremonies. They were probably influential over ritual practices and ritual practitioners. I also presume that Recuay chiefs held authority over a corporate body tethered to land and estates, with command over a sizable share of resources: crops and herds, kin relations, prestige goods, and/ or labor. Previous chapters have described the archaeological correlates of rank in Recuay society. Let us now examine how chiefly persons were contemplated and fashioned through material culture.

A Warfare Aesthetic

Recuay art and imagery emerged under the context of intergroup competition during the first millennium A.D. They flourished at a time when warriorhood emerged as a critical form of elite ideology and cultural production throughout the Central Andes. It is perhaps not surprising that much of the artistic expression and labor investment in the celebration of chiefly elites (and ancestors) appears to treat the practice of warfare and associated complexes, especially hunting, trophy-taking, and sacrifice.

Warfare was more than just a side or ceremonial activity. Fortified hilltop settlements were the predominant loci for economic and cultural life in the Recuay world. Although we have little evidence for physical combat, living in a fort and keeping a safe distance against raids, ambivalent neighbors, and theft clearly shaped the ancient mind-set. In particular, warfare formed its own aesthetic in material culture and was embedded in local understandings of leadership.

In addition to the culture's emphasis on weaponry, fortifications, and defensive settlement systems, the imagery of ceramics and stone sculpture consistently depicts warrior figures with weapons such as the mace, club, spear, and shield. They also chew coca (fig. 41) and hold small bags (fig. 34). Warriors also wear a range of headgear, probably denoting a form of military rank or achievement, perhaps warriors who have killed or captured enemies (Métraux 1949). Trophy heads were also prominent emblems of success in warfare: adorning headdresses or held in the hand, attached in small bags, or used as pectorals. Regardless of whether these were bona fide warriors or pretenders, warriorhood was wholly valorized in the ancient Recuay world. Early colonial accounts of groups in highland Ancash also suggest that local groups were warlike (e.g., Espinoza Soriano 1964: 12–13).

Evidence indicates that the Recuay shared commonalities in the thinking and doing of warfare with neighboring cultures. For example, Recuay artists showed the defeat and disabling of enemies in the same way as the Moche (and many other cultures) did, by grasping a frontal lock of their hair. The imagery seems to have privileged face-to-face contests, where clubs and shields were preferred over long-distance weaponry and combat methods. Another crucial connection concerns the imagery of warriors with elaborate accouterments and equipment, sometimes bearing hands and bodiless heads, probably as references to trophies of defeated enemies (Benson 1984; Disselhoff 1956; Lau 2004a; Schuler-Schömig 1979, 1981).

Some evidence indicates that enemies were viewed as a kind of enemy "prey" and that the activity of war was like a type of hunting, a common association in South American cultures (e.g., Descola 2001; Donnan 1997; Viveiros de Castro 1992). Besides the physical work which articulates many different notions (masculinity, teamwork, skill and stealth, preparation, danger, and violence to other beings), war and hunting in the Andean past seemed to emphasize the incorporation of external vitalities. Warfare can therefore be understood as a vital source for male personhood and chiefly standing in the Recuay world. This is why the male figures in Recuay art were almost always portrayed as warriors — a role that they chose themselves or that was given to them in commemoration by their descendants. Much warrior ideology was keyed to attire and headgear, which visually incorporated special elements from powerful prey/enemy beings, specifically in the form of human and animal trophies.

Architecture and representations of architecture constituted another key expression of the commitment to warfare. The elaborately modeled and painted fortified buildings in the ceramic architectural effigies resemble the high-walled compounds and fortifications found in the major Recuay settlements. Many of these constructions were overbuilt if they were only for defensive purposes; and the fortified form and features would be unnecessary if the construction was only ceremonial in function. At places such as Yayno and Pashash, the architects reveled in the materiality of their elaborate stonework, with its impregnable monumental walls, sloping batter, and fine stonemasonry arrangements of different hues and sizes.

It might be conjectured that Recuay leaders and buildings were also reinforced through their "chiefly" exteriors — a form of psychological combat. Just as chiefs desire through their attire, the enclosures of Yayno and Tinyash are overwhelming in the monumental elegance of their fortified façades. Such surfaces emerged as a cultural strategy, a technology, in the highly competitive milieu of highland Ancash during the first millennium A.D. (see the discussion below).

In addition to their strategic/military purposes, fortifications were the settings for structuring certain lifestyles, especially those promulgated by elites. Fortified hilltop centers should not be interpreted simply as defensive, with a single, fixed purpose and/or occupation; fortifications were often centers for community life and the locales in which most Recuay people were socialized.

Overall, the defensive posturing in settlement patterns complements the provocative imagery of Recuay artworks, reflecting sociopolitical conditions in the north highlands, in which the threat of intergroup violence was pervasive and capitalized upon by chiefly leadership ideology. Just as Homeric epics, medieval armor, and war memorials are highly elaborate and distinctive expressions of a society's engagement with warfare, various elements of Recuay culture — from vessels to architectural effigies to fortifications — express local value systems that make warfare a destructive yet prestigious and creative activity.

On Bodies: The Human Form of Persons, Places, and Things

Recuay represents the earliest highland style of the Central Andes to represent humans on a regular basis. Humanlike figures abound in the imagery of Chavín, the predecessor of the Recuay in highland Ancash, but these might best be called humanoid, given their mythical features. Such features referenced supernatural qualities or the potential for divine transformation. Humans appeared now and again in the stone sculpture and pottery of other highland Andean cultures, such as Pukara, Yaya-Mama, and Huarpa. But Recuay appears to have spearheaded a systematic interest in human representation of both men and women in the sierra. Just like a number of coeval coastal cultures, the Recuay used the human body as a crucial symbolic locus. This important artistic development was taken up later in the Middle Horizon with the spread of Wari culture from Ayacucho.

The innovation in reckoning and extending the human body into artistic representation holds important implications for reconstructing the social and political life of the Recuay. In particular, it elucidates how forms of social inequality, gender, and worldview are embodied in overtly human form through things and activities (e.g., Classen 1993; Houston et al. 2006; Joyce 1998). Perhaps most importantly, it is one of the few lines of evidence about ancient local understandings of such categories: the artistic representations help us reckon how Recuay people felt about themselves and social others. Viewed diachronically, they also reflect new forms of ranking and political strategies during the Early Intermediate Period, while eschewing preceding Early Horizon modes.

Personal, Interactive Monuments

The Recuay human form manifests principally in ceramics and stone sculpture. In both media the human figure is restricted to certain representational conventions, fixed themes or scenes, and a limited range of actions and/or action upon them. Recuay stone sculpture, in particular, is typified by a small repertoire of designs. Human and anthropomorphic figures constitute the primary subject, followed by feline and more abstract, geometric representations.

Human figures are almost always depicted frontally. They are shown in a standing or splayed position, with their legs spread apart. Others are depicted as sitting, sometimes cross-legged or with the legs tucked in, with their hands grasping their knees. While the figures may be portrayed cross-legged, foreshortening and other techniques are rarely used to show the superposition of body elements or perspective. Human figures also occur singly. Although they may be accompanied by feline/mythical creatures, very few examples of sculptures portray multiple humans or scenes of social interaction. Each stone slab was by and large the domain of one individual.

We do not have much evidence to consider representations of humans as shamans or priests, as the literature so often suggests. Furthermore, it is very unlikely that the imagery treats a single individual repeatedly. Rather, I believe that the stone-carved image marked a general honored status—ancestorhood—achieved by different individuals (Lau 2002). They were probably representations of celebrated progenitors, warriors, and leaders.

The imagery of stone sculpture highlights essentialized anatomical features: head, trunk, arms, genitalia, and legs. The main focus of Recuay sculptures is the head. It is portrayed frontally, ranges from a round to roundish triangular shape, and is always oversized. In Huaraz-style statues the head occupies nearly a third of the sculpture's height. The separation between the head and the torso is further emphasized by a tremendous lower jaw and chin. This transition often features the greatest removal of stone on sculptures and is especially marked when lit from above (fig. 33). Artists often exaggerated head elements, such as the size and shapes of the eyes, nose, and jaw. Noses are flattened and are rectangular, triangular, or *tumi*-shaped.[1] The wide-open eyes indicate that the figure is sentient and alert. In contrast, the artisans gave relatively little attention to the mouth and neck.

Overall, the rendering of the faces, especially of statues from Aija and Huaraz, resembles the form of funerary masks. The sloping planar aspect of the face, the massive jaw, and the eyes are all typical of masks used to adorn the heads of mummy bundles, such as along Peru's central coast and in the Chachapoyas region. Some Recuay sculptures, in other words, are most likely effigies of dead ancestors, sometimes in the form of funerary bundles.

The head often exhibits additional elements. These include ear spools (sometimes featuring a cross pattern) and great fanlike collars, probably a common type of mortuary adornment. The most important head ornamentation is the different headdresses worn by Recuay individuals. Some are round helmets, but the most common has a thick band adorned with different elements, including frontlets (human or animal heads), trophy paws or hands on either side, projecting round or square nubbins, and forehead crescents (fig. 34). The headdresses are also very pronounced on the sculptures featuring the central figure theme. The central figure on these often has a headdress or head appendages of a feline-serpent creature (*amaru*).

Human heads are frequently depicted disembodied in stone sculpture. Most often, single heads are portrayed as being pecked at or held by birds (Grieder 1978: figs. 145–147). Some reliefs feature multiple heads, as if collected in a box or container. Once disembodied, the heads are still powerful and desirable, but they appear to become objectified as dehumanized, vulnerable things which are seized. Most commonly, human figures hold heads, display them in bags, or hang them as body ornaments (fig. 41).

Recuay sculptors emphasized the sex of the human figures. Male sexual organs are presented as raised circles (usually one or three). Females may be represented by the presence of a notch in the lower pubis. Breasts are not customarily depicted. Males and females are further distinguished through apparel and accessories. In the Recuay sculptures from Aija (fig. 32) men are often shown as warriors wielding weapons, shields, and trophy heads. Women are sometimes represented with braided hair, a special type of shawl and associated pins, and pouches. In general, aside from the sexual organs, the postcranial elements are deemphasized. The limbs, for example, feature relatively little elaboration. On ceramics feet are frequently depicted as small projections extending away from the figure; sometimes they feature painted or incised toes. Footwear is rarely represented.

Overall, Recuay carvers worked human figures in a rigid, blocky style. Although some sculptures in the round were produced, most blocks are planar and were modified using a combination of bas relief and incision. Sometimes anatomical elements (heads, shoulders, limbs) are creatively configured and contorted to fit within the block or the action of the composition (fig. 37a). Kroeber (1949: 446, 1950: 195) observed that Recuay stone-carving was rarely naturalistic or "lifelike" and that the representations failed to render the figure "free from the boulder." He judges, rather pejoratively, that this reflected a lack of artistic skill and was a defect of the culture, holding sculptural verisimilitude as some type of yardstick of achievement.

Most Recuay stone-carving was meant to be set in buildings, which in part explains the focus on planar blocks. But the entanglement between stone and representation was more than simply a practical matter. A figure's essence was likely bound in the stone, for its enduring importance derived from being overtly made of stone and having stonelike qualities — divinities and ancestors are said to lithomorphose. Andeans could just as easily locate value or sacred essences in a pebble or a boulder as in fancy, finely made artifacts. Thus rendering a figure "free of the stone" need not have been a Recuay desire or imperative.

The medium of carving stone was ideal, because it fit well with the permanence and perpetual influence that ancestors were deemed to have. Lodged in buildings, in fields, and in ritual spaces in or near the village, the sculptures were monuments to place and territory. These ancestor effigies, male and female, assumed stonelike forms and characteristics:

anchored, heavy, and enduring. But in these nearby settings they were also interactive monuments, meant to be seen and engaged regularly. They were an idiom for remembering the past and, just as importantly, for experiencing and reproducing that past.

The Well-Attired Body

If stone was the material par excellence for expressing the place-based essence of ancestral monuments, ceramics acted as a much more pliable, portable, and surficially fertile medium for artistic expression. In particular, the human figure in ceramic ornamentation shows a greater range of forms, adornment, and potential for action. Both males and females are represented. Unlike the stone reliefs, however, they are not commonly depicted with sexual organs. Rather, the size, apparel, accouterments, and gestures of the figures enable determination of their gender and, more importantly, their relative positions and capacities.

MEN'S AND WOMEN'S WEAR

Some elements of male gear have already been described for stone sculpture. But men's wear becomes even more extravagant on pottery representations. The quintessential male garment is the shirt or tunic, which reaches down to at least the lower waist and more commonly to the thighs and knees. The front and back sides are decorated with elaborate designs: mythical beings and more geometric motifs. Sometimes the frontal designs are limited to the central part of the shirt or to two vertical bands (one band descending from each shoulder); more commonly, designs blanket the entire surface. Underneath, men often wear a skirtlike garment around the waist like a kilt, which drapes over the knee and flares outward (fig. 49). The basal border of this lower garment is often decorated with geometric designs, such as repeating triangles or step motifs. Over the tunic and skirt male figures sometimes wear a cloak, fastened near the neck and flaring at the hems, which frames a prominent triangular space around the chest and waist (fig. 50).

Male headdresses are also more detailed on ceramic representations. The great care in their forms and decoration suggests that these must have been very elaborate constructions in real life, probably made out of organic, perishable materials. There are a number of types. One of the most common is a kind of domed helmet and/or thick headband with one or more decorative projecting ornaments. Handlike or featherlike projections, occasionally scored, are sometimes laid flat, forming little brims (pl. 6); at other times they are attached vertically to the thick lower band

FIGURE 49. (*Top*) Modeled vessel of a male figure with a camelid. The male figure, wearing an animal effigy headdress and fringed ear ornaments, plays a flute, while next to him is a camelid with a rope around its neck. The representation likely commemorates a camelid sacrifice, a ceremonial practice common to native Andeans, perhaps in honor of the well-attired figure. (Staatliche Museen zu Berlin–Preussicher Kulturbesitz Ethnologisches Museum; photo by C. B. Donnan)

FIGURE 50. (*Bottom*) Modeled effigy jar in the form of a standing chiefly male. His headdress features upright trophy hand elements and a featherlike frontlet. The forehead projection also serves as the spout. The figure wears a cape-like garment which drapes over, only to form a curved triangular border around the front torso. The lower horizontal element represents the bottom fringe of his clothing. The jar and the regalia once featured resist-designs, now extremely faded. (Museo Arqueológico de Ancash, Huaraz)

(fig. 48). The heads and hands/paws of animals are common adornments —feline elements are most common, but birds are also shown. Human hands and serpents are sometimes used to adorn the base. A trophy head or a small blocklike projection is common on the front of the headband (forehead), while hand or paw elements are customarily found on the sides. Sometimes the frontal forehead projection also serves as the vessel's spout (fig. 50). In some cases the headdress mimics an entire body of the animal, with the wearer's head fitting directly into the animal's abdomen (fig. 49).

Several feathers or antlers may be inserted into the headdress just above the forehead. These may be made from different materials. Gold foil ornaments, including representations of plumed featherwork, for example, are known from Recuay burials (Wegner 1988). More commonly, the helmet is topped by a semicircular crest with radiating featherlike elements. The base is round or patty-shaped, encircling the wearer's head. Other examples are angular, with scored projections at the ends. Some tall, conical forms widen toward the top, while others consist of opposed step designs, a type found also on Gallinazo, Vicús, and Moche figures. Some unique headdresses are surmounted by marvelous crests, such as oversized versions of the fanlike element (fig. 51) or paired giant circles, resembling the eyes of an owl. Small anthropomorphic and animal figures, especially serpents and birds, are occasionally lodged within the headdress.

As in sculptures, male figures commonly wear ear ornaments. Usually these are round and painted with a central dot, a circle of dots with a dot in the middle, or an interior cross, dividing the circle into four wedges (sometimes with a dot in each wedge). The most elaborate ear ornaments have ridged or fringed outer edges as well as a central projecting element (fig. 49). Very few have been found in archaeological contexts, but some wooden examples exist. Metal ear ornaments are also known. In addition to whole spools, decorated metal discs and flanged edges were probably used to fashion composite earplugs (Grieder 1978: 129–131). The painted dots and the scored edges may refer to repoussé designs and scalloped/ fringed outer edges of metal pins. A central projecting figure, usually a mythical animal or human head, is also very common in Recuay metal pins.[2] Copper-metal alloys were the most common material for Recuay metalwork. Fancy ornaments were also made out of gold, sometimes in hammered sheets, such as frontlet ornaments and small circular laminas to be attached to clothing. Objects of copper-silver-gold composition are also known. In addition, the Recuay employed the technique of casting,

FIGURE 51. Modeled effigy of a male figure with a camelid. The male figure wears elaborate garments, ear spools, and a spectacular headdress, with feather-like plumes and painted mythical animal designs (from Lau 2000: fig. 10). (Museo Cassinelli, Trujillo)

probably the lost-wax method, to fashion personal items: pins and other ornaments, mace-heads, and axeheads.

The great diversity and elaboration of the head ornamentation suggest that it was a prominent indicator of social status among the Recuay, especially for males. Certain types of headdresses could only be worn by military leaders and captains (for example, among the Inka); they could be used to communicate their high rank and regional affiliation. Ear spools were worn only by high-status nobility, called fittingly *orejones*

FIGURE 52. Modeled effigy jar in the form of a standing chiefly male, flanked by two women. The female figures are represented frontally and wear low head coverings and tunics with a checkerboard pattern, which is usually reserved for women's apparel. The female figures also have face painting, just under their mouths. (Staatliche Museen zu Berlin–Preussicher Kulturbesitz Ethnologisches Museum; photo by C. B. Donnan)

(big ears). Also interesting is the great emphasis on animals in the headdresses. Perhaps this had something to do with titles or kin affiliations or with age/warrior grades. More generally, if body ornament concerns the disclosure of a person's "visible resources" for public interaction (Strathern 1979: 250), what could be more potent than incorporating elements of the outside world such as hard-won human and animal parts into an armature for the head, that locus par excellence of personal display?

In ceramics women also regularly wear luxury attire. Many designs worn by men can be found on the women's wear too. But some garments, patterns, and accouterments seem to have been favored by women. In contrast to males, headgear for women was more modest and spartan. Women most often wear a simple head covering (probably of textile fabric and thicker around the forehead), which falls over the neck and shoulders (figs. 28, 52). Plies of hair are also sometimes rendered in this manner.

Like men's faces, women's faces are almost always painted red, probably to distinguish a natural flesh tone.

Females typically wear a long tunic, which drapes down at least to the knees. Sometimes, as in the case of males, another garment is wrapped around the waist, like a flaring skirt. Women on pottery frequently wear a checkerboard design (Reichert 1978: 31). Large panels of the pattern can characterize the front or back sides of the outer garments. The shirts are sometimes fastened or adorned with garment pins (one on each shoulder). Most pins usually have circular nail-type heads (fig. 53). Some pins have alternative forms: a shaft with two curling anchorlike edges or a top view of the triangular heads. When affixed to garments, the sharp ends point toward the back, while the heads on the torso may be allusions to the figure's breasts. Many such pins made of copper-metal alloys and some of gold exist in collections, most from unprovenienced contexts. Some are plain, while others feature typical Recuay designs, especially double-headed serpents and other mythical figures.

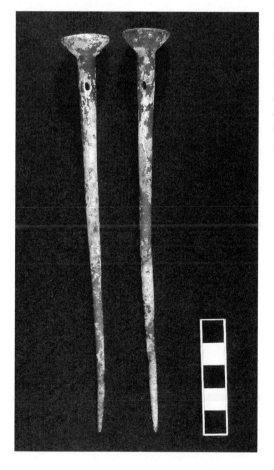

FIGURE 53. Copper-metal nail-head pins (*ticpis*) found as a pair in a Recuay burial cist at Poma-kayán. Thread run through the small holes attached the pins to the garments at shoulder-level. Recuay pins are also occasionally gold-plated and/or have conical heads, sometimes with cast designs. Note the slight size difference between the two elements of the complementary pair. (Museo Arqueológico de Ancash, Huaraz)

FIGURE 54. Modeled double-chambered effigy jar, in the form of a woman playing a drum flanked by a large avian, perhaps a duck. Note her slimmed waistline, cinched with a sash featuring a decorative circle pattern. (Staatliche Museen zu Berlin–Preussicher Kulturbesitz Ethnologisches Museum; photo by C. B. Donnan)

In ceramic effigies women are full-bodied like men, rotund like the globular vessel body. But often the potter constricted the vessel body to denote the slimming of the female waistline and accented this with a narrow sash or belt. The sash can be plain (pl. 5c) but frequently bears geometric designs (fig. 54), especially interlocking motifs. Although the faces of males and females are both marked by a dark red color, females regularly show additional face painting, usually in the form of a distinctive rectangular pendant beneath the mouth. The rectangle is typically in dark paint, painted with small light-colored designs, such as triangular heads and dots.

Overall, the ceramics and stone sculpture commemorated women and men of high chiefly status in Recuay society. The great conventionalization in clothing and accessories emphasizes the differentiation of individuals as well as the variable social roles accorded to men and women. Recuay individuals distinguished themselves from others on the basis of dress and the use of images.

Recuay imagery is typified by a suite of characteristic figural designs, which I treat as "iconic." The term is not employed here in the sense that these images or idols are worshipped. That meaning may perhaps apply for the Recuay, but at present this sense remains largely conjectural and secondary to my main usages. Rather, the iconic figures share in their strong emphasis of being separable and framed within distinct, modular fields. The term is useful because the designs are often regarded as representative of Recuay culture. Their capacity to be independent and exemplary images is the principal point here, and I contend that they articulated Recuay chiefly status in ancient times.

The imagery in question is of special beings who have both mythical and more naturalistic features. Because of substantial variability in representation, frequently on the same object or design field, it can be argued that these do not represent single divinities but form groups of cognate divinities or supernaturals. Indeed, some appear to change into other forms, and the image expresses only one status of its being. Six broad categories of such beings are distinguishable by their form.

Perhaps no one form in the ancient Andes is more identified with its culture than the crested animal (Group A), also sometimes called the "Recuay feline" (fig. 55a–b). The animal is most often represented as a quintessentially linear form. It is shown in a profile aspect, with large circular eyes, clenched claws on front and hind limbs, a tail, and a mythical appendage (crest) emerging from its head. The crest sometimes issues from the nose area and sometimes from the top of the head. It is frequently serrated or broken into segments with circular or half-circle finials, which can extend and arch over the animal's body. These representations are so varied that it is problematic to consider them all to be one creature or to be "felines" at all.

Scholars have debated the cultural origins and influence of Group A figures. Some prefer Recuay, while others point to north-coast origins in Salinar or Gallinazo (Bankmann 1988; Bruhns 1976; Mackey and Vogel 2003; Makowski and Rucabado Y. 2000; Nersesov 1987, 1993). Just as contentious is the identification of the animal prototype. It could be a fox, a dog, a viscacha, or a feline; even the feline may have different sources: jaguar, puma, and gato montés. The various names used to describe the design — the "moon animal," "dragon," "great crested being," and "rampant feline"— attest to its ambiguity. Group A figures are mythical in character because they feature natural and supernatural anatomical ele-

FIGURE 55. Iconic figures in Recuay imagery: Group A (a–b) resist-painted representations of crested felines on ceramics (redrawn from Tello 1923: Figs. 9, 12); Group B (c–e) representations of bodiless heads on ceramics (redrawn from Tello 1923: Figs. 22, 25, 28); Group C (f–k) ceramic and textile representations of feline-serpent creatures or amarus. (Adapted from Grieder 1978: 224; Levillier 1926: pl. B; Tello 1923: fig. 15, 18)

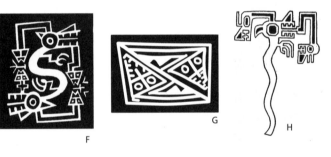

ments. Some scholars have associated their use in coastal cultures with the moon and lunar symbolism (Bruhns 1976), although such associations are less prominent in Recuay.

Another class of beings, Group B, is constituted by various images of a bodiless frontal face (fig. 55c–e). Krzysztof Makowski and Julio Rucabado (2000: 200) refer to this figure as "la divinidad radiante" (the radiant divinity), while Carolina Hohmann (2003) calls it the "rostro circular frontal de boca dentada" (frontal circular head with toothy mouth). The head is almost always circular, with a flat, tumi-like nose and a wide-open mouth with upper and lower rows of teeth. The design is most commonly rendered in resist black, sometimes over red slip and/or kaolin paste color, making the outlined face red or creamy white, respectively. Often the head features a headdress and/or wears ear ornaments, using the same designs typical of ear ornaments found on modeled human figures. In many cases, four symmetrically arranged appendages emanate out of the head. They typically terminate in serpent-feline heads.

Tello (1923) argued that this figure was a deified jaguar/feline, a solar and diurnal divinity, due to its radiating emanations (also Grieder 1978). He argued this at least in part because felinelike creatures were also represented with frontal aspects. Scholars conceive of this being as the "radiant divinity" (Makowski and Rucabado Y. 2000) and believe it to be the principal deity in the Recuay pantheon. Iconographic analysis by Hohmann (2003) emphasized the importance of central face beings in ceramic design compositions. She contended, in contrast to Tello's claim, that the figures were anthropomorphic divinities of a dark, nocturnal universe — manifested in negative painting — associated with women and the sea. It should also not be ruled out that the frontal bodiless heads may sometimes represent the frontal aspect of bodiless head objects, such as trophy heads or effigies of them.

Distinctive composite creatures that hybridize feline and serpent features represent another class of iconic imagery, Group C. These have two main forms, single-headed and bicephalic. Both frequently make use of feline heads and forelimbs, while the serpent features include a long forked tongue and a long, often humped body, typically without hind limbs (fig. 55f–k). Ceramic painted imagery shows great diversity in Group C creatures, and feline-headed serpents are found also in modeled effigy forms, textiles, and sculptures (pl. 7; figs. 56, 57). Bicephalic creatures are frequently represented from above, such that the heads are rendered in triangular form (Grieder 1978: 168–169), with the heads juxtaposed or "interlocked." It may be useful to call creatures of this group (which feature both serpent and feline elements) amarus (see Urton 1996: 241). Group A (crested animals) and Group B (frontal heads) often sprout appendages, which can take the form of Group C figures. Group C creatures also commonly issue appendages which take Group C forms.

The fourth group, Group D, consists of anthropomorphs depicted frontally. The figures are full-bodied, with hands held upward and legs splayed outward (fig. 58). Sometimes the torso features a cross-motif and the head has appendages. These are infrequent iconic representations on

FIGURE 56. (*Top*) Effigy vessel of a feline-serpent creature (amaru). (Museo Arqueológico de Cabana)

FIGURE 57. (*Bottom*) Sculpture of a bicephalic creature, probably from Pashash. Note the head appendages which terminate as creature heads. (Museo Arqueológico de Cabana)

ceramics but are very important single designs on vertical slab sculptures and as part of larger carved arrangements (with other figures or on the backs of statues) (figs. 40, 46). The heads of such figures also sprout or are topped by head appendages, which may terminate in amaru heads.

The fifth group, Group E, consists of avian figures. The bodies of birds

FIGURE 58. Tall ring-base cup, showing a frontal figure, representative of Group D iconic figures. (Museum für Völkerkunde, Berlin; photo by C. B. Donnan)

are represented in profile, usually with an aquiline hooked beak (pl. 5d). A protruding appendage above the upper beak of some representations strongly suggests the caruncle of the Andean condor (*Vultur gryphus*); the opposed digit on the claw seen in some representations is also consistent with the claws of condors. Other images emphasize owls; the bodies are in profile but the heads and massive pairs of large, round eyes turn toward the viewer. Sometimes Group E figures are depicted from a top view, showing both wings outstretched, but with an unusual angle to render the head, with a profile eye, split-representation of the beak, and caruncle-like nubbins (e.g., Grieder 1978: 236). Most avian figures feature only occasional hybridization with other creatures. Nevertheless, their tongues sometimes morph into Group C figures, in top view or in profile.

Finally, the sixth group, Group F, consists of iconic felines without explicit mythical characteristics, such as appendages or serpentine bodies.

The images are versatile in all the categories, especially Groups A to E. The figure can exist as a primary representation on its own. Thus it is

TABLE 3. Iconic Figures

Figure (gloss)	Iconic group	Transformation	Locus of Transformation
Crested animal	Group A	Group A + C	Crest, tail, tongue, feet
Bodiless head	Group B	Group B + C	Head
Feline-serpent (amaru)	Group C	Group C + C	Tongue, crest
Splayed anthropomorph	Group D	Group D + C	Head
Avian	Group E	Group E + C	Tongue
Feline	Group F	—	—

common to find single representations on relatively small, quadrangular stone panels. Iconic figures also adorned special design fields. One of the most important is the pectoral area of the tunics worn by frontal male humans or central figures; Group B images are very common there (see Hohmann 2003). These are framed: separated and given individual value. The images can also be combined and functionally integrated into a greater composition, with others of the same or different categories (see Lau 2006b: 234–236). Thus bicephalic creatures as well as crested animal figures are found on horizontal slabs; or multiple amarus may exist on a single panel on textiles. Hence any one image functioned and, presumably, signified on its own as well as through combination.

Following the pioneering interpretation of Tello (1923), most scholars would agree that the different beings are part of Recuay cosmovision and mythology. They are probably associated with celestial beings and phenomena (solar, lunar, stars, contrasts between nocturnal/diurnal), but the precise associations remain unclear.

Prehispanic Andean divinities are typified by their multiple and protean forms (e.g., Lau 2008; Makowski 2005). Thus it is noteworthy that an important quality of nearly all the iconic figures is their transformative capacity (table 3). It is important that most of the figures show appendages, and sometimes even those appendages morph into additional appendages. Even within the same iconic group, multiple beings have or project multiple aspects.

Care needs to be taken in distinguishing representational conventions for different beings (forms associated with profile view, top view, or split representation taken as distinct). Thus the Group B head may simply be a Group A feline head viewed frontally. Group A and Group B figures are both represented on the chests of chiefs, which indicates this equivalence and the ambiguity of contending whether one is more important than the other. Also, the head appendages can look very different when represented frontally, in profile, in top view, or as split representation. They are not necessarily different beings.

In sum, it may be premature to distinguish specific divinities. Neither do we have any indication of their domains of efficacy or their hierarchical importance within a Recuay pantheon or society. It is possible, however, to conclude that Group A–Group E figures all had overlapping representational features, mainly in Group C figures, that signify some form of supernatural status or mythical significance. What was conveyed is more difficult to glean. Having outlined their diverse form, let us see where such images are used. Alone or in the plural, these images enriched special surfaces of things, buildings, and people.

ELITE APPAREL AND SOCIALITY: GENRES OF ACTION

Most pottery representations with human figures are about chiefly sociality and ceremonial life. In scenes of festivities as well as of more reserved ritual, Recuay people wear elegant regalia, festooned with the iconic figures and geometric designs. Although their meanings remain elusive, the surficial elaboration can be conceptualized as what some anthropologists have termed the "social skin" (Strathern 1979; Turner 1980).

The modification of exterior surfaces is a strategic field for negotiating identity and an individual's place and image within a community. The myriad modes of body ornament (such as cosmetics, tattooing, hairdos, and attire) present contact zones for social interaction and communication of meanings, especially as related to personal capacities and relationships to social others. It is not surprising to find that the forms of surficial decoration found on human bodies are also common on other parts of the ceramic vessels and other media altogether. Such forms can be considered extensions of chiefly elites that help mediate crucial social relations. Even the so-called decorative, geometric designs are not inert, for they help signal the chiefly disposition of things and help saturate activities and spaces with their presence.

The apparel plays a prominent role in the representations, because the large majority of Recuay figural representations are depictions of lords in highly conventionalized forms of interaction with other beings, usually subjects. I suggest that the imagery performs as a visual record and proxy for chiefly sociality, which is constituted by different categories or genres of action (fig. 59).

Perhaps the most important genre of social interaction depicted in the ceramics was the veneration of chiefly figures. The depictions took different forms, but the typical examples highlight a male figure presid-

FIGURE 59. Diagram reconstructing Recuay chiefly sociality and genres of action, as reflected in effigy vessels. Arrows show the direction of action to or from subjects or both. Notably, the majority of social relations actions are directed to or received by the chiefly figure. It is also interesting that relations with other chiefs or persons of analogous standing (in scale/dress) are rarely if ever depicted in the ceramic representations.

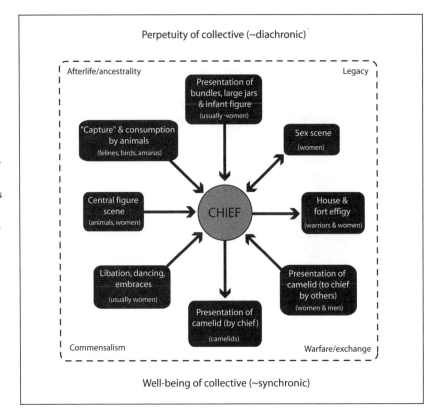

ing over a central location and subsidiary figures (fig. 60). He is typically standing, although seated poses also occur. The surrounding figures are probably kin and followers who make up the central figure's chiefly house, with its network of social relations and charges (Gero 2001). The central figure wears elaborate clothes and gear which connote his status and warriorhood. Attendants, who are usually smaller and less well attired, convene around the central figure and often bear items, such as cups or bundles, in supplicatory acts. The gestures are of libation, mourning, or reverence. The differential treatment of human figures in scale and elaboration is one of the best indicators of ranking in Recuay society.

Festive gatherings formed another important genre of social interaction. For Rebeca Carrión Cachot (1955: 69, pl. 15–18), group representations of merriment and feasting were parties and "scenes of dance and libation." Besides the offering of drink, Recuay artists on occasion represented figures gathered in festive huddles, embraces, or dances around the central figure. The personage is often standing or seated, assuming the de facto pose of a mummy bundle. Recuay pots also show figures who play musical instruments, probably for public ceremonial events and funerary rituals. Men handle flutes, while women usually play drums (pl. 6a; fig. 54) (Arriaga 1968 [1621]; Chaumeil 2007; Duviols 1986).

In another series of elaborately modeled pots, men stand next to camelids, leading them by a rope — most likely to their eventual sacrifice (figs. 49, 51). This sometimes occurs with onlookers, but more commonly the well-attired man is depicted alone with the camelid. Although these scenes of interacting bodies are quite distinct, it is reasonable to believe that they form episodes of a narrative focused on key moments in the life and reception of various chiefly leaders.

Women are also very prominent in Recuay funerary art (Gero 1999). The depictions are some of the earliest mimetic representations of women in the highlands. Earlier images are known from the north highlands (for example, from Chavín and Kotosh cultures), but they are usually highly stylized, focus on hybrid divinities, and reference mainly female characteristics (genitalia and hair). With the onset of Recuay, specific women are emphasized through funerary art and appear to play an increasingly explicit role in the constitution of highland society and status.

The group scenes in which females attend to a central male figure hint at the practice of polygamy and female mourning in ancient Recuay society (fig. 46). Early colonial census documents indicate that having multiple wives was widespread among native nobility during the sixteenth century. Lords (curacas) sometimes had more than a dozen wives,

FIGURE 60. Modeled effigy vessel, showing a chiefly person surrounded by smaller warriors. The central figure wears an elaborate headdress, topped by a large fan element, and a trophy head frontlet with serpents on the sides. He also carries a mace. Several of the warriors have face painting and trophy-head packs worn around the waist. (Staatliche Museen zu Berlin–Preussicher Kulturbesitz Ethnologisches Museum; photo by W. Schneider-Schütz)

whereas lesser elites, especially brothers of primary leaders, appear to have had at least several wives (Espinoza Soriano 1978; Varón Gabai 1980). In a world where labor, as opposed to money, was fundamental, extending kin relations by marriage alliances enhanced one's status and production. During colonial times in highland Ancash, native women held fame as wives of important curacas as well as particularly efficacious ritual practitioners (e.g., Mills 1994: 166–167).

In addition to multifigure scenes, women are often represented on their own. Females are most often seated, holding items in presentation poses: large jars, cups, bundles, and figurines or infants. Indeed, the jar carried by the female effigy using a headstrap is the physical vessel (pl. 5c). The association between female bodies and the large jars is notable, because the vessels were probably for the preparation and serving of chicha maize beer, a common element in many Andean religious and social activities. Chicha, of course, was also the obligatory drink provided by sponsors of festive work parties. Both men and women hold drinking goblets, but the large jars appear to be the domain of women — implicating them in the making and transport of maize beer. Their dutiful generosity is also shown in depictions of the offering and distribution of drink at ceremonies. Gero (2001: 50) contended that women, as co-providers in these activities, carried "social capital" and political sway independent of, but complementary to, those of male chiefs.

In some South American societies, chicha is the quintessential product of female labor yet is considered vital to the well-being and health of men, especially in rites which construct masculinity and proper male adult persons (Conklin 2001; Viveiros de Castro 1992). Indeed, chicha helps activate this relational interdependence, described as the "idea that for both sexes, sources of vitality and potency that create gendered capacities . . . lie outside the individual in interactions with others" (Conklin 2001: 167). Chicha, not surprisingly, is also a basic social lubricant and offering in Andean ritual focused on the dead (e.g., Allen 1988; Course 2007; Gose 1994).

One of the purposes of Recuay effigy vessels was to help reify chiefly persons and ancestors through periodic acts, gifts, and contributions of others. If the appropriation of vitality from others is essential to religious experience (Bloch 1992), then this is expressed in Recuay ceremonialism both in the fixed miniature figures accompanying the central figure and in the living people making, handling, and drinking the contents of the vessel, probably a special type of beverage. Like the drink, the vessel itself is an offering, a sacrifice. Furthermore, if negotiating understandings of one's place with unlike individuals generates the self and actualizes or enhances special capacities (Strathern 1988), then the activities just outlined are fundamental in constituting the chief, head of house, or ancestor. In death, such vessels performed as visual commemoration, an ancient biopic which acknowledged and "completed" a person by pulling together the different accounts of the deceased one's past social relations (see also Course 2007).

This is also a model for understanding the vessels which portray the human body in sexual intercourse. The imagery is limited to ceramics, and the activity is always between a female and male partner, who, because of their attire, are both of high rank (fig. 61). They are understood as an elite pairing. The preferred positions include the male on top (missionary style) or in a dual sitting style, face to face, with the female's legs wrapped around the male's waist. Crucially, in both positions the partners extend their arms to face each other, their eyes meeting in visual acknowledgment.

FIGURE 61. Modeled effigy bottle showing male-female sexual intercourse. Besides the act itself, the extension of arms to the partner (the male's is above the female's) and the eyes trained on each other demonstrate the union of complementary opposites and its visual acknowledgment. The figures perform in full regalia, including headgear; the woman also wears a checkerboard garment, while the man wears ear ornaments. (Staatliche Museen zu Berlin–Preussicher Kulturbesitz Ethnologisches Museum; photo by C. B. Donnan)

The sex scenes indicate a prejudice against depicting the genitals. Men and women are almost always shown dressed in elaborate textiles, even headdresses, or concealed by textiles or covers.[3] This contrasts, for example, with the sexual representations in Moche or Nasca pottery, where genitalia are explicit, often in an exaggerated or otherwise prominent manner. According to Gero (2004), sexual representations in the Central Andes express culture-specific practices and prerogatives of elites. Moche depictions, showing masturbation, anal sex, and the erect penis, privilege male orgasm and domination. In Recuay imagery, where both sexes are pleasured, copulation scenes emphasize gender interdependence and complementarity (Gero 2004: 20).

The sex scenes usually have been interpreted as specific historical acts: the consummation of a marriage, the production of heirs, or a specific ritual episode. Yet such imagery need not (or need not only) refer to ephemeral events. Rather, the scenes may serve as condensed statements, even forecasts, about the general pairing, its attendant social relations, and visual endorsement. A crucial point is that the eyes of both partners are always trained on each other in the act of witnessing. Moreover, the copulating pair is sometimes watched over or accompanied by attendants or children. Thus the attendants or children are also "witnesses," just like the handler of the vessel. They are the products of the pair, showing both the need for and proof of the union.

The sex scenes visualize the legacy of the line by conjoining female persons with chiefs. In brief, Recuay female imagery indicates that women were fundamental to the activities and objects of chiefly political fields: maize beer production, labor recruitment, cooking, and sex. These were all vital for Recuay social reproduction and would fit in with other classes of vessels which mark key biographical milestones that construct Recuay nobility.

It is notable that sexual organs, which are so significant in stone-carved images, are very rarely depicted in ceramics. Similarly, depiction of breasts or modeling of the torso to connote breasts was shunned by the potters. Even feline figures, which are always identifiably male in stone sculpture, are rarely represented with exposed sexual organs in pottery. This does not indicate an intentional gender ambiguity (e.g., Joyce 1996), because other conventions (such as apparel, ornaments, and the slimming of waists) clearly denote the figure as male or female; nor is there an intention to shame or humiliate the figure (e.g., Flannery and Marcus 1996; Hill 2000). Still, it is notable that nearly all figures in Recuay pots, with the exception of the head and limb extremities, are covered.

Several alternatives can be presented to account for the different media-based dispositions toward nudity. The difference could be attributed to artistic or regional variability: sculptors in the Huaraz area were simply more explicit in the gendering of figures. A difficulty with this approach is that it does not easily explain the absence of genitals on the feline imagery of ceramics, when they are very common in stone sculpture. Another possibility is that the stone monoliths were wrapped or covered with textiles or other materials, such as paint, plaster, or metals. Yet another alternative is that some regional sculptors sought to distinguish the gender of figures because of the potential ambiguities of the represented form — that is, they felt they needed to be more explicit about the identity of the figure. Even where gendered textiles or accouterments were present, it was not enough. Rather, it was vital to recognize the figure's identity and being through his/her physical sexual organs. Precisely why such differences existed remains hypothetical.

Perhaps another way to approach the conundrum, however, would be to rethink it: why bother wearing textiles at all? And were there special contexts for display of one's "social skin"?

CLOTH AND RELATED MATTER

Of the general classes of Recuay material culture, textiles are the least well known, in spite of the advanced technology of known examples as well as the economic importance of camelid and fiber production among Recuay villages (e.g., Lau 2007). Three main lines of data illuminate Recuay textile arts and their use: physical examples of textiles, representations of textiles (especially on pottery), and related evidence for fiber production and weaving.

Spindle whorls are the weights attached to the end of the spindle rods which, when spun, help propel the pulling action of the line and enable the transformation of raw fiber into spun, weavable yarn. In highland Ancash today, spinning is often done as a type of busy, complementary work by women and teenagers, especially while they watch their herds (for the importance of spinning, see Dransart 1995, 2002).

Whorls are common in Recuay sites, especially in high-altitude zones where herding benefited from proximity to puna grazing areas. Of the many whorls recovered through excavation at Chinchawas, for example, most were made expediently out of broken ceramic sherds, but examples of bone and fired pottery were also found. The finest examples, probably small luxury items, were ground down carefully out of diversely colored stones into disc and lenticular forms. Sometimes whorls were found as funerary offerings and were perhaps tools of the person who had died, for use in the afterlife. The frequency of spinning implements suggests that fiber production was one of the main economic activities of the small village. Such work enabled its inhabitants to exchange fiber products for marine shell, exotic pottery, obsidian, and other desirable goods from coastal and other highland groups.

Actual Recuay textiles are very rare. Fewer than a dozen examples have been published, and only a few specimens have archaeological provenience. Specialists have identified several types of Recuay textiles: plain-weaves and, more commonly, tapestry cloth (Garaventa 1978; Manrique P. 1999; Porter 1992). Designs are sometimes painted on cotton plain-weaves. Plain-weaves and tapestries of camelid fiber also have woven designs. In the tapestries, the warp threads (vertical on the loom and usually of cotton or combining cotton and camelid fiber threads) are covered over by weft threads (horizontal and typically of camelid fiber).

In the most elaborate Recuay cloths, the weavers used two-ply camelid fiber warps and interlocked wefts on a wide loom, typical of highland styles. The long rectangular cloths would then be sewn together, with the seam (for example, on a tunic) down the centerline; wide looms presume the collaboration of paired weavers. Other textiles were made by sewing various small tapestry panels together (pl. 7). Recuay cloths were probably the most technically advanced and labor-intensive of their time. Indeed, the technology — two-panel tapestry woven on a wide loom — would be adopted by Wari elites for their elaborate garments (Rodman and Cassman 1995: 34; Rodman and Fernández 2000: 126).

Recuay cloth fragments have been found mainly in the form of tunics. Smaller edged fragments could have been for belts or headwraps. A tapestry with Recuay designs has also been found as a "pillow," filled with plant fiber, on which rested a wrapped interment bundle (Bennett 1939: fig. 15a). Designs on Recuay cloths are rendered mainly in camelid fiber colors (dark and light browns, creamy white) and in yellow, black, and reds. Designs are often paired or symmetrical, with alternating colors or color reversals (pl. 7b).

In the existing corpus, the most important image was the frontal anthropomorphic head with four appendages (Group B figures). Chiefly figures in modeled ceramics often have a Group B figure in the pectoral area of the tunic. Frontal heads are typically the largest figures and occupy more central positions in the compositions. The heads are usually squarish, with rounded corners. They feature large round eyes, noses with curling nostrils, and simple mouths that are slightly ajar and show bare upper and lower rows of teeth. The heads commonly wear ear spools (typically a male accouterment), quartered into wedges of alternating color.

More than any other medium, cloth displayed the diversity of Group C amaru creatures in Recuay thought (pl. 7a). Several tapestry examples are blanketed with such figures (e.g., Levillier 1926: pl. A). Tongues, head crests, tails, and limbs morph into amaru appendages. Some amarus are single-headed, while others are double-headed; some figures are legless with snakelike bodies, while others sprout claws. One of the most distinctive variations is a bicephalic being, with two frontal anthropomorphic heads and a humped back (compare figs. 37d, 55j, 57).

Profile birds with aquiline beaks and curling claws (perhaps condor-like avians) are also depicted on textiles, sometimes as "filler" elements or sometimes as large designs alternating with frontal heads. More rarely, small profile anthropomorphic figures, holding staffs or long clubs, are represented on some textiles. Top-view figures of paired raylike creature heads are also known. Finally, the Recuay wove small geometric elements — paired quadrangles of different color, crosses, triangular elements, hourglass forms, crenellating bands, and comma-pairs — in the spaces between larger motifs (pls. 7a and 7b).

The technical virtuosity, combined with the profusion of bold patterns, designs, and color, must have set Recuay weavings and their wearers apart from their contemporaries. Attire and being appropriately dressed were of utmost importance: when displayed and worn, textiles enrobed persons and things in special surfaces. On the one hand, textiles present portable, temporary frontiers by which people display and promote their place in society; they offer a field for mediating social interaction and conveying meanings about identity and status (Turner 1980). On the other, using special textiles may offer a means of sanction and protection, a confidence, with sacred designs empowered through integrating, fortifying, or keeping within socio-magical essences of materials, what Adrienne Kaeppler (1997) called "entangling divinity" and Alfred Gell (1993) called "wrapping in images."

It may not be too far afield to impute similar understandings to the Recuay case. Textiles were privileged in ceramic representations and effigies. To be sure, textiles were valued, as most of them are known as funerary offerings. Wearing textiles and headdresses was emphasized even in circumstances where it would have been unusual if not downright awkward in practice. Even in the sex representations, partners perform under covers, fully dressed. In these ways, the textile is an object — but so is the person wearing it. In other words, what is at play is the depiction of two beings, in their respective "social skins," in the process of union. To strip the chiefly individual of his clothes would take away both the expression and a means of his chiefliness.

Recuay imagery is never simply documentary or mimetic: the wearing of fancy surfaces objectifies. Examining special people through their surfaces is important: for lords, as figureheads, are fundamentally artificial, in the sense of being composed, carefully constructed entities. They exist within a historical milieu but also frequently transcend it by fitting into a mythic, divine order (e.g., Houston and Stuart 1996; Sahlins 1985; Valeri 1985; Zuidema 1990).

Clothes, especially those worn in public, are vital in communicating this capacity because they literally wrap or cover persons in meanings. Textiles are wealth objects, in that they instance the ability to access labor. Because of the laborious use of threads and redundant motions, the production of tapestry cloths is especially costly in energy expenditure (Stone-Miller 1992). Just as importantly, in the Recuay case, chiefly leaders (for example, in central figure scenes) are meant to be understood as powerful individuals not only because of their size and centrality in scenes. They wear clothes redolent with potency and are "made" into representatives of special forces.

Cloth was also important because of its role in ancestor cults (pl. 6b; fig. 62). The veneration of mummies is essentially a ritual of renewal and reciprocity. Ancestors will continue to provide well-being and fertility, but the attention must be reciprocal, for descendants must also nourish the deceased. This was mainly achieved through ritual offerings of chicha, coca, and camelid meat. But new or additional layers of cloth were also common as gifts and sacrifices that were accorded to the key figures of highland descent groups, chiefs, and ancestors (Arguedas and Duviols 1966; Arriaga 1968 [1621]; Duviols 1967). The careful wrapping and handling of effigies must have been equally significant, because such gestures drew from dispositions of family and familiar devotion expected from descendants. They reciprocated for previous care to ensure future goodwill (Duviols 1986: 70, 105).

Textiles for the Recuay therefore were much more than simply garments or expressions of wealth. They wrapped and protected, demonstrated status, and imparted authority. Textiles enveloped people and in so doing helped to fashion them and actualize their capacities in social settings. Extraordinary textiles bolstered the image of those most public and assailable of objects: chiefs and ancestors. Nonetheless, it was the

FIGURE 62. Modeled effigy vessel showing a male figure covered in textile. He is wrapped like a mummy bundle (from Lau 2000: fig. 9). (Museo Nacional de Arqueología, Antropología e Historia, Lima)

choice of the descendants and associated artisans to be their advocates in the afterlife — they were responsible for spinning the narrative.

ON ENRICHED SURFACES: TECHNOLOGIES OF ENHANCEMENT

Certain technical dispositions suffused in Recuay culture affected the production and ancient reception of objects. Broadly, the Recuay stressed techniques to render special decorated surfaces. Stone sculpture is perhaps the most overt example. Carving stone reliefs presupposes that an image will be formed from a rough block of stone through reduction. The Recuay accomplished this in a number of ways. On rare occasions they sculpted in the round. Most works combined relief and incision on flat or fairly flat slabs. On some pieces, material was removed around the image, with the voids forming the background and the design in bas relief (figs. 43, 44). Crucially, Recuay ceramic surfaces were also "negativized" through resist or negative painting. In this process, a design in the original creamy white or red surface (or both) was revealed on a black background after a resist material was removed. This was done to create complex geometric and zoomorphic motifs and effected a visual play of different parts of the vessel or figures.

The importance of these creative dispositions is threefold. First, they seek to create by removing rather than adding on. What they accomplish is to resolve an image out of the original fabric, the void or background, which in a sense is coaxed out of the material — whether in raw stone or on the original cream or red slipped surface. Second, negativization privileges the original material itself and its external qualities, especially color and finish. Finally, we can sense an ancient logic about the generative capacity of materials. The interplay of inner and outer layers produces figure-ground contrasts, which accentuate — indeed help create — the designs.

A further elaboration on technical styles and value systems is important here. Unlike many early metallurgical traditions that focused on hardness, efficiency, or the durability of metalwork, what was precious and essential about metals for many Andeans was their color (Helms 1981; Lechtman 1977, 1984). Andean metallurgy also emphasized the incorporation of a material throughout its physical structure, in spite of greater costs. For example, although Andeans knew about gilding by plating or adding thin leaf, which is more economical in terms of material, they often preferred to alloy gold with copper metal and then hammer and burnish the desired product to enrich the gold and bring out its color on the surface. In doing so, much Andean metalwork sought to make gold surficial *and* integral to the structure of the material.

Interestingly, the process of surface enrichment, as this is sometimes called, can be compared to Recuay negative painting and stone-carving, because it attains the desired result of revealing design by removing. Important parallels between metalwork and other types of making are discussed below. These can be considered cognate expressions of a cross-media technological style based on enriching surfaces and on perceiving and rendering design through background/negative space.

While Recuay textile designs are woven directly into cloth, weaving can still be said to draw on this mode of enhancement. The "negativization" in textiles might be seen in alternating designs which toggle color and reverse color schemes on opposed panels/surfaces. It is not coincidental that the designs rendered in resist painting resemble precisely those found on textiles. The linear forms, the negativization of resist surfaces, and the framing of iconic designs through modular, panel-like cartouches may be following or reinforcing technical dispositions in weaving (see also Makowski 2004: 56).

But the same techniques further distinguish a type of value system which sets Recuay apart from other cultures of the Central Andes. Whereas the techniques that Heather Lechtman (1984) describes emphasize the incorporation of materials throughout the entire product's structure, Recuay techniques focused on the surficial; what was of paramount importance was the outer surface. A melánge of technical traditions, emphasizing integrity and surfaces, occurs in Recuay metallurgy, which employs both sheet-assembly styles typical for the Central Andes and electrochemical plating and lost-wax casting often described for the Northern Andes (e.g., Grieder 1978; Schindler 2000; Scott 1998). For example, the large garment pins of Pashash were made out of a copper alloy form, lost-wax cast, and then bathed in a coat of gold plating. As with resist painting, Recuay metalwork suggests interactions with groups of the Northern Andes.

Because of archaeological visibility, it is easy to discount the effect of other forms of making, such as pyroengraving gourds (*Lagenaria* sp.). Little direct evidence exists for such production in Recuay, but it was a common and ancient practice throughout the Andes (Jiménez Borja 1948; Spahni 1969). Some of the earliest evidence for gourd use comes from the Callejón de Huaylas (Lynch 1980c). Tello (1929), of course, argued that many pottery vessel forms in highland Ancash were modeled on gourd shapes. And it should be noted that gourd cups were often the preferred vessels, probably similar to ceramic open bowls for the Recuay, by which chicha was served in religious practices in colonial highland Ancash (e.g., Millones 1979: 248).

In many ways, negative painting reproduces the style of surfaces rendered by pyroengraving. Tendencies toward linearity, binary color schemes, and the capacity for raised designs on black backgrounds are inherent in the technique. The Wilkawaín resist style, used in the Callejón de Huaylas during the Middle Horizon, may have had its inspiration in coastal pyroengraving techniques and designs (Bennett 1944: fig. 8; Lau 2005: fig. 4g; Tello 1956: fig. 134).

The tendency to think and render in "negative" terms can be found in the fine black decorated wares at Yayno, of the Late Recuay period. In these examples, the entire surface except the design was painted in positive black, leaving the design in the original slip color (pl. 4l–m).

Most discussions of Recuay artworks focus on the meanings of the imagery, although some scholars have alluded to the relationships between Recuay designs and the technology. A. L. Kroeber (1949: 445), for example, hinted at a connection between technique and representation when he argued: "It may be suspected that the linearity or avoidance of mass and area in Recuay painting is the product of some feature of the technical process of negativizing. Linearity means that heads and bodies tend to be represented by lines, not merely that areas are bordered by lines."

Terence Grieder (1978: 182) provided the most explicit interpretations connecting style and different artistic expressions. He argued that Recuay art production was quintessentially corporate and of elite patronage: "The unity of the Recuay style is the result of [elite] pressure sufficient to blot out nearly all individuality in the expressive products." In regard to technique, he contended that the distinctive painting and figurine style, especially of Pashash, derived from the representational standards established by stone sculpture. Thus the simple facial features of painted and modeled ceramic heads took their form from tenon-heads. Similarly, the designs on metal jewelry originated from the forms of tenon-heads and relief slabs. Implicit in the observations is that the unity of the style and technique on different media helped aggrandize their patrons.

Fewer people (with several notable exceptions) have commented on the formal or sensorial qualities of Recuay surfaces or their implications for the use and reception of the objects. George Kubler (1962a: 245) provided a brief treatment in which he highlighted the culture's narrative propensities, the abstract modeling, and "absence of individuality." He compared Recuay artworks to interior-painted geometric designs found in tombs of the Northern Andes and pointed out the parallels between the "cipher"-like decorations. Kubler (1962a: 245) also noted the visual impact of the negative painting: "If the figural parts are resist-covered, they emerge in a light color on a dark ground, with the effect of making the ground visually more active than when the figure appears in dark upon light."

The notion of a "negative universe" put forth by Hohmann (2003: 150) merits consideration in this respect. In a study of the Group B figures (frontal faces) on ceramics, she noted that the figures are rendered as negative designs on dark backgrounds and contended that the images rendered in negative were of the principal divinity or divinities in the Recuay pantheon, who lorded over an alternate nocturnal world, associated with water and fertility, where only supernaturals resided. Insofar as the interpretation is limited to ceramics, the argument may be valid. Even in ceramics, however, different positive painted versions of bodiless heads are known. But the account cannot reconcile other media that have Group B figures, such as textiles, stone sculpture, or ceramics in later Recuay tradition, where frontal heads are not rendered against a dark background. Furthermore, although she argues that humans are not portrayed, it is likely that Group D figures, ancestral humans, also have a place in the "negative universe."

Nevertheless, the notion of a special space where supernatural beings are immanent and where they periodically emerge remains compelling. Perhaps what is at play is not so much a dark, nocturnal universe as a transformative surface for the presencing, the externalizing, of beings from hidden interiors. Recuay surfaces and their interactive quality were critical, because they performed on interactive objects and were mediated by chiefly persons.

Corporate Bodies: Vessels, Interiors, and Transactions

More complex relationships between vessels and bodies are expressed in the ceramic representations of buildings. Fewer than fifty such vessels have been published, and none has ever been found through systematic excavations. Stylistically they fall within the Middle and Late Recuay periods. The few examples with provenience information have been found in the southern Recuay area and the upper areas of the Pacific slopes. At present they have not been reported from the northern part or the Conchucos, where the best-known population centers (Pashash, Yayno) are located.

At their most basic, the pots are containers for liquids. They are typified by two spouts: a flaring larger one for pouring in and a short and smaller tubular one for pouring out. They are also fairly small; because of their size and thin walls of fine paste, they are also surprisingly light.

The pots are quite variable in terms of representation, but they all depict places with buildings, most with human figures in scenes of activity within them. Constructions may be fairly simple, such as those with a basic canopy, while others convey larger spaces, such as walled enclosures. The most common consists of an individual multistory structure, connected through staircases and ladders. The buildings usually feature rectangular plans, but several circular examples are known. Emphasis is often placed on an interior courtyard as well as a parapet or landing overlooking the courtyard. These spaces constitute the main areas where human figures are positioned and where their roles and relationships are actively constituted (pl. 8).

Architectural effigies show some of the greatest diversity of human representation in Recuay art. The most prominent is the large chiefly figure. Only the oversize head of the figure is shown in some vessels, with the torso and limbs of the figure (if present) encased within the architecture (fig. 63). Attendant figures, sometimes male but mainly female, often bear cups, held out in front with both hands. In some cases they hold packages or bundles, in a similar offering pose. At other times they stand by, empty handed. Occasionally warriors or armed sentries are

FIGURE 63. Modeled vessel showing a chiefly figure encased in a structure. The bird elements of his headdress mimic the bird figures on top of the flat canopy. The lower horizontal element, probably the stringcourse of buildings, resembles the flaring bottom borders common on male apparel. The two female side figures are seated; behind them (not shown) are several male warrior figures. The central figure performs literally as the head of the structure and collective. (Staatliche Museen zu Berlin–Preussicher Kulturbesitz Ethnologisches Museum; photo by C. B. Donnan)

also depicted, located strategically in different parts of buildings. Finally, the scenes sometimes include small dogs and birds.

Resist decoration is very common on the architectural vessels. All of the polychrome designs are typically reserved for the exterior façades of the buildings, with little painted elaboration of the interior except for the small figures. The iconic figures described above are used liberally. The buildings also often have a profusion of banded and more geometric designs, including bands, lattices, step and fret designs, and diamonds. Most of these same designs have analogues in stone sculpture and painted architectural decoration (figs. 22, 23, 46). The most prominent are the splayed anthropomorphs, mythical beings, and various geometric motifs.[4] Some finely worked stones also seem to have been architectural elements, such as blocks with channels and holes, blocks which look like moldings, and small squarish panels which probably formed decorative friezes and stringcourses. Where standing architecture is depicted, it often has stylistic correspondences with Recuay building techniques. Neighboring cultures appear to have had similar architectural detail, sometimes in stone and sometimes in adobe (e.g., Bennett 1950; Kauffmann Doig and Ligabue 2003).

The small worlds depicted in the architectural effigies disclose a formality and order in Recuay society. Such pots are focused on, indeed obsessed with, an interior domain (see also Allen 2002; Descola 2006). They contain few, if any, references to an "outside"— whether in terms of countryside features, wildlife or flora, or enemies. These are highly ordered, artificial universes. Even the small dogs and birds sometimes populating the buildings are familiar and tame. They too are ossified in formal poses and act more like props. Thus an exterior domain is excluded. It seems reasonable to draw comparisons with many Amerindian worldviews that emphasize strong distinctions between the self-sufficiency of civilized beings, things, and life within a controlled domain (for example, a house or community) and the unchartered wildness and flux outside.

These expressions of formal and social order are rather low key: the most arresting and active dimension resides not in the activity of the interior figures but in the painted decoration. It is instructive that the decoration occurs principally at the interfaces between the inner and outer worlds. Specific emphasis was given to suitable representation of the exterior walls of an interior whole; they were active boundaries for interchanges with social others.

What was transacted and why? Here again, the Recuay artists provide clues, for the central figure is more than just the center of action. His body is likened to the vessel, which in turn can embody different architectural forms (figs. 22, 63). In some cases the figure is physically enveloped by the structure, filling it but also becoming it. So the implication is that the central figure not only is like or occupies a structure but in fact is the structure. His face is the face of the house, his clothes double as the building's exterior, and his body implies his dwelling and social structure.

This is reinforced visually through metonymic elements and substitutions, such as the stringcourse or sloping projection of the structure, which also refers to the flanged hem of the figure's garment. Motifs are shared by the central figures as well as the buildings, in similar strategic places. Small figures of birds perch nonchalantly on headdresses as they do on rooftops. The figure's girth, probably connoting his vigor and prosperity, finds a happy match in the vessel's rotundity and a capacity to contain.

As functional pots with the ability to hold and pour liquids, these vessels were probably for special beverages, perhaps alcoholic chicha maize beer. Unlike the giant work-party feasts of the Inka, however, where chicha was at once obligatory and provided by the state in great volume, the small size of the Recuay vessels suggests small quantities of beverages offered in moderation, most likely to a more select group of recipients.

Most vessels depict houses and highlight the familiar or domestic content of the objects. Despite their technical sophistication, I would argue that the vessels were neither magical objects nor objects magically made (cf. Gell 1992), as much as they appear to have drawn significance through episodic use by people accustomed to their surfaces and meanings. The objects circulated in a special but limited ceremonial field. A habitual acquaintance and formal intimacy very likely existed between the objects and imagery and their human users/viewers.

The different forms of the effigy vessel, whether in anthropomorphic or architectural mode, highlight the figure's status and generosity. We might take the physical pouring of the vessels literally as "this well-dressed house provides drink," but now we can also see that this easily toggles with the notion that "this well-dressed figure (chief/ancestor) of the house provides drink." The metaphor is made more explicit in some vessels where the spout issues from the figure's headdress or from the very cup held in his hands. Hence, by distributing chiefly products, these vessels were sites where corporate and physical bodies were able to commingle and where fluid and figural transactions occurred, involving the chiefly person, his line, and his following. Gary Urton (1996: 253, emphasis in the original) writes that "society is consistently imagined, or seen metaphorically, as a body . . . while bodies are *individually* experienced, they are *collectively* socialized." Such objects at once marked and facilitated the social orbits of chiefs.

Ultimately, these artworks may fit as early expressions where important individuals assume multiple corporeal statuses in the Andes and where in one form they are embodied through physical architecture. They are very much related to how Andean peoples began thinking about and construing their fleshly leaders as transcendent beings — who continue to attend to their descendants in return for their devotion after biological death. This, of course, is the basic desire of ancestor cults. The ritual practices in which these objects took center stage were the domains of small collectivities, probably extended families or kin groups, actively commemorating their known deceased. It remains these small, familiar worlds that the vessels and their makers sought to contain and perpetuate.

The pattern of house-based, politico-ritual corporations, headed by founding lords, would reemerge in later, more centralized groups, such as the Chimu *ciudadela* (walled enclosure) and the Inka *panaca* (royal descent group). Both were identified through a large, palatial architectural complex and its court, ordered around a dead king/mummy who performed as the figurehead for both the collectivity (the "house") and the physical building (Moore 2005; Ramírez 1996). Architectural surfaces, adobe murals, and ashlar masonry were focal in all of these enterprises because they construct the social skin, that "frontier of the social self" (Turner 1980: 112). This was originally employed to understand body ornament, but it is also useful to understand the communicativity of other surfaces, especially given the formal equivalencies that the Recuay attributed to special vessels, buildings, and people.

Interactions with Animals:
Metaphors and Transformations

The other important figures in Recuay artworks are animals and animal-like creatures. The most recognizable animals are of highland species, both wild and domesticated. In addition to the treatment of the human figure, the emphasis on local fauna was one of the greatest changes in the elite arts of the time.

The Recuay's noted predecessors, the Chavín, opted for exotic animal prototypes, especially of tropical lowland areas. The bodies and anatomical features of jungle creatures such as the cayman and jaguar were crucial in Chavín art but played little or no explicit role in the art of the Recuay. The inhabitants of Chavín de Huántar subsisted almost exclusively on highland animals, such as camelids, deer, and small mammals. But rarely if ever do these show up in the monumental art. Chavín priests and artisans exploited the depiction of lowland fauna, probably because their fearsome and alien characteristics enhanced the intentional otherworldliness of the religion and its cultic practices (Miller and Burger 1995). Even the types of organic exotica highlighted by Chavín — such as lowland plants, San Pedro cactus, and marine shell (*Spondylus* and *Strombus* spp.) — disappear from later iconography. By Recuay times, elite arts depicted animals that were largely familiar to most highlanders: camelids, pumas, mountain cats, snakes, dogs, deer, condors, and owls. The animals they saw, hunted, or ate became incorporated into their representational world.

Some images of animals are difficult to identify, however, because similar representational conventions were used by Recuay artists to depict them. Thus what may be foxes, dogs, felines, viscachas, or some similar animal all sometimes share similar traits: claws, open mouths baring teeth, curling tails, and quadrupedal and rampant positions.

The use of animals in Recuay art is notable because the animals are always in interaction with human bodies. This is either depicted (human with animal figures), implied through juxtaposing chiefly surfaces and figural animals, or experienced through physical handling of the vessel. To be sure, animals occur alone, but they are not studies of animals in a natural habitat. More commonly, these same animals interact with humans in a series of different themes which allude to their interventions or appropriation in social activities and fields.

The effigy vessels depicting a man leading a camelid constitutes one such theme (fig. 49, 51). The male figure is always elaborately attired and made up, as if prepared for a public appearance. All of the diacritical elements of his dress serve to signal the man's status and rank. He leads the camelid by a rope, probably to its eventual sacrifice. In contrast to the human figure, the camelids are in general relatively plain both in the physical ornamentation and in the economy of detail used to render the animal. Camelids were sources of wealth and status, but they are not the focal point of the artwork. They are only vehicles for the implied action of their sacrifice and probable redistribution (the gifting and sharing of meat) in public feasting or offering contexts. Such acts helped to cultivate and reinforce the prestige of their handlers.

Dogs and birds in the architectural effigies are accessories of enclosed, houselike environments, where they help to mark off a type of controlled, safe space. These refer to their domesticity as well as to attention to the lord of the house. Sometimes animals occupy (or substitute for) the same positions as female attendants in central figure scenes. Thus these are figures who accompany the central figure, and their variable expressions again suggest the social relations of his authority and veneration.

As noted, animals or animal parts are also vital in the chiefly attire, especially on headgear. Animal parts, probably trophies from predation (of humans, serpents, foxes, felines, deer, and birds), are carefully integrated into headdresses and headgear. The headdresses with animal elements indicate acumen and ability in the hunt. They also express a type of social value predicated on the appropriation of materials as wealth and vitality from outside worlds. Such attire portrays the public image of chiefs as prosperous and privileged.

Animals or animal-like creatures in Recuay art are sometimes associated with violent, transformative actions on human bodies. One is the consuming of humans (fig. 64). Carnivorous birds and mammals (usually on ceramics) gorge merrily on the lifeless corpse with closed eyes, pulling out internal organs (Makowski 2000). Similar animals are often depicted in carved reliefs, pecking on heads (fig. 65). Another interaction is constituted by the "taking" of humans, where oversized animals, usually felines, grasp miniature human figures/effigies with both hands, as if in possession or presentation fashion (fig. 31, pl. 6c). Usually this gesture is reserved for animals who hold things on which they nibble or for human figures offering bundles, infants, and drinking goblets.

The precise significance of these scenes remains unclear. Do they invert normal human/animal hierarchies? Do they depict mythical, idealized notions or pinpoint historical events (such as defleshing or death by punishment)? Several have suggested, for example, that these scenes may treat the aftermath of ritual combat among the Recuay, one purpose of which was to heighten fertility (Makowski and Rucabado Y. 2000: 210). Whatever the case, animals appear to be vital in the physical transformation of fleshly bodies and as liminal agents between lived and supernatural worlds. One clue to interpreting the scene is the position of spouts on some vessels, depicting scenes of animals feasting on the human; the entry spout issues from the corpse's groin and sometimes doubles as his genitalia. The inference is that the human, despite his transformed (dead) state, is still a provider, a source of vitality. This notion recurs in the human-feline interactions of the central figure scenes.

FIGURE 64. (*Top*) Modeled vessel showing carrion birds, probably condors or vultures, eating from a corpse. (Staatliche Museen zu Berlin–Preussicher Kulturbesitz Ethnologisches Museum; photo by C. B. Donnan)

FIGURE 65. (*Bottom*) Quadrangular panel sculpture of a warrior figure whose head is being pecked by carrion birds, probably from Pashash. (Museo Arqueológico de Cabana)

Felines and Leaders

Felines and amaru creatures are perhaps the most common images on Recuay art. In contrast to a common occidental identification of cats with feminine qualities, Recuay culture emphasized their maleness. Felines, especially on stone sculpture, are shown as virile, male predators.

Felines are depicted in a number of ways which differentiate them from humans. For example, humans are almost always represented in frontal poses, whereas felines are typically represented in profile (fig. 66). Feline heads, though, are sometimes shown frontally, both in pottery and in sculpture (such as tenon-heads). Furthermore, unlike human mouths, which are rather plain, Recuay artists exaggerated the mouth and dentition on felines. Felines have their mouths wide open, baring their teeth. Erect phalluses and large testicles are pronounced and unequivocal statements of their sex. Also, unlike human portrayals, the limbs terminate in clenched claws. All the key spots for carved work—the eyes, open maw with interlocking fangs, claws, genitals, spiraling tail, and attack stances—convey the vital capacities of felines. They connote sexual and killing prowess, power, and agility. These qualities must have been attractive to Recuay leaders in programs of personal or group aggrandizement.

An explicit contrast exists, however, between the dynamic, tensed expression of felines (and feline action) and the rather lifeless, somewhat stoic and calm, appearance of the human figures. The chiefly figure rarely does more than preside in any scene—he is the recipient or pivot of action rather than the doer. This follows the argument that chiefs stand for ancestors: central, timeless, and of monumental bearing. But, as in other chiefly societies, purposefulness and poise—probably referencing the predatory stealth of cats—may have been valuable qualities of political leaders.

FIGURE 66. Sculpture s15 from Chinchawas, showing a central figure scene: a frontal warrior figure, adorned with a trophy-head ornament, flanked by profile feline creatures.

Some Recuay leaders fashioned themselves as being like felines by the types of juxtapositions and substitutions that appear in the art. This is most evident in the "central figure theme."[5] The essential design of the theme — a frontal human figure commanding the deference of the flanking figures — expresses the individual's authority. The flanking figures are usually feline (pl. 5a), but on ceramics large birds (raptors or vultures), serpents, or women are sometimes depicted in lieu of the felines (for example, fig. 52). The central figures differ in adornments but at least in stone sculpture are often depicted with genitals. The central personage in sculpture also often has serpent appendages emerging from his head or wears a headdress with comparable elements. Weapons and trophies often identify the central figures as warriors. Thus the general scene confronts the viewer with a formidable countenance: a chiefly warrior and master of subjects.

The qualities of the warrior figures are further accentuated by associations with the feline creatures. The calm, collected carriage of human figures contrasts with the exaggerated actions and growling expressions of the felines, yet they were metaphors of prowess in hunting and killing. Ritual human sacrifice was very weakly referenced in Recuay art: occasional representations of a head-taking sacrificer figure, severed heads, and perhaps the animal-gorging scenes. But the warrior figures became enhanced through their juxtaposition with and their command over the flanking felines. Perhaps most importantly, some chiefly figures are essentially dressed in the designs, the second skins, of felines: resist circle and dots on the upper legs and stripes/rings around the limb extremities. The comparison is particularly noteworthy between two vessels from the Jancu grave-lot, where they were likely to have been used in conjunction during chiefly rites (pls. 5a, b).

Most representations of felines in Recuay art were probably based on highland feline prototypes — the puma or the spotted gato montés (fig. 67) — rather than necessarily the oft-cited jaguar. Circular pelage markings, for example, are very rare in feline depictions of stone sculptures, although they do occur on ceramics along with other geometric designs. It should be mentioned that adult pumas are light brown, while puma cubs have spots on their bodies and rings around their tails. The gato montés is likewise often spotted, with tail rings.[6]

I follow the argument that the puma, which had associations with the highlands (cold), order, and governance, formed a more logical model to denote authority for different sierra cultures (Zuidema 1985). This is notable because creatures with jaguar features and their associations (hot-

ness, shamanism, wildness) were basic to the art of Chavín, the culture immediately antecedent to Recuay in highland Ancash.

Contrary to much thinking about Recuay culture, overtly shamanic practices and allusions in general are relatively rare in the art. It indicates little emphasis on the representation of the ecstatic religious practitioner and hallucinogens, as seen in other Pre-Columbian cultures (e.g., Cordy-Collins 1977; Reilly 1989; Stone-Miller 2004). Trance activities to induce shamanic journeys and visions left few traces (if any) in Recuay material culture and iconography. At the very least, Recuay developments showed little of the Chavín shamanic complex. This was a major disjunction between the use of feline imagery in Recuay and Chavín cultures. Rather, what seems to have been vital in Recuay representations of feline creatures is their association with leadership, both in life and in death.

The central figure scene includes various elements which refer to a process of supernatural transformation, consumption, and reemergence. Perhaps the most evident are the serpent appendages located above the head of the main figure. Most often the appendages issue from the head, growing out of a central stem. Sometimes no stem is present, and they appear more like a simple headdress (figs. 37a, 39). In other depictions the appendages are detached from the head, forming an independent figure above the human figure (fig. 37d). In still other representations feline-serpent appendages emerge out of nonfeline heads. Heads, as in many Andean societies, can be a critical symbolic locus for transformation and renewal.

The appendages also devour body parts. For example, serpent headdresses often have their feline heads juxtaposed with hands and fingers, as if to consume them. Limbs and appendages (tongues, tails, ears) terminate in creature heads which, in turn, form or eat other limbs and appendages. What seems to be emphasized is that the action, the process of change, is continual, in a series of iterations that has form but is never complete. The range of amaru creatures on textiles may further express this diversity.

Finally, sometimes transformation is shown by the replacement of the central figure characters with other characters. Thus the central figure and the flanking felines on sculptures can be complemented by or indeed replaced by more mythical-looking beings: double-headed creatures. Notably, the creature's heads are depicted frontally (like humans) and have not interlocking fangs but simple groove mouths, a feature characteristic of human representations. In the case of the central figure, I surmise that the bicephalic creature is what he is conceived to have turned into — an alternate or surrogate version of the original.

Feline features may represent an otherworldly capacity and form of ancestors. In different parts of the Andes and elsewhere in South America, the feline form is often considered a state of humans in the afterlife (Hernández Príncipe 1923; Sullivan 1988; Zuidema 1985). Interestingly, some Quechua groups of highland Ancash (especially in the Cordillera Blanca) consider pumas to be images of the recently deceased. Moreover, they are said to consume their victims and serve as vessels for human spirits (Walter 1997). Such oral traditions may relate to the depictions of felines and animals in general, who hold and devour different forms of human bodies (fig. 65, pl. 6c). The "eating" of humans can refer to the physical breakdown of the human body but also to its conversion into ancestorhood.

Thus in Recuay art animals were very often liminal creatures. They mark key transitions between common and special time and between lived and supernatural domains. Felines in particular serve as intermediaries between death and the afterlife. The feline imagery forms a critical dimension in Recuay visual culture because of its close relationship with the apotheosis and veneration of the honored deceased, probably chiefly leaders or kin group founders. They represent ancestors who are likened to felines for their superhuman qualities. But they are also consumed and made integral/reconstituted by feline creatures as part of the transformation from corpse to ancestor.

Discussion

The Performativity of Recuay Art: Visual Fields and Social Contexts

The principal media of the Recuay corporate art style, stone sculpture and ceramics, formed parts of small political programs of chiefs and their families. These media were crucial in two related but distinct cultural domains of public display: funerary cults and feasting activities. The objects were at once the backdrop and vital participants in these activities, because they performed as social agents for their makers and users.

Where did these images circulate? As noted, stone sculptures, although movable (with great effort), adorned special kinds of Recuay architecture. The most prominent were funerary buildings, in particular subterranean tombs and aboveground chullpas. Enclosures and high-status residences also occasionally featured stone reliefs. Fine ceramics were much more portable and were found especially in tomb contexts. The vessels also must have been prominent during political/ceremonial displays, most likely in many of the same contexts as the stone sculptures. Textiles, worn on live and dead bodies, were also essential forms of display.

Recuay festive events with food and drink were political strategies as well (Gero 1992; Lau 2002). In most societies food and eating form critical social and political fields (Bray 2003; Dietler and Hayden 2001). The festive provisioning of food and drink, especially an alcoholic beverage, in return for labor is a social strategy that is well known among societies of the Central Andes, ancient and historical (Hastorf and Johannessen 1993; Jennings et al. 2005; Mayer 2002; Morris 1979). It is essentially a form of exploitation understood within an idiom of generosity, reciprocity, and community (Godelier 1977). Through their hospitality, hosts incurred the debt of the guests, which could be converted at a later time to different forms of resources — such as food, luxuries, and, most often, labor. It is clear that fancy vessels were integral to the political-ceremonial life of the Recuay, because they depicted them in festive social scenes or as fundamental gear held in the hands of high-status individuals. Cups are held by both recipients and servers, and entire jars (probably for maize beer) are carried by women. The objects portray but also help facilitate the celebration of chiefly leaders and momentous acts in their lives: transitions in leadership, union of families, the birth of an heir, formal succession to office, and important public appearances.

The physical handling of the vessels must have reinforced different sorts of social relations between host and guest and host and kin. Pouring jars and pitchers, for example, commonly depict high-ranking individuals in the act of drinking, presenting a cup, or receiving cups from subsidiary figures — positions probably assumed by those receiving or offering drink (pls. 6b, 8). Drinking from effigy head cups (fig. 27) literally conveyed drinking from the head of this lord. The practice centered on generosity and the flow of ancestral well-being.

In the architectural effigies, where acts of presentation and reverence are offered to the deceased, Recuay artists effected different fields of interaction and visuality. Each is concerned with witnessing and reproducing the event. The first was the one created by the artist to represent, for example, the group scene, where the modeled figures interacted with each other. The second concerns the person who viewed the scene, who, in doing so, acknowledged the action. And the third involves the user of the vessel, a pourer (and perhaps a descendant), who distributed the contents of the vessel to others, in turn, to acknowledge the past event and in effect replicate past action in the present. This was therefore a peculiar type of memory practice, part inscribed (vessel representation) and part incorporated (using the vessel, being with it, witnessing, and mimesis of positions).

Recuay ceramic imagery therefore memorializes the past at the same time as it prescribes future sociality. Recuay objects were used strategically to reiterate special social relations associated with forms of status, kinship, and hierarchy. Through their performance, persons and roles were actively constituted.

Conclusions

The combination of simple yet forceful themes with imaginative execution makes Recuay one of the most recognizable art styles of ancient America. Add to these qualities technical savvy, spare yet powerful forms, and a distinctive aesthetic, and it becomes evident why the artworks have dominated the most important studies of the culture. In this chapter I have reviewed the diversity of Recuay art, focusing on a number of iconographic clusters which center on notions of personhood and the social relations of ethnic lords. The images emphasized a web of sociality (ancestors, women, animals, mythical beings, and males), which helped to construct proper chiefly individuals.

It is perhaps axiomatic to argue that many of the iconographic elements were shared among the various Recuay groups. Certain technical styles demonstrate that Recuay groups also produced arts and crafts in similar ways. Thus the comparison highlights techniques of elaborating surfaces and foregrounding images, based largely on reduction or removal of material. This is most prominent in ceramics and stone sculpture but can be extended to other media, such as architecture, metalwork, and weaving.

The repetition of Recuay designs helped to signify chiefly bodies and extend chiefly associations to different media and forms. Recuay groups highlighted exterior surfaces not simply to signpost wealth or enchant others. Such surfaces contained, nurtured, and transacted familiar but special contents. These were ancestral flows, concentrated in chiefly persons and other symbolic vessels. The physical presence of ancestors, in effigies and in surfaces, was particularly significant, because genealogy was a source of empowerment in Recuay society.

This discussion primarily describes the accrual of meanings by Recuay images through their social contexts. The imagery was meaningful principally through use and display in group ritual contexts. Recuay images do not exist on their own or have objective meanings but are constantly constructed or modified through the intervention of humans. The images which are the focus of this discussion were significant because they were used to engage with varying audiences, living and deceased, of different orders — from individual to family to lineage to community.

Stone sculptures with images of anthropomorphs occupied privileged positions in funerary monuments because they were received as tutelary manifestations of vigilant ancestors. The libation vessels, through their containment and offering of drink, alternatively constructed kin and ideological meanings through their conventionalized scenes of lords, women and attendants, houses, and creatures. The imagery of walls — in their forms and stone surfaces — protected interiors and intimidated enemies and allies alike through the idiom of warfare. Textiles and other artworks fashioned chiefly persons and ancestors in real life and in ceramic depictions. In all these instances, the objects' efficacy diminished as soon as believers lost interest in them, with their former potencies and meanings retreating back inside.

PLATE 1. Compounds at Yayno. (a) East façade of c41, a quadrangular compound. The façade is over 30 meters across and the wall stands over 10 meters high. The construction would have had at least three additional rows of boulder slab uprights (wankas). (b) Southeast façade of c50, a circular compound at Yayno. The wall stands over 11 meters high. In each compound, multistory interior rooms, built inside the walls around an open courtyard, were the dwellings of high-status inhabitants.

PLATE 2. Rock painting on a large boulder, near the entrance to Quebrada Quilcay-huanca, showing two anthropomorphs (a smaller one to the left of the large figure) with outstretched arms. Above them are crescent-shaped arcs, painted in red and yellow. Above the larger figure is a red plumelike element.

PLATE 3. Polychrome open bowls, with ring bases. (a, b) Positive and resist-painted bowls from Pashash. The repeated motifs (circle and dots, linked eye-like elements, and S-scrolls) are very common at Pashash and other areas in northern Ancash. (Museo de la Nación, Lima) (c) Bowl found at Pomakayán. The decoration includes red and orange paint over the creamy white paste surface. (Museo Arqueológico de Ancash, Huaraz)

PLATE 4. Fine pottery from Yayno. (a–f) Rayo-style kaolinite bowls; (g, h) Asuac-style bowls, fine paste; (i, j) Huanchac-style bowls, fine paste; (k–n) Black-linear redware-style vessels.

Ø15

A

Ø16

E

Ø16

B

Ø20

F

Ø18

C

Ø16

G

Ø14

H

Ø17

D

Ø15

I

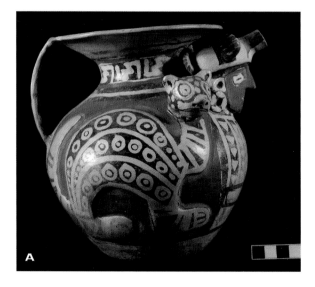

PLATE 5. Modeled polychrome vessels from Jancu tomb. (a) Effigy jar of profile feline (one of two which flank a frontal male, to the right). The main chiefly figure has a headdress that also serves as the pouring spout. (b) Effigy jar of a seated male figure, with resist designs that resemble feline pelage markings. The upper limbs of felines and males show circle and dot patterns while the limb extremities feature rings/stripes. By wearing such "skins," chiefly males of Jancu were probably perceived as being like feline creatures. (c) Effigy jar of a seated female carrying a vessel. She features shawl pins, narrowing of her waist, and a decorative head band which extends around the vessel. Historical records indicate that women were often charged with chicha production for public and funerary ceremonies. (d) Jar with framed representation of a bird (Group E iconic figure), probably a condor or condorlike figure. (Museo Arqueológico de Ancash, Huaraz)

A

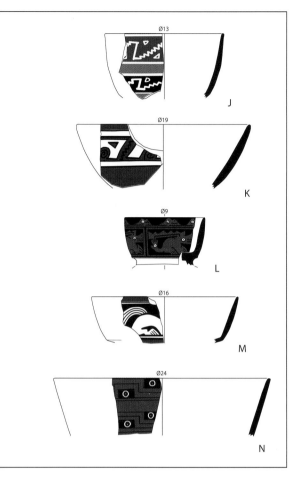

Ø13

J

Ø19

K

Ø9

L

Ø16

M

Ø24

N

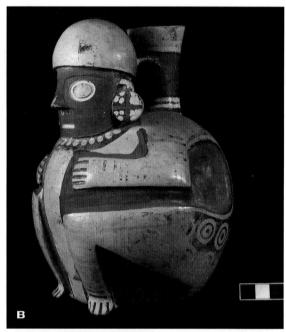

B

C

D

A

B

PLATE 6. Modeled polychrome vessels. (a) Effigy of a seated flute player, garbed in rich attire and intricate designs; he wears a tall hat with brim elements as well as ear ornaments. (Municipality of Chacas Collection) (b) Effigy vessel in the form of a seated male figure, wearing an elaborate tunic with circle designs and a headdress with scored elements laid flat, like brims. The figure raises a small cup, which also served as the pouring spout. The areas without clothing are painted red. The figure's mouth features teeth, which are unusual for such effigies. (Museo Regional de Caraz) (c) Effigy vessel showing a feline seizing or "taking" a human figure. (Musée du quai Branly, photo by Patrick Gries, reproduced with permission, Scala Group)

C

PLATE 7. Recuay-style textiles. (a) Large panel of tapestry tunic, made of cotton warps and camelid fiber wefts. The textile features a range of iconic figures in a single field. (Reproduced with permission from V&A Images/Victoria and Albert Museum, London [Museum No: T.89&A-1984]) (b) Reconstruction drawing of a plain-weave textile fragment, recovered from a cliff tomb context at Aukispukio. Note the alternations in color and design elements. (Museo Arqueológico de Ancash, Huaraz)

A

B

A

┈┈┈ Reconstructed

A

PLATE 8. Effigy vessel showing a drinking ceremony within an architectural setting. (a) View of exterior. (b) View of interior, with figures holding bowls. (Photographs by Christopher Donnan, Fowler Museum of Cultural History)

PLATE 9. Head representations in Recuay culture.
(a) Fragment of Recuay pottery vessel, showing a Moche style head (aquiline nose, stripped ear ornaments, round helmet, eyes), perhaps depicting a trophy object. From site of Pashash (Museo Arqueológico de Cabana)
(b) Stone sculpture of head with large banded helmet and ear ornaments, probably a warrior figure chewing coca (bulge in his left cheek). Today, the head adorns the foundations of the main church in Cabana, along with other sculptures from the ruins of Pashash.

CHAPTER EIGHT

A Prehistory of Recuay Culture

My goal in this concluding chapter is to produce a diachronic model of the character and workings of the culture which elaborates on different forms of evidence presented earlier. The discussion weaves two intersecting themes and data sets, organized chronologically. First, it describes the variability and development of Recuay political systems, as reflected in the archaeological record. This employs inferences from different data (including patterns in artifacts, monuments, and settlements) to describe the rise and decline of sociopolitical centers in different regions of the Recuay heartland. Second, the discussion considers the role of interaction between groups, as reflected in material style and the movement of special objects. Different patterns of frequency and distribution indicate interregional contacts and cultural transactions between Recuay settlements and political centers as well as their timing. Foreign interaction seems to have been fundamental to both the emergence of the Recuay style and its eventual demise. Relative insularity and remarkable regional diversification characterized the intervening time.

This chapter emphasizes the role of Recuay culture and history in the wider archaeological record of the Central Andes. In particular, I focus on different things of the culture — with regard to their making, style, and use — and review how they expressed, participated in, and affected the course of Recuay prehistory.

Emerging Recuay Style and Identity after Chavín

Elements of the Recuay culture emerged in the north highlands of Peru just as soon as Chavín culture began to disappear. Huarás style, the white-on-red pottery component of the Recuay tradition, was crucial in this respect.

Other white-on-red pottery cultures existed in the northern highlands and north central coasts at the time. Some scholars suggested the existence of a "white-on-red horizon" that followed Chavín's demise (Lumbreras 1974b; Willey 1945). Throughout, this pottery showed an emphasis on painted, white linear, and geometric designs on red paste ceramics, especially on the exteriors of bowls. Subsequent developments were associated with the diversification of local styles in various regions, such as Lima, Gallinazo, Moche, and Recuay.

The degree to which Huarás groups interacted with or contributed to the demise of Chavín people can be debated. But it is clear that Huarás culture was largely a conscious rejection of Chavín forms and meanings. It is possible that Huarás emerged in the Callejón de Huaylas and moved into the Chavín area (Lumbreras 1970: 72). Some of the elements of Huarás pottery, however, suggest coastal influences. For example, as in later Recuay styles, potters modeled human and animal figures on jars. In addition, whole vessels occasionally became effigies of the human form. This manner of representation was not part of any local Chavín-period repertoire and was more typical of the Gallinazo, Salinar, and Vicús styles of Peru's north coast and foothills. Geometric-linear designs and polished redware surfaces were also common decorative modes.

The dispersed presence of pre-Recuay occupations suggests that Huarás groups were fairly widespread across the Ancash highlands, but little of the wealth accumulation or demographic concentration characteristic of later Recuay settlements is present.

Some disagreement exists concerning the nature of relationships between Recuay and Chavín and contemporary cultures of the Early Horizon. Some have contended that Recuay originated directly out of the Chavín tradition. For example, John W. Smith, Jr. (1978: 90) argued that Recuay was an "end product or modification of the Chavín tradition," largely because of similar thematic content in the art (especially feline imagery) as well as in the production/forms of stone sculpture. Smith (1978: 121–126) followed his advisor, Richard Schaedel, in thinking that Recuay exploited an existing infrastructure, an interaction network abandoned by Chavín.

Huarás-period interregional exchange is not well understood, but clues are provided by the feline effigy vessel found in a post-Chavín level at Chavín de Huántar (Lumbreras 1974b: fig. 126a; Purin 1990: 15). Found with Huarás white-on-red materials, it is transitional to Recuay. The large eyes, lack of pelage markings, surface treatment, and modeling are extraordinary for Huarás, and the mythical theme is more characteristic of coastal cultures (such as Salinar, Gallinazo, or Vicús). This might suggest continued pilgrimage by coastal groups to the cult center after its height.

Terence Grieder (1978: 183) also believed that the Recuay were inheritors of a Chavín legacy: "The new [Pashash] elite inherited the language of power from the Chavín style, a language whose form was stone buildings ornamented with stone tenon-heads and relief sculptures, with pottery and metal ritual objects bearing sacred designs. Those elements were retained by the new patrons as heirs to Chavín power." In other words, Chavín forms persisted or were revived by the Recuay. Grieder (1978: 183) postulated that a small, early settlement at Pashash was taken over by a foreign elite class, probably from the south coast and Paracas culture. This was because of similarities in ceramic forms, techniques (resist painting), and common iconographic designs (especially felines, serpent creatures, and head appendages) in Paracas art.

The present evidence, however, indicates a very sharp break between the Chavín and Recuay traditions, in style as well as in sociopolitical arrangements. As noted, the religious meanings of the iconography showed little continuity. Feline depictions in particular were less openly associated with shamanism than with concerns about political leadership and the afterlife. The contexts of the production and use of the feline imagery —which extended far beyond pilgrimage centers to small villages and hilltop settlements of different size and complexity — indicate major ruptures. Thus it could be argued that religious imagery became popularized. Objects with feline imagery were much more restricted during the Chavín horizon, mainly limited to elites or religious practitioners.

Cultural connections with the north and north-central coast may have been more important during the initial development of Recuay culture (fig. 68). The section on settlement systems in chapter 2 has described the north-central coast as a key region for intensive multicultural relationships, probably between groups of different ethnicity. This is especially evident in the existence of buffer zones and special gateway settlements separating highland communities and coastal Moche and Gallinazo people (e.g., Millaire 2008; Proulx 1982; Topic and Topic 1982; Wilson 1988). In addition, defensible "gateway communities," located at key routes and constricted valley necks, articulated highland and coastal areas and were centers for the interchange of fancy ceramics from multiple prestige cultures (Czwarno 1983; Topic and Topic 1983). Some Middle Valley groups were responsible for very large defensible centers, distinguished by the prominence of highland-related kaolinite wares, such as at Cerro León

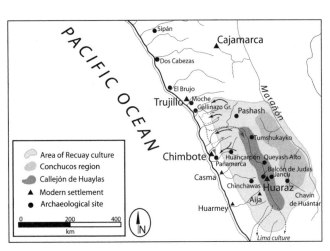

FIGURE 68. Routes and directions of interaction patterns during the early Early Intermediate Period (left) and Middle Horizon (right), at the beginning and end of Recuay culture, respectively.

(Moche) and Huancarpón (Nepeña). In terms of pottery, these appear coeval with Early Recuay and indicate strong interaction between different populations.

Significant connections between Recuay and Gallinazo (or Virú) populations existed at an early stage. Gallinazo culture developed on the north coast of Peru by the first centuries B.C. and prior to Moche florescence. A stratified society with militaristic dispositions, Gallinazo established its major center, known as the Gallinazo Group, in the Virú Valley. The culture extended into the Moche and Santa valleys and beyond (Bennett 1950; Fogel 1993; Kaulicke 1992; Larco Hoyle 1945; Makowski, Donnan, et al. 1994; Wilson 1988) but featured many stylistic elements shared by Recuay groups. Recuay and Gallinazo interaction emerged by the first centuries A.D. and was likely due to commercial interests associated with the exploitation of chaupiyunga mid-valley areas as well as the traffic of coast-highland products along the western slopes of the Andes.

Pottery associations, in forms and decoration, provide the best temporal and spatial markers for this interaction. One often-cited trait is the use of negative or resist painting. As for the Recuay, this painting technique was very common on the fancy range of pottery (bottles and serving wares) and was employed to fill design fields with repeated linear and banded designs. Unlike the Recuay, however, Gallinazo resist painting was usually executed as a bichrome resist black on the redware paste. Other distinctive commonalities include the use of special vessel shapes, including dipper and fancy bottle forms, as well as modeled human and animal figures. The marked resemblances in form and decoration led Rafael Larco Hoyle (1945, 1962) to contend that Recuay culture derived from coastal groups.

Another important Gallinazo-Recuay connection is the shared use of the crested animal design (Group A), described in chapter 7. The animal represents one of the most common motifs on Recuay funerary pottery and also appears in a number of other contemporary highland and coastal cultures. Like Recuay pottery, Gallinazo ceramics render the animal as a resist design on vessel walls — shown in profile, with prominent circular eyes, a long tail, and a mythical appendage (the "crest") emerging from its head.

The design appears often in the art of north-coast groups. Found in Salinar and Gallinazo, it later transforms in appearance and in composition (Bruhns 1976; Mackey and Vogel 2003). Early Moche examples, as full-figured effigies, include dramatic anthropomorphic depictions of the animal wielding a sacrificial knife and severed head. The creature appears to carry associations with death, ritual sacrifice, and decapitation that are common in later Moche imagery and funerary practices. The crested animal was one divinity in a wide range of supernatural beings in the Moche world. Spectacular wooden representations feature dual crested animals facing each other (Franco Jordán et al. 2005). In styles of the north coast, it is often shown inside a crescent form: hence the "moon animal" moniker. In Moche representations, the crested animal figure battles a fanged divinity in a mythic battle, perhaps associated with the perpetual movement and succession of celestial bodies. No such confrontations are represented in Recuay art. It seems likely that the crested animal had divergent specific meanings, or disjunctions, in spite of the similar form.

The growing popularity of shared imagery coincided with major social transformations during the Early Intermediate Period in northern Peru (e.g., Kaulicke 1992; Makowski, Donnan, et al. 1994). In particular, large townlike settlements and ceremonial centers seem to have been more centralized. This period is marked by the emergence of regional theocratic systems of rank and elite ideology. The sharing of stylistic and religious elements is noteworthy because the Gallinazo, Recuay, and Moche groups were in competition with each other. Radiocarbon measurements indicate that they were largely contemporaries. Multiethnic relations were probably common in specific coastal valleys by around A.D. 200–300. In the circumscribed river valleys of the north-central coast, they vied over agricultural and herding resources as well as finite supplies of water and land.

When Moche political power coalesced during Middle Moche times, the other two cultures and their respective communities seem to have been marginalized. Gallinazo, for example, eventually became absorbed or displaced as part of Moche expansion, presumably through military invasion — although Gallinazo-related ceramics and cultural elements continued in different north-coast areas throughout the Early Intermediate Period (e.g., Kaulicke 1992; Shimada 1994). Despite their interest in coastal resources, Recuay groups apparently never fully established colonies or settlements along the coast, on the scale of Pashash or Yayno, preferring trading relations in lieu of territorial takeover or because they were incapable of it. Notably, all three cultures seem to have valorized warfare in their culture and imagery. Settlement pattern studies demonstrate increasing reliance on fortified hilltop settlements and suggest that it was a time of great uncertainty and competition.

The Gallinazo also made architectural or house effigies. As in the Recuay examples, human figures populate these miniature spaces and are often presided over by a well-attired lord. The form of the buildings as well as architectural features are also very similar to those found on Recuay versions. It is interesting to note that the wall decoration resembles elaborate façades made out of stonemasonry, usually found in highland areas, or of adobe reliefs and mural work, located mainly in coastal areas (e.g., Bennett 1950; Bueno M. 2001; Thompson 1973). Besides the house effigies, Gallinazo shared with Recuay the emphasis on standing chiefly figures in various officious acts — offering, presentation, being venerated, and presiding over people and buildings. The metaphor linking chiefly leaders and house-based corporate groups is perhaps most explicitly made in effigies of Gallinazo lords, like some Recuay human figures, who wear headgear topped with paired step designs which are also used to adorn the gabled roofs of buildings (Grieder 1978: 135–137; Larco Hoyle 1945: 5). These were new tropes of action and authority for public figures in artworks, presumably sponsored by the figures and their respective corporate groups.

It is not coincidental that new political arrangements characterized these groups, with political power increasingly vested in the hands of chiefly leaders and their kin-based factions. What is at stake here is not the rise of social differentiation or the rise of chiefly societies, for both these phenomena can be documented in earlier Andean prehistory. Rather, a special form of leadership intensified during the power vacuum left in the wake of the collapse of Chavín and associated socio-religious centers during the transition between the Early Horizon and Early Intermediate Period. Earlier forms of ranking highlighted access to and knowledge of rare and finely made religious esoterica. The new ideology emphasized descent and predation and the social distinctions of chiefs and their respective collectives. Lordships began to fill in the political landscape in northern Peru, based on their command over "house" and warfare. Such corporate groups were almost certainly organized along descent lines. It can be hypothesized that they were also actively constituted through the activities of co-residence, commensalism, organized conflict against competitors, and artistic production. The chief, at once a physical and symbolic force, stood at the core of these cultural enterprises.

Some generalizations about Recuay sociopolitical developments during this early period can be enumerated. First, the extant data show that the most prominent developments occurred along the Pacific flanks and in the Callejón de Huaylas, especially along the northern fringes of these regions. At present we have scant evidence of Early Recuay presence farther to the south and to the east (in Conchucos). Pashash was already a thriving center by about A.D. 300; the Huaraz area saw less precocious development. And most of the stylistic interaction was with groups to the north, such as the Salinar, Gallinazo, Moche, and Vicús.[1] The convergence of many of the Recuay ceramic tradition's major components occurred along the frontiers of northern Ancash, along the foothills and the western flanks of the Andes. Soon thereafter the interaction was felt throughout the Recuay heartland, with widening production linked to status displays and funerary cults of aspiring elites and their increasingly powerful factions.

Contact Zones and Cultural Florescence, A.D. 300–600

The archaeological record of the Middle Recuay period indicates great changes in the geopolitics of highland Ancash. Pashash and then Huaraz wielded substantial cultural and probably economic clout over their territories, but settlements in surrounding areas emerged to compete with them. In the Callejón de Huaylas, strong chiefly polities emerged in the Katak, Carhuaz, and Caraz areas. In northern Ancash, La Pampa and Aukispukio were the largest settlements bordering the Pashash zone. In the Cordillera Negra, coeval polities, probably on a smaller scale, existed in Aija, the upper Nepeña, and the upper reaches of the Casma headwaters.

The principal shift was the sudden development of the northern Conchucos, just north of the Río Yanamayo, into an additional hotspot of Recuay settlement and local political integration. Yayno and the coeval major settlements of Huintoc, Marcajirca, and Rayogaga are all within a day and a half's walking distance of each other yet feature some of the largest and most impressive monuments of the ancient Andean world. Dominating productive lands below, they were fortress towns composed of elaborate compounds.

In all the principal zones of political centralization, monumental architecture, finewares, and other indices of accumulation of wealth mark the proliferation of local Recuay lordships. They shared a pervasive community ideology based on ritual and chiefly sanction. The best-known cases thus far are Pashash, Yayno, Katak, and Huaraz. Some of these communities consisted of internally diverse corporate groups. The fancy wares from the sites are discernibly Recuay but consist of regional strains rather than a unified style. They also all suggest high-status offering and commensal practices. The use of stone sculpture was another important prerogative, but it was not standard practice everywhere. Stone-carving was popular especially in the Callejón de Huaylas, Cabana, and Cordillera Negra regions for funerary cults and elaborating special high-status spaces. Because of the wide stylistic diversity and patchy distribution of material culture, combined with a lack of administrative architecture and settlement centralization, not much evidence exists for a Recuay "state." The present data suggest small town-based polities — large chiefdoms or curacazgos — characterizing different regions of a diverse Recuay commonwealth.

The Recuay flourished during a time when art and political power were fundamental dimensions of Early Intermediate Period cultures. Recent investigations, especially of elaborate tombs and temple structures, make it clear that finely made objects and elite architecture were central to the ideology of leadership along the northern Peruvian coast. Moche artworks formed elaborate expressions of elite political and religious ideology (e.g., Bawden 1996; Donnan 2004; Pillsbury 2001; Uceda and Mujica 2003). Elites stood out as they redramatized myths and appropriated mythical personas and attributes. The great temples — with their spaces for commemoration, subterranean tombs for burials, and plazas for feasting — were the stages for these performances. On the surface, it could be argued that such practices also characterized the Recuay.

A closer analysis, however, shows fundamental differences. One key issue concerns scale. Recuay ceremonial practices, limited to corporate groups and the local community, seem to have been fairly modest affairs compared to the large valley centers of the Moche, such as the Moche type site, El Brujo complex, and Pampa Grande. Unlike these ceremonial centers, which served urban populaces and associated hinterlands, even the largest Recuay towns never held more than 1,000–1,500 persons at their height. Highland populations were certainly considerable. But wide tracts of arable land, agro-pastoral orientations, and the predominant site type (the small hilltop village with households in immediately adjoining lands) meant that Recuay groups were characterized by greater dispersed settlement.

Furthermore, Recuay ceremonial centers do not appear to have been major interregional pilgrimage sites. They seem to have served local communities rather than groups from different regions and ethnicities. This contrasts with the earlier pattern in highland Ancash during the Chavín horizon, wherein Chavín de Huántar was established as an oracle and a paramount pilgrimage site for the region. The different tenor of Recuay ceremonialism derived from the later ritual prerogatives that centered on highly specific divinities: local ancestors. Recuay and Moche ceremonialism had a mythic basis in that ritual forms referred to and sometimes reenacted mythic narratives. But whereas Moche ceremonies served pan-Moche divinities, Recuay focused on chiefly ancestors who had potent but restricted domains of efficacy.

The trajectory of Recuay and Moche interaction represents one of the unique and richest histories of interethnic relations in the ancient Americas. They were neighboring cultural traditions during the greater portion of the first millennium A.D. Specific forms of interaction connected the two regions, despite each having a long period of relatively insular development. The interaction manifested in different ways, but the most prominent included trade, stylistic interaction, patterns of making, and sometimes patterns in armed conflict.

One crucial way to discern Recuay-Moche interaction is in the making of things. It is one of the exceptional cases in Andean prehistory of prestige culture emulation. This interaction resulted in a number of hybrid ceramic forms and images: Moche-produced vessels inspired by Recuay forms and thematic composition (Bankmann 1979; Reichert 1982b). Following typical Moche practice, the vessels are made out of redware not kaolinite, employ molds, and are rendered using the standard white and red color scheme; even the figures, in the modeling of their faces and bodies, are discernibly Moche (fig. 69). Yet the portrayal of the central figure theme and the vessel shapes are distinctively Recuay.

Why Moche potters reproduced Recuay types remains unclear. Some pots were mold-made, so a series of replicas was possible,[2] presumably for multiple audiences. This emulation is also curious because Recuay pottery only very rarely circulated in Moche settlements. Styles such as

FIGURE 69. Moche replica of a Recuay vessel, showing a central figure scene. Although the shape and subject matter emulated Recuay pottery dispositions, the paste, modeling, and color scheme are distinctively Moche. (Staatliche Museen zu Berlin–Preussicher Kulturbesitz Ethnologisches Museum; photo by C. B. Donnan)

Gallinazo and Cajamarca were more common, because they may have been the residues of different ethnic groups *within* Moche settlements (e.g., Shimada 1994; cf. Makowski 2008b). With some exceptions, Recuay culture did not commonly extend into lower valley areas except in mixed cemeteries. This is probably not an instance of a Moche potter working in the Recuay heartland, such as a captive, transplanted, or itinerant worker. Rather, these seem to be Moche imitations of an exotic highland style. Probably because of its prestige and political sway in Ancash, Recuay culture occupied a privileged position. Another highland tradition, Cajamarca, from Early Cajamarca times onward, featured pottery forms and designs which Moche potters also copied.

The sharing of stylistic elements in terms of vessel forms, decoration, and imagery constituted the main fields of early Recuay interaction with coastal groups (pl. 9a). Later Moche and Recuay interaction extended to the ways in which elite activities were perceived and represented.

One way consisted of converging styles of representing warriors, warrior-elites, and armed combat. Elsewhere (Lau 2004a) I have enumerated parallels in a burgeoning warrior ideology during the Early Intermediate Period. Specifically, they shared forms in high-status warrior attire and gear, conventionalized images of capture, and trophy ornaments—

which can be understood as belonging to the co-development of an ideological complex about warriors and violence. Actual physical evidence for armed combat is rare in the record. But the vital point is that this complex grew prominent more or less coevally for neighboring groups and became fundamental to their elite arts and aesthetics. Recuay, Gallinazo, and Moche were all implicated as well as other cultural traditions further abroad, such as Vicús and, less prominently, Cajamarca. It seems that success in warfare and related practices (hunting, trophy-taking) constituted a space for building the social capital of warriors and their chiefly leaders. Warriorhood became overtly part of a gendered sociality during the early portion of the Early Intermediate Period.

Some Moche fine-line scenes may show interethnic conflict. Moche groups may have wanted to reference Recuay-like foreigners, or enemies in general, in their art. In addition to being competitors for crucial land and resources (especially in the middle valley zones), enemies probably also embodied vital essences that were incorporable through violent capture and ritual killing. Such triumphs enhanced the authority of the Moche lords. It is not known whether a clash between Recuay and Moche groups ever occurred, as suggested in some imagery. But like other Moche narrative scenes, the subject matter of combat scenes probably had both mythical and religious undertones as well as a historical basis, in that they were performed by human actors. These scenes, I believe, memorialized Moche victories over the alien group, perhaps long in the past. These activities may have been staged and reenacted in ritual political performances using live captives in later times (Lau 2004a).

Another field of cultural interaction was in the imagery of sexual intercourse. The Moche are the better known for their sexual imagery. The Moche emphasis on oversized erect phalluses and vaginas, masturbation, sodomy, and fellatio has been interpreted as emphasizing a type of ancient birth control and deviant sexual habits (Kauffmann Doig 1979; Larco Hoyle 1965). Others highlight the fertility of the sexual representations, concerning supernaturals, the afterlife, or local concepts of procreative activity (Bergh 1993; Bourget 2006; Weismantel 2004). The Recuay sex scenes described in chapter 7 are, by comparison, rather less sensational but no less informative (Gero 2004). The Recuay interest in representing the body in coitus was not inherited from local Early Horizon (Chavín) sources. Like Moche scenes, the Recuay scenes probably owe their origins to cultures of the north coast (Vicús and Gallinazo). Especially in their form and tone, the Recuay representations are more similar to the imagery of these cultures, where the emphasis seems to have been on partners of complementary status and general visual acknowledgment of the union between chiefly persons.

In sum, the Recuay maintained rich interaction with other northern cultures during the early Early Intermediate Period. It is notable that the key innovations in representation during this time centered on changing attitudes toward human beings, activities, and their potencies in the different cultures. The artworks point toward the propagation of new, increasingly localized ideologies about the timelessness and power of secular leaders and their factions. This was perhaps the major transformation in Early Intermediate Period art: high-status factions represented themselves in conventionalized images depicting stylized bodies, individual and corporate, in action. In doing so, they distinguished themselves from social others.[3]

The Recuay also maintained cultural interaction with other regional groups. Most notably, peoples of the Central Coast and especially of Lima culture to the south show strong stylistic relationships during the middle and late parts of the Early Intermediate Period. The most common shared element is the bicephalic serpent motif in the ubiquitous interlocking imagery of Lima art (especially ceramics, murals, textiles, and wood sculpture), followed by emphasis on the frontal head with appendages. Even the crested animal is sometimes depicted. Because of the timing of the interaction (ca. A.D. 300–400) as well as the range of the images found in highland Ancash, most scholars feel that the influence moved from the north highlands to the central coast. Lima groups may have borrowed from the Recuay style, perhaps as ideological support for their own leaders (Makowski and Rucabado Y. 2000: 231–232).

The interlocking designs (Group C) in Recuay ceramics are commonly used to emphasize high-status attire and the surfaces of buildings. The designs are repeated in geometric profusion in Lima objects, blanketing the surface in an interlocking pattern. Lima designs are strongly planar and oftentimes geometric, replicating woven designs, so textiles may have been the predominant medium for the interaction. Because of their portability and value in negotiating identity, textiles, especially those made out of camelid hair fiber, played an integral role in cultural transactions between highland and coastal groups.

In general, we do not have much direct evidence for the exchange of bulk food/resources such as meat, camelid fiber, and marine resources between Recuay and coastal groups during the Early Intermediate Period. Corrals and ancient routes do exist in coastal valley areas, but few pertinent studies of food remains have been published. Fish and shellfish remains are rare in the faunal assemblages from highland Recuay tradition settlements (Lau 2007; Rofes 1999).

To be sure, the preservation and the visibility of organic remains bias the current record. More work in the future will clarify the degree to which food products were traded between the coast and highland regions. Nevertheless, strict verticality models — of discontiguous resource zones controlled by a single group — do not necessarily map well with the patterns of coast-highland networks prevalent in Ancash during the first millennium A.D. (see Schaedel 1985). The different periods of strong interaction do not fit well with models of major population displacements or movements, such as conquest, diasporic, or settler forms.

Prestige goods were very occasionally brought into the Recuay heartland. Some Moche items were acquired, but little importation from neighboring Gallinazo or Lima cultures seems to have occurred. The cases are associated mainly with Recuay occupations of the Cordillera Negra and the Pacific Andean flanks, the geographical interface between Recuay and coastal and middle valley groups.[4] In the few known cases, Moche-style items were popular as grave goods as well as in contexts of public display. Obsidian is relatively rare at Early Intermediate Period sites in highland Ancash, compared to periods of greater availability and consumption during the Early Horizon and Middle Horizon (Burger et al. 2006).

Overall, the emergence of large settlements during middle Recuay times does not seem to have coincided with strong interregional trade of sumptuaries. Stylistic interaction certainly took place, but the physical exchange of imports appears to have been fairly restricted. This was true even at the most powerful of Recuay centers, Pashash, which was fairly close to Moche and Gallinazo groups in the Santa Valley. Though they had knowledge of their neighbors, Recuay elites were either uninterested in their prestige goods or unable to acquire them. Moreover, it seems that the development of Recuay centers, the seats of large, valley-based chiefdoms, occurred without much foreign input or competition from ethnic outsiders.

Within the Recuay heartland, however, settlement patterns and defensive location indicate that internecine warfare was likely a decisive factor in the formation of the town-based polities. Very large proto-urban settlements developed suddenly and in unprecedented fashion in the fourth century A.D. Earlier large settlements in the north-central highlands had arisen around ceremonial centers. Some Recuay centers, such as Yayno, grew through a process of agglutination. A strategic location provided a defensible core, wherein a number of compounds — the residential complexes of corporate groups of variable size — contributed to a larger fortified community. The incentives for this practice probably included safety in numbers, trained organization in arms and leadership, and public performances; these articulated the paramount leader, factions, and community beliefs.

Late Recuay Transformations

The terminal developments of the Late Recuay period are perhaps the best known of the cultural tradition. Despite regional distinctions, profound changes in the material culture of Recuay groups characterized the end of Early Intermediate Period and the beginning of the Middle Horizon. The gradual dissolution of the pottery style by the seventh century A.D. coincided with wider cultural transformations which heralded the end of the Recuay tradition.

By this time Pashash and the settlements of Katak and Aija were less intensively occupied, perhaps even abandoned. Although Yayno maintained its power in the northern Conchucos, its inhabitants continued to have little ability to access fancy wares and other long-distance trade items.

Settlements near strategic trade routes in the Callejón de Huaylas and the Cordillera Negra grew increasingly important. Not surprisingly, these were also the strategic areas with clear Wari influence. Multipurpose settlements with funerary, public, and residential sectors were the main vectors for early Wari interaction. Sites such as Honcopampa, Wilkawaín, and Chinchawas all had relatively sudden and major local-style building programs during this time. Honcopampa may have been used as an administrative center; but it is now clear that the forms of the buildings (the rectangular compounds and D-shaped niched structures) were not unequivocal Wari intrusive forms. Yayno's rectangular compounds in particular are earlier and more elaborate than those at Honcopampa.

A surge of long-distance exchange also marked this period. For example, Cordillera Negra groups at Chinchawas during the seventh century A.D. had access to Late Moche and Early Wari polychrome wares. People in the Callejón de Huaylas also had greater access to rare artifacts and materials, as seen in the diverse pottery assemblages of Pierina area sites and Ichik Wilkawaín. The interaction focused mainly on prestige goods for display and ritual offerings, which emphasized exotic, unfamiliar preciosities and the imagery of powerful societies. Raw rare materials such as marine shell as well as obsidian also began to be transacted. Therefore both the range of sources and the frequency of exotics increased considerably, demonstrating the groups' growing ability and desire to acquire rare sumptuary items from different exotic and politically sovereign areas. This was a highly selective practice to assert political power and economic wherewithal and probably to reinforce the distinctive tastes of increasingly competitive factions.

What was transacted? Some Late Moche pottery was imported into highland Ancash, such as sites in the areas of Chinchawas, Huaricoto, and Pierina. Middle Cajamarca cursive styles also entered into highland Ancash in small quantities—a precursor to more intensive presence later. Other nonlocal wares were imported from adjacent upper valleys of the Pacific flanks as well as the neighboring highlands. Perhaps most notable were occasional imports of Wari polychrome styles in Late Recuay contexts (Bennett 1944; Isbell 1989; Lau 2005, 2006a; Ponte R. 2001).

The period was therefore highlighted by significant interaction focused on the physical exchange of luxury goods, especially from neighboring highland and coastal areas. They most commonly appeared in funerary contexts as elite grave offerings, but they also served as luxury items for status display. Some must have been acquired through economic transactions as commodities or perhaps through other means. For example, some may have been pilgrimage offerings, the plunder of raids, or diplomatic gifts.

It is important to note that even small, fairly modest communities managed to acquire objects bearing Wari and Wari-related motifs. These items apparently were not the exclusive purview of wealthy elites. Wari forms and imagery were important for a range of groups with different socioeconomic capacities. Wari items may have been desirable for their religious or cosmological content that could be appreciated across factional, rank, or ethnic boundaries. Many later groups in highland Ancash borrowed Wari-inspired designs and decorative modes.

The greater availability of obsidian from southern Peru was part of the intensification of interregional trade practices during the early Middle Horizon. Notably, obsidian has not been reported from the large centers such as Pashash, Honcopampa, and Yayno but rather from fairly small villages such as Chinchawas and Ancosh Punta. These sites featured obsidian mainly from the Quispisisa source (Ayacucho), with one sample from the Alca source in Arequipa (Burger et al. 2006).

An understudied topic is the degree of mutual stylistic interaction among highland groups, especially during the end of the Early Intermediate Period. Most scholars assume that the impact of Wari expansion in the provinces was largely one-directional: Wari to province. But this presupposes an already-fixed state style and a stable, hierarchical political relationship. To be sure, new motifs and forms (especially in ceramics) evince Wari stylistic influence on later Ancash groups, usually late into the Middle Horizon; but Late Recuay groups also adopted technical and design dispositions in pottery production from other cultures, such as those associated with Cajamarca and coastal press-molded wares (Lau 2004b, 2006a).

Limited evidence suggests that Recuay groups interacted with their south-central Andean neighbors before the Middle Horizon. The possible transmission of wide-loom tapestry technology has already been noted, but we have additional lines of evidence. Stone sculpture, for example, was one of the possible vectors of Recuay influence on southern Andean cultures, including Wari. This is especially evident in the central-figure theme and in high-relief stone carving, which Schaedel (1952, 1993: 231–236) found similar to that of the northern Recuay.

In addition, some Recuay motifs of supernatural beings are very similar in form to polychrome pottery designs found in the Ayacucho area before Middle Horizon Wari expansion (Lumbreras 1959; Menzel 1964).[5] Mythical beings in proto-Wari pottery have ties to Recuay images: bicephalic creatures with humped backs, top-view serpent-feline heads on appendages, and other creatures with top-view or split-represented heads.[6] Such designs, many found at Pashash, are dated to the Middle Recuay period, by at least A.D. 400. Split-representation and top-view perspectives on Wari polychromes were very likely holdovers from Huarpa and Late Nasca antecedents; and bicephalic creatures, avian figures, and humped animals are known from Nasca types (e.g., Proulx 2006: figs. 5.39, 5.73). But it is still important that similar mythical creatures and ways of representation were shared between the regions in question prior to Wari centralization. The shared conventions and imagery imply partly overlapping cosmological beliefs. In all likelihood, the common ideas were part of the initial appeal of Wari for Recuay people and a strategy of Wari religious expansion during the Middle Horizon.

In sum, the main consumers of long-distance trade during the Late Recuay period at present seem to have been groups in the Cordillera Negra and Callejón de Huaylas, especially in the zone between Huaraz and Caraz. The available evidence indicates that trade was less prominent in the Conchucos, the Cabana region (northern Recuay area), and southern Callejón de Huaylas (Katak, Aija). Crucially, very little Wari presence existed in the Conchucos area, suggesting that it was largely outside the main routes for Wari-associated exchange and expansion found in the intermontane valleys west of the Cordillera Blanca.

Older centers lost their power, while others came to the fore. Settlements with an intensive Wari presence were located in strategic areas for trade and politico-religious interaction. Wari influence, especially in religious imagery and ways of rendering pottery, certainly reached many parts of the Callejón de Huaylas and the Central Andes at this time. Direct control of the region by Wari cannot be ruled out, but the present evidence in Ancash does not demonstrate the infrastructure of administration and extraction that would provide positive evidence for widespread territorial domination. For example, Inka roads, satellite centers, strongholds, ceremonial offerings, and storehouses are all present from the short period of Inka colonialism in highland Ancash. If the Wari expanded through conquest, the material correlates appear different from those recognized for the Inka. Wari's initial push into highland Ancash centered on elite alliances in key zones and exchange of rare and prestige objects.

Finally, it should be emphasized that Wari styles constituted only a part of the commodities exchange during the Late Recuay period. Other styles were also desirable, such as Late Moche, Cajamarca, and other kaolinite wares of the north highlands. Wari certainly became more important later in the region, but its initial intervention in the Recuay world was through a cosmopolitan, polythetic prestige economy with interested and able partners.

The Demise of the Recuay Culture and Polities

The Wilkawaín period in highland Ancash coincided with the demise of Recuay tradition polities. Unprecedented changes in domestic and ceremonial material culture occurred in most areas. Kaolinite pottery, the most common diagnostic of Recuay culture, disappeared. Stone sculptural production apparently either ceased, such as at Aija, or was characterized by new dispositions in imagery, such as at Chinchawas. Major transformations also took place in public ceremony, which grew increasingly focused on aboveground chullpa mausolea.

In addition, long-distance exchange was typified by new patterns. During the later period of Wari presence in the Callejón de Huaylas, groups of the Cordillera Negra and the Callejón de Huaylas favored intensification of trade and cultural interaction with coastal groups. This was an important time for transaction of various styles of exotic pottery from many neighboring areas (Lau 2005). Obsidian from the Ayacucho highlands was used in considerable quantities, indicating that contacts with groups in the south continued to be strong to acquire the material (Burger et al. 2006). Long-distance trade was especially prominent when economic interaction intensified, almost certainly due to Wari expansion.

Local material culture showed increasing appropriation of coastal imagery and nonlocal technical styles in some areas — such as production of fancy polished redwares and blackwares and the use of press-molding techniques for special serving vessels. Stylistic interaction also grew, with local wares adopting foreign traits, especially from the coveted Cajamarca and Wari styles. By the mid to late Middle Horizon (ca. A.D. 800) coastal-style exotics — press-molded and polished monochrome wares — became more important to groups of the Cordillera Negra and Callejón de Huaylas.

Local highland Ancash groups emulated prestigious Wari styles during and directly after the Wilkawaín period, which paralleled similar developments in other parts of the Andean world. The regional manifestations of this process in highland Ancash were varied. Nonetheless the source material for local potters and other artisans likely derived from Wari imagery and cosmology. Its intervention in different parts of Ancash resulted in the adoption of new painted design motifs and color combinations (for example, pendant designs, interior open bowl decoration, polychrome painting, and band/meanders), which had been distinctive parts of the Wari stylistic vocabulary. Again, the character and distributions of the present data suggest that Wari-inspired things were valuable to elites and commoners alike in societies across the Andes. In a short span of about a century the new innovations eclipsed earlier Recuay practices.

The settlement evidence does not indicate major population declines during the Middle Horizon. Profound changes in the occupations of Recuay settlements took place, however, especially in the former seats of political and religious power. Pashash's decline began earlier, but it was largely abandoned by A.D. 700. The groups at Yayno did not continue to build large, elaborate compounds. Monumental building programs in the Recuay style ceased across highland Ancash, being superseded by other forms of special constructions. In particular chullpas and their attendant ritual complex became much more prevalent. Important changes in the scale of collective ritual also occurred. Taken together, decisive changes marked the end of the Recuay tradition: the shared cultural dispositions that once had brought together the widespread groups of the commonwealth disintegrated.

The Causes of Recuay's Demise: A Trial Account

The causes for the demise of Recuay culture remain far from clear. Nevertheless, it is possible to attempt a systemic account. Any working model at this stage remains conjectural but serves to implicate a series of interlinked variables and evidence. Alternative trajectories exist, and new data will refine the points here. I should note that I am mainly referring to the end of the Recuay material style. Any sociodemographic conclusions need to wait for skeletal and DNA evidence.

On the basis of ice-core data from Huascarán, colder conditions prevailed especially during the sixth and eighth centuries A.D. The time was comparable to the Little Ice Age, which pushed snowlines, typical vegetation cover, and agricultural zones to lower elevations. While such conditions probably improved herding economies, existing agricultural pursuits may have suffered due to frosts, decreased yields, and shorter growing seasons associated with colder weather.

Little migration was possible because of habitual practice, ancestral ties to land, and circumscription. Any intermontane areas that were productive agriculturally had long been settled and continued to be occupied, especially at lower elevations. Conflict between neighboring groups, probably due to resource disputes, had long fueled the predominant settlement type in highland Ancash: the defensive hilltop center. People at settlements such as Yayno (located far above the current upper limits of agriculture at 4,150 masl) would be farther from their fields. In effect, they would have needed to travel farther and worked more for less. By the eighth century A.D. major occupation and building programs at Yayno ceased. Earlier centers such as Pashash, Queyash Alto, and Aija had already been deserted. In contrast, places at lower elevations, such as Huaraz and Honcopampa, swelled.

The economic uncertainties, new knowledge of other cultures, and demographic flux probably evoked questions about the efficacy and closed character of Recuay faiths. Local ancestral divinities, the customary agents of abundance, were not effective. This was a sentiment in small and large communities alike. Groups at large centers probably grew dissatisfied with their chiefs, the earthly representatives of ancestors.

The traditional ideology of the Recuay — focused on group exclusion, descent privileges, and lavish consumption — was outmoded. On the one hand, the growth of settlements such as Huaraz and Yayno probably fueled difficulties in reconciling the interests of different factions/enclaves. On the other, the economic trouble unmasked chiefly exploitation, especially in light of their continued failures to ensure good production. Large community rituals, associated with fancy venues for conspicuous displays, fell out of favor. Human and architectural effigy ceramics were discontinued, replaced by simpler bowl and jar forms made of nonkaolin clays. At the same time when the imagery was growing increasingly geometricized and abstract, it muted or displaced the former aesthetic centered on the techniques and conventions of imaging the chiefly body.

Funerary cults dedicated to ancestors continued to be fundamental. But they focused on new kinds of objects, imagery, and spaces. Chullpas, in particular, proliferated and were used by both wealthier and lower-status groups as symbolic centers and overt markers of ancestry. Stone-carving continued, but with slightly modified imagery. Tenon-heads shifted from specific human to feline forms, and reliefs focused on frontal splayed anthropomorphs. Other finely made things such as Recuay-style metalwork and stonemasonry disappeared. These products were all indicative of heavy labor and resource costs. While existing strategies of labor recruitment (such as commensalism) were not abandoned, their intensity and scale were certainly more restrained by the Middle Horizon.

Wari culture and ideology, with its general emphasis on fertility, must have been particularly inviting, indeed buoyant, in this context. Recuay religion already included some elements of the Wari worldview, making them at least somewhat compatible. People in the region had also worshipped a staff god many generations before. For the Recuay, they were giants, made remarkable monuments, and moved and carved stone with impossible precision.[7] They must have been favored by their supreme divinity — a storm god, bringer of lightning, master of creatures and rain. Even though their buildings and sculptures lay in ruins, they remained sacrosanct enough for the Huarás and Recuay to bury their dead in their midst.

Now a new faith, drawing on similar precepts, was being recast by Wari, a looming power to the south, based in a great and extensive settlement. Their representatives were always successful in having or transacting valuable, ideologically potent materials, such as brilliantly painted pots, lapis, turquoise, obsidian, and marine shell. For at least a century they had traversed through the Callejón de Huaylas, making forays into northern lands for their unusual objects and the much-cherished fiery red *Spondylus*. They were surely powerful, for they also wore and commanded dazzling textiles, which equaled or surpassed even the finest Recuay weavings. Just as importantly, neighboring groups, especially elites, were becoming visibly successful due to their alliances with Wari people. Moche, Cajamarca, and Lima/Nievería styles all became increasingly Wari. Their initiatives always commanded attention, because they could be backed by religious and military might.

Wari relations proliferated along routes of exchange: the Callejón de Huaylas and western slopes of the Cordillera Negra, targeting vital north-south and coast-highland corridors, respectively. Initially, local lords and their corporations were the main mediators of Wari imported objects. But because their imagery had little to do with direct ancestors or chiefly entitlement, elites could not claim exclusive right to it. Opting in, as in local choice or as in not resisting, meant a new ideological space for elites, full of *Spondylus*, brilliantly painted pottery, textiles, and useful obsidian — all with sanction from the Wari capital in the south. For commoners, it was the promise of abundance. Indeed, after a century or so even nonelites could have a stake in Wari culture through local potters, carvers, and weavers. Wari culture and ideology thus spread like wildfire, erasing the last vestiges of the Recuay style.

The current archaeological record reinforces elements of this narrative, but additional lines of evidence are needed. In particular, more site-based research would fill out the regional diachronic picture of local trajectories of culture change and subsistence practices. Settlement data also beg for greater chronological precision, especially the identification of subphases. The paleoclimatic data are suggestive, but more fine-grained proxy data about environmental conditions are needed to relate to relative chronologies and cultural patterning.

For the model to work, future research can focus on corollaries about land use and settlement patterning. First, we should expect that lower-elevation areas should have more intensive settlement during the early Middle Horizon. Huaraz constituted one such place, but others should exist. Lower-elevation sites or those strategic for exchange might also demonstrate evidence for greater stylistic interaction and trade (Huaraz, Honcopampa, Chinchawas). Alternatively, fewer large residential sites should have been established in higher locations, such as the puna. Life at the upper limits of agriculture and above would have been increasingly difficult. This might be demonstrated where high sites are abandoned or show intensification of high-altitude resources.

Any plausible narrative requires assessment of internal and external factors. The environmental context for modeling cultural transformations is essential, but it is neither a prime mover nor the systemic kick for the process. Indeed, the eight centuries of the Recuay cultural tradition were typified by change rather than stasis, which cannot be reduced to paralleling environmental change.

Multiple factors led to cultural change during the Middle Horizon. In the Recuay case, these factors had to do with new opportunities and changing value systems, at a time when dissatisfaction with older paradigms was growing. This took place in the midst of new pressures and opportunities promoted by the religious and politico-economic expansion of the Wari state. I would also locate the transformation in new forms of sociality, which became increasingly important because of the competitive and relatively independent nature of Recuay communities. Just as with the beginning of the style, its end pivoted on people's changing ways of doing and interacting with things — making, using, circulating, consuming them — perceived as better or more effective in comprehending and managing their worlds. Given the present data, this works as a better scenario than ascribing the transformations to totalizing sociodemographic ruptures associated with conquest, migration, climate change, or diffusion.

In large part, then, the same things that contributed to the distinctive character of Recuay culture were also the reason for its eventual downfall. The chiefly ideology and lifestyles which had long characterized groups of the Recuay commonwealth could no longer be sustained by the Middle Horizon. In this fashion, the material culture and imagery were not only crucial in understanding the past. They helped make it: they effected events and were willful in prehistory.

CHAPTER NINE

Epilogue

In most societies, it takes some doing to erase the memory of past groups and their cultures. Ancient places and things have different potentials of becoming again. They reintegrate into other traditions, participate in new narratives, become received wisdoms, and fall in and out of favor in the literature. Sometimes an element can be useful and meaningfully redeployed (pl. 9b). Usually they remain latent, with unpredictable afterlives.

My examination here has concentrated on the diverse flows of ideas characterizing Recuay groups, as reflected in material remains. Some were borrowed, some were invented, but all were shaped for their own ends. By A.D. 800 only a few lingering ideas seemed to have any Recuay substance, basis, or presence at all. Perhaps techniques in herding and camelid use were one such instance. Stone sculptures also continued to be made and used in the interest of ancestor cults. Otherwise, few material things or techniques can exemplify a legacy owed to the Recuay tradition.

In the flow of ideas, do cultures leave lasting marks? I have frequently wondered why, for example, the images and meanings which underwrote the Recuay's elaborate iconography largely disappeared from highland Peru. Why was the crested animal evacuated from later local styles? Why did the innovation in human representation not continue into other highland styles and cultures? I am skeptical of interpretations that might see the receding of ideas as "nonadaptive," absolute, or final. Rather, I suppose now that such dispositions did not disappear at all — they remain dormant, nascent in the flows of Andean culture and history.

Recuay pots and stone sculptures surface in towns, villages, and the countryside from time to time, often found accidentally during construction. In one recent case two superbly preserved monoliths were found in Huaraz during routine excavations to widen a street, which led to a controversy over their status as private property of the landowner or as part

FIGURE 70. Three cast replicas of Recuay stone sculptures, serving as pylons blocking automobile access in Huaraz. Jirón José Olaya is one of the only streets in the city that survived the major 1970 earthquake with most of its old buildings intact.

of the national cultural patrimony (Bazán del Campo 2008). Replicas of stone sculptures, meanwhile, are sold to tourists, who take them home to adorn gardens and country estates. They also provide the livelihood for their modern carvers. Quite unexpectedly, even as curiosities, ancient sculptures have reentered Andean social life and the local imaginary.

Replicas also line various zones of modern Huaraz as short pylons (fig. 70) or centerpieces of sidewalk benches. Most people would be hard pressed to recognize what the replicas are, except to rest on them for a break. Nothing suggests that the ancient prototypes are of Recuay style, date to around A.D. 400, and stand only a few hundred meters away in the nearby archaeological museum. Nor is there much contemplation that passersby may somehow be related to or even be descendants of the original figures. Yet they are certainly implicated now as monuments, subtle as they are, to the Recuay past. Their contemporary use recontextualizes their ancestral import: they perform as interactive embodiments, simulacra of the originals, serving the community and their descendants to improve well-being in overall social life. In effect, a peculiar convergence of ancient meaning and intention is manifested today, despite the delay.

I close by reiterating one of the main convictions of this study. Ancient art and culture are neither mere reflections of historical patterns nor only stuff through which past behaviors are inferred. Material things, to be sure, are frequently physical expressions of the past. But they are often much more: they are agents, intended or otherwise, of that past. They contribute to the flows of history and help shape their courses and contours.

APPENDIXES

APPENDIX 1. Demographics in the Department of Ancash

Province of Ancash	Capital	General Geographic Distribution	Total Area (ha)	Agricultural Area Used, 1994 (ha)	% Area Cultivated	Pop. (1993)	Pop. (2002 est.)	% Urban (2002 est.)	Density Persons/ Ha Used	Density Persons (1993)/ Province Area	Density Persons (1993)/ Total Ha Cultivated
Carhuaz	Carhuaz	Callejón de Huaylas	80,395	11,689	14.5	40,796	46,231	29.4	3.49	0.51	0.16
Recuay	Recuay	Callejón de Huaylas	230,419	7,753	3.4	19,824	20,363	59.4	2.56	0.09	0.08
Yungay	Yungay	C. de Huaylas/ Cordillera Negra	136,148	19,341	14.2	51,663	59,210	18.9	2.67	0.38	0.21
Huaraz	Huaraz	C. de Huaylas/ Cordillera Negra	249,291	24,075	9.7	124,960	145,732	66.1	5.19	0.50	0.50
Huayla	Caraz	C. de Huaylas/ N. Ancash/Cord. Negra	229,278	17,932	7.8	52,158	62,039	35.0	2.91	0.23	0.21
Aija	Aija	Cordillera Negra	69,672	5,102	7.3	8,936	9,298	19.4	1.75	0.13	0.04
Ocros	Ocros	Cordillera Negra/ S. Ancash	194,507	7,162	3.7	7,178	7,192	47.3	1.00	0.04	0.03
Bolognesi	Chiquián	S. Ancash	315,480	15,979	5.1	28,945	29,751	55.1	1.81	0.09	0.12
A. Raimondi	Llamellín	East of Cordillera Blanca	56,161	14,992	26.7	19,440	20,817	24.0	1.30	0.35	0.08
Asunción	Chacas	East of Cordillera Blanca	52,866	2,939	5.6	10,106	10,844	16.6	3.44	0.19	0.04
C. F. Fitzcarrald	San Luis	East of Cordillera Blanca	62,425	12,315	19.7	21,592	22,584	9.7	1.75	0.35	0.09
Huari	Huari	East of Cordillera Blanca	277,190	35,743	12.9	65,870	68,332	42.4	1.84	0.24	0.26
M. Luzuriaga	Piscobamba	East of Cordillera Blanca	73,058	12,449	17.0	23,943	27,636	15.6	1.92	0.33	0.10
Pomabamba	Pomabamba	East of Cordillera Blanca	91,405	17,978	19.7	26,990	28,046	28.2	1.50	0.30	0.11
Sihuas	Sihuas	East of Cordillera Blanca	145,597	24,238	16.6	32,780	36,082	25.2	1.35	0.23	0.13
Corongo	Corongo	N. Ancash	98,801	7,224	7.3	9,104	9,587	45.9	1.26	0.09	0.04
Pallasca	Cabana	N. Ancash	210,121	14,397	6.9	29,272	31,550	47.5	2.03	0.14	0.12
Casma	Casma	Coast	226,103	10,851	4.8	36,400	41,875	65.7	3.35	—	—
Huarmey	Huarmey	Coast/Cordillera Negra	390,842	7,480	1.9	24,519	27,054	71.3	3.28	—	—
Santa	Chimbote	Coast/Cordillera Negra	400,499	34,689	8.7	349,201	403,605	91.9	10.07	—	—

Source: Garayar et al. 2003.   *Note:* ha = hectares; pop. = population.

APPENDIX 2. Radiocarbon Dates from Highland Ancash

Site	Reference	Lab No.	14C Age (yrs B.P.)	1-Sigma Cal. Range	2-Sigma Cal. Range	Phase Association	Context and Material
Amá	—	AA32486	520±55	A.D. 1333–1438	A.D. 1304–1453	Cotojirca III	Funerary structure A, with copper (charcoal)
Ancosh Punta	Ponte R. 1999a	AA32481	1195±55	A.D. 734–937	A.D. 686–981	Cotojirca IV	Outside habitation Unidad z2 (charcoal)
Auquish Corral	Ponte R. 1999b	AA32483	250±50	A.D. 1637–1796	A.D. 1494–1947	Cotojirca V/Aquillpo	Hearth in patio (charcoal)
Carhuac Punta	Ponte R. 1999a	AA32482	535±50	A.D. 1330–1433	A.D. 1303–1444	Cotojirca V/Aquillpo	Locus 641 (charcoal)
Chavín de Huántar	Lumbreras 1989	HAR-1104	2640±70	832–791 B.C.	919–562 B.C.	Huarás	Tomb 7, in stone fill (charcoal)
Chavín de Huántar	Lumbreras 1989	HAR-1109	2480±70	787–409 B.C.	801–398 B.C.	Huarás	Midden on house floor (charcoal)
Chavín de Huántar	Amat 1976a	Gif-1079	2100±100	350 B.C.–A.D. 16	390 B.C.–A.D. 123	Huarás	Old temple atrium, NE sector, Lev. 5 (plant carbon)
Chinchawas	Lau 2001	AA32365	1710±50	A.D. 256–408	A.D. 229–429	Kayán	Burnt area, OP9 Level J, Terrace 1 (charcoal)
Chinchawas	Lau 2001	AA32369	1395±45	A.D. 622–664	A.D. 598–689	Chinchawasi 1	Base of midden, OP19 Level L (wood/bone)
Chinchawas	Lau 2001	AA32371	1375±45	A.D. 642–677	A.D. 602–763	Chinchawasi 1	Under batán, house, OP49 Level D (charcoal)
Chinchawas	Lau 2001	AA32368	1305±45	A.D. 663–773	A.D. 652–801	Chinchawasi 1	Floor refuse deposit, OP31 Level H (charcoal)
Chinchawas	Lau 2001	AA32376	675±50	A.D. 1283–1386	A.D. 1263–1400	Chinchawasi 1	Tomb ST-3, OP65 Level B (charcoal)
Chinchawas	Lau 2001	AA32367	1290±45	A.D. 668–776	A.D. 657–863	Chinchawasi 2	Refuse deposit, OP4 Level G (charcoal)
Chinchawas	Lau 2001	AA32366	1250±45	A.D. 689–863	A.D. 664–891	Chinchawasi 2	Refuse/fill, OP21 Level I (charcoal)
Chinchawas	Lau 2001	AA32372	1180±45	A.D. 778–940	A.D. 694–980	Chinchawasi 2	Top of refuse deposit, OP26G (charcoal)
Chinchawas	Lau 2001	AA32373	1170±55	A.D. 778–960	A.D. 692–994	Warmi	Refuse on floor, OP36G (charcoal)
Chinchawas	Lau 2001	AA32374	1160±45	A.D. 781–961	A.D. 730–985	Warmi	Burnt refuse on floor, OP43I (charcoal)
Chinchawas	Lau 2001	AA32370	1150±50	A.D. 782–977	A.D. 731–998	Warmi	Burnt pit, OP20 Level F (charcoal)
Chinchawas	Lau 2001	AA32377	655±50	A.D. 1288–1392	A.D. 1276–1405	Warmi	Chullpa tomb CT-2, OP57 Level A (human bone)
Chonta Ranra Punta	Ponte R. 1999a	AA32484	2230±55	386–201 B.C.	399–124 B.C.	Huarás	Locus 137 (charcoal)
Gotushjirka	Herrera 2005	AA13210*	1495±90	A.D. 440–644	A.D. 345–690	Phase II (EIP/MH)	Cut P1, circular enclosure, base of inner wall (charcoal)

Site	Reference	Lab No.	14C Age (yrs B.P.)	1-Sigma Cal. Range	2-Sigma Cal. Range	Phase Association	Context and Material
Guitarrero Cave	Lynch 1980b	Si-1504	2315±125	517–204 B.C.	790–52 B.C.	Huarás-Recuay	Unit 47, fire-drill hearth (wood)
Honcopampa	Isbell 1989	n/a 3	1380±70	A.D. 618–687	A.D. 541–777	Late E.I.P./MH1	Patio-group AC-8, Exc.2, floor hearth (charcoal)
Honcopampa	Isbell 1989	n/a 2	1330±100	A.D. 640–778	A.D. 539–943	Huarás-bearing	Patio-group AC-5, Exc. 1, Lev. 11 (charcoal)
Honcopampa	Isbell 1989	n/a 5	1280±70	A.D. 663–804	A.D. 642–937	Middle Horizon 1–2	Patio-group AC-2, Exc. 4, broken floor (charcoal)
Honcopampa	Isbell 1989	n/a 1	1240±90	A.D. 673–892	A.D. 642–993	Middle Horizon 2	Patio-group AC-5, Exc.1, SW floor (charcoal)
Hornojirca C	Ponte R. 1999b	AA32491	615±50	A.D. 1298–1402	A.D. 1284–1421	Cotojirca IV	Subterranean tomb (human bone)
Intiaurán	Lane 2006a	A13211[†]	350±40	A.D. 1480–1640	A.D. 1450–1640	Inka/Colonial	Destruction level above floor, cent. structure, Sector A
La Pampa	Terada 1979	TK-173	640±50	A.D. 1293–1396	A.D. 1279–1410	White-on-red	RCC structure, upper floor (charcoal)
La Pampa	Terada 1979	TK-193	500±70	A.D. 1334–1445	A.D. 1302–1609	(Late) Caserones	Contents of vessel under floor (charcoal)
Llaca Amá Caca	Ponte R. 1999a	AA32489	1300±55	A.D. 662–776	A.D. 644–880	Cotojirca IV	Hearth with ashy sediment (charcoal)
Llaca Amá Caca	Ponte R. 1999b	AA32485	535±70	A.D. 1325–1438	A.D. 1296–1476	—	Rockshelter, Capa 1, Sector IV (charcoal)
Marcajirca (Huari)	Ibarra, pers. com.	LTL2624A[§]	891±45	A.D. 1040–1220	A.D. 1020–1230	Late Interm. Period	Associated with chullpa contexts
Marcajirca (Huari)	Ibarra, pers. com.	LTL2625A[§]	701±45	A.D. 1260–1390	A.D. 1220–1400	Late Interm. Period	Associated with chullpa contexts
Marcará area	Ziółkowski et al. 1994	I-1352	2086±225	393 B.C.–A.D. 131	777 B.C.–A.D. 419	White-on-red	(charcoal/bone)
Marcará area	Ziółkowski et al. 1994	I-1350	1851±135	A.D. 5–340	168 B.C.–A.D. 527	—	(charcoal)
Marcará area	Ziółkowski et al. 1994	I-1359	1621±145	A.D. 255–601	A.D. 81–676	Recuay	(charcoal)
Marcará area	Ziółkowski et al. 1994	I-1353	1541±125	A.D. 401–644	A.D. 240–758	—	(charcoal)
Marcará area	Ziółkowski et al. 1994	I-1355	991±110	A.D. 904–1180	A.D. 780–1274	Late Honco	(charcoal)
Marcará area	Ziółkowski et al. 1994	I-1358	956±210	A.D. 888–1279	A.D. 658–1411	Late Honco	(charcoal)
Marcará area	Ziółkowski et al. 1994	I-1354	896±115	A.D. 1019–1263	A.D. 897–1298	Late Honco	(charcoal)

APPENDIX 2 (Continued)

Site	Reference	Lab No.	14C Age (yrs B.P.)	1-Sigma Cal. Range	2-Sigma Cal. Range	Phase Association	Context and Material
Marcará area	Ziółkowski et al. 1994	I-1356	586±110	A.D. 1291–1436	A.D. 1224–1489	—	(charcoal)
Marcará area	Ziółkowski et al. 1994	I-1357	501±105	A.D. 1325–1473	A.D. 1286–1640	—	(charcoal)
Queyash Alto	Gero 1992	Beta-31354	2220±150	403–54 B.C.	763 B.C.–A.D. 79	Huarás	White-on-red level (charcoal)
Queyash Alto	Gero 1992	Beta-31357	2140±90	357–46 B.C.	396 B.C.–A.D. 54	Huarás	White-on-red level (charcoal)
Queyash Alto	Gero 1992	Beta-31353	1360±90	A.D. 618–768	A.D. 537–886	Post-Recuay	Post-Recuay association (charcoal)
Queyash Alto	Gero 1992	Beta-30112	1350±80	A.D. 640–768	A.D. 543–879	Post-Recuay	Post-Recuay association (charcoal)
Queyash Alto	—	Beta-30115	1210±80	A.D. 690–942	A.D. 659–998	Post-Recuay	Post-Recuay association (charcoal)
Queyash Alto	—	Beta-30114	1160±80	A.D. 776–982	A.D. 679–1022	Post-Recuay	Post-Recuay association (charcoal)
Quitapampa C	Ponte R. 1999b	AA32488	2305±55	401–262 B.C.	478–262 B.C.	Recuay	Burned circular structure, outside tomb (charcoal)
Pashash	Grieder 1978	TX-944	1640±80	A.D. 263–534	A.D. 237–601	Quinú	Fill above Quinú level, Cut 4 Level 4 (charcoal)
Pashash	Grieder 1978	TX-1332	1610±170	A.D. 243–638	A.D. 34–768	Quinú	Stone fill, Cut 9 Level 4, white-on-red (charcoal)
Pashash	Grieder 1978	TX-1824	1590±60	A.D. 411–540	A.D. 264–616	Recuay-Yaiá	Fill over La Capilla burial, Cut 12 Level 4 (charcoal)
Pashash	Grieder 1978	TX-942	1580±70	A.D. 411–559	A.D. 263–639	Recuay	Alluvium, Cut 3 Level 2 (charcoal)
Pashash	Grieder 1978	TX-940	1500±90	A.D. 433–647	A.D. 386–685	Recuay	Alluvium over surface, Cut 3 Level 2 (charcoal)
Pashash	Grieder 1978	TX-941	1490±70	A.D. 475–643	A.D. 420–664	Huacohú	Burned roof beams, Cut 4 Level 2 (charcoal)
Pashash	Grieder 1978	TX-1329	1400±60	A.D. 604–669	A.D. 541–765	mid-Recuay (Yaiá)	Fill in doorway to burial, Cut 12, Level 6 (charcoal)
Pashash	Grieder 1978	TX-943	1380±100	A.D. 600–764	A.D. 435–886	Yaiá	Fill over house structures, Cut 3 Level 4 (charcoal)
Pashash	Grieder 1978	TX-1331	1110±270	A.D. 658–1216	A.D. 412–1401	Huacohú	Fill under house floor, Cut 9 Level 3 (charcoal)
Pashash	Grieder 1978	TX-1330	420±80	A.D. 1425–1622	A.D. 1331–1649	Colonial	Base of wall, Cut 7 Level 4 (charcoal)
Tecliomachay	Malpass 1985	B-8556	2310±60	406–209 B.C.	513–195 B.C.	n/a	Rock-lined hearth
Tecliomachay	Malpass 1985	B-8555	1750±60	A.D. 241–379	A.D. 144–417	Early Interm. Period	Ash layer

Site	Reference	Lab No.	14C Age (yrs B.P.)	1-Sigma Cal. Range	2-Sigma Cal. Range	Phase Association	Context and Material
Urpaycoto	Ponte R. 1999b	AA32492	3060±50	1405–1224 B.C.	1430–1131 B.C.	Ancosh	Locus 3924 (ceramic)
Yarcok	Ponte R. 1999a	AA32490	1125±50	A.D. 886–983	A.D. 778–1018	Middle Horizon	Chullpa tomb, Tumba 11, Capa 2 (human bone)
Yayno	Lau 2010	AA74404*	1556±33	A.D. 434–545	A.D. 423–574	Recuay (G1)	Operation 8, Level G (charcoal)
Yayno	Lau 2010	AA74401*	1524±29	A.D. 533–595	A.D. 433–604	Recuay (G1)	Operation 3, Level J (charcoal)
Yayno	Lau 2010	AA74402*	1508±33	A.D. 538–604	A.D. 435–636	Recuay (G1)	Operation 4, Level I (charcoal)
Yayno	Lau 2010	AA74400*	1473±33	A.D. 563–622	A.D. 542–646	Recuay (G1)	Operation 1, Level I (charcoal)
Yayno	Lau 2010	AA74403*	1447±33	A.D. 593–645	A.D. 559–653	Recuay (G1)	Operation 7, Level G (charcoal)
Yayno	Lau 2010	Beta-225518*	1330±40	A.D. 652–694	A.D. 645–772	Late Recuay (G2/3)	Operation 14, Level E (charcoal)
Yayno	Lau 2010	Beta-269995*	1330±40	A.D. 660–690	A.D. 640–770	Recuay	Operation 5, Level H (charcoal)
Yayno	Lau 2010	Beta-269996*	1330±40	A.D. 660–690	A.D. 660–810	Late Recuay (G2/3)	Operation 9, Level F (charcoal)
Yayno	Lau 2010	Beta-225517*	1290±50	A.D. 668–771	A.D. 652–867	Late Recuay (G2/3)	Operation 11, Level F (charcoal)
Yayno	Lau 2010	Beta-269994*	1190±40	A.D. 780–890	A.D. 710–960	Late Recuay (G2/3)	Operation 3, Level E (charcoal)
Yurakpecho	Lane 2006a	A13212†	660±35	A.D. 1290–1390	A.D. 1280–1400	Late Interm. Period	Offering pit, Structure 1

Note: all calibrated with Calib 3.0.3c, except * (Calib 5.0.1, intcal04.14c), † (OxCal v3.10), and § (OxCal v3.5).

NOTES

Chapter 1. Toward a Recuay Prehistory

1. As expressed in the term *illa* (or *ylla*), referring to something traditionally treasured.
2. By "tributarios," the administrative records meant a tribute- or tax-paying individual, most often an able-bodied male adult (married) head of household. Such patterns were also almost certainly affected by Inka conquest and reorganization during the Late Horizon.

Chapter 2. Land and Settlement in Ancient Ancash

1. Weather stations at Yungay (2,585 masl; 1953–1969), Huaraz (3,050 masl; 1950–1954), and San Lorenzo (3,750 masl; 1965–1970) averaged 295.8, 773.7, and 853.3 millimeters annually (ONERN 1973: 3).
2. One account describes how a Catequil idol was brought furtively to Cabana, where a new shrine was constructed for it after the original was destroyed by the Inka (Topic 1998; Topic et al. 2002).
3. Sites are known mainly from reports filed with the Instituto Nacional de Cultura — Ancash, Huaraz.
4. Variations occur from valley to valley, and scholars also define these areas somewhat differently. For example, for the Moche Valley, Theresa Topic and John Topic (1982: 2) define the mid-valley, ca. 200 to 1,000 masl, as beginning where the valley narrows into a gateway. For Proulx (1985: 21–22) and Daggett (1985), in contrast, the valley neck in Nepeña coincides with the beginning of the upper valley at Tomeque, ca. 385 masl (compare also Billman 1996: 30–33, Wilson 1988: 32–33).

Chapter 4. Ritual Buildings and Landscapes

1. This is perhaps the fundamental difference between Recuay "galleries" and many of those at Chavín de Huántar, for example, where it is possible to stand upright and appreciate and interact with a religious image such as the Lanzón.

Chapter 5. Pottery and Society

1. When Bennett (1944) used "Andean Archaic," this was actually a misreading on his part. Tello used "Andean Archaic" to describe a number of ceramic styles, including the "primitive technique" of Copa, the classic "Recuay" of the Macedo collection, and Chavín-style wares. In contrast, Kroeber (1944:

93) acknowledged Tello's intent and called the "primitive technique" of the Callejón de Huaylas the "Lagenaria-type."

2. The pot used to illustrate the "Pashash-Recuay" style (Bueno M. 1989: pl. 7) may be a fake (see Reichert 1982a).

Chapter 6. Objects of Stone

1. I also refer to previous reports and corpuses, which developed using their own criteria (e.g., Schaedel 1952: 1).

2. Wooden examples are also known (see Smith 1977).

3. A number of whole and broken examples, as yet unreported, can also be found in the Museo Arqueológico de Ancash, Huaraz, and Museo Regional de Cabana.

4. At the Sahuanpuncu site near Carhuaz, Steven Wegner and I encountered a tenon-head within a zone of chullpas (Bennett 1944: 62–63). Anthropo-morphic heads were described at the site of Huambo, south of Katak, including one example found on the interior wall of an ancient building (Schaedel 1952: 130).

5. See Guaman Poma (1980: folio 289) for a depiction of a "typical" interment in Chinchaysuyo (the northern quadrant of Tawantinsuyo) which shows the distinctive seated position and apparel, including an arching head ornament and wide fanlike collar.

Chapter 7. Chiefly Worlds in Artworks and Imagery

1. A tumi is a metal axe-shaped object common to the north coast of Peru. It frequently has a convex, crescent-shaped edge and concave sides, narrowing toward the head.

2. It is possible that metal "garment" pins may also have been worn in the ears. A representation at Pashash (Grieder 1978: 122) shows a male wearing ear-rings or perhaps metal pins with the shafts bent around (as some were found at the site). Furthermore, some painted representations of Pashash ceramics show frontal anthropomorphic ears simply with a curl (Grieder 1978: 213–215), which may allude to the curving shaft.

3. Like ancestor effigies in other world cultures, Recuay sculptures may have been wrapped or covered with precious textiles, paints, or other materials in periodic renewal rites. In this way the figure is for the most part concealed.

4. See Bennett (1944); Grieder (1978); and Lau (2006b), among others. It should be noted that some zoomorphic designs are limited to sculpture, while some geometric motifs occur only in the painted models. In addition, not all the painted designs have correspondences in Recuay architecture.

5. Some evidence suggests that the central figure theme emerged first in ceram-ics (by Middle Recuay) and was then transferred to stone sculpture, certainly by Late Recuay times (see Lau 2006b).

6. High-altitude communities in Isluga, in northern Chile, also perceive the gato montés as a camelid herder, often an agent of human herders who guides camelids by whistling at them (Dransart 2002). Members of the com-

munity had tame gatos montés living in their homes (Penny Dransart, personal communication, 2008).

Chapter 8. A Prehistory of Recuay Culture

1. Each of these represents a cultural tradition; I am mainly referring to associations with: (1) Early to Middle Gallinazo, roughly Gallinazo I and II (Bennett 1950; Fogel 1993); (2) the complex associated with Vicús (Kaulicke 1992; Lumbreras 1987; Makowski, Donnan, et al. 1994); (3) Late Salinar (Kaulicke 1992); and (4) Early Moche, encompassing Moche I and II.

2. Several hybrid vessels are known to have been made by the same mold (see Reichert 1982b).

3. Philippe Descola (2006) would term this type of social identification or ontology typical of certain societies "analogic," where the members of a given society find discontinuities in the interiority (mind/soul) and physicality (body/surface) between humans and other existing beings.

4. Amat (1976a: 535) has referred to some early Moche objects from Recuay tombs in the Mosna Valley but never described the materials systematically. Possible Moche-style pottery and a spindle whorl were encountered at the site of Pashash (Grieder 1978: 72–73). Moche vessels have been identified in Recuay funerary contexts in Nepeña (Gambini 1984; Proulx 1982). Moche ceramics, including bichrome vessels, impressed wares, and modeled representations of a pelican and a fanged decapitator (both of coastal association), have also been found in late Recuay contexts, especially as grave offerings and objects used in status display (Lau 2001; Ponte R. 2001).

5. These designs are frequently classified as Chakipampa A (Menzel 1964) or Rudaqasa style of the "Transicional" period between the Early Intermediate Period and Middle Horizon (Lumbreras 1959).

6. Steven Wegner (personal communication 2004, 2007). Less distinctive commonalities include frontal heads with paired or four appendages, filler elements (repeating S-shapes on their sides, lattices, eyes with dots, sausages with dots), and anthropomorphic effigy pots.

7. I am referring to the common thinking of ancients and forebears (*los antepasados*) as giants among some Cordillera Blanca groups (see Yauri Montero 2000; Walter 2006).

REFERENCES

Adelaar, Willem F. H.

1988   Search for the Culli language. In *Continuity and Identity in Native America: Essays in Honor of Benedikt Hartmann*, edited by Maarten Jansen, Peter van der Loo, and Roswitha Manning, pp. 111–131. Leiden: Brill.

Alba H., C. Augusto

1946   La provincia de Huaylas en la historia. In *Monografía de la Provincia de Huaylas*, edited by F. García Cuéllar, pp. 21–44. Caraz: Antena 7.

Alcalde M., Angélica

2003   Reconocimiento arqueológico en la cuenca alta del río Santa. In *Arqueología de la sierra de Ancash: propuestas y perspectivas*, edited by Bebel Ibarra A., pp. 371–404. Lima: Instituto Cultural Runa.

Aldenderfer, Mark S., editor

1993   *Domestic Architecture, Ethnicity and Complementarity in the South Central Andes.* Iowa City: University of Iowa Press.

Allen, Catherine J.

1988   *The Hold Life Has: Coca and Cultural Identity in an Andean Community.* Washington, D.C.: Smithsonian Institution Press.

1997   When pebbles move mountains: iconicity and symbolism in Quechua ritual. In *Creating Context in Andean Cultures*, edited by Rosaleen Howard-Malverde, pp. 73–84. Oxford: Oxford University Press.

1998   When utensils revolt: mind, matter and modes of being in the pre-Columbian Andes. *Res* 33: 17–27.

2002   The Incas have gone inside: pattern and persistence in Andean iconography. *Res* 42: 180–203.

Amat, Hernán

1976a   Estudios arqueológicos en la cuenca del Mosna y en el Alto Marañón. *Actas del XLI Congreso Internacional de Americanistas (Mexico, 1974)* 3: 532–544.

1976b   Las formaciones agropecuarias de los períodos Formativo, Desarrollo Regional, Imperio Huari y Estados Regionales de Ancash. Ph.D. dissertation, Universidad Nacional de San Agustín, Arequipa.

2003   Huarás y Recuay en la secuencia cultural del Callejón de Conchucos: Valle del Mosna. In *Arqueología de la sierra de Ancash: propuestas y perspectivas*, edited by Bebel Ibarra, pp. 97–120. Lima: Instituto Cultural Runa.

Ames, Alcides
1998   A documentation of glacier tongue variations and lake development in the Cordillera Blanca, Peru. *Zeitschrift für Gletscherkunde und Glazialgeologie* 34: 1–36.

Andrade Ciudad, Luis
1995   La lengua Culle: un estado de la cuestión. *Boletín de la Academia Peruana de la Lengua* 26: 37–130.

Antúnez de Mayolo, Santiago
1935   Las ruinas de Tinyash (Alto Marañón). *Revista de la Escuela Nacional de Artes y Oficios* 5.
1941   Las ruinas de Tinyash: exploración arqueológica, febrero 1934. *Boletín de la Sociedad Geográfica de Lima* 58: 193–220.

Antúnez de Mayolo R., Santiago Erik
1986   Riego en Aija. *Allpanchis* 28: 47–71.

Apolín G., Donato
2004   Yayno, portentosa ciudad pre-inca. *Kordillera* 16: 10–11.

Appadurai, Arjun
1986   Introduction: commodities and politics of value. In *The Social Life of Things*, edited by Arjun Appadurai, pp. 3–63. Cambridge: Cambridge University Press.

Arguedas, José María, and Pierre Duviols, editors
1966   *Dioses y hombres de Huarochirí: narración quechua recogida por Francisco de Avila (¿1598?)*. Lima: Instituto de Estudios Peruanos.

Arkush, Elizabeth, and Charles Stanish
2005   Interpreting conflict in the ancient Andes: implications for the archaeology of warfare. *Current Anthropology* 46: 3–28.

Arnold, Denise Y.
1997   Making men in her own image: gender, text and textile in Qaqachaka. In *Creating Context in Andean Cultures*, edited by Rosaleen Howard-Malverde, pp. 99–131. Oxford: Oxford University Press.

Arriaga, Pedro J. de
1968   [1621] *The Extirpation of Idolatry in Peru*. Lexington: University of Kentucky Press.

Ashmore, Wendy, and Arthur Bernard Knapp, editors
1999   *Archaeologies of Landscape: Contemporary Perspectives*. Malden: Blackwell Publishers.

Astuhuamán G., César W., and Dina Araceli Espinoza C.

2005   Una aproximación a la arqueología de Sihuas, Periodo Intermedio
        Temprano y Horizonte Tardío. In *La complejidad social en la Sierra
        de Ancash*, edited by Alexander Herrera, Carolina Orsini, and Kevin
        Lane, pp. 63–83. Milan: Castello Sforzesco.

Avendaño, Fernando de

2003   [1617] Relación de las idolatrías de los indios de Fernando de Aven-
        daño. In *Proceso y visitas de idolatrías: Cajatambo, siglo XVII*, edited
        by Pierre Duviols, pp. 713–719. Lima: Instituto Francés de Estudios
        Andinos.

Bankmann, Ulf

1979   Moche und Recuay. *Baessler-Archiv*, n.s. 27: 253–271.
1981   Zwei Skulpturen aus dem Callejón de Huaylas, Peru, im Museum zu
        Basel. *Verhandlungen der Naturforschenden Gesellschaft in Basel* 92:
        39–46.
1988   Recuay-Studien, I: Früheste Abbildung einer Keramik des Recuay-
        Stils. *Baessler-Archiv* n.s. 36: 99–108.

Bawden, Garth

1996   *The Moche*. Oxford: Blackwell Publishers.

Bazán del Campo, Francisco

2007   La veneración a los huancas en el Callejón de Huaylas. *Hirka* 4: 2–6.
2008   Monolitos hallados en el sector de Batán en la ciudad de Huaraz.
        Hirka 16: 1–4.

Bazán del Campo, Francisco, and Steven Wegner

2006   La veneración a la huanca en el Horizonte Temprano. *Integración:
        Cultura Ancashina* 3: 21–22.

Beckwith, Laurie A.

1990   The Function of the Circular Galleries at Marcahuamachuco,
        Peru. M.A. thesis, Department of Anthropology, Trent University,
        Peterborough.

Bennett, Wendell C.

1939   *Archaeology of the North Coast of Peru: An Account of Exploration
        and Excavation in Viru and Lambayeque Valleys*. Anthropological
        Papers 37(1). New York: American Museum of Natural History.
1942   *Chavin Stone Carving*. New Haven: Yale Anthropological Studies 3.
1944   *The North Highlands of Peru: Excavations in the Callejón de Huaylas
        and at Chavín de Huántar*. Anthropological Papers 39(1). New York:
        American Museum of Natural History.
1946   The archaeology of the Central Andes. In *Handbook of South Ameri-
        can Indians, Volume 2: The Andean Civilizations*, edited by Julian
        H. Steward, pp. 61–148. Bureau of American Ethnology, Bulletin 143.
        Washington, D.C.: Smithsonian Institution.

1948   The Peruvian co-tradition. In *A Reappraisal of Peruvian Archaeology*, edited by Wendell C. Bennett, pp. 1–7. Memoirs 4. Menasha, Wisc.: Society for American Archaeology.

1950   *The Gallinazo Group, Virú Valley, Peru.* Publications in Anthropology 43. New Haven: Yale University.

Bennett, Wendell C., and Junius B. Bird

1949   *Andean Culture History.* New York: American Museum of Natural History.

Benson, Elizabeth P.

1984   The men who have bags in their mouths. *Indiana* 9: 367–381.

Bergh, Susan E.

1993   Death and renewal in Moche phallic-spouted vessels. *Res* 24: 78–94.

Billman, Brian R.

1996   The Evolution of Prehistoric Political Organizations in the Moche Valley. Ph.D. dissertation, University of California at Santa Barbara. Ann Arbor: University Microfilms.

Bingham, Hiram

1913   In the wonderland of Peru: the work accomplished by the Peruvian Expedition of 1912. *National Geographic Magazine* 24: 387–573.

1916   Further explorations in the land of the Incas: the Peruvian Expedition of 1915 of the National Geographic Society and Yale University. *National Geographic Magazine* 29: 431–473.

Bloch, Maurice

1992   *Prey into Hunter: Politics of Religious Experience.* Cambridge: Cambridge University Press.

Bodenlos, Alfred J., and John A. Straczek

1957   *Base-Metal Deposits of the Cordillera Negra Departamento de Ancash, Peru.* Bulletin 1040. Washington, D.C.: United States Geological Survey.

Bonavia, Duccio

1968   *Las ruinas del Abiseo.* Lima: Universidad Peruana de Ciencias y Tecnología.

1991   *Perú: hombre e historia — de los orígenes al siglo XV (tomo I).* Lima: EDUBANCO.

Boone, Elizabeth H.

2000   *Stories in Red and Black: Pictorial Histories of the Aztecs and Mixtecs.* Austin: University of Texas Press.

Borchers, Philipp

1935   *Die Weisse Kordillere.* Berlin: Scherl.

Bourget, Steve

2001   Rituals of sacrifice: its practice at Huaca de la Luna and its represen-
        tation in Moche iconography. In *Moche Art and Archaeology in An-
        cient Peru*, edited by Joanne Pillsbury, pp. 89–109. Washington, D.C.:
        National Gallery of Art.

2006   *Sex, Death, and Sacrifice in Moche Religion and Visual Culture*. Aus-
        tin: University of Texas Press.

Bradley, Richard

1998   *The Significance of Monuments: On the Shaping of Human Experience
        in Neolithic and Bronze Age Europe*. London: Routledge.

2000   *An Archaeology of Natural Places*. London: Routledge.

Bray, Tamara L., editor

2003   *The Archaeology and Politics of Food and Feasting in Early States and
        Empires*. New York: Kluwer.

Bruhns, Karen Olsen

1976   The moon animal in northern Peruvian art and culture. *Ñawpa
        Pacha* 14: 21–40.

Brush, Stephen B.

1976   Man's use of an Andean ecosystem. *Human Ecology* 4: 144–166.

1977   *Mountain, Field, and Family: The Economy and Human Ecology of
        an Andean Valley*. Philadelphia: University of Pennsylvania Press.

Bueno M., Alberto

1989   Arqueología de Ancash: nuevas perspectivas. In *Ancash: Historia y
        cultura*, edited by Alberto Bueno M., pp. 31–43. Lima: CONCYTEC.

2001   Excavaciones arqueológicas en Tumshukaiko: informe preliminar.
        In *XII Congreso Peruano del Hombre y La Cultura Andina*, edited by
        Ismael Pérez, Walter Aguilar, and Medardo Purizaga, pp. 30–53. Aya-
        cucho: Universidad Nacional de San Cristóbal de Huamanga.

Burger, Richard L.

1985a   Archaeological investigations at Huaricoto, Ancash, Peru: 1978–1979.
        National Geographic Society Research Reports 19: 119–127.

1985b   Prehistoric stylistic change and cultural development at Huaricoto,
        Peru. *National Geographic Research* 1: 505–534.

1992   *Chavín and the Origins of Andean Civilization*. London: Thames and
        Hudson.

Burger, Richard L., George F. Lau, Victor M. Ponte R., and Michael D. Glascock

2006   The history of prehispanic obsidian procurement in highland Ancash.
        In *La complejidad social en la Sierra de Ancash*, edited by Alexander
        Herrera, Carolina Orsini, and Kevin Lane, pp. 103–120. Milan: Civiche
        Raccolte d'Arte Applicata del Castello Sforzesco.

Burger, Richard L., and Thomas F. Lynch

1987   Gary S. Vescelius (1930–1982). *Andean Past* 1: 1–3.

Burger, Richard L., and Lucy Salazar-Burger

1993　The place of dual organization in Early Andean ceremonialism: a comparative review. In *El mundo ceremonial andino*, edited by Luis Millones and Yoshio Onuki, pp. 97–116. Osaka: National Museum of Ethnology.

Buse, Hermann

1965　*Introducción al Perú*. Lima: Imprenta del Colegio Militar "Leoncio Prado."

Byers, Alton C.

2000　Contemporary landscape change in the Huascarán National Park and buffer zone, Cordillera Blanca, Peru. *Mountain Research and Development* 20: 52–63.

Cadier, Eric, and Bernard Pouyaud, editors

1998　*Variations climatiques et ressources en eau en Amérique du Sud: importance et conséquences des événements El Niño*. Bulletin 27(3). Lima: Institut Français d'Études Andines.

Campana, Cristóbal

2000　Estudio de un edificio Recuay: formas y símbolos. *Arkinka* 57: 88–96.

Cardich, Augusto

1985　The fluctuating upper limits of cultivation in the Central Andes and their impact on Peruvian prehistory. *Advances in World Archaeology* 4: 293–333.

Carey, Mark

2005　Living and dying with glaciers: people's historical vulnerability to avalanches and outburst floods in Peru. *Global and Planetary Change* 47: 122–134.

Carneiro, Robert

1985　The chiefdom: precursor of the state. In *The Transition to Statehood in the New World*, edited by Grant Jones and Robert Kautz, pp. 37–79. Cambridge: Cambridge University Press.

Carrión Cachot, Rebeca

1955　El culto al agua en el antiguo Perú: la paccha, elemento cultural panandino. *Revista del Museo Nacional de Antropología y Arqueología* 2: 50–140.

1959　*La religión en el antiguo Perú (norte y centro de la costa, período postclásico)*. Lima: Tipografía Peruana.

Carsten, Janet, and Stephen Hugh-Jones, editors

1996　*About the House: Lévi-Strauss and Beyond*. Cambridge: Cambridge University Press.

Castillo, Luis Jaime, Andrew Nelson, and Chris Nelson

1997　"Maquetas" mochicas de San José de Moro. *Arkinka* 22: 120–128.

Castillo, Luis Jaime, and Santiago Uceda C.

2008   The Mochicas. In *Handbook of South American Archaeology*, edited by Helaine Silverman and William H. Isbell, pp. 707–729. New York: Springer Science.

Chapdelaine, Claude

1998   Excavaciones en la zona urbana de Moche durante 1996. In *Investigaciones en la Huaca de la Luna 1996*, edited by Santiago Uceda, Elías Mujica, and Ricardo Morales, pp. 85–115. Trujillo: Universidad Nacional de La Libertad.

Chaumeil, Jean-Pierre

2007   Bones, flutes and the dead: memory and funerary treatments in Amazonia. In *Time and Memory in Indigenous Amazonia: Anthropological Perspectives*, edited by Carlos Fausto and Michael Heckenberger, pp. 243–283. Gainesville: University Press of Florida.

Childe, V. Gordon

1929   *The Danube in Prehistory*. Oxford: Oxford University Press.

Choronzey, Jonathan

2009   Présence et identité Gallinazo dans la basse vallée de Santa, côte nord du Pérou. M.A. thesis, University of Montreal.

Church, Warren B.

1996   Prehistoric Cultural Development and Interregional Interaction in the Tropical Montane Forests of Peru. Ph.D. dissertation, Yale University. Ann Arbor: University Microfilms.

Cisneros Velarde, Leonor, and Luis G. Lumbreras

1980   *Historia general del ejército peruano*. Lima: Comisión Permanente de la Historia del Ejército del Perú.

Clark, John E., and Michael Blake

1994   The power of prestige: competitive generosity and the emergence of rank in Lowland Mesoamerica. In *Factional Competition and Political Development in the New World*, edited by Elizabeth Brumfiel and John W. Fox, pp. 17–30. Cambridge: Cambridge University Press.

Classen, Constance

1993   *Inca Cosmology and the Human Body*. Salt Lake City: University of Utah Press.

Clothier, William J., II

1943   Recuay pottery in the lower Santa Valley. *Revista del Museo Nacional* 12: 239–242.

Cobbing, Edward. J., Wallace S. Pitcher, John J. Wilson, John W. Baldock, William P. Taylor, William McCourt, and Norman J. Snelling

1981   *The Geology of the Western Cordillera of Northern Peru*. Memoir 5. London: Institute of Geological Sciences Overseas.

Cobo, Bernabe
1990   [1653] *Inca Religion and Customs*. Austin: University of Texas Press.

Collier, Donald
1955   *Cultural Chronology and Change as Reflected in the Ceramics of the Virú Valley, Peru*. Fieldiana (Anthropology) 43. Chicago: Chicago Natural History Museum.
1962   Archaeological investigations in the Casma Valley, Peru. *Akten de 34. Internationalen Amerikanisten Kongresses, 1960 (Wien)*: 411–417.

Conklin, Beth A.
2001   Women's blood, warriors' blood and the conquest of vitality in Amazonia. In *Gender in Amazonia and Melanesia*, edited by Thomas Gregor and Donald Tuzin, pp. 141–174. Berkeley: University of California Press.

Connerton, Paul
1989   *How Societies Remember*. Cambridge: Cambridge University Press.

Cook, Anita G.
2001   Huari D-shaped structures, sacrificial offerings and divine rulership. In *Ritual Sacrifice in Ancient Peru*, edited by Elizabeth P. Benson and Anita G. Cook, pp. 137–163. Austin: University of Texas Press.

Cook, Noble David
1977   La visita de los Conchucos por Cristóbal Ponce de León, 1543. *Historia y Cultura* 10: 23–45.
1981   *Demographic Collapse: Indian Peru, 1520–1620*. Cambridge: Cambridge University Press.

Coote, Jeremy, and Anthony Shelton, editors
1992   *Anthropology, Art, and Aesthetics*. Oxford: Clarendon Press.

Cordy-Collins, Alana
1977   Chavín art: its shamanic/hallucinogenic origins. In *Pre-Columbian Art History*, edited by Alana Cordy-Collins and Jean Stern, pp. 353–362. Palo Alto: Peek Publications.

Course, Magnus
2007   Death, biography and the Mapuche person. *Ethnos* 72: 77–101.

Cummins, Thomas B.
2002   *Toasts with the Inca: Andean Abstraction and Colonial Images on Kero Vessels*. Ann Arbor: University of Michigan Press.

Czwarno, Robert M.
1983   Ceramic Indications of Cultural Interaction: Evidence from Northern Peru. M.A. thesis, Trent University, Peterborough.

Daggett, Richard E.

1985   The Early Horizon–Early Intermediate Period transition: a view from the Nepeña and Virú Valleys. In *Recent Studies in Andean Prehistory and Protohistory*, edited by D. Peter Kvietok and Daniel H. Sandweiss, pp. 41–65. Ithaca, N.Y.: Cornell Latin American Studies Program.

D'Altroy, Terence N.

2002   *The Incas*. Malden: Blackwell Publishers.

DeLeonardis, Lisa, and George F. Lau

2004   Life, death and ancestors. In *Andean Archaeology*, edited by Helaine Silverman, pp. 77–115. Oxford: Blackwell Publishers.

DeMarrais, Elizabeth, Timothy Earle, and Luis Jaime Castillo

1996   Ideology, materialization, and power strategies. *Current Anthropology* 37: 15–31.

Denevan, William M.

1992   The pristine myth: the landscape of the Americas in 1492. *Annals of the Association of American Geographers* 82: 369–385.

2001   *Cultivated Landscapes of Native Amazonia and the Andes*. Oxford: Oxford University Press.

Descola, Philippe

1986   *In the Society of Nature: A Native Ecology in Amazonia*. Cambridge: Cambridge University Press.

2001   Genres of gender: local models and global paradigms in the comparison of Amazonia and Melanesia. In *Gender in Amazonia and Melanesia*, edited by Thomas A. Gregor and Donald Tuzin, pp. 91–114. Berkeley: University of California Press.

2006   Beyond nature and culture. *Proceedings of the British Academy* 139: 137–155.

Diaz, Henry F., Jon K. Eischeid, Chris Duncan, and Raymond S. Bradley

2003   Variability of freezing levels, melting season indicators, and snow cover for selected high-elevation and continental regions in the last 50 years. *Climatic Change* 59: 33–52.

Diaz, Henry F., and Vera Markgraf, editors

2000   *El Niño and the Southern Oscillation: Multiscale Variability and Global and Regional Impacts*. Cambridge: Cambridge University Press.

Diessl, Wilhelm

2004   *Huantár — San Marcos — Chavín: sitios arqueológicos en la sierra de Ancash*. Lima: Instituto Cultural Runa.

Dietler, Michael

1996   Feasts and commensal politics in the political economy: food, power and status in prehistoric Europe. In *Food and the Status Quest: An*

Interdisciplinary Perspective, edited by Polly Wiessner and Wulf
Schiefenhövel, pp. 87–125. Providence: Berghahn Books.

2001   Theorizing the feast: rituals of consumption, commensal politics
and power in African contexts. In *Feasts: Archaeological and Ethnographic Perspectives on Food, Politics and Power*, edited by Michael
Dietler and Brian Hayden, pp. 65–114. Washington, D.C.: Smithsonian
Institution Press.

Dietler, Michael, and Brian Hayden, editors

2001   *Feasts: Archaeological and Ethnographic Perspectives on Food, Politics
and Power*. Washington, D.C.: Smithsonian Institution Press.

Dietler, Michael, and Ingrid Herbich

1998   *Habitus*, techniques, style: an integrated approach to the social under-
standing of material culture and boundaries. In *The Archaeology of
Social Boundaries*, edited by Miriam Stark, pp. 232–263. Washington,
D.C.: Smithsonian Institution Press.

Disselhoff, Hans Dietrich

1956   Hand- und Kopftrophäen in plastischen Darstellung der Recuay-
keramik. *Baessler Archiv*, n.s. 4: 25–32.

Donkin, R. A.

1979   *Agricultural Terracing in the Aboriginal New World*. Viking Fund
Publications in Anthropology 56. Tucson: University of Arizona
Press/Wenner-Gren Foundation.

Donnan, Christopher B.

1965   Moche ceramic technology. *Ñawpa Pacha* 3: 115–138.

1971   Ancient Peruvian potters' marks and their interpretation through
ethnographic analogy. *American Antiquity* 36: 460–466.

1992   *Ceramics of Ancient Peru*. Los Angeles: Fowler Museum of Cultural
History.

1997   Deer hunting and combat: parallel activities in the Moche world. In
Spirit of Ancient Peru, edited by Kathleen Berrin, pp. 51–59. New York:
Thames and Hudson.

2004   *Moche Portraits from Ancient Peru*. Austin: University of Texas Press.

Donnan, Christopher B., and Donna McClelland

1999   *Moche Fineline Painting: Its Evolution and Its Artists*. Los Angeles:
Fowler Museum of Cultural History, University of California.

Doughty, Paul L.

1968   *Huaylas: An Andean District in Search of Progress*. Ithaca: Cornell
University Press.

Doyle, Mary Eileen

1988   Ancestor Cult and Burial Ritual in Seventeenth and Eighteenth Century Central Peru. Ph.D. dissertation, University of California at Los
Angeles. Ann Arbor: University Microfilms.

Dransart, Penny

1995   Inner worlds and the event of a thread in Isluga, northern Chile. In *Andean Art: Visual Expression and Its Relation to Andean Beliefs and Values*, edited by Penny Dransart, pp. 228–242. Aldershot: Avebury.

2002   *Earth, Water, Fleece and Fabric: A Long-term Ethnography of Camelid Herding in the Andes.* London: Routledge.

Duviols, Pierre

1967   Un inédit de Cristóbal de Albornoz: la instrucción para descubrir todas las guacas del Piru y sus camayos y haziendas. *Journal de la Société des Américanistes* 56: 7–39.

1973   Huari y llacuaz, agricultores y pastores: un dualismo prehispánico de oposición y complementaridad. *Revista del Museo Nacional* 39: 153–191.

1977   Un symbolisme andin du double: la lithomorphose de l'ancêtre. *Actes du XLIIe Congrès International des Américanistes (Paris)* 4: 359–364.

1978   *Camaquen upani:* un concept animiste des anciens Péruviens. *Collectanea Instituti Anthropos* 20: 132–144.

1979   Un symbolisme de l'occupation, de l'aménagement et de l'exploitation de l'espace: la monolithe "huanca" et sa fonction dans les Andes préhispaniques. *L'Homme* 19: 7–31.

1986   *Cultura andina y represión: procesos y visitas de idolatrías y hecherías Cajatambo, siglo XVII.* Cuzco: Centro de Estudios Rurales Andinos "Bartolomé de las Casas."

2003   *Procesos y visitas de idolatrías: Cajatambo, siglo XVII.* Lima: Instituto Francés de Estudios Andinos.

Earle, Timothy K.

1987   Chiefdoms in archaeological and ethnohistorical perspectives. *Annual Review of Anthropology* 16: 279–308.

Eisleb, Dieter

1987   *Altperuanische Kulturen IV: Recuay.* Berlin: Staatliche Museen Preussischer Kulturbesitz, Museum für Völkerkunde.

Eliade, Mircea

1959   *The Sacred and the Profane: The Nature of Religion.* New York: Harcourt Brace.

Enock, C. Reginald

1907   *The Andes and the Amazon: Life and Travel in Peru.* New York: C. Scribner's Sons.

Erickson, Clark L.

2008   Amazonia: the historical ecology of a domesticated landscape. In *Handbook of South American Archaeology*, edited by Helaine Silverman and William H. Isbell, pp. 157–183. New York: Springer Science.

Espejo Núñez, Julio

1951   Exploraciones arqueológicas en las cabeceras del Pukcha (Peru). *Cuadernos Americanos* 10: 139–152.

1957   Primeros indicios arqueológicos del estilo cultural Huaylas (Recuay) en la cuenca del Pukcha (Perú). *Cuadernos Americanos* 91: 137–150.

1959   Katayok y Molle-Ukru. *Perú Indígena* 8: 91–98.

Espinoza Soriano, Waldemar

1964   El curacazgo de Conchucos y la visita de 1543. *Bulletin de l'Institut Français d'Etudes Andines* 3: 9–31.

1978   *Huaraz: poder, sociedad y economía en los siglos XV y XVI — reflexiones en torno a las visitas de 1558, 1594 y 1712.* Lima: Seminario de Historia Rural Andina, Universidad Nacional Mayor de San Marcos.

1987   *Artesanos, transacciones, monedas y formas de pago en el mundo andino: siglos XV y XVI.* Lima: Banco Central de Reserva del Perú.

Falcón, Víctor

2004   Los orígenes del huanca como objeto de culto en la época precolonial. *Allpanchis* 64: 35–54.

Falcón, Víctor, and Patricia Díaz

1998   Representaciones líticas de Tinyash. *Andesita* 1: 57–64.

Finkel, Irving, editor

2007   *Ancient Board Games in Perspective.* London: British Museum Press.

Flannery, Kent, and Joyce Marcus

1996   *Zapotec Civilization.* New York: Thames and Hudson.

Flannery, Kent V., Joyce Marcus, and Robert G. Reynolds

1989   *The Flocks of the Wamani: A Study of Llama Herders on the Punas of Ayacucho, Peru.* San Diego: Academic Press.

Fogel, Heidy

1993   Settlements in Time: A Study of the Social and Political Development during the Gallinazo Occupation of the North Coast of Peru. Ph.D. dissertation, Yale University. Ann Arbor: University Microfilms.

Ford, James A.

1949   Cultural dating of prehistoric sites in the Virú Valley, Peru. In *Surface Survey of the Virú Valley, Peru*, edited by James A. Ford and Gordon R. Willey, pp. 29–89. Anthropological Papers 43(1). New York: American Museum of Natural History.

Ford, James A., and Gordon R. Willey, editors

1949   *Surface Survey of the Virú Valley, Peru.* Anthropological Papers 43(1). New York: American Museum of Natural History.

Franco Jordán, Régulo G., Cesar Galvez M., and Segundo Vásquez Sánchez

2005   *El Brujo: pasado milenario.* Trujillo, Perú: Ediciones SIAN.

Fraser, Douglas
1966   The heraldic woman: a study in diffusion. In *The Many Faces of Primitive Art: A Critical Anthology*, edited by Douglas Fraser, pp. 36–99. Englewood Cliffs, N.J.: Prentice-Hall.

Gade, Daniel W.
1999   *Nature and Culture in the Andes.* Madison: University of Wisconsin Press.

Gambini, Wilfredo
1984   *Santa y Nepeña: dos valles, dos culturas.* Lima: Imprenta M. Castillo.

Garaventa, Donna M.
1978   Peruvian textiles: textiles from Lowie Museum of Anthropology and California Academy of Sciences. *Pacific Discovery* 31: 21–26.

Garayar, Carlos, Hugo Vallenas, and Walter H. Wust, editors
2003   *Atlas departamental del Perú (tomo 4): Ancash-Huánuco.* Lima: Ediciones PEISA.

Gell, Alfred
1992   The technology of enchantment and the enchantment of technology. In *Anthropology, Art and Aesthetics*, edited by Jeremy Coote and Anthony Shelton, pp. 40–67. Oxford: Clarendon Press.
1993   *Wrapping in Images: Tattooing in Polynesia.* Oxford: Clarendon Press.
1998   *Art and Agency: An Anthropological Theory.* Oxford: Clarendon Press.

Gelles, Paul H.
2000   *Water and Power in Highland Peru: The Cultural Politics of Irrigation and Development.* New Brunswick, N.J.: Rutgers University Press.

Georges, Christian
2004   20th-century glacier fluctuations in the tropical Cordillera Blanca, Perú. *Arctic, Antarctic, and Alpine Research* 36: 100–107.

Gero, Joan M.
1990   Pottery, power, and . . . parties! *Archaeology* 43(2) (March/April): 52–56.
1991   Who experienced what in prehistory?: A narrative explanation from Queyash, Peru. In *Processual and Postprocessual Archaeologies: Multiple Ways of Knowing the Past*, edited by Robert W. Preucel, pp. 126–139. Occasional Paper No. 10. Carbondale: Center for Archaeological Investigations, Southern Illinois University.
1992   Feasts and females: gender ideology and political meals in the Andes. *Norwegian Archaeological Review* 25: 15–30.
1999   La iconografía Recuay y el estudio de género. *Gaceta Arqueológica Andina* 25: 23–44.
2001   Field knots and ceramic beaus: interpreting gender in the Peruvian Early Intermediate Period. In *Gender in Pre-Hispanic America*, edited by Cecilia Klein, pp. 15–55. Washington, D.C.: Dumbarton Oaks.

2004   Sex pots of ancient Peru: post-gender reflections. In *Combining the Past and the Present: Archaeological Perspectives on Society*, edited by Terje Oestigaard, Nils Anfinset, and Tore Saetersdal, pp. 3–22. International Series 1210. Oxford: BAR.

Gillespie, Susan D.
2000   Rethinking ancient Maya social organization: replacing "lineage" with "house." *American Anthropologist* 102: 467–484.

Godelier, Maurice
1977   *Perspectives in Marxist Anthropology*. Cambridge: Cambridge University Press.

Goldstein, Paul S.
1993   Tiwanaku temples and state expansion: a Tiwanaku sunken-court temple in Moquegua, Peru. *Latin American Antiquity* 4: 22–47.
2000   Exotic goods and everyday chiefs: long-distance exchange and indigenous sociopolitical development in the South Central Andes. *Latin American Antiquity* 11: 335–362.
2005   *Andean Diaspora: The Tiwanaku Colonies and the Origins of South American Empire*. Gainesville: University Press of Florida.

González Carré, Enrique, Enrique Braygarac Dávila, Cirilo Vivanco Pomacanchari, Vera Tiesler Blos, and Máximo López Quispe
1999   *El templo mayor en la ciudad de Wari: estudios arqueológicos en Vegachayoq Moqo-Ayacucho*. Ayacucho: Universidad Nacional de San Cristóbal de Huamanga.

Gorbak, Celina, Mirtha Lischetti, and Carmen Paula Muñoz
1962   Batallas rituales de Chiaraje y del Tocto de la provincia de Kanas (Cuzco-Perú). *Revista del Museo Nacional* 31: 245–304.

Gose, Peter
1994   *Deathly Waters and Hungry Mountains: Agrarian Ritual and Class Formation in an Andean Town*. Toronto: University of Toronto Press.

Graeber, David
2001   *Toward an Anthropological Theory of Value: The False Coin of Our Own Dreams*. New York: Palgrave.

Grieder, Terence
1978   *The Art and Archaeology of Pashash*. Austin: University of Texas Press.

Grieder, Terence, Alberto Bueno Mendoza, C. Earle Smith, Jr., and Robert M. Malina
1988   *La Galgada, Peru: A Preceramic Culture in Transition*. Austin: University of Texas Press.

Guaman Poma de Ayala, Felipe

1980 *El primer nueva corónica y buen gobierno.* Edited by John Murra, Rolena Adorno, and Jorge Urioste. Mexico City: Siglo Veintiuno.

Guillet, David

1987 Terracing and irrigation in the Peruvian highlands. *Current Anthropology* 28: 409–430.

Hastenrath, Stefan, and Alcides Ames

1995 Diagnosing the imbalance of Yanamarey Glacier in the Cordillera Blanca of Peru. *Journal of Geographical Research* 100: 5105–5112.

Hastorf, Christine A., and Sissel Johannessen

1993 Pre-Hispanic political change and the role of maize in the central Andes of Peru. *American Anthropologist* 95: 115–138.

Heckenberger, Michael

2007 Xinguano heroes, ancestors, and others: materializing the past in chiefly bodies, ritual space and landscape. In *Time and Memory in Indigenous Amazonia: Anthropological Perspectives*, edited by Carlos Fausto and Michael Heckenberger, pp. 284–311. Gainesville: University Press of Florida.

Heggarty, Paul, and David Beresford-Jones

2010 What role for language prehistory in redefining archaeological "culture"?: a case-study on new horizons in the Andes. In *Investigating Archaeological Cultures: Material Culture, Variability, and Transmission*, edited by B. Roberts and M. Vander Linden. New York: Springer.

Helms, Mary W.

1981 Precious metals and politics: style and ideology in the Intermediate Area and Peru. *Journal of Latin American Lore* 7: 215–235.

Hernández Príncipe, Rodrigo

1923 Mitología andina — idolatrías en Recuay. *Inca* 1: 25–78.

Herrera, Alexander

1998 Acerca de un tercer fragmento de la estela de Yauya. *Baessler-Archiv* 46: 231–253.

2003 Arte lítico de la región de los Conchucos, Ancash, Perú. *Arqueológicas* 26: 107–130.

2005 Territory and Identity in the Pre-Columbian Andes of Northern Peru. Ph.D. dissertation, Cambridge University.

2006 Territorio e identidad: apuntes para una modelo de la complejidad social andina. In *La complejidad social en la sierra de Ancash: ensayos sobre paisaje, economía y continuidades culturales*, edited by Alexander Herrera, Carolina Orsini, and Kevin Lane, pp. 3–18. Milan: Civiche Raccolte d'Arte Applicata del Castello Sforzesco.

Heyden, Doris

1981   Caves, gods and myths: world-view and planning in Teotihuacan. In *Mesoamerican Sites and World-views*, edited by Elizabeth Benson, pp. 1–39. Washington, D.C.: Dumbarton Oaks.

Hill, Erica

2000   The embodied sacrifice. *Cambridge Archaeological Journal* 10: 317–326.

Hohmann, Carolina

2003   El rostro circular frontal de boca dentada en la iconografía Recuay. *Arqueológicas* 26: 131–152.

Horkheimer, Hans

1944   *Vistas arqueológicas del noroeste del Perú*. Trujillo: Instituto Arqueológico, Universidad de La Libertad.

Hoskins, Janet

1998   *Biographical Objects: How Things Tell the Stories of People's Lives*. London: Routledge.

Houston, Stephen D., and Tom Cummins

2004   Body, presence and space in Andean and Mesoamerican rulership. In *Palaces of the Ancient New World*, edited by Susan Toby Evans and Joanne Pillsbury, pp. 359–398. Washington, D.C.: Dumbarton Oaks.

Houston, Stephen D., and David Stuart

1996   Of gods, glyphs and kings: divinity and rulership among the Classic Maya. *Antiquity* 70: 289–312.

Houston, Stephen D., David Stuart, and Karl Taube

2006   *The Memory of Bones: Body, Being and Experience among the Classic Maya*. Austin: University of Texas Press.

Hyslop, John

1984   *The Inka Road System*. New York: Academic Press.

Ibarra A., Bebel

2003   Arqueología del Valle del Puchca: economía, cosmovisión y secuencia estilística. In *Arqueología de la sierra de Ancash: propuestas y perspectivas*, edited by Bebel Ibarra, pp. 251–330. Lima: Instituto Cultural Runa.

Ingold, Tim

1993   The temporality of the landscape. *World Archaeology* 25: 152–174.

1999   *The Perception of the Environment: Essays on Livelihood, Dwelling and Skill*. London: Routledge.

Inomata, Takeshi

2006   Plazas, performers and spectators: political theaters of the Classic Maya. *Current Anthropology* 47: 805–842.

Isbell, William H.

1977   Cosmological order expressed in prehistoric ceremonial centers. *Proceedings of the 42nd International Congress of Americanists* 4: 269–297.

1989   Honcopampa: was it a Huari administrative centre? In *Nature of Wari: A Reappraisal of the Middle Horizon Period in Peru*, edited by R. Michael Czwarno, Frank M. Meddens, and Alexandra Morgan, pp. 98–114. International Series 525. Oxford: BAR.

1991   Honcopampa: monumental ruins in Peru's North Highlands. *Expedition* 33: 27–36.

1997   *Mummies and Mortuary Monuments: A Postprocessual Prehistory of Central Andean Social Organization*. Austin: University of Texas Press.

Jackson, Margaret A.

2008   *Moche Art and Visual Culture in Ancient Peru*. Albuquerque: University of New Mexico Press.

Jennings, Justin D., Kathleen L. Antrobus, Sam J. Atencio, Erin Glavich, Rebecca Johnson, German Loffler, and Christine Luu

2005   "Drinking beer in a blissful mood": alcohol production, operational chains and feasting in the ancient world. *Current Anthropology* 46: 275–304.

Jiménez Borja, Arturo

1948   Mate peruano. *Revista del Museo Nacional* 17: 34–73.

Jomelli, V., D. Grancher, D. Brunstein, and O. Solomina

2007   Recalibration of the yellow Rhizocarpon growth curve in the Cordillera Blanca (Peru) and implications for LIA chronology. *Geomorphology* 93: 201–212.

Joyce, Rosemary A.

1996   The construction of gender in Classic Maya monuments. In *Gender and Archaeology*, edited by Rita B. Wright, pp. 167–195. Philadelphia: University of Pennsylvania Press.

1998   Performing the body in pre-Hispanic Central America. *Res* 33: 147–165.

Julien, Daniel G.

1988   Ancient Cuismancu: Settlement and Cultural Dynamics in the Cajamarca Region of the North Highlands of Peru, 200 B.C.–A.D. 1532. Ph.D. dissertation, University of Texas, Austin.

1993   Late pre-Inkaic ethnic groups in highland Peru: an archaeological-ethnohistorical model of the political geography of the Cajamarca region. *Latin American Antiquity* 4: 246–273.

Kaeppler, Adrienne

1997   Polynesia and Micronesia. In *Oceanic Art*, edited by Adrienne Kaeppler, Christian Kauffman, and Douglas Newton, pp. 21–155. New York: Abrams.

Kaser, Georg

1999   A review of the modern fluctuations of tropical glaciers. *Global and Planetary Change* 22: 93–103.

2001   Glacier-climate interaction at low latitudes. *Journal of Glaciology* 47: 195–204.

Kauffmann Doig, Federico

1956   Las ruinas de Chopijirca (Vicos, Ancash). *Revista de Museo Nacional* 25: 120–139.

1966   *Mochica — Nazca — Recuay en la arqueología peruana.* Lima: Universidad Nacional Mayor de San Marcos.

1970   *Arqueología peruana: visión integral.* Lima: Editorial Promoción Inca.

1979   *Sexual Behaviour in Ancient Peru.* Lima: Kompaktos.

1980   *Manual de arqueología peruana.* Lima: Ediciones PEISA.

2002   *Historia y arte del Perú antiguo (Vol. 3).* Lima: PEISA–La República.

Kauffmann Doig, Federico, and Giancarlo Ligabue

2003   *Los Chachapoya(s).* Lima: Universidad Alas Peruanas.

Kaulicke, Peter

1992   Moche, Vicús Moche y el Mochica temprano. *Bulletin de l'Institut Français d'Etudes Andines* 21: 853–903.

Kembel, Silvia R.

2001   Architectural Sequence and Chronology at Chavín de Huántar, Peru. Ph.D. dissertation, Stanford University. Ann Arbor: University Microfilms.

2008   The architecture at the monumental center of Chavín de Huántar: sequence, transformations and chronology. In *Chavín: Art, Architecture and Culture,* edited by William J. Conklin and Jeffrey Quilter, pp. 35–81. Los Angeles: Cotsen Institute of Archaeology Monograph 61.

Kemper Columbus, Claudette

1990   Immortal eggs: a Peruvian geocracy, Pariaqaqa of Huarochirí. *Journal of Latin American Lore* 16: 175–198.

Kinzl, Hans

1935   Altindianische Siedlungsspuren im Umkreis der Cordillera Blanca. In *Die Weisse Kordillere,* edited by Philipp Borchers, pp. 262–295. Berlin: Verlag Scherl.

1954   *Cordillera Huayhuash, Perú.* Innsbruck: Verlag Tiroler Graphik.

Kinzl, Hans, and Erwin Schneider

1950   *Cordillera Blanca (Perú).* Innsbruck: Wagner.

Klein, Andrew G., Geoffrey O. Seltzer, and Bryan L. Isacks

1999   Modern and last local glacial maximum snowlines in the Central Andes of Peru, Bolivia, and Northern Chile. *Quaternary Science Reviews* 18: 63–84.

Kolata, Alan L.

1983   Chan Chan and Cuzco: on the nature of the ancient Andean city. In
         Civilization in the Ancient Americas: Essays in Honor of Gordon R.
         Willey, edited by Richard Leventhal and Alan Kolata, pp. 345–371. Al-
         buquerque: University of New Mexico Press.

Kopytoff, Igor

1986   The cultural biography of things: commoditization as process. In *The*
         Social Life of Things: Commodities in Cultural Perspective, edited by
         Arjun Appadurai, pp. 64–91. Cambridge: Cambridge University Press.

Kosok, Paul

1965   *Life, Land, and Water in Ancient Peru*. New York: Long Island Univer-
         sity Press.

Kroeber, A. L.

1926   *Archaeological Explorations in Peru, Part I: Ancient Pottery from Tru-*
         jillo. Anthropological Memoirs 2(1). Chicago: Field Museum of Natu-
         ral History.

1930   *Archaeological Explorations in Peru, Part II: The Northern Coast.*
         Anthropological Memoirs 2(2). Chicago: Field Museum of Natural
         History.

1944   *Peruvian Archeology in 1942*. Publications in Anthropology 4. New
         York: Viking Fund.

1949   Esthetic and recreational activities: art. In *Handbook of South Ameri-*
         can Indians, Volume 5: The Comparative Ethnology of South American
         Indians, edited by Julian Steward, pp. 411–492. Bulletin 143. Washing-
         ton, D.C.: Bureau of American Ethnology.

1950   A local style of lifelike sculptured stone heads in ancient Peru. In *Bei-*
         träge zur Gesellungs- und Volkerwissenschaft, Professor Dr. Richard
         Thurnwald zu seinem achtzigsten Geburtstag gewidmet, pp. 195–198.
         Berlin: Verlag Gebr. Mann.

Krzanowski, Andrzej

1986   Cultural chronology of northern Andes of Peru (the Huamachuco-
         Quiruvilca-Otuzco region). *Acta Archaeologica Carpathica*: 231–264.

Kubler, George

1962a   *Art and Architecture of Ancient America*. Harmondsworth: Penguin.
1962b   *The Shape of Time: Remarks on the History of Things*. New Haven:
         Yale University Press.

Lane, Kevin J.

2006a   Engineering the Puna: Hydraulics of Agro-Pastoral Communities
         in a North Central Peruvian Valley. Ph.D. dissertation, University of
         Cambridge.

2006b   Through the looking glass: re-assessing the role of agro-pastoralism
         in the north-central Andean highlands. *World Archaeology* 38:
         493–510.

Lanning, Edward P.

1965   Current research: highland South America. *American Antiquity* 31:
        139–140.

1967   *Peru before the Incas*. Englewood Cliffs, N.J.: Prentice-Hall.

Larco Hoyle, Rafael

1945   *La cultura Virú*. Buenos Aires: Sociedad Geográfíca Americana.

1948   *Cronología arqueológica del norte de Peru*. Buenos Aires: Sociedad
        Geográfíca Americana.

1960   La cultura Santa. In *Antiguo Perú: espacio y tiempo*, pp. 235–239.
        Lima: Librería Editorial Juan Mejía Baca.

1962   *La cultura Santa*. Lima: Litografía Valverde S.A.

1965   *Checán: Essay on Erotic Elements in Peruvian Art*. Geneva: Nagel
        Publishers.

1966   *Peru*. Cleveland: World Publishing.

n.d.   *Escultura lítica del Perú pre-colombino*. Lima: Instituto de Arte
        Contemporáneo.

Lau, George F.

2000   Espacio ceremonial Recuay. In *Los dioses del antiguo Perú*, edited by
        Krzysztof Makowski, pp. 178–197. Lima: Banco de Crédito.

2001   The Ancient Community of Chinchawas: Economy and Ceremony in
        the North Highlands of Peru. Ph.D. dissertation, Yale University.

2002   Feasting and ancestor veneration at Chinchawas, North Highlands of
        Ancash, Peru. *Latin American Antiquity* 13: 279–304.

2004a   Object of contention: an examination of Recuay-Moche combat imag-
        ery. *Cambridge Archaeological Journal* 14: 163–184.

2004b   The Recuay culture of Peru's north-central highlands: a reappraisal
        of chronology and its implications. *Journal of Field Archaeology* 29:
        177–202.

2005   Core-periphery relations in the Recuay hinterlands: economic interac-
        tion at Chinchawas, Peru. *Antiquity* 79: 78–99.

2006a   Northern exposures: Recuay-Cajamarca boundaries and interaction.
        In *Andean Archaeology III: North and South*, edited by William H.
        Isbell and Helaine Silverman, pp. 143–170. New York: Plenum/Kluwer
        Publishers.

2006b   Recuay Tradition sculptures of Chinchawas, North Highlands of An-
        cash, Peru. *Zeitschrift für Archäeologie Aussereuropäischer Kulturen* 1:
        183–250.

2006c   Status and social differentiation in Recuay culture: a review. In *La
        complejidad social en la Sierra de Ancash: ensayos sobre paisaje,
        economía y continuidades culturales*, edited by Alexander Herrera,
        Carolina Orsini, and Kevin Lane, pp. 121–138. Milan: Civiche Raccolte
        d'Arte Applicata del Castello Sforzesco.

2007   Animal resources and Recuay cultural transformations at Chincha-
        was (Ancash, Peru). *Andean Past* 8: 449–476.

2008   Ancestor images in the Andes. In *Handbook of South American Ar-*

chaeology, edited by Helaine Silverman and William H. Isbell, pp. 1025–1043. New York: Springer Science.

2009   Correspondencias entre las lenguas y los antiguos desarrollos culturales de la sierra norcentral del Perú. Paper presented at VII Simposio Internacional de Arqueología "Lenguas y sociedades en el antiguo Peru: hacia un enfoque interdisciplinario," Pontificia Universidad Católica del Perú (Lima).

2010   House forms and Recuay culture: residential compounds at Yayno (Ancash, Peru), a fortified hilltop town, AD 400–800. *Journal of Anthropological Archaeology* 29: 327–351.

Lau, George F., and Gabriel Ramón

2007   Yayno, cima del mundo: ciudadela fortificada de la tradición Recuay. *Gaceta Cultural del Perú* 27: 26–28.

Laurencich, Laura, and Steven Wegner, editors

2001   *El Museo de Chacas*. Bologna: Editrice Compositori.

Laurencich-Minelli, Laura, Alberto Minelli, and Carolina Orsini

2001   Una ciudadela estilo Recuay en el valle de Chacas (Perú): el sitio Pinchay-Riway—una nota preliminar. *Journal de la Société des Américanistes* 87: 325–338.

Lawrence, Denise, and Setha Low

1990   The built environment and spatial form. *Annual Review of Anthropology* 19: 453–505.

Lechtman, Heather N.

1977   Style in technology—some early thoughts. In *Material Cultures: Styles, Organization and Dynamics of Technology*, edited by Heather Lechtman and Robert Merrill, pp. 3–20. St. Paul: West.

1980   The Central Andes: metallurgy without iron. In *The Coming of the Age of Iron*, edited by Theodore A. Wertime and James D. Muhly, pp. 267–334. New Haven: Yale University Press.

1984   Andean value systems and the development of prehistoric metallurgy. *Technology and Culture* 25: 1–36.

1993   Technologies of power: the Andean case. In *Configurations of Power: Holistic Anthropology in Theory and Practice*, edited by John S. Henderson and Patricia A. Netherly, pp. 244–280. Ithaca: Cornell University Press.

Lehmann, Walter, and Heinrich Ubbelohde-Doering

1924   *Kunstgeschichte des alten Peru*. Berlin: E. Wasmuth Staatliche Museen zu Berlin.

Lemonnier, Pierre

1993   *Technological Choices: Transformation in Material Cultures since the Neolithic*. London: Routledge.

León Gómez, Miguel Angel

2003   Espacio geográfico y organización social de los grupos étnicos del Callejon de Conchucos durante los siglos XVI y XVII. In *Arqueología de la sierra de Ancash: propuestas y perspectivas*, edited by Bebel Ibarra A., pp. 457–466. Lima: Unay Runa.

Levillier, Roberto

1926   *Nueva crónica de la conquista del Tucumán, Tomo I (1542–1563)*. Madrid: Sucesores de Rivadeneyra, Colección de Publicaciones Históricas de la Biblioteca del Congreso Argentino.

Lévi-Strauss, Claude

1983   *The Way of the Masks*. London: Jonathan Cape.

Lumbreras, Luis G.

1959   Esquema arqueológico de la Sierra Central del Perú. *Revista del Museo Nacional* 28: 64–117.

1969   *De los pueblos, las culturas y las artes del antiguo Perú*. Lima: Francisco Moncloa Editores.

1970   *Los templos de Chavín*. Lima: Corporación Peruana de Santa.

1974a   Informe de labores del proyecto Chavín. *Arqueológicas* 15: 37–55.

1974b   *The Peoples and Cultures of Ancient Peru*. Washington, D.C.: Smithsonian Institution Press.

1977   Excavaciones en el templo antiguo de Chavin (sector R): informe de la sexta campana. *Ñawpa Pacha* 15: 1–38.

1978   *Arte precolombino: escultura y diseño (segunda parte)*. Lima: Banco de Crédito.

1987   *Vicús: colección arqueológica*. Lima: Museo Banco Central de la Reserva.

1989   *Chavín de Huántar en el nacimiento de la civilización andina*. Lima: Ediciones INDEA.

Lynch, Thomas F.

1980a   Artifacts made from stone and other inorganic materials. In *Guitarrero Cave: Early Man in the Andes*, edited by Thomas F. Lynch, pp. 175–232. New York: Academic Press.

1980b   *Guitarrero Cave: Early Man in the Andes*. New York: Academic Press.

1980c   Guitarrero Cave in Its Andean context. In *Guitarrero Cave: Early Man in the Andes*, edited by Thomas F. Lynch, pp. 293–320. New York: Academic Press.

MacCormack, Sabine

1991   *Religion in the Andes: Vision and Imagination in Early Colonial Peru*. Princeton: Princeton University Press.

Macedo, José M.

1881   *Catalogue d'objets archéologiques du Pérou de l'ancien empire des Incas*. Paris: Imprimerie Hispano-Américaine.

Mackey, Carol, and Melissa Vogel

2003   La luna sobre los Andes: una revisión del animal lunar. In *Moche:
        hacia el final del milenio*, edited by Santiago Uceda and Elías Mujica,
        pp. 325–342. Lima: Pontificia Universidad Católica del Perú.

Makowski, Krzysztof

2000   Dos cántaros en estilo Recuay: guerreros y ancestros de la sierra de
        Ancash. *Iconos* 4: 60–61.

2004   *Primeras civilizaciones.* Vol. 9. Lima: El Comercio Enciclopedia Temá-
        tica del Perú.

2005   La religión de las altas culturas de la costa del Perú prehispánico. In
        Religiones andinas, vol. 4 of *Enciclopedia Iberoamérica de Religiones*,
        edited by Manuel M. Marzal, pp. 39–88. Madrid: Editorial Trotta.

2008a   Andean urbanism. In *Handbook of South American Archaeology*,
        edited by Helaine Silverman and William H. Isbell, pp. 633–657. New
        York: Springer Science.

2008b   Poder e identidad étnica en el mundo moche. In *Señores de los reinos
        de la luna*, edited by Krzysztof Makowski, pp. 55–76. Lima: Banco de
        Crédito.

Makowski, Krzysztof, Iván Amaro, and Otto Eléspuru

1994   Historia de una conquista. In *Vicús*, edited by Krzysztof Makowski.
        Lima: Banco de Crédito del Perú.

Makowski, Krzysztof, Christopher B. Donnan, Luis Jaime Castillo, Magdalena
        Diez Canseco, Iván Amaro, Otto Eléspuru, and Juan Antonio Murro,
        editors

1994   *Vicús.* Lima: Banco de Crédito del Perú.

Makowski, Krzysztof, and Julio Rucabado Y.

2000   Hombres y deidades en la iconografía Recuay. In *Los dioses del antiguo
        Perú*, edited by K. Makowski, pp. 199–235. Lima: Banco de Crédito.

Malpass, Michael

1985   Two Preceramic and Formative occupations in the Cordillera Negra:
        preliminary report. In *Recent Studies in Andean Prehistory and Proto-
        history*, edited by Daniel H. Sandweiss and D. Peter Kvietok, pp. 15–40.
        Ithaca: Cornell Latin American Studies Program.

Manrique P., Elba

1999   Textilería Recuay. In *Tejidos milenarios del Perú*, edited by José Anto-
        nio de Lavalle and Rosario de Lavalle de Cárdenas, pp. 251–258. Lima:
        AFP Integra.

Mantha, Alexis

2006   Late prehispanic social complexity in the Rapayán Valley, Upper
        Marañón drainage, Central Andes of Peru. In *La complejidad social
        en la Sierra de Ancash: ensayos sobre paisaje, economía y continui-
        dades culturales*, edited by Alexander Herrera, Carolina Orsini, and

Kevin Lane, pp. 35–61. Milan: Civiche Raccolte d'Arte Applicata del Castello Sforzesco.

Marcus, Joyce, and Jorge E. Silva
1988   The Chillón Valley "coca lands": archaeological background and eco-
        logical context. In *Conflicts over Coca Fields in XVIth-Century Peru*,
        edited by María Rostworowski, pp. 1–32. Memoirs, No. 21. Ann Arbor:
        Museum of Anthropology, University of Michigan, Number 21.

Mark, Bryan G.
2008   Tracing tropical Andean glaciers over space and time: some lessons
        and transdisciplinary implications. *Global and Planetary Change* 60:
        101–114.

Mark, Bryan G., and Geoffrey O. Seltzer
2005   Evaluation of recent glacier recession in the Cordillera Blanca, Peru
        (AD 1962–1999): spatial distribution of mass loss and climatic forcing.
        Quaternary Science Reviews 24: 2265–2280.

Márquez Zorilla, Santiago
1965   *Huari y Conchucos*. Lima: Imprenta "El Cóndor."

Masferrer Kan, Elio R.
1984   Criterios de organización andina: Recuay siglo XVII. *Bulletin de
        l'Institut Français d'Etudes Andines* 13: 47–61.

Masuda, Shozo, Izumi Shimada, and Craig Morris, editors
1985   *Andean Ecology and Civilization: An Interdisciplinary Perspective
        on Andean Ecological Complementarity*. Tokyo: University of Tokyo
        Press.

Matsumoto, Ryozo
2006   Arqueología de Llanganuco: resumen de las excavaciones desde el año
        2002 al 2004. Paper presented at the II Conversatorio Internacional
        de Arqueología de Ancash, Instituto Nacional de Cultura — Ancash
        (18–21 August), Huaraz.

Mayer, Enrique
1985   Production zones. In *Andean Ecology and Civilization*, edited by
        Shozo Masuda, Izumi Shimada, and Craig Morris, pp. 45–84. Tokyo:
        University of Tokyo Press.
2002   *The Articulated Peasant*. Boulder: Westview Press.

McCown, Theodore D.
1945   *Pre-Incaic Huamachuco: Survey and Excavations in the Region of
        Huamachuco and Cajabamba*. Publications in American Archaeology
        and Ethnology 39. Berkeley: University of California.

Meddens, Frank M., and Anita G. Cook
2001   La administración Wari y el culto a los muertos: Yako, los edificios en
        forma "D" en la sierra sur-central del Perú. In *Wari: arte precolombino*

peruano, edited by Pedro Bazán, pp. 213–228. Lima: Fundación El Monte.

Mejía M., Zenobio

2006 Leyenda sobre la destrucción del pueblo de Marcuncunca. In *Huandoy y Huascarán: narraciones orales clásicas de Ancash*, vol. 1, edited by Aníbal Jesús Paredes Galván, pp. 9–14. Huaraz: Círculo Literario Bohemia Santiaguina.

Mejía Xesspe, Toribio

1941 Walun y Chinchawas: dos nuevos sitios arqueológicos en la Cordillera Negra. *Chaski* 1: 18–24.

1948 Los soterrados de Katak. In *El Comercio* (Lima), 7 January, p. 9.

1957 Chullpas precolombinas en el área andina. *Revista de la Universidad Nacional de la Plata* 2: 101–108.

Menzel, Dorothy

1964 Style and time in the Middle Horizon. *Ñawpa Pacha* 2: 1–105.

1977 *The Archaeology of Ancient Peru and the Work of Max Uhle*. Berkeley: Lowie Museum of Anthropology.

Menzel, Dorothy, John Howland Rowe, and Lawrence E. Dawson

1964 *The Paracas Pottery of Ica: A Study in Style and Time*. Publications in American Archaeology and Ethnology 50. Berkeley: University of California.

Meskell, Lynn

2004 *Object Worlds in Ancient Egypt: Material Biographies Past and Present*. New York: Berg Publishers.

Métraux, Alfred

1949 Warfare, cannibalism, and human trophies. In *Handbook of South American Indians, Volume 5: The Comparative Ethnology of South American Indians*, edited by Julian H. Steward, pp. 383–410. Bulletin 143. Washington, D.C.: Bureau of American Ethnology, Smithsonian Institution.

Middendorf, Ernst W.

1895 [1893–1895] *Peru: Beobachtungen und Studien über das Land und seine Bewohner während eines 25 jährigen Aufenthaltes*. Berlin: R. Oppenheim.

1973 *Perú: observaciones y estudios del país y sus habitantes durante una permanencia de 25 años*. Lima: Dirección Universitaria de Biblioteca, Universidad Nacional Mayor de San Marcos.

Millaire, Jean-François

2008 Beware of highlanders: coast-highland interactions in the Virú Valley, Peru. Paper presented at the 73rd Annual Meeting of the Society for American Archaeology, Vancouver.

Miller, George R., and Richard L. Burger
1995   Our father the cayman, our dinner the llama: animal utilization at Chavín de Huántar, Peru. *American Antiquity* 60: 421–458.

Millones, Luis
1979   Religion and power in the Andes: idolatrous curacas of the Central Sierra. *Ethnohistory* 26: 243–263.

Mills, Kenneth
1994   Especialistas en rituales y resistencia cultural en la región norcentral del Peru, 1642–1672. In *En el nombre del Señor: shamanes, demonios y curanderos del norte del Peru*, edited by Luis Millones and Moisés Lemlij, pp. 148–183. Lima: Biblioteca Peruana de Psicoanálisis.

Mitchell, William P., and David W. Guillet, editors
1993   *Irrigation at High Altitudes: The Social Organization of Water Control in the Andes*. Washington, D.C.: American Anthropological Association.

Montell, Gosta
1929   *Dress and Ornaments in Ancient Peru*. Göteborg: Elanders Boktryckeri Aktiebolag.

Moore, Jerry D.
1995   Archaeology of dual organization in Andean South America: a theoretical review and case study. *Latin American Antiquity* 6: 165–181.
1996a   Archaeology of plazas and the proxemics of ritual: three Andean traditions. *American Anthropologist* 98: 789–802.
1996b   *Architecture and Power in the Ancient Andes: The Archaeology of Public Buildings*. Cambridge: Cambridge University Press.
2005   *Cultural Landscapes in the Ancient Andes: Archaeologies of Place*. Gainesville: University Press of Florida.

Morales Arnao, Benjamin
1998   Desglaciación y disminución de recursos hídricos. *Boletín de la Sociedad Geográfica de Lima* 111: 7–20.

Morales Arnao, Benjamin, and Stefan Hastenrath
1998   Glaciers of South America — glaciers of Peru: with sections on the Cordillera Blanca on landsat imagery and Quelccaya ice cap. *U.S. Geological Survey Occasional Paper* 1386 (I): 151–179.

Morris, Craig
1979   Maize beer in the economics, politics, and religion of the Inca Empire. In *Fermented Food Beverages in Nutrition*, edited by Clifford F. Gastineau, William J. Darby, and Thomas B. Turner, pp. 21–34. New York: Academic Press.

Moseley, Michael E.

1983   Good old days were better: agrarian collapse and tectonics. *American Anthropologist* 85: 773–799.

1992   *The Incas and Their Ancestors: The Archaeology of Peru*. New York: Thames and Hudson.

Moseley, Michael E., and Kent C. Day, editors

1982   *Chan Chan: Andean Desert City*. Albuquerque: School of American Research.

Moseley, Michael E., and Robert Feldman

1982   Vivir con crisis: percepción humana de proceso y tiempo. *Revista del Museo Nacional* 46: 267–287.

Munn, Nancy D.

1986   *The Fame of Gawa: A Symbolic Study of Value Transformation in a Massim (Papua New Guinea) Society*. Cambridge: Cambridge University Press.

Murga Cruz, Antonio

1983   Estudios arqueológicos en el Cerro Agopampa. Informe de Proyecto Los Angeles. Universidad Nacional de Trujillo, Trujillo.

Murra, John V.

1972   *El "control vertical" de un máximo de pisos ecológicos en la economía de las sociedades andinas*. Huánuco: Universidad Hermilio Valdizán.

Nersesov, Y.

1987   The Recuay monster and the dragon: two mythical beings on Moche vessels in the collection of the Pushkin State Museum of Fine Arts. In *Pre-columbian Collections in European Museums*, edited by Anne Marie Hocquenghem, Peter Tamási, and Christiane Villain-Gandossi, pp. 240–249. Budapest: Akadémiai Kiadó

1993   The Recuay monster in the art of Mochica culture. *Rossiiskaia Arkheologiia* 3: 57–67.

Netherly, Patricia J.

1977   Local Level Lords on the North Coast of Peru. Ph.D. dissertation, Cornell University. Ann Arbor: University Microfilms.

NRC (National Research Council)

1989   *Lost Crops of the Incas: Little-Known Plants of the Andes with Promise for Worldwide Cultivation*. Washington, D.C.: National Research Council and National Academy Press.

Obregón Velázquez, Víctor

2007   Garway. *Revista Informativa de la Municipalidad de Huayllán* 1: 8–9.

Ochatoma, José, and Martha Cabrera

2001   Arquitectura y áreas de actividad en Conchopata. *Boletín de Arqueología PUCP* 4: 449–488.

Offler, R., L. Aguirre, B. Levi, and S. Child

1980   Burial metamorphism in rocks of the Western Andes of Peru. *Lithos* 13: 31–42.

Oliver, José

2005   The proto-Taíno monumental cemís of Caguana: a political-religious "manifesto." In *Ancient Boriquen: Archaeology and Ethnohistory of Native Puerto Rico*, edited by Peter E. Siegel, pp. 230–284. Tuscaloosa: University of Alabama Press.

ONERN (Oficina Nacional de Evaluación de Recursos Naturales)

1972   *Inventario, evaluación y uso racional de los recursos naturales de la costa: cuencas de los Ríos Casma, Culebras y Huarmey*. Lima: Oficina Nacional de Evaluación de Recursos Naturales (ONERN).

1973   *Estudios de suelos del Callejón de Huaylas (semidetallado)*. Lima: Oficina Nacional de Evaluación de Recursos Naturales (ONERN) y Comisión de Rehabilitación y Reconstrucción de la Zona Afectada (CRYRZA).

1975a   *Estudios de suelos del Callejón de Conchucos*. Lima: Oficina Nacional de Evaluación de Recursos Naturales (ONERN) y Comisión de Rehabilitación y Reconstrucción de la Zona Afectada (CRYRZA).

1975b   *Estudios de suelos del Callejón de Huaylas*. Lima: Oficina Nacional de Evaluación de Recursos Naturales (ONERN) y Comisión de Rehabilitación y Reconstrucción de la Zona Afectada (CRYRZA).

Onuki, Yoshio

1985   The yunga zone in the prehistory of the Central Andes: the vertical and horizontal dimensions in Andean ecological and cultural processes. In *Andean Ecology and Civilization*, edited by Shozo Masuda, Yoshio Onuki, and Craig Morris, pp. 339–356. Tokyo: University of Tokyo Press.

Orsini, Carolina

2003   Transformaciones culturales durante el Intermedio Temprano el valle de Chacas: hacia el desarrollo de asentamientos complejos en un área de la sierra nor-central del Perú. In *Arqueología de la sierra de Ancash: propuestas y perspectivas*, edited by Bebel Ibarra, pp. 161–174. Lima: Instituto Cultural Runa.

2006   ¿Metáforas de complejidad social? Huari, llacuaz, organización del territorio y especialización económica en Chacas (valle de Chacapata, Perú). In *La complejidad social en la Sierra de Ancash: ensayos sobre paisaje, economía y continuidades culturales*, edited by Alexander Herrera, Carolina Orsini, and Kevin Lane, pp. 151–163. Milan: Civiche Raccolte d'Arte Applicata del Castello Sforzesco.

2007   *Pastori e guerrieri: I Recuay, un popolo preispanico delle Ande del Peru*. Milan: Jaca Books.

Ortega, Eudoxio

1956   *Los Konchukos*. Lima: Libreria "D. Miranda."

Oyuela-Caycedo, Augusto

1998   Ideology, temples and priests: change and continuity in house socie-
         ties in the Sierra Nevada de Santa Marta. In *Recent Advances in the
         Archaeology of the Northern Andes: Papers in Memory of Gerardo
         Reichel-Dolmatoff*, edited by Augusto Oyuela-Caycedo and J. Scott
         Raymond, pp. 39–53. Los Angeles: Institute of Archaeology, University
         of California.

Paerregaard, Karsten

1987   Death rituals and symbols in the Andes. *Folk* 29: 23–42.

Paredes, Juan, Berenice Quintana, and Moisés Linares

2001   Tumbas de la época Wari en el Callejón de Huaylas. In *Huari y Tiwa-
         naku: modelos vs. evidencias, primera parte*, edited by Peter Kaulicke
         and William H. Isbell, pp. 253–288. Lima: *Boletín de Arqueología
         PUCP* 4.

Paredes G., Aníbal, editor

2006   *Huandoy y Huascarán: narraciones orales clásicas de Ancash*. Vol. 1.
         Huaraz: Círculo Literario Bohemia Santiaguina.

Paredes Olvera, Juan

2007   Redescubriendo Willkawaín e Ichic Willkawaín. *Boletín Informativo
         Mensual* 3: 2–3.

Parker, Gary J., and Amancio Chávez R.

1976   *Diccionario quechua, Ancash-Huailas*. Lima: Ministerio de
         Educación.

Parsons, Jeffrey R., Charles M. Hastings, and Ramiro Matos M.

1997   Rebuilding the state in highland Peru: herder-cultivator interaction
         during the Late Intermediate Period in the Tarama-Chinchaycocha
         region. *Latin American Antiquity* 8: 317–341.

2000   *Prehispanic Settlement Patterns in the Upper Mantaro and Tarma
         Drainages, Junín, Peru: The Tarama-Chinchaycocha Region*. Memoirs
         34. Ann Arbor: University of Michigan Museum of Anthropology.

Paternosto, César

1996   *The Stone and the Thread: Andean Roots of Abstract Art*. Austin:
         University of Texas Press.

Paul, Anne

1990   *Paracas Ritual Attire: Symbols of Authority in Ancient Peru*. Norman:
         University of Oklahoma Press.

Pérez Calderón, Ismael

1988   Monumentos arqueológicos de Santiago de Chuco, La Libertad. *Bole-
         tín de Lima* 60: 33–44.

1994   Monumentos arqueológicos de Santiago de Chuco, La Libertad. *Boletín de Lima* 91–96: 225–274.

Pillsbury, Joanne, editor
2001   *Moche Art and Archaeology in Ancient Peru*. Studies in the History of Art 63. Washington, D.C.: National Gallery of Art.

Platt, Tristan
1986   Mirrors and maize: the concept of yanatin among the Macha of Bolivia. In *Anthropological History of Andean Polities*, edited by John Murra, Jacques Revel, and Nathan Wachtel, pp. 228–259. New York: Cambridge University Press.

Ponte R., Víctor M.
1999a   Análisis de los asentamientos arqueológicos en el área de influencia de la Mina Pierina. Report submitted to Mina Barrick Misquichilca and the Instituto Nacional de Cultura, Huaraz, Peru.
1999b   Excavaciones arqueológicas en el área de Marenayoc. Report submitted to Mina Barrick Misquichilca and the Instituto Nacional de Cultura, Huaraz, Peru.
2001   Transformación social y política en el Callejón de Huaylas, siglos III–X d.C. In *Huari y Tiwanaku: modelos vs. evidencias, primera parte*, edited by Peter Kaulicke and William H. Isbell, pp. 219–252. Lima: *Boletín de Arqueología PUCP* 4.

Porter, Nancy K.
1992   A Recuay style painted textile. *Textile Museum Journal* 31: 71–81.

Protzen, Jean-Pierre
1992   *Inca Architecture and Construction at Ollantaytambo*. New York: Oxford University Press.

Proulx, Donald A.
1968   *An Archaeological Survey of the Nepeña Valley, Peru*. Research Report 2. Amherst: Department of Anthropology, University of Massachusetts.
1982   Territoriality in the Early Intermediate Period: the case of Moche and Recuay. *Ñawpa Pacha* 20: 83–96.
1985   *An Analysis of the Early Cultural Sequence of the Nepeña Valley, Peru*. Research Report 25. Amherst: Department of Anthropology, University of Massachusetts.
2006   *A Sourcebook of Nasca Ceramic Iconography: Reading a Culture through Its Art*. Iowa City: University of Iowa Press.

Prządka, Patrycja, and Miłosz Giersz
2003   *Sitios arqueológicos de la zona del valle de Culebras: Valle Bajo (vol. 1)*. Warsaw: Sociedad Polaca de Estudios Latinoamericanos.

Pulgar Vidal, Javier
1972   *Los ocho regiones naturales del Perú*. Lima: Editorial Universo.

Purin, Sergio, editor

1990   *Inca-Perú: 3000 ans d'histoire*. Brussels: Musées Royaux d'Art et d'Histoire and Imschoot.

Raimondi, Antonio

1873   *El Departamento de Ancachs y sus riquezas minerales*. Lima: Imprenta El Nacional.

1874–
  1880   *El Perú*. Lima: Imprenta del Estado.

1942   *Notas de viaje para su obra* El Perú *(1874–1880), primer volumen*. Lima: Imprenta Torres Aguirre.

Ramírez, Susan E.

1996   *The World Upside Down: Cross-Cultural Contact and Conflict in Sixteenth-Century Peru*. Stanford: Stanford University Press.

Ravines, Rogger

1984   Tinyash: un pueblo prehispánico de la puna. *Boletín de Lima* 31: 31–37.

2000   La cultura Recuay. In *Las culturas prehispánicas*, edited by Bernardo Roca Rey Miró Quesada, pp. 81–88. Lima: Empresa Editora El Comercio y Universidad Ricardo Palma.

Ravines, Rogger, and Juan José Alvarez Sauri

1967   Fechas radiocarbónicas para el Perú. *Arqueológicas* 11: 1–58.

Redmond, Elsa

1994   *Tribal and Chiefly Warfare in South America*. Memoirs 28. Ann Arbor: Museum of Anthropology, University of Michigan.

Reichel-Dolmatoff, Gerardo

1985   *Los Kogi: una tribu de la Sierra Nevada de Santa Marta, Colombia*. Bogotá: Procultura.

Reichert, Raphael X.

1977   The Recuay Ceramic Style: A Reevaluation. Ph.D. dissertation, University of California, Los Angeles.

1978   Ceramic sculpture of ancient Peru. *Pacific Discovery* 31: 28–32.

1982a   A counterfeit Moche-Recuay vessel and its origins. In *Falsifications and Misreconstructions of Pre-Columbian Art*, pp. 51–62. Washington, D.C.: Dumbarton Oaks.

1982b   Moche iconography — the highland connection. In *Pre-Columbian Art History: Selected Readings*, edited by Alana Cordy-Collins, pp. 279–291. Palo Alto: Peek Publications.

Reilly, Kent, III

1989   The shaman in transformation pose: a study of the theme of rulership in Olmec Art. *Record of the Art Museum, Princeton University* 48: 4–21.

Reina Loli, Manuel

1959   Arqueología huaracina: el adoratorio de Pumacayán. *Actas y trabajos del II Congreso Nacional del Peru* 1: 114–122.

Reinhard, Johan

1985   Chavín and Tiahuanaco: a new look at two Andean ceremonial cen-
        ters. *National Geographic Research* 1: 345–422.

Reiss, Wilhelm, and Alphons Stübel

1880   *The Necropolis of Ancón in Peru.* Berlin: A. Asher and Co.

Rice, Prudence M.

1987   *Pottery Analysis: A Sourcebook.* Chicago: University of Chicago Press.

Rick, John W.

2005   The evolution of authority and power at Chavín de Huántar, Peru.
        In *Foundations of Power in the Prehispanic Andes*, edited by Kevin J.
        Vaughn, Dennis E. Ogburn, and Christina A. Conlee, pp. 71–89. Ar-
        chaeological Papers 14. Washington, D.C.: American Anthropological
        Association.

2008   Context, construction and ritual in the development of authority at
        Chavín de Huántar. In *Chavín: Art, Architecture and Culture*, edited
        by William J. Conklin and Jeffrey Quilter, pp. 3–34. Monograph 61.
        Los Angeles: Cotsen Institute of Archaeology.

Rivera, Limber

2003   *Las cordilleras Raura y Huayhuash: su importancia geoeconómica.*
        Huánuco: Instituto de Investigación y Desarrollo Comunal.

Rivet, Paul

1949   Les langues de l'ancien diocèse de Trujillo. *Journal de la Société des
        Américanistes* 38: 1–52.

Rodman, Amy Oakland, and Vicky Cassman

1995   Andean tapestry: structure informs the surface. *Art Journal* 54: 33–39.

Rodman, Amy Oakland, and Arabel Fernández

2000   Tejidos de Huari y Tiwanaku: comparaciones y contextos. *Boletín de
        Arqueología PUCP* 4: 119–130.

Rofes, Juan

1999   Análisis de los restos de fauna vertebrada recuperados por el Proyecto
        Arqueológico Pierina en Huaraz, Ancash. In Análisis de los asenta-
        mientos arqueológicos en el área de influencia de la Mina Pierina,
        edited by Victor Ponte R. Report submitted to Mina Barrick Mis-
        quichilca and the Instituto Nacional de Cultura, Huaraz, Peru.

Roosevelt, Cornelius Van S.

1935   Ancient civilizations of the Santa Valley and Chavín. *Geographical
        Review* 25: 21–42.

Rostworowski, María

1988   *Conflicts over Coca Fields in XVIth-Century Peru.* Memoirs 21. Ann
        Arbor: Museum of Anthropology, University of Michigan.

Rostworowski, María, and Pilar Remy, editors

1992   *Las visitas a Cajamarca 1571–72/1578.* Vols. 1–2. Lima: Instituto de
        Estudios Peruanos.

Rostworowski de Diez Canseco, María

1999   *History of the Inca Realm.* Cambridge: Cambridge University Press.

Rowe, John Howland

1946   Inca culture at the time of the Spanish conquest. In *Handbook of
        South American Indians, Volume 2: The Andean Civilizations*, edited
        by Julian Steward, pp. 183–330. Bulletin 143. Washington, D.C.:
        Bureau of American Ethnology.

1963   Urban settlements in ancient Peru. *Ñawpa Pacha* 1: 1–27.

1967   Stages and periods in archaeological interpretation. In *Peruvian
        Archaeology: Selected Readings*, edited by John Howland Rowe and
        Dorothy Menzel, pp. 1–15. Palo Alto: Peek Publications.

1979   Standardization in Inca tapestry tunics. In *Junius B. Bird Pre-
        Columbian Textile Conference*, edited by Junius B. Bird, Ann P. Rowe,
        Elizabeth P. Benson, and Anne-Louise Schaffer, pp. 239–264. Wash-
        ington, D.C.: Textile Museum.

Rowe, John Howland, and Dorothy Menzel, editors

1967   *Peruvian Archaeology: Selected Readings.* Palo Alto.: Peek
        Publications.

Russell, Glenn S., Banks L. Leonard, and Jesus Briceño

1998   The Cerro Mayal workshop: addressing issues of craft specialization
        in Moche society. *MASCA Research Papers in Science and Technology
        (Supplement)* 15: 63–89.

Sahlins, Marshall

1985   *Islands of History.* Chicago: University of Chicago Press.

Salomon, Frank

1986   *Native Lords of Quito in the Age of the Incas: The Political Economy of
        North Andean Chiefdoms.* Cambridge: Cambridge University Press.

1991   Introductory essay: the Huarochirí Manuscript. In *The Huarochirí
        Manuscript: A Testament of Ancient and Colonial Religion*, edited by
        Frank Salomon and George Urioste, pp. 1–38. Austin: University of
        Texas Press.

1995   "Beautiful grandparents": Andean ancestor shrines and mortuary rit-
        ual as seen through colonial records. In *Tombs for the Living: Andean
        Mortuary Practices*, edited by Tom D. Dillehay, pp. 315–353. Washing-
        ton, D.C.: Dumbarton Oaks.

2004   Andean opulence: indigenous ideas about wealth in colonial Peru.
        In *The Colonial Andes: Tapestries and Silverwork, 1530–1830*, edited
        by Elena Phipps, Johanna Hecht, and Cristina Esteras Martín,
        pp. 114–124. New York: Metropolitan Museum of Art.

Salomon, Frank, and George Urioste, editors

1991   *The Huarochirí Manuscript: A Testament of Ancient and Colonial Religion*. Austin: University of Texas Press.

Sandweiss, Daniel H., Kirk A. Maasch, Richard L. Burger III, James B. Richardson, Harold B. Rollins, and Amy Clement

2001   Variations in Holocene El Niño frequencies: climate records and cultural consequences. *Geology*: 603–606.

Sawyer, Michael J.

1985   An Analysis of Mammalian Faunal Remains from the Site of Huaricoto, PAN3-35. M.A. thesis, Department of Anthropology, California State University, Hayward.

Schaedel, Richard P.

1948a   The Callejón de Huaylas of Peru and its monuments. *Archaeology* 1: 198–202.

1948b   Stone sculpture in the Callejón de Huaylas. In *A Reappraisal of Peruvian Archaeology*, edited by Wendell C. Bennett, pp. 66–79. Memoirs 4. Menasha, Wisc.: Society for American Archaeology.

1951   Major ceremonial and population centers in northern Peru. *Civilizations of Ancient America: Selected Papers of the XXIXth International Congress of Americanists* 1: 232–243.

1952   An Analysis of Central Andean Stone Sculpture. Ph.D. dissertation, Yale University. Ann Arbor: University Microfilms.

1966   Incipient urbanization and secularization in Tiahuanacoid Peru. *American Antiquity* 31: 338–344.

1985   Coast-highland interrelationships and ethnic groups in Northern Peru (500 B.C.–A.D. 1980). In *Andean Ecology and Civilization: An Interdisciplinary Perspective in Ecological Complementarity*, edited by Shozo Masuda, Izumi Shimada, and Craig Morris, pp. 443–474. Tokyo: University of Tokyo Press.

1993   Congruence of horizon with polity: Huari and the Middle Horizon. In *Latin American Horizons*, edited by Don S. Rice, pp. 225–261. Washington, D.C.: Dumbarton Oaks.

Schindler, Helmut

2000   *The Norbert Mayrock Art Collection from Ancient Peru*. Munich: Staatlische Museum für Völkerkunde.

Schmidt, Max

1929   *Kunst und Kultur von Peru*. Berlin: Propyläen-Verlag.

Schuler-Schömig, Immina von

1979   Die "Fremdkrieger" in Darstellungen der Moche-Keramik. Eine ikonographische Studie. *Baessler Archiv*, n.s. 27: 135–213.

1981   Die sogenannten Fremdkrieger und ihre weiteren ikonographischen Bezuge in der Moche-Keramik. *Baessler Archiv*, n.s. 29: 207–239.

Scott, David A.

1998   Technical examination of ancient South American metals: some examples from Colombia, Peru and Argentina. *Boletín, Museo del Oro* 44: 79–105.

Scully, Vincent

1975   *Pueblo: Mountain, Village, Dance.* New York: Viking Press.

Seler, Eduard

1893   *Peruanische Alterthümer.* Berlin: n.p.

Serna Lamas, Cesar

2009   Proyecto Arqueológico Pumacayán: investigación, conservación y puesta en valor. *Pumakayán* 1(2): 5.

Shimada, Izumi

1994   *Pampa Grande and the Mochica Culture.* Austin: University of Texas Press.

Shimada, Izumi, Lonnie G. Thompson, Ellen Mosley-Thompson, and Crystal B. Schaaf

1991   Cultural impacts of severe droughts in the prehistoric Andes: application of a 1,500-year ice core precipitation record. *World Archaeology* 22: 247–270.

Sievers, Wilhelm

1914   *Reise in Peru und Ecuador, Ausgeführt 1909.* Munich and Leipzig: Duncker und Humblot.

Sillar, Bill

1996   The dead and the drying: techniques for transforming people and things in the Andes. *Journal of Material Culture* 1: 259–289.

Silva Santisteban, Fernando

1986   La lengua culle de Cajamarca. In *Historia de Cajamarca (Vol. 2): Etnohistoria y lingüística*, edited by Fernando Silva Santisteban, Waldemar Espinoza Soriano, and Rogger Ravines, pp. 365–369. Cajamarca: Instituto Nacional de Cultura.

Silverman, Helaine

1993   *Cahuachi in the Ancient Nasca World.* Iowa City: University of Iowa Press.

Silverman, Helaine, and Donald A. Proulx

2002   *The Nasca.* Malden: Blackwell Publishers.

Smith, John W., Jr.

1977   Recuay gaming boards: a preliminary study. *Indiana* 4: 111–137.
1978   The Recuay Culture: A Reconstruction Based on Artistic Motifs. Ph.D. dissertation, University of Texas, Austin.

Solomina, Olga, Vincent Jomelli, Georg Kaser, Alcides Ames, Bernard Berger, and Bernard Pouyaud

2007   Lichenometry in the Cordillera Blanca, Peru: "Little Ice Age" moraine chronology. *Global and Planetary Change* 59: 225–235.

Soriano I., Augusto

1940   Algo sobre la arqueología de Ancash. *Actas y Trabajos Científicos del XXVII Congreso Internacional de Americanistas (Lima, 1939)* 1: 473–483.

1941   Monografía de Ancash, Nepeña (Provincia de Santa). *Revista del Museo Nacional* 10: 263–277.

1947   Breve monografía de Ancash. *Fanal* May: 5–12.

1950   *Memoria del director del Museo Arqueológico de Ancash.* Huaraz: Imp. El Lucero.

Soto Verde, Lilyan

2003   Waullac y el Intermedio Temprano en el Callejón de Huaylas. In *Arqueología de la Sierra de Ancash: propuestas y perspectivas*, edited by Bebel Ibarra A., pp. 175–192. Huaraz: Instituto Cultural Runa.

Spahni, Jean-Christian

1969   *Los mates decorados del Perú.* Lima: Peruano-Suiza, S.A.

Steward, Julian H., editor

1946   *Handbook of South American Indians, Volume 2: The Andean Civilizations.* Bulletin 143. Washington, D.C.: Bureau of American Ethnology.

Steward, Julian H., and Louis C. Faron

1959   *Native Peoples of South America.* New York: McGraw-Hill.

Stone-Miller, Rebecca

1992   Creative abstractions: Middle Horizon textiles in the Museum of Fine Arts, Boston. In *To Weave for the Sun: Ancient Andean Textiles in the Museum of Fine Arts, Boston*, edited by Rebecca Stone-Miller, pp. 35–42. New York: Thames and Hudson.

2004   Human-animal imagery, shamanic visions, and ancient American aesthetics. *Res* 45: 47–68.

Strathern, Marilyn

1979   The self in self-decoration. *Oceania* 29: 241–257.

1988   *Gender of the Gift: Problems with Women and Problems with Society in Melanesia.* Berkeley: University of California Press.

Strong, William Duncan, and Clifford Evans, editors

1952   *Cultural Stratigraphy in the Virú Valley, Northern Peru: The Formative and Florescent Epochs.* New York: Columbia University Press.

Strong, William Duncan, Clifford Evans, and Rose Lilien

1952   Appendix 1: description of pottery types. In *Cultural Stratigraphy in the Virú Valley, Northern Peru: The Formative and Florescent Epochs*, edited by William Duncan Strong and Clifford Evans, pp. 253–351. New York: Columbia University Press.

Sullivan, Lawrence E.

1988   *Icanchu's Drum: An Orientation to Meaning in South American Religions.* New York: MacMillan.

Swenson, Edward R.

2006   Competitive feasting, religious pluralism and decentralized power in the Late Moche period. In *Andean Archaeology III: North and South,* edited by William H. Isbell and Helaine Silverman, pp. 112–142. New York: Springer Science.

Taussig, Michael

1993   *Mimesis and Alterity: A Particular History of the Senses.* London: Routledge.

Taylor, Gerald

1976   *Camay, camac* et *camasca* dans le manuscrit quechua de Huarochirí. *Journal de la Société des Américanistes* 63 (1974–1976): 231–244.

2000   *Camac, camay y camasca y otros ensayos sobre Huarochirí y Yauyos.* Travaux 126. Lima: L'Institut Français d'Etudes Andines.

Tello, Julio C.

1923   Wira Kocha. *Inca* 1(1): 93–320; 1(3): 583–606.

1929   *Antiguo Perú: primera época.* Lima: Comisión Organizadora del Segundo Congreso de Turismo.

1930   Andean civilization: some problems of Peruvian archaeology. *Proceedings of the 23rd International Congress of Americanists (New York, 1928):* 259–290.

1940   Origen y desarrollo de las civilizaciones prehistóricas andinas. *Actas y Trabajos Científicos del XXVII Congreso Internacional de Americanistas (Lima, 1939)* 1: 589–720.

1956   *Arqueología del Valle de Casma: culturas Chavín, Santa o Huaylas Yunga y Sub-Chimú.* Lima: Editorial San Marcos.

1960   *Chavín: cultura matriz de la civilización andina.* Lima: Universidad Nacional Mayor de San Marcos.

Terada, Kazuo, editor

1979   *Excavations at La Pampa in the North Highlands of Peru, 1975.* Tokyo: University of Tokyo Press.

Terada, Kazuo, and Ryozo Matsumoto

1985   Sobre la cronología de la tradición Cajamarca. In *Historia del Cajamarca: Tomo 1 (Arqueología),* edited by Fernando Silva S., Waldemar Espinoza S., and Rogger Ravines, pp. 67–89. Cajamarca: Instituto Nacional de Cultura.

Thompson, Donald E.

1966   Archaeological investigations in the Huarmey Valley, Peru. *36th International Congress of Americanists* 1: 541–548.

1973   Investigaciones arqueológicas en los Andes orientales del norte del Perú. *Revista del Museo Nacional* 39: 117–126.

Thompson, Donald E., and Rogger Ravines

1973   Tinyash: a prehispanic village in the Andean Puna. *Archaeology* 26: 94–100.

Thompson, Lonnie G.

2001   *Huascarán Ice Core Data, IGBP PAGES/World Data Center A for Paleoclimatology Data Contribution Series #2001-008*. Washington, D.C.: NOAA/NGDC Paleoclimatology Program.

Thompson, Lonnie G., Keith A. Henderson, Ellen Mosley-Thompson, and Ping-Nan Lin

2000   The tropical ice core record of ENSO. In *El Niño and the Southern Oscillation: Multiscale Variability and Global and Regional Impacts*, edited by Henry F. Diaz and Vera Markgraf, pp. 325–356. Cambridge: Cambridge University Press.

Thompson, Lonnie G., and Ellen Mosley-Thompson

1987   Evidence of abrupt climatic change during the last 1500 years recorded in ice-cores from the tropical Quelccaya ice cap. In *Abrupt Climate Change*, edited by W. H. Berger and L. D. Labeyrie, pp. 99–110. NATO ASI Series C, Vol. 216. Norwell: D. Reidel.

1989   One-half millennia of tropical climate variability as recorded in the stratigraphy of the Quelccaya ice cap, Peru. *Geophysical Monograph* 55: 15–31.

Thompson, Lonnie G., Ellen Mosley-Thompson, Willi Dansgaard, and Pieter Grootes

1986   The Little Ice Age as recorded in the stratigraphy of the tropical Quelccaya ice cap. *Science* 234: 361–364.

Thompson, Lonnie G., Ellen Mosley-Thompson, Mary E. Davis, Ping-Nan Lin, Keith A. Henderson, J. Cole-Dai, J. F. Bolzan, and K.-B. Liu

1995   Late glacial stage and Holocene ice core records from Huascarán, Peru. *Science* 269: 46–50.

Thompson, Lonnie G., Ellen Mosley-Thompson, Mary E. Davis, Ping-Nan Lin, Keith A. Henderson, and Tracy A. Mashiotta

2003   Tropical glacier and ice core evidence of climate change on annual and millennial time scales. *Climate Change* 59: 37–155.

Thompson, Lonnie G., Ellen Mosley-Thompson, and Benjamin Morales

1984   El Niño–Southern Oscillation events recorded in the stratigraphy of the tropical Quelccaya ice cap, Peru. *Science* 203: 50–53.

Thompson, Lonnie G., Ellen Mosley-Thompson, and P. A. Thompson

1992   Reconstructing interannual climatic variability from tropical and subtropical ice-core records. In *El Niño: Historical and Paleoclimatic Aspects of Southern Oscillation*, edited by Henry F. Diaz and Vera Markgraf, pp. 295–322. Cambridge: Cambridge University Press.

Tilley, Christopher

1994   *A Phenomenology of Landscape: Places, Paths and Monuments.* Oxford: Berg Publishers.

Tilley, Christopher, and Wayne Bennett

2004   *The Materiality of Stone: Explorations in Landscape Phenomenology.* Oxford: Berg Publishers.

Topic, John R.

1998   Ethnogenesis in Huamachuco. *Andean Past* 5: 109–127.

Topic, John R., and Theresa L. Topic

1983   Coast-highland relations in northern Peru: some observations on routes, networks, and scales of interaction. In *Civilization in the Ancient Americas: Essays in Honor of Gordon R. Willey*, edited by Richard Leventhal and Alan Kolata, pp. 237–259. Albuquerque: University of New Mexico Press.

1987   The archaeological investigation of Andean militarism: some cautionary observations. In *The Origins and Development of the Andean State*, edited by Jonathan Haas, Shelia Pozorski, and Thomas Pozorski, pp. 47–55. Cambridge: Cambridge University Press.

1997   Hacia una comprensión conceptual de la guerra andina. In *Arqueología, antropología e historia en los Andes: homenaje a Maria Rostworowski*, edited by Rafael Varon Gabai and Javier Flores Espinoza, pp. 567–595. Lima: Instituto de Estudios Peruanos.

Topic, John R., Theresa Lange Topic, and Alfredo Melly Cava

2002   Catequil: the archaeology, ethnohistory, and ethnography of a major provincial huaca. In *Andean Archaeology I: Variations in Sociopolitical Organization*, edited by William H. Isbell and Helaine Silverman, pp. 303–336. New York: Kluwer Academic/Plenum.

Topic, Theresa L.

1982   The Early Intermediate Period and its legacy. In *Chan Chan: Andean Desert City*, edited by Michael E. Moseley and Kent C. Day, pp. 255–284. Albuquerque: School of American Research, University of New Mexico.

Topic, Theresa L., and John R. Topic

1982   *Prehistoric Fortifications of Northern Peru: Preliminary Report on the Final Season, January–December 1980.* Peterborough, Ontario: Trent University Department of Anthropology.

1984   *Huamachuco Archaeological Project: Preliminary Report of the Third*

Season, June–August 1983. Occasional Papers in Anthropology 1. Peterborough, Ontario: Trent University.

Torero, Alfredo
1974   *El quechua y la historia social andina.* Lima: Universidad Ricardo Palma Dirección Universitaria de Investigación.
1989   Areas toponímicas e idiomas en la sierra norte peruana: un trabajo de recuperación lingüística. *Revista Andina* 7: 217–257.

Tosi, Joseph A., Jr.
1960   *Zonas de vida natural en el Perú.* Boletín Técnico 5. Lima: Instituto de Ciencias Agrícolas de la OEA, Zona Andina.

Townsend, Richard F., editor
1992   *The Ancient Americas: Art from Sacred Landscapes.* Chicago: Art Institute of Chicago.

Trigger, Bruce G.
1990   Monumental architecture: a thermodynamic explanation of symbolic behavior. *World Archaeology* 22: 119–132.

Troll, Carl
1980   [1931] Las culturas superiores andinas y el medio geográfico. *Allpanchis* 15: 3–55.

Tschauner, Hartmut
2003   Honco Pampa: arquitectura de élite del Horizonte Medio del Callejón de Huaylas. In *Arqueología de la sierra de Ancash: propuestas y perspectivas,* edited by Bebel Ibarra, pp. 193–220. Lima: Instituto Cultural Runa.

Turner, Terence
1980   The social skin. In *Not Work Alone: A Cross-cultural View of Activities Superfluous to Survival,* edited by Jeremy Cherfas and Roger Lewin, pp. 112–140. London: Temple Smith.

Uceda, Santiago, and Elias Mujica, editors
2003   *Moche: hacia el final del milenio.* Lima: Pontificia Universidad Católica del Peru.

Uhle, Max
1903   *Pachacamac: Report of the William Pepper, M.D.L.L.D., Peruvian Expedition of 1896.* Philadelphia: Department of Anthropology, University of Pennsylvania.
1914   The Nazca pottery of ancient Peru. *Proceedings of the Davenport Academy of Sciences* 13: 1–46.

Urton, Gary
1993   Actividad ceremonial y división de mitades en el mundo andino: las batallas rituales en los carnavales del Sur del Perú. In *El Mundo*

Ceremonial Andino, edited by Luis Millones and Yoshio Onuki, pp. 117–142. Lima: Editorial Horizonte.

1996　The body of meaning in Chavín art. *Res* 29: 237–255.

Valeri, Valerio

1985　*Kingship and Sacrifice: Ritual and Society in Ancient Hawaii.* Chicago: University of Chicago Press.

Valladolid Huamán, Clide María

1990　Auquis Marca — (Pueblo Viejo). *Boletín Informativo* 4: 10–11. Huaraz: Museo Arqueológico de Ancash.

Varón Gabai, Rafael

1980　*Curacas y encomenderos: acomodamiento nativo en Huaraz, siglos XVI–XVII.* Lima: P. L. Villanueva.

1993　Estrategias políticas y relaciones conyugales: el comportamiento de Incas y Españoles en Huaylas en la primera mitad del siglo XVI. *Bulletin de l'Institut Français d'Etudes Andines* 22: 721–737.

Vaughn, Kevin J.

2005　Crafts and the materialization of chiefly power. In *Foundations of Power in the Ancient Andes*, edited by Kevin J. Vaughn, Dennis E. Ogburn, and Christina A. Conlee, pp. 113–130. Archaeological Papers 14. Washington, D.C.: American Anthropological Association.

Verano, John W.

2001　War and death in the Moche world: osteological evidence and visual discourse. In *Moche Art and Archaeology in Ancient Peru*, edited by Joanne Pillsbury, pp. 111–125. Studies in the History of Art 63. Washington, D.C.: National Gallery of Art.

Villacorta O., Luis Felipe

2006　Antonio Raimondi y el departamento de Ancash: historia y construcción de un vínculo científico, personal y simbólico. In *El departamento de Ancachs y sus riquezas minerales (1873, por Antonio Raimondi)*, edited by Luis Felipe Villacorta O., pp. 21–96. Lima: Universidad Nacional Mayor de San Marcos.

Viveiros de Castro, Eduardo

1992　*From the Enemy's Point of View: Humanity and Divinity in an Amazonian Society.* Chicago: University of Chicago Press.

1998　Cosmological deixis and Amerindian perspectivism. *Journal of the Royal Anthropological Institute*, n.s. 4: 469–488.

2004　Exchanging perspectives: the transformation of objects into subjects in Amerindian ontologies. *Common Knowledge* 10: 463–484.

Vuille, Mathias, and Raymond S. Bradley

2000　Mean annual temperature trends and their vertical structure in the tropical Andes. *Geophysical Research Letters* 27: 3885–3888.

Vuille, Mathias, Raymond S. Bradley, Martin Werner, and Frank Keimig
2003   20th century climate change in the tropical Andes: observations and model results. *Climatic Change* 59: 75–99.

Wallace, Dwight T.
1991   Chincha roads: economics and symbolism. In *Ancient Road Networks and Settlement Hierarchies in the New World*, edited by Charles D. Trombold, pp. 253–263. Cambridge: Cambridge University Press.

Walter, Doris
1997   Comment meurent les pumas: du mythe au rite à Huaraz (centre-nord du Pérou). *Bulletin de l'Institut Français d'Etudes Andines* 26: 447–471.
2002   *La domestication de la nature dans les Andes péruviennes*. Paris: L'Harmattan.
2006   Los sitios arqueológicos en el imaginario de los campesinos de la Cordillera Blanca (Sierra de Ancash). In *Complejidad social en la arqueología y antropología de la sierra de Ancash, Perú*, edited by Alexander Herrera, Carolina Orsini, and Kevin Lane, pp. 177–190. Milan: Comune di Milano-Raccolte Extra Europee del Castello Sforzesco.

Wegner, Steven A.
1982   Hacia una definición de la cultura Recuay. *Universidad Nacional Mayor de San Marcos Serie Investigaciones* 5: 1–8.
1988   *Cultura Recuay*. Exhibit pamphlet. Banco Continental and Museo Arqueológico de Ancash (Lima, September–October).
2000   *Arqueología y arte antiguo de Chacas*. Huaraz: Instituto Cultural Ancashwain.
2001a   Exhibition pamphlet for "Auquis Puquio: un refugio antiguo, hijo de la tierra" (9 November–8 December). Huaraz: Banco Wiese Sudameris.
2001b   Síntesis de la historia cultural antigua de Chacas. In *El Museo de Chacas*, edited by Laura Laurencich Minelli and Steven Wegner, pp. 11–36. Bologna: Editrice Compositori.
2002   Las esculturas prehispánicas de Chacas. *El Pregonero* 20: 17–18.
2003   Identificando el área de dominio Recuay: un extendido inventario cerámico para la identificación de asentamientos Recuay. In *Arqueología de la sierra de Ancash: propuestas y perspectivas*, edited by Bebel Ibarra, pp. 121–134. Lima: Instituto Cultural Runa.
2009   Antonio Raimondi y las esculturas antiguas de Huaraz. *Pumakayán* 1(3): 12–13.

Weiner, James, editor
1994   *Aesthetics Is a Cross-cultural Category*. Manchester: Group for Debates in Anthropological Theory, Department of Social Anthropology.

Weismantel, Mary
2004   Moche sex pots: reproduction and temporality in ancient South America. *American Anthropologist* 106: 495–505.

Wells, Lisa E., and J. S. Knoller

1999 Holocene coevolution of the physical landscape and human settlement in northern coastal Peru. *Georarchaeology* 14: 755–789.

Wiener, Charles

1880 *Pérou et Bolivie: Récit de voyage suivi d'études archéologiques et ethnographiques et de notes sur l'écriture et les langues des populations indiennes.* Paris: Librairie Hatchette.

1993 [1880] *Perú y Bolivia.* Lima: Instituto Francés de Estudios Andinos.

Willey, Gordon R.

1945 Horizon styles and pottery traditions in Peruvian archaeology. *American Antiquity* 11: 49–56.

1946 The Chiclín conference for Peruvian archaeology, 1946. *American Antiquity* 12: 132–134.

1953 *Prehistoric Settlement Patterns in the Virú Valley, Peru.* Bulletin 155. Washington, D.C.: Bureau of American Ethnology, Smithsonian Institution.

1988 *Portraits in American Archaeology.* Albuquerque: University of New Mexico Press.

Wilson, David J.

1987 Reconstructing patterns of early warfare in the Lower Santa Valley: new data on the role of conflict in the origins of north coast complexity. In *The Origins and Development of the Andean State*, edited by Jonathan Haas, Shelia Pozorski, and Thomas Pozorski, pp. 56–69. Cambridge: Cambridge University Press.

1988 *Prehispanic Settlement Patterns in the Lower Santa Valley, Peru: A Regional Perspective on the Origins and Development of Complex North Coast Society.* Washington, D.C.: Smithsonian Institution Press.

1995 Prehispanic settlement patterns in the Casma Valley, north coast of Peru: preliminary results to date. *Journal of the Steward Anthropological Society* 23: 189–227.

Yauri Montero, Marcos E.

2000 *Leyendas ancashinas.* 6th ed. Lima: Taller Gráfico Lerma Gómez.

2004 Literatura oral andina: aculturación y carencia. *Asterisco* 17: 40–60.

Yoffee, Norman

2005 *Myths of the Archaic State.* Cambridge: Cambridge University Press.

Young, Kenneth R., and Blanca León

1999 *Peru's Humid Eastern Montane Forests: An Overview of Their Physical Settings, Biological Diversity, Human Use and Settlement, and Conservation Needs.* Oyacachi: Centre for Research on the Cultural and Biological Diversity of Andean Rainforests.

Young, Kenneth R., and Jennifer Lipton

2006   Adaptive governance and climate change in the tropical highlands of western South America. *Climate Change* 78: 63–102.

Zaki, Andrzej

1987   Zoomorphe Steinskulpturen aus Santa Cruz (Peru): Ein Beitrag zum Raubtiermotiv in der vorkolumbischen Kunst. *Schweizerische Amerikanisten-Gesellschaft Bulletin* 51: 7–18.

Zimmerer, Karl S.

1996   *Changing Fortunes: Biodiversity and Peasant Livelihood in the Peruvian Andes.* Berkeley: University of California Press.

Ziółkowski, Mariusz S., Mieczysław F. Pazdur, Andrzej Krzanowski, and Adam Michczyński

1994   *Andes: Radiocarbon Database for Bolivia, Ecuador and Peru.* Warsaw, Poland: Andean Archaeological Mission of the Institute of Archaeology, Warsaw University and Gliwice Radiocarbon Laboratory of the Institute of Physics, Silesian Technical University.

Zuidema, R. Tom

1977   Shaft-tombs and the Inca empire. *Journal of the Steward Anthropological Society* 9: 133–178.

1985   Lion in the city: royal symbols of transition in Cuzco. In *Animal Myths and Metaphors in South America*, edited by Gary Urton, pp. 183–250. Salt Lake City: University of Utah Press.

1990   Dynastic structures in Andean culture. In *Northern Dynasties: Kingship and Statecraft in Chimor*, edited by Michael E. Moseley and Alana Cordy-Collins, pp. 489–505. Washington, D.C.: Dumbarton Oaks.

INDEX

(plates and pages of figures in italics; plate numbers are indicated with *pl.*)

adobe, 54, 103, *168*, 229
aesthetics, 6, 19, 253
agriculture, 21–28, 35, 38, 44, 57–58, 59–61, 120; agro-pastoralism, 38, 43, 44, 121; crop rotation, 27; oral tradition, 186; rainy season, 27; scheduling, 122; upper limits of, 24, *25*, 34–35, 60, 261. *See also* cereals, irrigation, legumes, tubers
Aija: pottery, 129; region, 30, 42, 94, 166, 249, 256, 259, 261; reservoirs, 78; stone sculptures, 42, *161*, 165, 169, 173, 183, 198; style, 129
Alca, 257
alcoholic drink, 156, 230, 239
algae, 25
aluvión landslides, 36, 125
amaru, 198, 209, *210*, 212, 221, 235, 238
Amat, Hernan, 41, 50, 131, 132, 134–135, 142, 148, 279; pottery seriation, 148–149
Amazonia, 21, 26, 29, 122, 193
Ancash, 2, 18, 21–23, 26–32, 131, 174; agricultural potential, 27–28; altitude, 21–28; climate change, 33–35, 119–120; coastal, 22–23, 26, 30–31, 44–46; disasters, 35–36, 55, 125; economic practices, 21, 35; elevation, 27; environment, 18, 21–22; ethnohistory, 14, 32, 41, 44, 47, 56–61, 85, 90, 96, 124, 193, 195, 215–216; geographic boundaries, 21–22, 28–32, 123; land use, 21–28, 35, 37; life zones, 22, 22–24, *25*, 26; populations, 28; preservation, 54; rainfall, 7, 22–28, 33–35, 277; resources, 22–26, 64; seasonality, 27, 125; sierra, 24, 28, 29, 31, 130; size, 21;

soils, 27; tectonism, 35; temperatures, 27, 33–36; transportation routes, 28, 30–31, 45, 123; water rights, 35
ancestors: ancestor cults, 20, 44, 49, 111, 124, 162, 185, 189, 231, 239; effigies, 124, 184–189, 199, 278; idol-making, 187–189; materiality, 162, 199; monuments, 55, 124, 186, 200; progenitors, 111, 114, 184, 189, 197–198; sculptural imagery, 167–168, *185*; stone uprights, 85–86, 88, 185–189; symbolism, 114–115; veneration, 20, 44, 49, 53, 54–55, 88, 90, 100, 110–113, 117, 157, 162, *185*, 187, 222. *See also* lithomorphosis, mortuary practices, *pacarinas*
Ancosh Punta, 41, 257
Andes: Andean Archaic pottery, 129; Central, *1*, 11, 21, 25, 28, 38, 56, 65, 86, 111, 153, 180, 225, 239, 243; Northern, 24, 193, 226; *páramo* Andes, 24–25; *puna* Andes, 24–25; south-central, 33
animals, 122, 231–238; sheep, 24. *See also specific animals*
Antajirca, 41, 169
anthropomorphs, *163*, *168*, 170, *171*, 173, 197–198; body ornament, 198; clothing, 162, 170; genitalia, 198, 199; head characteristics, 198; headdresses, 198
Antúnez de Mayolo, Santiago, 50
architectural characteristics: access, 69, 72, 74, 87, 89; antechambers, 93–96, 113, 114; arclike rooms, 87; batter, 105; benches, 68, 87; burial compartments, *96*, 97, 98; cantilevered, 99; columns, 100, 109; concentric walls, 70–73, 87; corbelling, 99; cornices, 109; courtyards, 70; doorways, 68, 69, 72, 73, 87, 89, 98, 100, 109, 112, 113; drainage canals, 69, 107; fencing, 103;

floors, 103; gabled roofs, 99, 109; galleries, 72, 74, 97, 109, 114; jambs, 95, 99, 109, 115, 167, 175; lighting, 94, 113; lintels, 72, 90, 99, 109, 115, 162, 172, 175; masonry facing, 105; mud-based construction, 102–103; mud-plaster walls, 100, 106, 115; niches, 72, 94, 95, *96*, 97, 107, 113; open interior spaces, 69, 70, 74, 109; ornament, *108*, 109, 115; painted walls, 96, 100; patios, 68–70, 72, 90, 100; pavements, 89, 100, 103, 106–107; perimeter walls, 69, 74, 77, 79, 97, 101, *108*, 112; *pirca*, 105; platforms, 68, 85, 88, 89, 101, 109; rafters, 103, 106; roofs, 99, 103, 104, 106, 109; slab doors, *96*, 97, 113; slab roofs, 92, 93–95, *99*, 106; staircases, 68, 69, 88, 89, 97, 106–107, 109, 167, *168*; stringcourses, 106, 109, 228, 230; vestibules, 93

architectural forms: ceremonial enclosures, 88–91; *chullpas*, 98–102; circular, 70–73, 91; compounds, 69–75; corrals, 38, 46, 48, 60, 76–77, 90, 121; fortifications, 78–83; houses, 67–75; patio-groups, 72, 91; plazas, 88–91, 107, 155; quadrangular, 70–73, 89; room complexes/clusters, 68, 70, 74, *168*; shrines, 85–87. *See also* subterranean tombs

architecture, 18, 41; aesthetics, 105–106; experience of mortuary buildings, 114–115; functions, 102, 116–117, 122; monumental, 37, 40, 50, 69, 82–83, 88, 103, 116, 117, 123–124; pottery representations of, *pl. 8*, 107–110, *108*, 122, 145, 148, 151, 195, 227, *228*, 229–231; preservation of, 103; social boundaries, 75

art, 2, 5–7, 19, 127, 193; aesthetics, 6, 19, 253; agency, 6, 117, 187–188, 221, 239; corporate art style, 191, 226, 239; cross-media emphasis, 226, 241; formalism, 6; Great Art, 173; intertextuality, 8; media, 239; sociality, 213–219, 240; value systems, 7–8, 19, 225

art imagery, 4, 5, 13, 19, 29, 191, 240–241, 254; animal symbolism, 231–238; biographical implications, 215, 218; central figure theme, *167*, 198, 236, 277;

chiefly display, 239–240; differences between media, 218–219; genres of action, 213, *214*; human attire, 200–206; human body ornamentation, 198; in stone, 196–200; mimesis, 185–189, 240, 254; negativized surfaces, 223–227; social skin, 213, 219, 221, 231; witnessing, *217*, 218, 240. *See also* iconic figures

ashlar, 104, 177, 231
Asuac pottery, 151
Aukispukio, 42, 51, 60, 98, 249
Ayacucho, 197, 257, 258, 260
ayllu, 41, 75–76
Aztec, 180

Balcón de Judas, 40, 51, 129, 133, 150
barley, 24
beans, 24, 38, 42, 178, 180–181. *See also* legumes
Bennett, Wendell C., 39, 66, 95, 101, 114, 129–131, 134, 137, 142, 152, 163, 277
birds, 23–25, 37. *See also* art imagery
Blanco-sobre-rojo, 137
body, 191, 196–206, 253. *See also* art imagery
bofedales, 24, 29
Bolivia, 64, 163
bone tools, 90, 122, 168; camelid crania spoons, 89, 90; ribs, 90; spindle whorls, 178, 219
bottle gourds, 143, 225
boulders, 70–72, 76, 85–88, 92, 93, 96, 98–101, 106, 115, 125
Bueno, Alberto, 97, 132–133, 149
buffer zones, 45, 245
Burger, Richard, 41
burials. *See* mortuary practices
burning, 85, 87

Cabana, 22, 47, 165, 171, 250, 258
caches, 85, 97, 156
caciques (native lords), 14, 193
cactus, 24, 232
Cajamarca: pottery style, 11, 111, 150, 153, 252, 253, 257, 258–260, 263; region, 24, 26, 29, 32, 81, 123, 131; town, 26
Cajamarquilla, 43, 44, 166, 169
Callejón de Huaylas, 26–31, 38, 39–42,

ice-cores, 33–35, 37; Huascarán cores, 33–34, 261; Quellcaya cores, 33–34. *See also* climate change

Ichik Wilkawaín, 40, 54, 66, 93, 94, 100, 101, 112, 113, 153, 256. *See also* Wilkawaín

ichu, 103

iconic figures, *208*; Group A, 207, *208*, 212; Group B, *208*, 209, 212, 220, 226–227; Group C, *208*, 209, *210*, 213, 221, 254; Group D, 209–210, *211*, 227; Group E, 210–211, *pl. 5d*; Group F, 211

idolatries, 96, 187

illa, 277

imagery, 19; bicephalic creatures, 162, 173; birds and owls, 162, 173, *234*; central figure theme, 162, *167*, 174, 198, *235*; crested animal, *172*, 173; felines, 162, *164*, *167*, 170, 182, 183, 235–236; forehead crescent, *163*, 198; frontlets, 198; head with four appendages, *173*; human heads, *164*, 174, 198; mummy bundles, *163*, 166, 185–187, 198; pottery representations, *109*, 110, *185*; rainbows, 173, 177; serpents, 170; step designs, 173, 177; trophy paws/hands, 198; trophy heads, 161, *172*, 198; warriors, *pl. 9b*, 50, *161*, *163*, 167, 170, *172*, 174, 236; weapons, *161*, *163*, *171*, 199; whirling crosses, *173*, 177; women, *161*, 162, *168*. *See also* anthromorphs

Ingold, Tim, 119

Inka, 15, 31, 32, 43, 57, 66, 76, 77, 124–125, 131, 176, 203, 230, 231, 277; architectural representations, 180; architecture, 57, 63, 89, 107, 115; Capac Ñan (road system), 77; *capacocha*, 124; *panaca*, 231; statecraft, 57, 77, 259; stone masonry, 104; sun worship, 87

Inkawaín, 42

interaction, 15, 30–31, 38–39, 46, 121, 245, *246*; boundaries, 123; caravans, 46, 60, 77, 121–122; coast-highland, 30–31, 44, 60, 220, 245–246, 254; interaction sphere, 15, 16, 133; stylistic, 15, 30; trade, 21, 31, 38–39, 44, 46, 49, 121, 153, 220, 254–255, 256

interior/exterior distinction, 122

Inti Watana, 87

irrigation, 12, 23, 24, 42, 66, 76, 78, 121; oral traditions, 124, 186

Isabelita Stone, 86

Isluga, 278

jaguars, 122, 207, 209, 231, 236

Jancu, 40, 45, 54, 86, 96–97, 107, 110, 111, 113, 114, 115, 117; groundplan, *96*; pottery, *pl. 5a–d*, *147*, 150, 156, 236

Jangas, 41, 86

janka, 22

Japanese Expedition, 133

Jatungaga, 53; subterranean chamber tomb, 93–94

Jimbe, 45

Junín, 57, 81

Kaeppler, Adrienne, 221

kanchas, 70

kaolinite pottery, 30, 39, 43, 44, 46, 50, 77, 97, 130, 131, 132, 137, 138, 139, 141, 148, 149, 150–153, 155, 245, 251, 259

Karachuko, 166

Karway, 48, 103

Katak, 39, 67, 95–96, 107, 113, 127, 129, 152, 163, 249, 250, 256, 259; pottery designation, 129

Katiamá, 51, 100, 101, 169, 183

Kauffmann Doig, Federico, 131, 166

Kayán pottery, 133

Kekamarca, 40, 182

kinship relations, 14, 26, 41, 75, 110–111, 112, 115, 184, 194, 216, 240

Kotosh, 215

Kroeber, A. L., 129, 132, 199, 226, 277

Kubler, George, 5–6, 226

Kuntur Wasi, 116

La Banda, 50

La Galgada, 64

La Libertad, 150, 174

La Merced, 42, 161

La Pampa, 68, 70, 73, 74, 133, 249; Rondán Circular Construction, *68*, 73

labor: festive, 155, 216, 239; input, 35, 67, 73, 82, 117, 118; recruitment, 89, 155, 218; tax, 9, 14

lakes, 24, 25, 30, 36, 37, 124–125

Lane, Kevin, 121

sexual imagery, 253; warfare imagery, 195, 252, 253

monoliths. *See* stone sculpture, *wankas*

monuments. *See* architecture

Moore, Jerry, 119

mortar, 76, *99*, 104–105

mortuary practices, 20, 54, 55, 67, 75–76, 87, 91, 92–102, 110–116, 118; architecture, 39, 40, 41, 42, 44, 46, 47–48, 50, 103, 111, 112–116, 118, 123–126; *ayllu* relationships, 75–76; burial positions, 112; ceremonial paraphernalia, 94, 96, 97, 113; cosmology of, 110, 112–116, 123–126, 238; diversity, 110; drinking, 216; emphasis on place, 111, 112; experience of mortuary buildings, 114–115; funerary bundles, 93; grave-lots, 45, 111, 149, 178; ideology, 113, 118, 238; reuse, 112–114; social boundaries, 75, 251; visibility, 101, 111. *See also* ancestors, *chullpas*, subterranean tombs

Mosna, 50, 133, 152, 279

mountains, 17, 25, 29, 30, 32, 41, 79, 80, 82, 87, 123, 124. *See also* Cordillera Blanca, Cordillera Huayhuash, Cordillera Negra

mourning, 214, 215

mud: mud brick construction, 102–103; *tapia*, 103; wall facing, 100. *See also* adobe

mummy bundles, 93, 112, 114, 125, *163*, 166, 185, 186, *187*, 198, 214, 223

Murra, John, 26

muscoid flies, 151

Nasca, 1, 11, 17, 134, 147, 218, 258

Nepeña, 44, 45, 130, 249, 277, 279

nevados, 30. *See also* glaciers, Cordillera Blanca

Nievería, 111, 263

north coast, 37

Nuevo Tambo, 100

obsidian, 38, 255–257, 260

oca, 24, 38

Ocros, 186

offering pits, 85

offerings, 13, 18, 40, 47, 51, 79, 85–89, 94, 96–97, 110, 113, 114, 116–118, 123, 130, 138, 141–143, 147, 149, 153, 155–157, 162, 173, 178, 187, 216, 220–222, 256–257, 259

olluco, 24, 38

oracle, 32, 44

Orojirca, 40

outcrops, 85–87, 124–125, 175, 185, 186

owls, 173, 202, 211, 232

oxygen isotopes, 33–34

pacarinas, 90, 124, 186

pachillas, 65, 71, 87, 105. *See also wanka-pachilla* stonework

Pacific flanks, 22, 29, 30, 39, 44–47, 79, 249, 255, 257. *See also* middle valley (coast)

Pacific Ocean, 22, 28, 31

Pacopampa, 116

painting, 101; on rocks, 86; on walls, 100, 110. *See also* pottery

Pallasca, 22, 25, 28, 29, 32, 47–48, 57, 165; stone sculpture style, 171–173

Pampa Grande, 250

panaca, 231

panpipes, 89

Paracas, 1, 245

páramo, 24

Paredes, Juan, 101, 152

Pashash, 14, 45, 47, 51, 53, 54, 56, 65, *69*, 78, 82, 107, 110, 111, 112, 116–118, 226, 245, 248–249, 250, 255–258, 260, 261, 278, 279; El Caserón, *69*, 105, 106; La Capilla, 47, 79, 80, 97, 106, 113, 156, 173; metalwork, 225; pottery, *pl. 3a–b*, 132–133, 137, 141–142, 146, 150, 155, 277; stone masonry, 106–107, 196; stone sculpture, 165, 171–173, 182, 183, *234*; tomb, 97–98

pasture, 29, 44, 58, 60, 78, 100, 121, 122

patio groups, 70, 72

Pativilca Valley, 22, 30

Pax Mochica, 46

Pierina area, 133, 152, 166, 256, 257

pigments, 86, 100, 115, 139–140, 151, 152

pilgrimage, 42, 44, 55, 121, 245, 251, 257

Pincos, 32

pins, 98, 162, 199, 202–203, *205*, 225, 278

Pira, 30, 43, 44, 55, 166, 176

pirca, 105

Piscobamba: ethnic group, 32; town, 170

plants. *See* agriculture, cereals, legumes, trees, tubers

platform-mounds, 116

plazas, 88–91, 107, 155

polygamy, 215–216

Pomabamba, 48, 70, 165, 170

Pomakayán, 40, 42, 55, 87–88; cist burials, 93; Early Horizon shrine, 88; pins, *205*; pottery, *pl. 3c*

Pongor, 40, 41, 169

Ponte, Víctor, 133, 167

potatoes, 24, 34, 38, 186

pottery, 18; alternative designations, 28, 127–133; blackwares, 138; chronological relationships, 66–67; designs, 140, 148–152, 200; discard, 154–155; distribution, 22, 28, 127; duration, 134; firing, 139–140, 141, 145; grave-lots, 149, 150, 155; kaolinite pottery production, 138–140, 152; makers' marks, 141–142; painting, 139, 149, 151, 152, 156; plainwares, 132, 134, 136, 138, 142, 154–155; plastic decoration, 140, 141, 143, 145, 148, 149; potter's wheels, 139; primitive technique, 128, 129, 132, 277; production, 146–147, 152; redwares, 138, 139, 148; resist painting, 138–140, 145, 148, 149, 209, 224, 226, 246–247; seriation, 132, 148; slip, 138–140, 144, 149–151, 209, 226; subphases, 132, 147–151; Recuay I, 150; Recuay II, 150–151; Recuay III, 151; typologies, 129; vent holes, 139; wasters, 139

pottery forms: bottles, 143; bowls, 89–90, 138–140, 149–152, 155; colanders, 89, 155; composite shapes, 142; corniform handles, 143, *144*; cups, 142, 149; dippers, 142, 150–151; donut-shaped, 145; doubled-chambered vessels, 145, 146, *147*, 151; effigy vessels, 146, 156; handled bowl, 143, *144*, 152; incurving bowls, *143*; jars, 89–90, 140, 143, 152; kancheros, 143, 152; ladles, 143, *144*, 155; long tube spout, 145, *146*; miniatures, 142; neck flanges, 145; ollas, 155; pacchas, 143, 151, 152; ring bases, 142, 143, 149; skeuomorphs, 132, 143, 225; spoons, 138, 143, 155; spouts, 143; square, 146; tall cups, 143; triangular, 146; triple-tube, 145

pottery functions: containers, 142–143, 154, 156; cooking, 154, 155; feasting, 155, 157; grave offerings, 150, 155–156, 257; hygiene, 154; infusions, 146; libations, 143, 147, 155–157; offerings, 142, 147, 155–157, 257; pouring, 143; reuse, 154; serving, 142–143, 147, 154; storage, 145, 147, 154, 155; trade items, 154

pottery imagery: architecture, *pl. 8,* 107–110, *108*, 122, 145, 148, 151, 227, *228, 229*–231; bicephalic creatures, *144*, 205; birds, *pl. 5d*, 144, 145, 202, 228, *234,* 236; camelids, 122, 145, 146, *201, 203*, 215, 232; central figure theme, *pl. 5a*, 167, *204*, 212; chiefly embodiments, 229–231; dancing, 145, 214; deer, 144; ear ornaments, *201, 202, 203*; face painting, 205, 206; feathers, *203*; felines, *pl. 5a, pl. 6c,* 144, 145, *147*, 202, 218; frontlets, 202; genitalia, 218, 233, 253; genres of action, 213; hair, *143, 204*; headdresses, 146, 200, 202, 204; heads, *pl. 9a, 143, 144*; iconic figures, 207, *208*, 209, 210, *211, pl. 5d,* 212, 213, 226–227, 247; libations, 145, 156, 214; male figures, *pl. 5a–b, pl. 6a–b,* 144, 145, 146, 148, *192*, 200, *201,* 202–204, 212, *215,* 228; mummy bundles, 214, *223*; musicians, *pl. 6a, 201, 206*; owls, 202; ritual gatherings, 145, 148, *185,* 214; serpents, 202, 236; sexual intercourse, 145, 146, *217*, 218, 221, 253–254; trophy elements, 202, 204, 233; veneration, 145, 213, *215*; warriors, *108, 192*, 236; witnessing, 217–218; women, *pl. 5c, 144, 147, 204*, 205, 206, 216, 236

Preceramic period, 26

predation, 195, 233, 249

preservation, 7, 103, 115, 127, 160, 255, 265

press-molded pottery, 111, 258, 260

prestige goods, 14, 118, 153, 194, 245, 255, 256, 259

priests, 116, 197, 232

primitive technique, 128, 129, 132, 277

privacy, 72

processions, 116

production zones, 38, 58, 120

progenitors, 111, 114, 184, 189, 197–198. *See also* ancestors